DERBY INNOVATOR

DERBY INNOVATOR

The Making of Animal Kingdom

Barry Irwin

Library of Congress Control Number:		2016904432
ISBN:	Hardcover	978-1-5144-7626-0
	Softcover	978-1-5144-7625-3
	eBook	978-1-5144-7624-6

Print information available on the last page

Rev. date: 05/13/2016

To order additional copies of this book, contact:
Xlibris
1-888-795-4274
www.Xlibris.com
Orders@Xlibris.com
736215

CONTENTS

Photo Credits

Photo credits in appearance order

1. Irwin Family Photo Collection
2. Irwin Family Photo Collection
3. Irwin Family Photo Collection
4. Bill Mochon
5. Irwin Family Photo Collection
6. Bill Mochon
7. Megan Jones
8. Joe DiOrio
9. Bill Mochon
10. Benoit Photo
11. Steve Stidham
12. Bob Coglianese
13. Benoit Photo
14. Andrew Watkins
15. Andrew Watkins
16. J C Photos
17. HKJC Photo
18. AP Photo/David J. Phillip
19. Andrew Watkins
20. Wendy Wooley
21. Tibor Szlavik

COVER PHOTO Anne Eberhardt
AUTHOR PHOTO Kamran Jebreili

CHAPTER 1

We Win the Derby

NBC color commentator Bob Neumeier stopped me in my tracks as I tried to cross the Churchill Downs racetrack and head toward the winners' circle after Animal Kingdom won the 2011 Kentucky Derby. I was champing at the bit to find my wife Kathleen and see my friends. The last thing I wanted at that moment was to be prevented from reaching my group by a television interviewer. I tried to press on but Neumeier had a hold of me and was insistent. So I waited as patiently as I could until his feed went "live."

"Barry Irwin was once a former sportswriter," Neumeier began when he was given his cue.

I joked around with him, saying, "I still *am* a former sportswriter!"

Ignoring my comment, Bob went right on with the interview. "What are the headlines that you are going to write on this one, Mr. Irwin?"

"I CAN'T BELIEVE IT!" was my headline offering.

Neumeier said, "There's a tear in your eye. Obviously I know you spent a lot of money. You've put a lot of effort into this game."

I said, "I'm overwhelmed. And I'm just thrilled for all of my clients and my family."

I hoped the interview was over because I desperately wanted to move on. But the man with the mic was just getting warmed up.

Neumeier said, "You made a move to go to Graham Motion the trainer. It paid off big time. How did you make that move?"

I said, "Well, I just was tired of other trainers lying to me and I wanted a guy that would tell me the truth."

"Really?" exclaimed Neumeier, who genuinely appeared to be caught off guard.

"Yeah."

"How many trainers lied to you?" asked Neumeier.

"Plenty. Anyway, gotta go," I said, and I walked away to join my fellow winners.

Neumeier, taken aback by my choice of words, closed with this—"Barry Irwin... Team Valor... honest guy." His inflection indicated that, although he was surprised by what he heard, he approved of my candid response to his question.

Little did I realize that my remarks would create such a contretemps.

In the days, weeks, months and, yes, years since my remarks were first uttered on that fateful May 7, they have been talked about, written about, scrutinized, lambasted, hailed, despised, revered, called into question, cherished, and blown completely out of proportion.

I had spoken to Bob Neumeier many times over the years and I treated his question as I would have if we had been shooting the breeze in the stable in the morning.

I always try to be as candid as possible. I was a reporter, editor and columnist for several years for *Daily Racing Form*, *The Blood-Horse* and dozens of other racing and breeding publications around the world. I have interviewed many people and I never liked it when they hemmed and hawed, aimed for political correctness or were evasive. So in my own life, I try to be as forthcoming as I hoped my interviewees would be. Anybody who knows me realizes this is my style.

Dale Romans, who is a personal friend and long-time trainer of mine, responded to a *Daily Racing Form* reporter's question about my post-Derby comments by saying, "That's just Barry being Barry."

So when Bob Neumeier interviewed me, I was not on guard.

I had not planned to utter what came out of my mouth in that post-Derby interview. What I said surprised me as much as anybody else. Why I had chosen, on the biggest stage in racing and after my greatest achievement, to use that moment was a surprise to me.

As a fiction writer in an earlier part of my life, I knew the power of the subconscious and I relied on it to form thoughts better than I was able to consciously. When I would sit down at the typewriter early in the morning, words just flowed onto the page from a wellspring that worked out all of the intricacies during my sleep.

So in retrospect, I should not have been surprised by what I said because what I said was the truthful answer to Neumeier's question. It became immediately apparent to me that those feelings I had were held just beneath the surface of my consciousness and must have reflected how I felt about the subject. It was not the politically correct thing to say at that time and place. But, hey, that's the way I have always lived my life.

Turf Writer Joe Drape wrote in *The New York Times*:

"Bob Baffert, the Hall of Fame trainer, has never worked with a Team Valor horse but recognized in Irwin's remarks a universal truth that continues to haunt a fractious industry. 'I think that was his inner voice talking,' said Baffert, a three-time Derby winner. 'We all do it (from) time to time. I have never been a big fan of his, but he is pretty sharp and has brought a lot of good people into the game. It's only natural in our business that we hate everyone that wins a lot.'"

Even though I had been interviewed several times over the years after some important triumphs, such as two Breeders' Cup wins, I had never been interviewed when I was so emotionally vulnerable.

When Animal Kingdom crossed under the wire to win the Kentucky Derby, I was shaking like a leaf. I was sobbing uncontrollably as my wife and I hugged each other. Tears were streaming down my cheeks and lips. When I walked downstairs from our seats in the grandstand, my legs were weak and kept buckling.

I had only experienced this sensation once before, twenty-two years earlier when our horse Martial Law sprang an upset to return $103.40 for a $2 bet to win the $1-million Santa Anita Handicap, the race made famous by Seabiscuit in 1940.

On that occasion, I was sobbing even more uncontrollably and my wife at the time had to literally prop me up on our way to the winners' circle. Fortunately for me, she was a very strong woman. When I got there, I was an emotional wreck.

When one grows up in Southern California, the biggest race by far to dream about winning is the legendary Big 'Cap and we had just won it with a most improbable horse. That day, my partner Jeff Siegel, who was excited but not a basket case like me, had to manage the winners' circle proceedings, grabbing an ear of the trophy, posing for photographs and doing most of the post-race interviews.

When the dust settled after Animal Kingdom's victory, it gradually became apparent that my post-Derby comment about the lying trainers had taken on a life of its own. *Daily Racing Form* ran a story in which a few of my former trainers were interviewed. People connected to these trainers uttered their dismay at my remarks.

Everybody, it seemed, wanted to register his or her reaction to my comments, be it on air, on paper or online.

Those who found my remarks objectionable did so on grounds that I had committed the unpardonable sin of airing racing's dirty laundry in public, or that I had trashed the sport by badmouthing it.

Others who found my comments worthwhile said or wrote that what I had to say was refreshing for its accuracy and candor. These folks welcomed the remarks and thanked me for my courage in making them.

The naysayers, many of whom basically wanted to hijack the conversation away from my achievement of winning the Kentucky Derby in an unprecedented manner, used my remarks to conduct a public hearing on exactly how big of an asshole I was.

Nothing these folks came up with was anything I had not heard since I began working in racing 42 years earlier.

Since my early youth, I had looked askance at authority figures that I considered to be full of crap or seemed to be taking advantage of their position to push an untidy agenda. I rarely hesitated in making my feelings known.

Whether it was a teacher, a coach, a rabbi or a friend's parents, I did not hold back. Sarcasm became my weapon of choice against anybody who held themselves falsely above the crowd.

I was among millions of young people worldwide who felt an immediate kinship with Holden Caulfield when I read *The Catcher in the Rye* for the first time. It changed my life.

As an adult, it was more of the same.

I had found a real-life hero to worship when Kent Parrot Hollingsworth hired me to write for *The Blood-Horse* magazine in 1969. He was a lawyer-turned-writer who edited the trade magazine for horse breeders and I thought he was the most admirable man I had ever met.

I was not so fortunate in my next job in racing as I worked for a far less ethical boss, who used fear and anger to manipulate his employees. He was the general manager of the Breeders' Association in California and I worked directly under him as editor of the organization's magazine. I quit that job when I discovered that having to do his bidding was adversely impacting my mental health.

So I wound up writing a nationally syndicated column in *Daily Racing Form*. When I left that position to enter the world of racehorse ownership and bloodstock sales nine years after entering the Thoroughbred industry, I used the occasion to write a lengthy piece in the non-trade magazine *New West*, which was similar to *New York* magazine.

In the *New West* piece, which was inspired by a *Sports Illustrated* piece detailing a wide swath of corruption that had been cut through the racing game by a racketeer named Tony Ciulla, I focused on the soft job racing journalists did in exposing corruption in the industry. I cited numerous examples of bad behavior that had been ignored by racing writers and editors, whom I said were partially to blame for guys like Ciulla being able to run their scams in racing.

I loved racing so much that I wanted to do whatever I could to expose the bad parts in the hopes that it would lead to improvements, both in the game and in racing journalism.

A lot of the same types of comments I heard after my post-Derby statements had been uttered about my *New West* piece. Instead of readers focusing on the merits of what I had written in *New West* or said after the Kentucky Derby, it seemed that a lot of my critics were more interested in nailing me for airing my sport's failings.

Among the things I wrote in *New West* was that the leading trainer and jockey of the at the time routinely used races early in a horse's career to school the animals, rather than trying to win with them. These remarks were made in an era of low prize money. All around the world, wherever prize money is meager, the incidence of corruption is higher, as horsemen and jockeys manipulate their horses to set up betting coups because cashing bets keeps them above water financially.

Gordon Jones, a *Herald-Examiner* handicapper and turf writer, challenged me to join him on Bud Furillo's *The Steam Room* radio talk program. A degenerate gambler who was always tapping out, Jones was generally believed to be in the pocket of Hollywood Park racetrack owner Marje Everett, who was a great supporter of all-time great trainer, Charlie Whittingham, and his regular jockey Bill "The Shoe" Shoemaker.

Speaking with all the incredulity he could muster, Prof. Jones asked, "Are you telling me that Bill Shoemaker holds horses in races?"

To which I replied, "Are you telling me that he doesn't?"

Fellow *Herald-Examiner* sports writer Furillo laughed out loud because anybody who regularly attended the races in Southern California knew that Shoemaker—especially when he rode inexperienced horses for Whittingham—routinely "stiffed" them until the trainer felt a horse was ready to run a winning race. Whittingham loved to cash a bet and he had his own runner, Mickey Sheraldi, to place his bets at the track so that nobody knew when Charlie was wagering.

Whittingham had become very wealthy by virtue of his unprecedented success as a racehorse trainer. We shared the same bank manager, who once told me that Charlie had most of his wealth at his branch of Bank of America in $100,000 certificates of deposit. Whittingham tried to cash bets for fun, not because he needed the money. To him, it was all part of an elaborate game.

One of the most exciting happenings that would take place in the press boxes on the Southern California circuit in the 1970s occurred when The

Shoe would let loose a youngster for "The Bald Eagle" (Whittingham had no hair). Virtually to a man, everybody would leap from his seat and yell, "It's a go!" Those who bet the winner were overjoyed, those who did not get on were pissed off and those who were neutral were entertained wildly. It was a laugh riot every time!

In *New West* I also wrote about jockeys who exchanged betting information for illegal drugs. I think I was among the first sportswriters who put this notion in print.

The "human cry" (hue and cry) from racing's establishment about my story made the post-Derby hubbub look like a parlor game.

Johnny Longden, the Kentucky Derby-winning trainer and rider, who held the world record for the most wins by a jockey until it was broken by Shoemaker, asked the Horsemen's Benevolent and Protective Association to "take my license away," whatever that meant. He thought it was outrageous for me to suggest that jockeys would use drugs, let alone trade information to gangsters for them. A trainer who attended the HBPA told me meeting that somebody took Longden aside and updated him on the recreational habits of modern day riders.

It did not hurt my credibility when, shortly after my piece appeared in *New West*, a young jockey named Ronnie Franklin was arrested in the parking lot at Disneyland for cocaine possession. He wound up losing the mount on one of the greatest Thoroughbred racehorses of all time, Spectacular Bid, which he had ridden nine days earlier in a failed Triple Crown bid in the 1979 Belmont Stakes. Shoemaker took over on "The Bid" and proceeded to ride him to twelve wins in his next thirteen starts, including the only "walkover" (one horse in a contest) in the modern era of racing.

Although sycophants like "The Professor" and "The Pumper" (Longden) got hot under the collar over what I had written about Whittingham and Shoemaker, I never received any flak from either of the principals. I suspect they both realized that what I wrote was accurate and that nothing they could say was likely to improve their situation.

Charlie Whittingham later trained some horses for my first racing partnership. And Bill Shoemaker later rode horses for me. I spoke with both of them on a regular basis in the years after my *New West* piece and the subject of that story never came up.

Interestingly, although many racing insiders feared that my revelations in *New West* would damage racing, the fact is that many things I wrote about underwent improvement over the next few years.

Whittingham and Shoemaker, for example, gradually stopped "schooling" horses in races. Today it would be unthinkable for a trainer such as Todd Pletcher or Shug McGaughey or Bill Mott to not try to win with a horse first time out if the horse was up to the task.

Because racing is a high-dollar sport, the potential for increase in the value of a good horse makes the cashing of any bet pale in comparison. So today, most trainers, jockeys and owners want to win at every opportunity. Nowadays, in a game with much better economic fundamentals, a trainer and rider are more concerned with their winning percentages, breeding rights and sales commissions than in stiffing a horse to cash a bet.

Racing today has other problems, such as trainers who cheat by using illegal performance enhancing drugs (PEDs). I have been writing and speaking out about these and other problems in the media for five decades.

So I guess I was surprised that anybody who knew me would be stunned by my post-race comments. I am equally puzzled that anybody would be surprised to learn that trainers lie.

What a lot of people did not realize was that, before I stopped using a group of trainers and moved all of my domestic stock to one trainer, Graham Motion, in the fall of 2011, I had strongly considered quitting the game.

I was totally fed up with being lied to by some of my trainers. I have a great responsibility to my 350 or so clients. They rely on me to be on top of what is going on with their investments. When trainers purposely lie or commit the sin of omission, it puts me in the dark, which is an unacceptable situation. I came very close to simply shutting down my operation.

But I was able to work out a suitable arrangement with Graham to train our stock and I decided not only to stay in the game, but also to up the ante by putting an investment group together to buy and renovate a forty-stall barn at Fair Hill training center in Northern Maryland.

Interestingly, it was not in my role as a victim of dishonesty that was the focus, but rather my sheer audacity in exposing that such a situation actually existed. How dare I!

I have appeared on national television to express my views on the problems that racing faces. I have given testimony before the United States Senate. I have written my views in *The New York Times*.

Half a century ago, racing was among the most popular sports in the United States. But since that time, other sports have emerged that Americans have found to be more appealing.

Racing has always been an insider's game. And its insistence against opening it up to a public that now craves transparency has kept the game stuck in the mud. Racing is divided into two camps: insiders, who want to keep to the status quo, and the rest, who want to strive for improvement. I cast my lot with the latter camp several decades ago.

CHAPTER 2

Bitten by the Bug

When I think back to my early fascination with horses, I do so in snapshots. I am, after all, a child of the Saturday matinee. Even in my twenties, when I devoted myself to fiction writing, I wrote in cinematic scenes, having been influenced as much by film as by prose.

One image invariably pops onto my inner screen. Location: my ninth grade Latin class. I am seated at my desk. I am supposed to be working on a lesson. Looking down with utter incredulity is my teacher. Instead of doing my declensions, I am in the throes of creating a *Daily Racing Form* chart of a fictitious race, involving some of my favorite horses.

It would have been embarrassing enough if I had been writing about English literature while seated in a Latin class. And, to somebody unfamiliar with matters of the turf, names like Round Table, Iron Liege, General Duke and Bold Ruler might very well have belonged in King Arthur's court at Camelot.

But, alas, they were the names of racehorses—some of the greatest of all time—and they were all competing as 3-year-olds that season in 1957, when I was in my last year at Louis Pasteur Junior High School.

That this vintage crop of Thoroughbreds inspired me infinitely more than Julius Caesar's first-hand account of the Gallic Wars pretty much summed up my priorities. Yes, I know, "Gallia est omnis divisa in partes tres"—Gaul is divided into three parts. Yadda, yadda, yadda. But hey, lady, so is the Triple Crown!

The only classics I cared about took place at Churchill Downs, Pimlico and Belmont Park, not on the battlefields of what became France, Switzerland and Belgium.

I was 14 in 1957 and I had been interested in horses and horse racing from the time I could walk. Shift the scene to a few years earlier and I see myself on my hands and knees in our family's garage annex in Beverlywood, California, where my brother and I set up our own miniature racetrack and stable area, complete with a roster of some of the finest racehorses that competed regularly at Santa Anita, Hollywood Park and Del Mar.

I loved racing, my brother loved games, and we combined our interests to come up with a fantasy stable that indulged both of our passions.

I was not some sort of oddball pre-teen; I had friends who shared my interests just as passionately. The scene shifts again, this time to a ground-floor studio behind the house of my friend Steve Kallman and his younger brother Frank. They had a tape recorder that we used to practice race calls and mimic radio touts that produced a never-ending stream of winners without any losers for fees that astounded us kids.

Steve was a first generation American whose parents came from Germany. His mother was the only Jewish woman in our neighborhood who worked as a domestic. My parents had no use for Steve's father, a salesman, because while his wife "slaved away cleaning other people's houses, that no-goodnik of a husband was at the racetrack losing his wife's hard-earned money on horses!"

What my parents never knew was that Steve and I sold racing tips on the corner of Robertson and National Boulevards. Steve had been selling newspapers on that heavily trafficked intersection on the northeast corner for years, right across from the first house my parents ever owned and an apartment building we later occupied between moves.

Steve and I would pore over the next day's card, make our selection, write the name down on a piece of paper, fold it several times, secure it so nobody could see it without paying for it, and offer it to regular newspaper customers for a fee of 25 cents. We did that until Steve began to worry that somebody would complain and it might cost him his newspaper gig, which was more important to him. We were 12 years old at the time.

But Steve's was not the only family in our neighborhood with a black sheep who blew money gambling on the pferdel (horses). My own family had one, too. On my father's paternal side was the tragic case of my uncle Fischel, who fled Russia during the 1917 revolution along with my dad's father Moishe.

Whereas Moishe and his Romanian-born wife Mary operated a Jewish delicatessen on famed Fairfax Avenue in the heart of the Borscht Belt, as well as on Third Street and later down the block from my high school on Robertson Boulevard, Fischel preferred to run bakeries.

My hunch is that he went into baking instead of fresh food because bakers work at night, leaving them free during the daytime, when a person, if such a person had a desire, could attend and even participate in the leisurely pursuit of backing one's opinion on the outcome of a sporting event in which the focal point was a horse.

Fischel worked hard, built a business that was comprised of three Borscht Belt bakeries and reached a level of affluence that allowed him to delegate work to others at night.

That Fischel could barely speak English, let alone read a racetrack program or write his name, did not stop him from being at the races every single day they were open. Had Damon Runyon been situated on Fairfax Boulevard instead of Broadway, he undoubtedly would have made Fischel into one of his unforgettable characters.

It was a sad circumstance in the oral history of our family when Fischel moved into our home on Gibson Street to die. We all knew he was going to die. He looked very sickly upon arrival. He was a sweet old gentleman. He was grateful and deferential. He looked frail and weak. But he had a little twinkle in his eye, especially when the subject of horse racing came up.

Fischel, the legend went, had "lost his three bakeries to the pferdel." A broken man now ravaged by illness, Fischel came to live with our family. He had nowhere else to go, as the rest of the family had ostracized him because of his gambling addiction. My dad hated that Fischel was a diseased gambler, but my father was a soft touch with a big heart.

In the brief time Fischel lived with us before he passed on to that big racetrack in the sky, I spent as much time with him as I could.

Fischel's arrival was a source of considerable aggravation in our household, as my mother was already concerned about my focusing too much attention on horse racing. Fortunately for Fischel and my dad, my mom did not have a leg to stand on because our family had recently played host to my maternal aunt's son, who was back from military duty.

My soldier cousin's explicit tales about his sexual escapades while in the military actually posed more of an immediate threat to her son's innocence than did the broken down gambler's musings. Oh the vagaries of a mother trying to protect the delicate psyche of her hormone-infused teenager! What is a mother to do, I ask you?

The old guy wore those glasses with lenses that looked like the bottom of Coca-Cola bottles. He could not read English and it is questionable whether he could even see anything in order to read it through those spectacles.

Fischel, it turned out, really was a degenerate gambler. He knew very little about horse racing. He based his bets on a horse's number on the track program or the colors of a jockey's silks, which is a province usually reserved for first-time visitors to a racetrack. The guy was downright embarrassing, even to a Bar Mitzvah-aged youth.

Before he died, Fischel gave me his beat-up binoculars, which I used for more than 20 years until I lost them one day at the track.

Fischel was not my only relative to buck up against my parents' mania to keep me as far away from horseracing as possible. My dad's sister Bertha occasionally attended the races, but only in the company of a date, if that fellow happened to take her to Hollywood Park or Santa Anita for an afternoon's entertainment.

Bertha was the "perfume lady" at Saks Fifth Avenue on Wilshire Boulevard in Beverly Hills. Every Beverly Hills playboy worthy of the title knew "Boitha." In an era when gossip seekers relied on newspaper columns and radio snippets from Sheila Graham and Hedda Hopper, Bertha knew the skinny on all the goings-on in Hollywood, thanks to the frequenting of her cosmetic counter by many of the entertainment industry's biggest players.

Matronly for her age, Bertha was far from prime dating material and she knew it. In her thirties she looked more like a middle-aged grandmother than the high-heeled hotties behind today's fragrance counters.

Her self-esteem took regular hits on the home front, where she still lived with her mother and father, who would "hak" her "a chainik" (talk incessantly) about when she was going to "find a nice Jewish man, get married and settle down like a regular person."

Consequently, when she had any opportunity to go on a date—regardless of whether the suitor was a schmo, a yutz or even a schlub—Bertha gladly seized the chance, if only to escape those human suction cups that passed themselves off as her parents.

One such boyfriend, who in the judgment of my entire household was a "first class jerk," did have one saving grace—the guy was a horseplayer! I was 9 years old and this guy would bet for me at the track.

I hated the guy because he refused to let me in his car one afternoon with a guppy I had managed to coax into a Dixie cup at the park. He made me put the guppy back in the pond so that I would not spill water on the carpet of his car.

When he let me place bets with him, I cut him some slack, although in the back of my mind he was still a putz for not letting me take that fish home in his car!

My first bet was a winner. Gesticulator won a race. When I saw my aunt, she discreetly slipped me the cash from the bet, less the two dollars her male friend bet for me. I was off to the races!

My interest in horses began at a young age, before I was in elementary school in Los Angeles. I had the obligatory photo op astride a pinto pony that was led through our neighborhood by its owner.

I regularly begged my grandmother to drive me "all the way over" Laurel Canyon to the "far off" San Fernando Valley so that I could whinny at horses boarded at the farms located on land that today has been developed into a bustling residential and commercial community.

Back then, at the midpoint of the 20th century, this drive might have taken only about 35 or 40 minutes, but measured in terms of culture, it would have felt more like eons to my family. "The Valley" represented a far-off farmland peopled by Okies, who had arrived from the Dust Bowl in covered wagons, and other assorted goyim who did not have enough sense to live in the city where they could get a decent corned beef sandwich at a proper delicatessen.

So, this act of schlepping a horse-crazed kid over The Great Divide between LA and The Valley was a genuine demonstration of love by my grandparents. And, when one of the horses whinnied back at their 6-year-old grandson, it made their challenging trip immensely worthwhile.

I made my grandparents, my aunt and my parents drive me to any venue where Hopalong Cassidy appeared, so that I could get the promotional silver coins sought after by devotees of the cowboy radio and movie star. "Enough with the Hoppy gelt already!" shrieked my exasperated grandmother after having to brave the crowds at Bullock's department store. They soon began referring to Hoppy as "Schlepalong." His contemporary Roy Rogers was, of course, "Roy the Goy."

I could not get enough of movies or television shows that had anything to do with horses. When I was in the first grade at Virginia Road Elementary School in Los Angeles, I successfully lobbied my parents to buy me a red cowboy outfit that included a matching hat. My mom put it high up on a closet shelf and cautioned me not to wear it or take it outside without her permission. It was a low point in my relationship with my parents when I not only scaled the closet shelves to reach the cowboy outfit, but also wore it to my school playground one weekend. Some older bullies took the outfit from me and I was never able to get it back.

Exactly how and when I first caught the racing bug is a mystery. My parents were dead set against this interest, but I sought out stories about racing in the library, watched any movie or TV program about racing and followed the sport in the newspaper, on radio and on weekends on our Philco.

My father ran the high and low hurdles both in high school and college and was a huge fan of track and field. It is quite apparent that my interest in horse racing stems from a combination of my dad's love of racing and my own interest in any type of horse.

The only activities permitted by my parents that involved horses were ones they considered to be "wholesome." There were weekend visits to Beverly Park, where I rode ponies around a small hoop at Ponyland. "Three rounds on Gypsy, fast please!" I would tell the lady who operated the concession. There were occasional family drives "all the way out" to Pomona to watch Arabian horses being put through some startling and exciting routines at the Kellogg Ranch. I loved watching the tricks those riders were able to do with the dish-faced horses.

And there was the annual trip the Los Angeles County Fair in Pomona, where in addition to a large barn with a representative of seemingly every breed of horse, I was able to watch horses racing. In those days, there were a couple of Quarter Horse races, a few harness races with pacers and trotters, and several races with Thoroughbreds on a bullring track. Naturally, my parents tried to keep me close by their side and as far away from the racetrack as possible. But there is nothing more exciting than being close to the rail at a bullring and feeling the rush of speed and power as those Thoroughbreds fly by.

The great racehorses Native Dancer and Swaps became my TV heroes. I followed them in all the media and could not wait to see them race on TV. To this day, Swaps is my all-time favorite racehorse.

By the time Kentucky Club pipe tobacco instituted a naming contest that offered a 2-year-old Thoroughbred as the winning prize, I was completely hooked on horse racing in the spring of 1954, the year that California-based Determine won the Kentucky Derby. Swaps won the Run for the Roses the following year, causing a 12-year-old kid to feel a great pride in being a racing fan in California.

Always entrepreneurially minded, I had shown a great facility--even as a pre-teen--for finding ways to raise capital when a specific need for the green stuff presented itself.

In order to send in a name for the Kentucky Club tobacco contest, one had to obtain a wrapper from a tobacco pack. My parents both smoked, but neither my dad nor any adult in my circle of acquaintances or relatives smoked a pipe. This meant that I would have to find a way to buy the product myself. And, in order to buy a pouch, I needed cash.

Aside from my usual money-making schemes that included collecting wire clothes hangers from housewives in my neighborhood and selling them to the local dry cleaner for a penny a piece, collecting soft-drink bottles and collecting the two-cents return deposit from the grocery store, and doing the odd chores for neighbors, I set up shop a block from my home to offer some choice condiments to local passers by.

I constructed a stand with a few wooden orange crates covered with a tablecloth that I borrowed from my mother's kitchen drawer, and topped it off with a hand-drawn sign. Among my products were bottles of Rikki salad dressings. The Roquefort and bleu cheese offerings were high-end products from a specialty food line my father sold to grocery stores throughout Southern California.

Sales were brisk as my pricing represented an astronomical savings compared with the retail price at the local market. My only fear was that I would run out of product! The entire enterprise, however, blew up in my face one fine afternoon when one of the passers by—no doubt a do-gooder—stopped by the stand, questioned me at length about the source of my product acquisition and promptly escorted me home, whereupon he explained to my mother what I was up to.

Anyway—long story short—by using all of the tools at my disposal, I was able to earn enough to fund the purchase of several pouches of Kentucky Club pipe tobacco. The next step was to find a suitable adult to actually buy the pipe tobacco for me. Back in the early 1950s, it was easy to tell an adult a true story and have them enable a youngster in his quest of winning a prize Thoroughbred. So I wound up filing several entries in the contest. I entered that contest every year until Kentucky Club ceased the promotion in the late 1960s.

Location: Santa Anita Park, Arcadia, California. In my mind's screen, I see myself grabbing on to a chain-link fence and catapulting myself onto the grounds at Santa Anita for an afternoon of racing excitement.

Location: Hollywood Park, Inglewood, California. I see myself and my friend Steve Robbins trying to convince an adult at Hollywood Park to place a bet for us minors. Our interest in racing had been fueled by a teacher who brought a copy of *Daily Racing Form* to school on Fridays as he geared up for Saturday racing less than 30 minutes away from Alexander Hamilton High School in Beverlywood. While the rest of the class studied, Steve and I took turns sitting next to the teacher's desk and going over the *Form* with the teacher.

By the time I graduated from high school and was ready to move on to college, horse racing was in my blood to stay.

CHAPTER 3

Competitive Edge

Walking on the treadmill in the fitness center near my home in Versailles, Kentucky and listening to tunes on my iPod, I am suddenly arrested by the staccato sounds of the bongo drums that precede Bobby Freeman asking me if I "wanna dance."

My mind flashes back to 1957 and the grass football field at Dorsey High School, where I high jumped in my first real track meet outside of my junior high school.

"Do You Wanna Dance?" was blaring loudly from a boombox forerunner that had been brought to the meet by one of the several black jumpers from the communities neighboring Dorsey, which was located between downtown Los Angeles and the Westside. Dorsey served as a buffer school between unofficial black residential neighborhoods and white ones.

My dad had driven me to the Crenshaw district for the Saturday meet that was a second stage qualifier for a sort of Junior Olympics conducted by the Los Angeles Parks and Recreation Department. I had "won" the first qualifier, as the lone entrant in an impromptu meet at my local park that was conducted as a favor to me by the playground director, who was a high school buddy of my father. In order to jump at Dorsey, I needed a qualifying mark at the playground.

In a makeshift set up, I jumped over a bamboo pole and landed on a couple of canvas mats that had been dragged over from the gym. At Dorsey, there was a regulation high jump pit with a regulation sawdust landing.

I was the only white kid in the high jump. Actually, when I think about it, I may have been the only white kid on the entire field. The other kids were intimidating as they fixed long-lasting stares on me and turned up the volume on their radio when it was my turn to jump.

My dad actually was on the field with me, which was pretty strange since none of the other kids had their parents on the field. My dad reckoned I needed support.

When it was my turn to jump, muscle memory took control of my body. My spaced-out psyche thankfully was eliminated from the equation. I jumped 5 feet 4 inches to win. I was a 9th grader, which in LA city made me a senior in junior high, but a freshman had I attended a county high school. The black kids were impressed, even though it was not cool for them to show it. Nobody wanted to get beat by some skinny 130-pound Jewish kid wearing tennis shoes instead of spikes.

I was pumped and feeling pretty good about myself. The following weekend was my favorite of the entire year—the first Saturday in May. The USC vs. UCLA dual track meet was in direct competition with the Kentucky Derby so it was nearly impossible to see both.

Since my dad was a devoted track and field fan, I invariably wound up going to the dual meet. It was the absolute best of times and now, a week after the famed dual meet, I was heading to the city finals in the same venue at the Los Angeles Memorial Coliseum, the 100,000-plus-seat stadium where the 1932 Olympics had been held.

I loved the Coliseum, where later in high school I became a vendor of popcorn and soft drinks. I had also attended each session of the 4-day NCAA track meet there two years earlier when I was 12 years old. Two years after the Dorsey meet I sold concessions when the Dodgers faced the Chicago White Sox in the first World Series played on the West Coast.

However something happened that after all of these years still perplexes me.

My dad told me the city finals had been postponed and later canceled. The reason he gave sounded plausible at the time.

But I always had the feeling my dad was not telling me the truth. I sensed then, as I still do today, that my dad was trying to protect me from disappointment. Subsequent events only served to bolster this notion.

The following year, in my first season in high school, I was the star athlete on the track and field team at Alexander Hamilton in Los Angeles. I never lost a high jump competition and, after I learned to hurdle, I rattled off several victories in a row.

My dad reluctantly agreed to act as my hurdle coach, showing me some of the techniques he learned when he was a hurdler at Roosevelt High School and Los Angeles City College. But for reasons that were at first difficult to understand, he never really got behind my athletic pursuits.

I will go to my grave believing that somehow he held me out of the city finals to spare me the agony of defeat. Apparently he knew a lot about defeat.

To my dad's everlasting credit, he attended every competition I entered in high school. He found a way to sneak away from work for an hour or two to watch me run and jump. He obviously was conflicted about my passion for track and field and I think he blamed himself for getting me interested, because I became a track and field nut to the exclusion of everything else, including school and my Hebrew studies. About the only thing I found time for other than track and field was being the class clown.

On at least three or four occasions, after I had finished a race in the 120-yard low hurdles, my dad was there right after the finish to console me for my loss, telling me that, "You just can't win 'em all, so don't be disappointed."

Oddly enough, I won each one of these races, just inching out my high school buddy Arnie Weiner. Yet, there was my dad, who was right on the finish line, and he could not see that his own son had won. He was always quick to console a loser.

I myself knew that I had won. When you are racing, no matter how close it is, the runner invariably knows if he has won. So when my dad came up to me and began to console me, I was incredulous.

The one race I did lose in the hurdles that ended a several-race winning streak came in the Western League Finals at University High School in West Los Angeles, when I struck into the last hurdle, stumbled badly and was able to finish only fifth.

A rule in place that allowed each of the several leagues in the Los Angeles Unified School District to advance one unqualified athlete to the Los Angeles City track and field championships preliminaries afforded me the opportunity to run in the hurdles at East Los Angeles Junior College, not far from where my dad had gone to high school. All I had to do was ask my high school coach to nominate me, after which the Western League officials would decide from among the applicants.

My dad counseled me against asking for this accommodation, arguing that a) I should concentrate on the high jump and b) there was no way that I would be able to keep up with all of those fast kids from the Southern League (South Central Los Angeles). I went against my dad's advice. My coach applied for the exception and the Western League officials granted it, since I had gone through the league season unbeaten in the low hurdles.

My dad was right in this instance, as I was dusted in my heat at East Los Angeles Junior College. I had the form over the hurdles, but I lacked the quickness between them to keep up with the South Central hurdlers.

I was not discouraged and I was glad that I had tried, because I wanted to test myself against the best kids in the city. I was up for the challenge.

At the same meet, I was among a group of high school kids that qualified to come back the following week to compete for the Class C Los Angeles City championship in the high jump. Back in those days, there were three divisions competing in track and field in the State of California. Based on a sliding scale that gave points for height, weight and age, the athletes were divided into Class C, Class B and Class A (varsity).

Since I was 14 when the season began, weighed only about 132 pounds and stood around 5 feet 7 inches, I was in Class C, befitting my skinny stature and young age. Even though I was a Class C competitor, I was the best high jumper in my school, the best Class C high jumper in the Western League and a contender for the City title.

I was the only jumper left with the bar at 5 feet 8 ¾ inches after all of those who had successfully cleared the previous heights had missed all 3 of their attempts at the final height of the competition.

I remember the competitors to this day. There was a rail-thin black boy who used a straight leg approach to power over the bar like Olympic champion Charlie Dumas of USC. He wore the purple colors of Manual Arts, an athletic powerhouse near the Los Angeles Coliseum. There was another black kid named James Adams who took your breath away as he seemed to walk up to the bar and suddenly explode straight up like a hovercraft. He wore the red singlet with the flying "F" of perennial kingpin Freemont High School in downtown LA.

There was a Filipino kid named Legaspi from Banning who used the outdated Western Roll, going over the bar on his side instead of straddling it like the rest of us. And there was the best one of all, James Watson of Narbonne High School, a former juvenile delinquent with a big scary reputation from his days at Riis Junior High School, which was the equivalent of a reform school in the LA County system. He had a powerful straight lead leg action, but he had not yet mastered the technique. When he did in the following year, he developed into one of the nation's premier high school jumpers.

Most of these kids had better marks than my 5'10" Hamilton High School record, but on the day none of them was able to clear the last height. Just before my final jump, the Manual Arts jumper walked up to me, clasped my hands in his at the level of my heart and wished me good luck. If I had missed, that kid would have tied for first with me. But he seemed genuine in wishing me good fortune. I was impressed with his sportsmanship.

I cleared the bar cleanly. It was all very dramatic, what with my having the last jump. The pressure was on me. And I didn't choke.

When I walked out of the East LA stadium with my mom and dad, a kid from the Western League who had not been following the drama asked how I had done. "I won," I said in a non-celebratory fashion.

My mom was surprised by my modest attitude and my dad seemed at a loss for words after I not only won the championship in a tough battle with kids who were better than I was, but I did not choke. He just could not relate to it, because all during the season, I surpassed anything he had ever done in high school.

Instead of being thrilled for me, he seemed more conflicted about it than anything else. To his friends and our family, he acted the part of my biggest supporter. But, in his solitary thought, he was amazed at what I had been able to accomplish compared to himself. He was still overly concerned about protecting my delicate psyche should I lose and, now that I was a success, he became worried that I was directing all of my energies and putting my entire focus on high jumping.

My father, having seen me grow up, knew me a lot better than I knew myself in certain respects, and he noticed in me a passion that was characterized by a penchant for going all in on any venture that captured my imagination. He did not want to me to focus on something as micro as high jumping to the exclusion of something macro like my education. He proved this by "benching" me during my junior year in high school midway through the season when my grades were embarrassingly poor.

My dad's main focus was not on risk taking and competition. That is where my dad and I differed, not only in sports but also in life.

My dad was a very talented guy in many respects. He won a citywide Shakespearean acting competition in Los Angeles. He edited the high school newspaper. He could have gone on to do many things that would have enriched the lives of himself and his family.

But he was afraid to lose and consequently uncomfortable taking risks. He died at 41 from heart problems resulting from a serious bout of scarlet fever as a child.

I really think the engine that drives me to be successful is the fear of becoming like my father—a guy who would not do what was necessary to fulfill any of his dreams. My dad was one of the most well liked people I have ever known. When he died, there must have been 300 cars in the funeral procession. Everybody liked him because he had a warm personality and great sense of humor. But beneath the veneer of happiness was an unhappy and unfulfilled guy who did not have the stomach to take risks and race after his dreams.

Unlike my dad, I have never been afraid to get beat. I do not like to lose. I am competitive to a fault. But I can tell you that it has only been through failure and losing things—people, possessions and contests—that I learned what it took to become a winner and to be successful.

When my dad gave me his reasons for not wanting me to run the hurdles in the LA City prelims, he challenged me without knowing he had done so. Over the years, when somebody has scoffed at the notion that I would be able to achieve a goal, I have always felt challenged.

And when I am challenged, I respond by redoubling my efforts. I do not like to lose at anything. So when I am challenged, there is no telling what I am apt to do in response.

This competitiveness manifests itself in some unusual ways. For instance, in the summer of the year Animal Kingdom won the Kentucky Derby, I pulled up near a small empty parking space in downtown Saratoga Springs, New York. I asked my passengers if they thought I could fit into the spot. My wife knew better than to say no, because she knew it would have challenged me. But the other passenger, a brand new Team Valor International employee named Bradley Weisbord, had not known me long enough to prevent him from blurting out "No way!"

By painstakingly making several incremental back-and-forth movements, which took about 5 minutes, I was finally able to maneuver the car into the space, with probably an inch to spare both in front and back, all to the protestations of young Mr. Weisbord, who kept yelling out such things as, "Are you crazy, you're gonna scrape the bumper!" That there were a few new scrapes to the front and rear bumper of my car was inconsequential and secondary to the fact that I was challenged, I rose to the challenge and I proved my point, no matter how inane, inappropriate or meaningless it may have been.

Another time, when I had just moved from Southern California to the Bluegrass in 1999, a bloodstock agent presented a horse to me that I wanted desperately to buy. The agent, however, was unable to strike a final deal with the prospective seller. Adding insult to injury, he told me that he wanted to wait another day, as he was sure he could sell the horse to a top trainer instead of me for more money. I suggested to the agent that he create a deadline for the seller that would add some urgency to the sale.

The agent said the owner was "an old guy, well into his eighties" and that the fellow was intractable. The agent reiterated that if a deal could be done, it would have to wait until the next day. Well, naturally, I took this as a challenge. Even though I was no longer operating a bloodstock agency as I had from 1978 to 1987, I retained all of my bloodstock agent instincts and guile.

I called the "old timer" myself, informed him that I liked his 2-year-old very much and wanted to buy him, but unless I could do a deal that very evening, I would be unable to complete any transaction, as I was slated to fly the very next day to Europe. If I got a signed contract to buy the colt, however, I would consider postponing my trip for a day.

The horse in question was at Calder. I told the owner that I never buy a horse sight unseen and the only way I would be able to finish the deal is if he gave me enough confidence to fly to Miami in the morning by signing a contract that evening.

It was after midnight and the guy did not have a computer or a fax machine. I told him that I would fax a contract to a Kinko's store about 25 minutes from his house. I told him he could drive over there, sign the agreement and fax it right back.

The fellow was reluctant because his trainer had told him that he could get a couple hundred thousand dollars more for the horse if he just waited until the morning. I was able to convince the guy that a bird in the hand was worth two in the bush.

I liked the horse, but even more, I was getting revved up on the fact that I could make the guy jump through hoops after midnight and drive half an hour away to sign a contract, thereby convincing my bloodstock agent friend not to tell me that something possible was impossible.

The guy jumped through the hoops, I inspected the horse in the morning, called the owner and told him that we had a deal. Then I let the bloodstock agent sell the horse to his other client for a tidy profit to me of $200,000. I never had to pay for the horse. I just used the contract to tie up the horse. This incident was more about making a statement to the agent than a financial event. I felt badly for the agent, who is a friend of mine, so I paid him $50,000 to soothe any hurt feelings. But I proved my point emphatically.

The horse went on to become a well-known Grade 2 winner in Southern California for one of the biggest trainers in the game.

So when I hear the sound of those bongo drums increasing in intensity and Bobby Freeman asking me if I "wanna dance," my response is "Ab-so-loootley I wanna dance!" Especially if it is a challenge and there is some risk involved.

CHAPTER 4

The Turf Writer

In a period of a few days in the autumn of 1969, my world as a writer came crashing down. I received a rejection slip from *The New Yorker* for a piece that had been with them for 8 months. Then I got a handwritten note from the editor of the Los Angeles-based literary magazine *Ante* informing me that the first of my five stories that had been accepted months earlier for publication would not see the light of day, as the magazine had folded when its funding "angel" had flown the coop.

Bearer of the bad tidings about my short stories was my instructor in a creative writing class I had taken for two years at the University of California at Los Angeles. Isabelle Ziegler was my biggest fan. She liked my "uniquely Irwinian" stories and scolded *The New Yorker* for not publishing my story, especially after mulling it over so long. But by accepting my five stories, Isabelle had taken them off the market for a considerable period of time, at least temporarily ending the possibility that another magazine might publish them. It was a lot of bitter pills to swallow at once and it left a horrible taste in my mouth for speculative writing. Never again would I write anything without being secure in the knowledge that it would be published.

I had spent the previous seven or eight years honing my craft as a short story writer and had nothing to show for it except a kind note from a staffer at *The New Yorker*, the admiration of my UCLA teacher and a correspondence with the *Kansas City Review*, which had been ready to publish one of my stories until I took a childishly intractable stance about one passage that the editor thought needed some clarification. When I informed them that Ernest Hemingway would not tolerate such a situation, they told me what I could do with the piece!

Earlier that summer I had started a novel—a "Holden Caulfield runs away to the race track" sort of thing.

My lone attempt at a non-fiction piece, which I had envisioned appearing in a Thoroughbred trade publication such as *The Blood-Horse*, also had fizzled. I had been reading *The Blood-Horse* since finding my first copy in a used book and magazine store on Alvarado Boulevard, next door to a pawnshop where, when I tapped out at the track or had a hot horse I wanted to bet, I used to regularly hock items such as my typewriter and my wife's engagement ring.

Robert "Bob" Hebert seemed to be living the type of life that appealed to this 25-year-old budding short story writer in 1968. He had his day job, as a handicapper and turf writer for the leading Los Angeles newspaper, and on weekends he filed reports on major Southern California races for *The Blood-Horse*.

I thought, "Hey, what a great gig. I could spend my week writing fiction, then go racing on weekends and get paid to write about the races. That might even lead to some freelancing. Sign me up!"

So I wrote a piece analyzing the dilemma Kentucky breeders faced when deciding whether to breed a mare to the new stallion Boldnesian, which was good enough to win the Santa Anita Derby and gain prominence as a winter-book favorite for the Kentucky Derby, but had only raced five times. At the time, there was a substantial prejudice against breeding to horses that failed to stand training after only a few outings. Today, a Santa Anita Derby winner of four of five starts would have just about achieved a full career in racing! How times have changed.

I sent the piece to Hebert, seeking his opinion. I thought I had done a thorough job. Bob, a well-mannered Southern gentleman and a quality human being, tried to let me down as gently as possible, but basically said the theme had been written about many times and my approach failed to bring anything fresh to the table. He gently unplugged my life support unit when he suggested that it was possible to be passionate about one's hobby of horse racing without contributing to it professionally as a writer. At the time it felt like piling on. I needed to be taken out of the game and given some bench time.

So there I was in September of 1969. I felt worthless and rudderless. I had been totally blown out of the water as a writer of both fiction and non-fiction. The comments by Hebert convinced me that the novel I had begun would amount to nothing but a joke, because obviously I did not know as much about horse racing as I thought.

In a spur-of-the-moment decision that completely changed my life, I quit my job of five years as a Group Supervisor of juvenile delinquents with the Los Angeles Probation Department and decided to drive to Lexington, Kentucky to see what it was like.

My first cross-country driving attempt ended after only about 3 hours, when my pathetic, wimpy little Karmann Ghia failed to climb all the way to the top of a steep incline leaving the desert community of Barstow, California.

Crap! Barstow again. I had gone there a year earlier with my wife for a job interview as sports editor of the *Desert Dispatch*. Barstow, a sparsely populated little hellhole out in the Mojave Desert, was basically a large truck stop exactly halfway between Los Angeles and Las Vegas. The job was mine for the taking, but my first wife could not abide living in the "middle of nowhere."

With my Karmann Ghia dead, I signed the registration certificate, placed it under the windshield wiper and abandoned the car in the dirt median of the highway. While walking back toward the small downtown, I was picked up by a couple of teenagers who offered to drive me to the Greyhound station in their dune buggy. These two rednecks had their fun with me first, though, as they shot out into the Mojave Desert and did some crazy-ass off-roading in an effort to scare the bejesus out of a city boy. They eventually dropped me off at the bus station. Real jerks.

Not having a car did not deter me from making a second attempt to drive to Kentucky; after all, I was nothing if not resourceful. I found a company that solved the needs of car owners who wanted their vehicles cheaply delivered to far off locations by pairing them with drivers in need of inexpensive ways of traveling. I was paired with a soldier who wanted his souped-up Dodge driven from Southern California to Fort Knox in Kentucky. All I had to do was pay for the gas.

Equipped with a big air intake scoop on the hood, the black Dodge exuded power and rumbled like a tank. Man, was that car ever a powerhouse. At one point, while driving through Wyoming or Montana where there was no posted speed limit, I got that sucker up to 125 miles an hour. I thought I was really hauling ass until a cop car flew by me like I was parked! God only knows how fast he was traveling.

My first stop across the country was in Las Vegas. I had been there many times as a kid with my parents. I had spent 10 days in Las Vegas on my honeymoon at the original Mob-owned Flamingo hotel thanks to a connection my uncle Sol Rubin had with the entertainer Danny Thomas, father of "That Girl" sitcom star Marlo Thomas and the founder of St. Jude Children's Research Hospital in Memphis.

This time, however, I stopped to test a gambling theory one of my co-workers at Juvenile Hall touted me on. It went like this: play roulette; wait for an odd or even number or a black or red color to come up three consecutive times; then bet against it because with each spin, the odds became more and more in favor of the opposite number or color occurring. That of course was in theory.

Starting out with a small bankroll, I was up more than $3,000 in less than a couple of hours. I figured I had found a way to fund the purchase of a new car. I called my wife, explained the gambling theory and my luck, and told her that I had decided to stick around for a couple of days to beef up my bankroll before heading on to Kentucky. She was unfazed an hour later to receive a second call announcing that I had lost most of my profit, was still slightly ahead and was getting back in the Dodge. I did manage to cash a bet on a filly named Title, a regally bred Bold Ruler filly out of Round Table's dam Monarchy, so I blew town with more money than I had arrived with.

When I made it to Lexington, my first stop was the offices of *The Blood-Horse*. I wanted to get a map showing the locations of Keeneland racetrack and the hundreds of breeding farms that surrounded the city. The first person that greeted me was Erbert Eades, an advertising executive who single-handedly would revolutionize promotion within the industry and provide funding for the magazine to improve dramatically in its coverage of racing and breeding both domestically and internationally. He was a great asset to the magazine and a good friend to me.

The Blood-Horse was started in 1916 by a small horsemen's group and sold to the predecessor of its current owner in 1935. Eventually, the Thoroughbred Owners and Breeders Association took it over. Founder Thomas B. Cromwell continued to operate a successful insurance company in offices located directly above the magazine's headquarters on Alexandria Drive.

The Blood-Horse had become a great part of my life in the mid-1960s. I could not wait until the next issue arrived at the newsstand on Las Palmas Avenue in Hollywood. If it arrived a day late, I would suffer withdrawal symptoms. I read the magazine from cover to cover, including all of the editorial copy, statistics and advertisements, discovered who all of the major industry players were and was simply fascinated by the world of racing and breeding.

Eades handed me a map and asked what I was up to. I told him that I was a writer. I was working on a racing novel. And I just wanted to come to Kentucky and see what the bluegrass was like. He asked me to hang around for a bit. When he returned, he said that Kent Hollinsgworth wanted to talk to me.

I was ushered into the private office of the editor of *The Blood-Horse* and directly confronted with the real-life image of the man whose editorials I had been devouring and admiring for the past few years.

Hollingsworth was an outgoing fellow. He was boyish, yet dressed conservatively in a suit and tie like an adult. He smoked a pipe and laughed and smiled a lot between puffs. He had an infectious personality. Kent Parrot Hollingsworth had charisma.

We hit it off instantly because we both had an offbeat sense of humor. As much as he tried to put me at ease, I was too excited and intimidated to relax. He asked about my stories. He asked what my goals were. I said that someday I would like to work as a correspondent for *The Blood-Horse* just like Bob Hebert.

Hollingsworth asked how much I knew about racing. First question out of his mouth was "Who is the leading sire in North America?" I knew the answer as well as I knew my 1-year-old daughter's name. But performance anxiety prevented me from coming up with the answer. Under less intimidating circumstances, I could have recited his lineage, race record and sire stats. Hell, he was in my fantasy *Daily Racing Form* chart that I designed that afternoon in Latin class! Not to mention I had just cashed a bet on his daughter Title in Las Vegas.

I eventually was able to answer several other questions. He asked if I had any examples of my work with me. I gave him one from the trunk of the Dodge. It was the story ultimately rejected by the *Kansas City Review* about some track and field athletes that was inspired by my days as a hurdler and high jumper at Los Angeles City College. He asked where I was staying. I told him that I did not know yet but that when I did I would call the office and leave my number for him.

The next day Hollingsworth phoned me at the Yokum Motor Lodge on the corner of Waller and Nicholasville, right across the street from the campus of the University of Kentucky. He offered me a job. I had not expected anything like that to happen. I thanked him, told him that I would confer with my wife and get right back to him. I also apologized for not being able to immediately come up with the name of leading sire Bold Ruler. He said he completely understood.

My wife Shelly Phyllis Hilton Irwin was still reeling from my sudden job resignation with the Probation Department. Even though we had no money and a 1-year-old daughter, I asked her to move from Los Angeles to Kentucky.

She had seen me receive one rejection slip after another. Now she saw me accepted for something and realized how much it meant to me.

Shelly was a brilliant young lady. But she had a troubled childhood. Her father was English-born James Hilton, the best-selling novelist and screenwriter who is best remembered for writing *Goodbye, Mr. Chips* and coining the word *Shangri-La*, a name Hilton gave to a fictional utopia in the Himalayan Mountains from his popular novel and movie *Lost Horizon* starring Ronald Coleman.

Shelly only got to know her father a bit when she was able to spend some time with him in England as a pre-teen. Hilton had quickly divorced Shelly's mother, who had donned a blonde wig when she played clarinet in Ina Ray Hutton's all-girl band. Natalie Robin née Rabin aka Rabinowitz was a 5-timer as a bride and eventually developed more interest in her own gender, a circumstance that led my own mother to be checked into a sanitarium for a short period of time after Shelly's mom had propositioned my mother and my aunt on the eve of my nuptials with my first wife.

Shelly was artistic and she was beautiful enough to be a model as a teenager. Fortunately for me, she was willing to show her husband of six years some solid support. What I asked her to do was not easy: we would be leaving a city where we both had spent all of our lives, where all of our family and friends lived, to move to a place where our liberal politics and Jewish backgrounds put us in a minority smaller than black people.

I had been earning $400 a week in the Probation Department. Hollingsworth offered me $100 a week. Neither Shelly nor I knew if we could possibly live on that little money. I mentioned this to Kent, who told me that living expenses in the Bluegrass were considerably cheaper than in Los Angeles.

Money and comfort meant very little to me in October of 1969. I wanted to make the move and work for *The Blood-Horse*. Thankfully my wife indulged me.

When I told the owner of the Yokum Motor Lodge that The Blood-Horse had hired me, she wasted no time in asking if I could sell a yearling she had bred. I would learn soon enough that seemingly everybody in Lexington had a yearling for sale. The 1-year-old horse in question had no pedigree and I did not know the first thing about selling a horse.

My term at *The Blood-Horse* lasted from October of 1969 through May of 1970. I learned how to write. I received a crash-course education that has served me well ever since. The method employed by *The Blood-Horse* to initiate a new writer into the Thoroughbred industry was baptism by fire.

Within weeks of my arrival, I was sent to Keeneland to cover the November Breeding Stock Sale. I had never been to a horse sale, only read about them. I had never met a single player at the sale, only read about them. It was daunting and exhilarating to be able to walk up to an icon like

A. B. "Bull" Hancock, the master of mighty Claiborne Farm, and ask him a question.

Prefacing any question with the introduction that I worked for *The Blood-Horse* afforded me instant credibility. The magazine was held in the highest regard by professional horsemen because of Kent Hollingsworth and the previous editor Joe Estes, who is credited with establishing the statistical criteria still used by the industry to measure its racing and breeding stock. Estes' lifelong friend Joe Palmer, a turf writer who began his career in racing at the magazine, elevated the genre as a contributor to the Lexington-based publication. Edward Bowen, who now lives a block away from me in Versailles, also maintained the high editorial standards of the magazine and had left a couple of years before my arrival to edit another publication.

Hollingsworth was listed as the editor. In point of actual fact, as the Irish put it, Kent's contribution to the magazine was his weekly column entitled "What's Going On Here." The man that did all of the actual editing and was responsible for managing the editorial content of the magazine was Lawrence K. (Larry) Shropshire, a United Press International editor that totally admired Hollingsworth's writing talent and followed him to the magazine.

Shropshire was a hard-nosed editor with a merciless blue pencil that could cut the life out of a sentence quicker than Jack The Ripper could slit the throat of a London hooker. It was incredibly difficult for me to get over the hump of tolerating Shropshire. He was a highly capable editor, but he had a gruff exterior, a most intimidating stare and a manner of speaking that was bone chilling and had the effect of belittling its target.

If he had been a boys' vice-principal and a maladjusted student had an option of being stared down by Shropshire or smacked in the butt with a large wooden paddle with holes in it, the paddle would have ruled as the prohibitive betting choice!

He also had some unusual habits. For instance, when he had worn down his pencil to the nub, he would reach into his desk, pull out a roll of previously worn-down pencil nubs rubber-banded together into what looked like rounds of ammunition and add the new nub to the roll. Then he would carefully place it back in his desk. I had a fantasy of Shropshire one day pulling out a huge roll of pencil nubs, draping them across his chest in the crisscross manner of a Mexican bandito and opening fire on his disappointing underlings in *The Blood-Horse* editorial office.

Shropshire was not liked by anybody at the magazine who worked directly under him. Shropshire's demanding ways resulted in a revolving door policy that saw new writers come into the office just as fired writers were shown the way out.

During the short period of time I worked at the magazine, several writers were relieved of their posts. It reminded me of a program instituted by the Scoutmasters at the Boy Scout camp named Emerald Bay on Santa Catalina Island. I spent two summers at Emerald Bay and loved nearly every second of it.

The part I did not care for was one in which a few boys—perhaps 3 or 4—were sent into the wilderness wearing nothing but swim trunks and Indian war paint on their faces. The lads had to stay out all night, fend for themselves, create their own shelter and find their own grub. At that time, the island was inhabited by wild boar. If the scouts were successful in keeping away from the camp until breakfast, they were inducted into a select group of previous survivors. The ones who returned prematurely faced considerable humiliation and derision.

That is what working at *The Blood-Horse* under Larry Shropshire was like for me—survival on a raw level. My job basically consisted of writing mini-stories about stakes winners and their connections each week. I typed the stories and placed them in Shropshire's basket. He edited them, sent them off to the print shop, which made galley proofs, and then Miss Pat Doyle and I proofed them. We took turns, with one of us reading from the galley and the other holding Shropshire's edited manuscript.

At week's end, it was up to me to re-read everything I had written, analyze why Shropshire had made his edits and try to learn from my mistakes. That is exactly how I learned to write. Shropshire never spoke to me about writing. I had to have the smarts to figure out how not to repeat my mistakes.

Shropshire allowed one spelling error a week. A writer who made two in one week would find himself walking out the front door prior to closing hours. In my entire tenure at the magazine, I had one spelling error. One afternoon, Shropshire fixed that long, penetrating stare on me under those dark eyebrows and glared at me with a disgust that was palpable.

"How do you spell Reuben?" he growled at me, holding one of my freshly written stories in his hands.

"R-u-b-i-n," I said, repeating the spelling of my uncle Sol Rubin, which was a lone point of reference based on my own experience.

Shropshire barked back "R-e-u-b-e-n is the normal way."

Okay, so the guy finally nailed me for a spelling error. Well hip-hip-hooray for him! I could handle the beat down. But when he said "the normal way" it took all of my control not to defend myself. But I kept my pie hole shut, because I wanted to continue working at the magazine. Anybody that dared to talk back to Shropshire was asking for an early trip to the front door. Charles Dickens would have adored this guy.

I must have been doing something right. After just a couple of months, Shropshire and Hollingsworth held a meeting, after which they took me to lunch at the members-only Thoroughbred Club of America in the bowels of the Springs Motel.

Following the meal, Shropshire took me aside back at the office, put his arm around me and said that both he and Hollingsworth were very impressed with my work ethic and my ability to learn the job quickly. He said that he wanted to "let go" a young man whom I shared my writing duties with and both he and Kent figured I was capable to handling both of our assignments. They were so grateful, they did not to wait the usual 6 months or a year, but just 3 months, to give me a raise.

Professionally, I was ecstatic to be praised by both of my superiors. When I came home and told Shelly about the raise, it was all she could do not to laugh at the largesse exhibited by the higher ups, who had increased my weekly salary by a whopping $5. My take-home pay rose by about $3.50. That was precisely enough to allow Shelly and me to buy tickets and one bag of popcorn at the lone theatre in downtown Lexington.

The anemic raise was insignificant compared to my acceptance as a full-fledged member in good standing of *The Blood-Horse* writing staff. I was living a dream. I was crazy about working at the magazine and furthering my knowledge both of writing and matters of the Turf.

In the days before the Internet, I would return to work after dinner and pore over old news clippings that comprised the magazine's "morgue." Hollingsworth often suggested books for me to read. I contributed reviews of books that had been sent to the editorial offices.

The road to becoming a competent writer on all aspects of racing and breeding was not without its bumps. The first farm story Shropshire assigned to me was a piece on a broodmare barn at Darby Dan Farm. Upon the death in the late 1940s of four-time Kentucky Derby winning owner Col. E. R. Bradley, his estate was acquired privately. Within a few years, the property and horses were divided among a group of prominent racing men and women, including Ogden Phipps (Bessemer Trust) and Robert Kleberg (King Ranch of Texas).

Darby Dan, the centerpiece of the physical property of Bradley's Idle Hour Stock Farm, became the Kentucky headquarters of John W. Galbreath, whose hardboot farm manager Olin Gentry would utilize great bloodlines acquired by Galbreath to win the Kentucky Derby twice and give the world English Derby winner Roberto, one of the most influential stallions of all time. Galbreath named him after Roberto Clemente, a Hall of Fame baseball player for his Pittsburgh Pirates baseball club.

Swaps, my all-time favorite racehorse, stood at Darby Dan Farm, so I knew a lot about the place and revered its heritage. But what I knew about the finer points of a broodmare barn would not fill a thimble. My attempt at the story was pathetic. Shropshire rewrote it and saved my sorry butt.

As with all of my failures, I was able to learn from my mistakes and improve the next time. The process of learning to write and gaining knowledge about racing and breeding was one of trial and error. The only way I learned was by making mistakes, having these mistakes shown to me (if not explained) and correcting my thought process to avoid repeating my errors.

It probably would have made me feel better about myself and a lot less afraid of Shropshire if he had taken the time to personally show me where I had erred and exactly how to avoid mistakes the next time.

But that was not his way. He wanted people to fully accept responsibility for their actions, to be forced to learn on their own and not to be coddled. In the end, of course, the old coot was 100 percent correct. But, partly because of my own hang-up with authority figures and the editor's insensitivity, I grew to despise his techniques, his condescending attitude and his lack of appreciation of horse racing.

Oddly, Shropshire cared nothing about horse racing. To hear him tell it, there were winners, there were losers and there were only a few ways a winner could accomplish a win; so verbose accounts of how a horse managed to cross first under the wire were classified by him as a complete waste of time, ink and foolscap paper. The only reason he was at the magazine was because of his love of Hollingsworth.

I will admit to a certain sense of satisfaction whenever Shropshire threw me a bone to compliment a turn of phrase or a particularly good lead, but in the end the man's misanthropy was too much for me.

When my daughter developed fluid in her ears as a result of allergies in the spring of 1970, local doctors were unable to help clear it up and we decided to return home to Los Angeles.

I did not protest and agreed with Shelly that it was time to return to the "real world." I would not miss working under Mr. Shropshire. Another episode that took place during this time also made it a lot easier to leave *The Blood-Horse*. One afternoon I overheard a phone conversation in which Shropshire was hiring a new correspondent from New England to cover racing in that area for the magazine.

When the writer asked about pay, Shropshire told him that he would start him out at $35 per story, but that "the sky's the limit from there. Why we have one writer that's been with us for years who makes up to $100 per story." I was shocked to find out that writers received a check as puny as

$35 and that the ceiling on payment was so low. I was tired of working for peanuts. I made more money as a part-time box boy in a supermarket as a high school senior in Beverly Hills than I was making as an adult with a wife and child at *The Blood-Horse* as a full time writer. It was time to move on.

We had no money to get back home. We had no suitable car to drive. So I began playing three-horse show parlays with a $15 stake each day. I hit for something like 23 days in a row. But it was nerve racking. I found myself driving in the snow at night to check results at the downtown offices of the *Lexington Herald-Leader* where my friend Jim Williams worked. I was becoming completely obsessed with gambling.

My wife designed and sewed some Chanel knockoffs and sold them to a local boutique. After 30 days we had generated enough money to fly home.

Once again, I was a young man without a job. But this time I had marketable skills. The first job I applied for upon my return home yielded me a position nearly identical to the one I had left, this time with *The Thoroughbred of California* magazine.

The California Thoroughbred Breeders Association really needed some editorial help. Right after my interview with general manager Brian Sweeney, he introduced me to the magazine's managing editor Giles E. Wright.

"Did you see the Belmont Stakes?" Wright asked about the third leg of the Triple Crown that had been run the weekend before.

I told him that I had not seen it in person, just on television.

"That's good enough," he responded.

He walked me into an adjacent room, where there was a typewriter on a desk, some paper and a chair. "Sit down and knock out a story to fill one published page," Wright said. "Let's see what you can do!"

So in my typically rapid fashion, I pounded out a story and handed it to Wright, who showed it to Sweeney, and they offered me a job. The salary allowed my wife and me a chance to live like normal people for the first time in a year.

I worked at *The Thoroughbred of California* for 5 years. As was the case at *The Blood-Horse*, I eventually wound up doing the jobs of three people: I served as the editor, the lone staff writer and advertising manager. I completely threw myself into the task. I was a workaholic. I thrived on doing the work. I tried to delegate authority and get Sweeney to hire people to assist. But it never seemed to work out. He knew he had a good thing in me and lacked the financial motivation to spend money on workers whose job I was doing at no additional cost.

My career at *The Thoroughbred of California* began well enough, but after a period of time I found I could no longer work under Giles E. Wright.

He was an old guy who failed to leave his mark as a newspaperman at the Hearst publication in Los Angeles, the *Herald-Examiner*. His wife was a more prominent newspaper writer than he. So he developed a chip on his shoulder. He spent most of our time together trying to impress me.

He bragged about his intimate relationships with famous players in the game. In reality, few horsemen knew or respected him. He seemed to lack the skills and personality to put his subjects at ease in order to get the best results from an interview.

In an unbelievably embarrassing situation, he drove me out to the Chino ranch of Rex C. Ellsworth, the cowboy breeder of Swaps. Giles had gone on forever about how close he was with the famously taciturn Ellsworth. When we arrived at the ranch, Ellsworth barely spoke a word to Wright, other than to remind him how Giles had gotten him in trouble for writing about a stallion Ellsworth owned in partnership that injured a foot on a scale. Had Giles not written about it, the partner would never have known. Ellsworth was still pissed off after several months.

I told Sweeney that I could no longer work under Wright. Sweeney said he wanted to make me the editor, but I was only 27. Wright was near retirement age and Sweeney needed 6 months to work on his board of directors before easing the senior citizen out of the building. He told me to find temporary employment elsewhere and in six months he would hire me back as the editor.

So once again I was unemployed a year after returning to work in Southern California. Sweeney did help me get a seasonal job in publicity at Santa Anita, where I proofed the daily program, wrote news releases and manned the mic in the morning at Clocker's Corner to announce when certain horses were on the track or working.

When Santa Anita's meet ended and the action moved to Hollywood Park, I once again was out of work. Rollin Baugh, a young bloodstock agent, hired me to assist him at his office in Newport Beach. I lived in Pasadena, an hour's drive from the offices of California Thoroughbred Consultants. I did not have a car that could be counted on to make the journey on the three days a week that I was hired to work for Baugh.

But Rollin was a great guy; he loved helping out people who he thought would be valuable assets to the industry and he made an investment in me. Rollin paid me $25 a day and bought a small white Chevy Luv truck for me to drive. I worked for Baugh for 6 months before he could no longer afford the $25 a day. He was just starting out and things were going slowly for him. He had only recently left the employ of the California Thoroughbred Breeders Association. People owed him money for services rendered, and a yearling he bought at Keeneland on spec had failed to find a home. It was completely understandable that he had to let me go.

While working at CTC, I sold my first horse. Rollin had received a call from a friend telling him about three extraordinarily well-bred Claiborne Farm fillies. Rollin asked me if I could find somebody to buy one of them.

"I don't know," I replied. "I've never tried before. What do you do?"

He advised me to think of a guy I knew in the Bluegrass, give him a call, tell him about the filly and ask if he knew anybody who would buy her. My first and only call was to my pal Jim Scully, who had my job at *The Blood-Horse* just before I arrived in Lexington. He was working as an independent bloodstock agent.

I called Jim. He phoned me right back to say that he would buy the filly named Chain for $50,000 plus a commission. Incomprehensibly, the person whom Scully sold Chain to was George Harris, who not only was a close business associate, but a fellow bloodstock agent whom Rollin Baugh spoke with on a daily basis.

Rollin was beside himself. He had not immediately thought to mention Chain to Harris. He was really mad at himself. Now he had to split commissions with Jim Scully and me for a horse he easily could have sold directly to his pal George Harris.

My commission was $1,000. At that moment in my life, $1,000 was like $500,000 to me today. Rollin was so upset, it took him 6 months to bring himself around to pay me. But pay me he did. And, for that $1,000, plus the $25 a day three times a week and the use of his white truck, I remain ever grateful to a guy who threw me a bone when he needed money himself. It was a selfless gesture that I have never forgotten.

After Rollin had to let me go, I was unemployed again. More than six months had passed since I had left the employ of the CTBA so I visited Brian Sweeney to get an update on my future job as editor of the magazine.

Sweeney, in fact, had done nothing to send Giles Wright to pasture. I told him that I had no job. I had gone down to the unemployment office with no luck in finding temporary work. I said things had gotten to such a pretty pass that I had suffered the indignity of having a welfare worker interview my wife and me at our apartment in order to qualify for food stamps. Jews in Southern California on food stamps was unheard of!

Hope that my tales of despair would hasten Wright's departure faded when Sweeney urged me to go ahead and qualify for the food stamps, because after he re-hired me, he said "You could probably continue to use them for up to six months!"

That was the last straw for me. I gave him a deadline. I was serious, too. The ploy worked, as Sweeney manned up to his promise, removed Wright and brought me back into the building.

My time away from the CTBA was difficult on my wife and me, but it turned out to be a benefit to my career, as I picked up valuable experience at Santa Anita and with CTC, working yearling sales, meeting many players in the game and expanding a network of contacts that would help me later on.

During my stint at *The Thoroughbred of California* magazine, I bought my first Thoroughbred, a 21-year-old mare named Brookwood that had made 132 starts, earned about $50,000 and had already produced a New York stakes winner named Recall, who had won the Interborough Handicap. A few friends joined me in this modest 4-figure venture. She had one foal for us.

In 1974, I left the magazine. I wanted to be a real journalist, not a claque working for a house organ. Too many of my projects were being rejected, so I threw in the towel.

I opened my own advertising agency, which I named after the great racehorse and stallion Eclipse. I worked primarily for Westerly Stud in the Santa Ynez Valley, where I specialized in promotion and advertising for stallions. It was a great gig while it lasted. But one day the Japanese-born-and-based wife of the Scandinavian furniture designer who hired me showed up. It immediately became apparent who wore the pants in that family.

In a newsletter I prepared for Westerly, I had featured a story on George A. Pope, a prominent California breeder and successful campaigner of horses both at home and abroad. Pope was standing a minor stallion at Westerly, which was a fledgling operation with no track record. I reasoned that, by showing that a guy of Pope's stature would support Westerly Stud, it imbued the entire operation with a sense of history, continuity and quality. The woman failed to see it from my point of view, arguing that I should be promoting her and not others, and she canned me.

Once again, I was back looking for a job.

CHAPTER 5

Daily Racing Form

In the spring of 1975 I got a call from Don "The Flamingo" Fleming, editorial chief of the Los Angeles office of the *Daily Racing Form* on Bimini Place, just down the street from Los Angeles City College, where I ran track, met my first wife and occasionally attended classes.

The Flamingo, as he was known behind his back, called to discuss hiring me. I went down to the office for an interview. He was looking for somebody to do a notes column on the Southern California racing circuit at Hollywood Park, Santa Anita and Del Mar.

"I know you can write and I know you know your way around the backstretch," he explained, "but what I don't know is if you can restrict yourself to writing notes or whether you are even interested in doing notes. Notes can be fun and lively if they're short and punchy. We're not looking for a columnist per se. We have one of those already. And I can't promise you that you'll ever have that chance.

"But I know you are looking for something and this may be it. It's not the opportunity you probably want, but it's a foot in the door at *Daily Racing Form*."

The problem was that I had never aspired to work for *Daily Racing Form* because I thought it was more or less a step down. The quality of writing on the West Coast was a joke. They were publishing stuff by Oscar Otis, Eunice Walkup and Pat Rogerson. Nobody in racing respected them. It was somewhat embarrassing.

But I missed being involved, I missed writing about horses and I wanted a steady paycheck again. So I took the job.

My first notes column appeared in the *Form* on April 17, 1975, four days before my 32nd birthday. On my first day in the press box, director of publicity Bob Benoit led me into his office, shut the door and said, "Barry I'm glad you got this job. But I must be honest with you and tell you that I don't like your being here. And I told your editor so.

"I've got the best guy in racing back there (in the stable area) everyday, turning out positive notes and stories. There is nobody better. He can find out things faster than anybody. All you'll be able to find out are negative things. That won't help us or racing. I'm so sure you won't be able to find out anything that's positive, I'll make you an offer of $50 for everything positive you can find out before Nat (Wess)."

Bob was a publicist. I was a reporter. We were on opposite ends of the news. Bob was not used to working with writers that he did not have in tow. I was a wild card. I scared the shit out of him. And, as he later found out, he had good reason to fear me.

Hollywood Park's publicity director had already gotten a little taste of what I was capable of when I made some pointed comments about Marjorie L. Everett in a story in *The Thoroughbred of California*. My boss Brian Sweeney was traveling when the issue containing the story went to press and I was able to slip in a provocative piece about Hollywood Park's operator.

A control freak way ahead of his time in trying to manage the news, Benoit did his best to eliminate the jobs of turf writers working for daily newspapers by offering stories and columns generated by Nat Wess and others in his publicity office. The editorial content was given gratis to newspapers in the hopes that editors would consider using it to supplement the output of their own writers. Eventually Hollywood Park increased its content to encourage editors to eliminate the jobs of turf writers. This was tantamount to the Republican National Committee generating news copy for the *New York Times*. Richard Nixon would have loved this guy.

The writers who did remain employed were always targets of Bob'n boss Mrs. Everett, who succeeded in corrupting the *Herald-Examiner's* turf writer Gordon Jones, a former college instructor who billed himself as "Professor" Gordon Jones. Handsome, well-educated and a gifted talker, Jones had all the tools to become successful as a promoter in any field he chose; but the man was hooked on the ponies and he had a gambling addiction that overtook his life. Because he was in a constant state of tapping out, he made himself vulnerable to Mrs. Everett's constant attentions. He sold out big time.

Bob Benoit ran his publicity department the way major motion picture moguls ran their studios in the 1930s and 1940s and the way political operatives run campaigns today. The only news that is generated comes from them. They identify what they consider to be news and write releases.

My duties for *DRF* consisted of writing advances, which were stories about impending races, and doing a notes column. Hollywood Park preferred that the media use the track's own versions of stakes advances instead of fresh material written by *DRF* writers. And many writers basically did just that: they would use virtually all the copy the publicity department handed to them, changing only the headline and the lead, while adding a byline.

My job, as I saw it, was to write about racing for the readers of the *Daily Racing Form*. But the owners of *DRF* were too cozy with the racetracks because of their reliance on each other, so the *Form's* interest in hard news and inside information was limited at best.

I saw myself as the third point in a triangle. Truth be told, I drove my superiors at *DRF* as crazy as I did the owners of racetracks. I had a real problem representing the *DRF* and the tracks at the direct expense of my readership, comprised mainly of horseplayers and racing fans that relied on me to provide them with reliable and unbiased information.

Back then, Hollywood Park and *Daily Racing Form* played a silly game that involved pretending that a famous horse would be running in an upcoming race, when the track knew for sure the horse would stay in the barn and *DRF* either knew or had a pretty good idea what was going on.

But once a patron had bought his copy of *Daily Racing Form* and had paid the admission price to enter the track, the game had been won. Score: *DRF*/track 1, patron 0. And *DRF* and the track were not content to do it once or twice. They ran up the score all season long.

Horseplayers and racing fans are an exceptionally resilient bunch. They are used to getting the short end of the stick on a daily basis. But they hate being hoodwinked and treated as marks. Upon hearing an announcement halfway through the program that Affirmed, for example, would not be racing that afternoon, the sense of deflation was palpable. Bob Benoit failed to understand or internalize this concept. He was a barker at the carnival, intent only on getting the suckers into the tent to see the bearded lady. It mattered not one whit to him that she turned out to be a guy wearing a bra and falsies!

Big horses draw big crowds and Hollywood Park knew it. So they put as much pressure as they could on trainers to get them to run at their track. And, in some cases, if the trainer was unable to oblige, Hollywood expected him to play along with them in pretending the horse would be running, just to get people out to the track.

The best illustration I can give of this phenomenon occurred one season in 1978 at Hollywood Park with Affirmed, the last horse to win the Triple

Crown until American Pharaoh did it in 2015. Cuban-born Lazaro Sosa Barrera trained the homebred for Louis and Patrice Wolfson's Harbor View Farm of Florida. I was close to Laz, regularly visited him in New York, covered him for stories in many publications, had him as a guest on my radio and television programs, and later managed a top racehorse that he trained.

On a Monday, which was my one confirmed day off from work at *Daily Racing Form*, Hollywood Park staged—and I use this word with utter precision—a press conference at the track. They knew nobody would be there because it was a "dark day," meaning no racing was scheduled. There were no entries being taken that day for races later in the week. Truth be told, Hollywood Park really only wanted a representative from *Daily Racing Form* to be there and I was the most likely candidate.

Focus of the news conference was to announce that Affirmed would be racing at the Inglewood, California oval the coming weekend. Affirmed had not been pointed for a race that weekend. I was puzzled. Because I wanted to have Monday off, I phoned Barrera to ask him if Affirmed was really going to run. He said "no." Then I told him that there was going to be a news conference, at which time it would be announced that Affirmed would be entered to run. It turned out that Nat Wess wanted Barrera to help them finesse the situation by indicating the colt was under serious consideration for the race. Barrera's stance was that he would do anything he could to help the track, but he would not be put in a position to lie. He had been invited for "lunch" at the track, but told me he would cancel those plans in light of what he learned from me.

I phoned The Flamingo, updated him on my conversation with Barrera, and asked if I could skip the press conference. "No," he said. "You have to go." So I drove over to Hollywood Park, went into the room where the press conference was set up and waited. The only person who showed up was Nat Wess. I told him point blank what I thought of his stupid scam. He handed me a press release and I went home. It was a complete charade to trick people into coming to Hollywood Park on the weekend, while Affirmed wound up staying in his stall. You know that tree they always talk about that falls in the forest and everybody wonders whether anybody hears it? Well, I was there and I missed the tree, but I was able to hear about it later!

Stuff like this did not go on at other major racetracks. Certainly, Saratoga, Belmont, Churchill Downs and Keeneland did not do it. I worked at Santa Anita and they did not do it. Hollywood Park stood alone and I placed most of the blame on Marje Everett. She ran the track like a despot and prompted her underlings to create and spew out propaganda.

Marje Everett was the adopted daughter of Benjamin F. Lindheimer, a Chicagoan who operated Arlington and Washington Park racetracks, as well as a minor league football team named the Los Angeles Dons. Marje took over the tracks, which she ran with an iron fist. In 1969, she was implicated in bribing Illinois Governor Otto Kerner, who spent three years in federal prison for accepting stock options in Everett's racetrack; in return, the governor granted her track choice racing dates.

Rumors also circulated that Marje did deals with organized crime figures and had once even had a man killed. Old-timers tell of Marje sitting on the bench at Dons games and telling the coach which plays to run. Whether it was true or not, the story, at the very least, indicated what a micro-manager she was.

Bob Benoit and Nat Wess, both fearful of losing their jobs, complied with Everett's wishes. I got to know Bob very well years later and he was a great guy who loved racing. I always found Nat Wess to be a pleasant enough fellow and a true professional. But like the willing accomplices in Germany involved in the Third Reich, they exhibited a remarkable degree of gusto in carrying out the plots of Der Führer.

When I ran a note in my *DRF* column about a horse she had bought, I got a close-up glimpse of the fear that Mrs. Everett was able to instill in some of the most powerful men in racing. Mike Hirsch was the bloodstock agent involved in selling Secretariat's half-brother Somethingfabulous to Mrs. Everett. He wanted credit in print for the transaction, but he made me swear that I would never reveal that he was my source, as Ms. Everett hated him (and with good reason). So I ran the note, and mentioned his name, but did not attribute it to a source. To say all hell broke loose was an understatement.

On the day the note appeared in my column, I wound up having individual meetings at the track with *Daily Racing Form* publisher Michael Sandler, Marje Everett herself and her trainer Charlie Whittingham. I did not know Sandler very well at that time. I had a good relationship with Charlie as, between marriages, I was dating one of his top exercise riders. I had no relationship whatsoever with Mrs. Everett.

Mike Sandler asked me where I got my information about the sale. I refused to tell him. On the one hand he respected me as a newspaperman, but on the other hand he became very frustrated because Mrs. Everett was a tyrant who always got her way. She demanded an apology and an explanation from me because she said that she no longer did business with bloodstock agent Mike Hirsch. Apparently, there was bad blood between Everett and the mother of the agent, whose father Buddy Hirsch trained for King Ranch of Texas. Charlie just wanted me to appease Everett and end the matter as quickly as possible. "You don't know this woman," he said "or what she is capable of doing."

When I met with Charlie, I was taken aback by how unnerved he was. Charlie Whittingham, an ex-Marine, was a "man's man," tough as nails, a giant in the industry and as no-nonsense a guy as anybody would ever expect to meet. Yet he was shaken up because he had compromised his relationship with Everett by doing a deal with the devil to buy a horse that he really wanted. Mike Hirsch was well known as a scoundrel and Everett had unsatisfactory dealings with him. Charlie was between a rock and a hard place.

When I met Mrs. Everett, I told her that I was sorry with the unexpected turn of events. "I apologize if this comment upset you," I said. She replied, in her Elmer Fudd way of speaking, "I want a com-pweet we-twaction because it is not twoo! I didn't buy this horse from Mike-ooh Huuuesh."

I told Mrs. Everett that I had checked the facts before I had written my note, believed them to be accurate and told her that I did not plan to write a retraction. She was not a happy person.

Agitating Bob Benoit and Nat Wess became something of a hobby for me. Each spring Benoit flew to Louisville for the Kentucky Derby. It was a week of partying and hustling Eastern-based connections to consider shipping their stock to Hollywood Park for the remainder of the annual spring-summer race meet.

One year Benoit brought Wess with him. But both Benoit and Wess wound up missing the Run for the Roses, as they were summoned back to Hollywood Park because the young man they had left in charge of the publicity office had been the subject of a prank perpetrated by none other than that rapscallion Barry Irwin.

Pete Bellas, the kid in charge, was a nice guy. But he worked for Bob Benoit, which made him the enemy. Knowing what a control freak Benoit was, I came up with a stunt to cause a bit of chaos around the press box. Benoit hated anybody getting a scoop on the publicity office. So I created my own scoop.

I "accidentally" left something in the publicity office's copy machine: a fictitious breaking news story I had just written about a serious leg injury to the top handicap horse on the grounds, the stretch-running white sensation Vigors. The story, with my byline on it, reported that the horse would be forced to miss a major upcoming race at Hollywood Park.

There were so many enjoyable aspects to this short, sweet little vignette in the press box, it really is hard to single out the highlight. But my favorite part might have been in the very beginning, when I watched Pete discover the document, read it, look around the press box as nonchalantly as he could, and contemplate his first move. It was simply exquisite to watch. Pete took the bait and proceeded to do his best to get the news on the wires of AP and UPI before my story surfaced around 5 p. m. in *Daily Racing Form.*

Benoit's press deputy first phoned Lou Eilken, the executive in charge of the racing program for Marje Everett's track. He was genuinely heartsick to hear the bad news, but was puzzled as to why the trainer did not notify him first. That expectation in and of itself illustrates the power Hollywood Park had over the horsemen of that era. He bemoaned the loss of the highlight of his "entire handicap program for the meeting!"

Eilken phoned his regrets to Vigors' owner W. R. "Fritz" Hawn, the twenty-year president of Del Mar racetrack and co-owner of the Dallas Cowboys. Hawn had no idea what the racing secretary was talking about. He suggested that Eilken call Larry Sterling, the horse's trainer. Sterling also expressed no knowledge of any injury.

Finally, Eilken called me. I spilled the beans and told him what we did and why we did it. He was so relieved that he did not get mad at me.

Fortunately for all concerned, Pete Bellas did not put his own version of the Vigors injury on the news wires.

Incidentally, "Fritz" Hawn later hired me to book mares to his stallions and to do his Thoroughbred advertising. Trainer Larry Sterling got a big laugh out of the whole thing. Around the track, only Benoit and Wess were sour on the prank.

Howard Senzell, who worked with me at *DRF*, helped me pull off the stunt and we both rejoiced in the amount of traction we were able to generate.

What neither of us knew at the time was the ripple effect from our little funfest.

The Flamingo told me that publisher Mike Sandler had summoned me to come down to the Bimini Place office for a meeting. I could tell The Flamingo was conflicted between his admiration of what I had done to Benoit and his being dressed down by the publisher.

Sandler chewed me out royally and said everything a parent would say to a wayward son: that what I did was inappropriate and reflected poorly upon *DRF* and everybody who worked there. He suspended me for a week.

When I returned to work, I was surprised to receive a message from my field supervisor Joe Hirsch, the legendary executive columnist for DRF. He requested my presence for a meeting in the hotel where he was staying since his arrival the day before from the East Coast.

Joe was charged with the task of shaping me up. I had known Joe for half a dozen years or so and admired him, as did every other turf writer in America, for his ability to turn out a prodigious amount of work leading up to and through the Triple Crown. He was such an omnipresent force.

My friend Jeff Siegel wrote a one-paragraph send up of him that he passed around the press box. The headline read "Joe Hirsch Wins Annual Joe Hirsch Award." The byline? Who else—Joe Hirsch! That pretty much summed up the stature of the man.

I was not, however, intimidated by him. Joe had a very cosmopolitan way about him. A master interviewer, he had a great knack for setting his subject at ease, wading through the muck in a very logical pattern, then driving home his point without getting so much as a pinky soiled.

He told me that I had a great future as a turf writer, that I could rise to the top at *DRF* and it was time to grow up.

I will say that most of my superiors at *Daily Racing Form* were always very supportive of my writing talent. With the exception of The Flamingo, all the rest of them—including Mike Sandler, Joe Hirsch and Bill Dow always went out of their way to praise my writing.

But in the end, the praise and the promises just were not enough. I wanted to work for a real newspaper, not a claque that hid things from the public.

Daily Racing Form back then was not anything like it is today. Back then it had a monopoly on "past performances" used to analyze races. Its news division treated the national sport as though it were a parlor game. It was owned by Walter Annenberg's Triangle Publications, which also included *The Morning Telegraph*, *TV Guide* and *Seventeen*. *Annenberg's notorious father Moe had acquired Daily Racing Form in 1920.*

Moe Annenberg was a gangster with real ties to organized crime. He operated the infamous "wire" used by illegal bookmakers to obtain quick horse racing results. Annenberg died thirty-nine days after spending two years in Federal prison for tax evasion. As was the case with his former associate Al Capone, tax evasion was all they could nail him on. He paid a fine of $9.5 million, which in today's dollars would amount to about $157 million.

His son Walter Annenberg was also indicted by the Feds, but in a plea bargain that sent Moe directly to jail; Walter was allowed to remain free. He operated the nation's third-oldest active daily newspaper, the *Philadelphia Inquirer*, and created the fabulously successful *Seventeen* magazine. He sold his empire for $3 billion to Rupert Murdoch and devoted himself to philanthropy in an effort to erase the stain on the family's name. Richard Nixon sent him to the Court of St. James as the American ambassador to England.

Early one afternoon in the summer of 1976 at Del Mar racetrack, I received a phone call in the press box with a tip to beat it downstairs to the valet parking area near the main entrance gate of the seaside track.

When I got down there, the Del Mar security officers were just wrapping up an incident involving Y. Charles "Chet" Soda, one of the original partners of the Oakland Raiders who always spent his summers at the beach. The chairman of the California Horse Racing Board was a tall, heavy-set gentleman who wore the kind of thin mustache favored by actors of an earlier era. The 68-year-old had pulled his car up to the front gate at Del Mar. In order to proceed to the restricted parking area, he needed a credential for his car, which he did not have.

Soda tried to explain to the two officers in charge that he had taken his wife's car and he was anxious to get inside to play the daily double. One officer spoke to Soda while the other officer stood directly in front of the car. Soda must have really wanted to get down on the double, because at one point, out of frustration, he took his foot off of the brake, and proceeded to prop one of the security officers onto the hood of his car.

The other officer, enraged, opened the driver's door, pulled Soda from the car, pushed him down to the ground and cuffed him. Soda then was escorted to a holding cell in the security office. He was "released on his own recognizance" later that evening.

I interviewed the officers and witnesses, sprinted back to the press box elevator, phoned The Flamingo and told him what happened. I then asked him what to do. I had the scoop. I was excited to have a real-life breaking news story to write. If I worked for a real newspaper, I would not have had to make that call. But I worked for the national house organ for racing, aka *Daily Racing Form*.

The Flamingo thought about it and finally said "Hmm. You go ahead, go ahead and write it, but just sit on it. I will phone you back."

I had not finished writing my report by the time The Flamingo called back to tell me "the Ambassador doesn't want to run that story."

Interestingly, the following morning, the major San Diego daily newspaper put the incident where nobody could miss it as its front-page headline story. Yet, *Daily Racing Form*--self-proclaimed as "America's Turf Authority since 1894"—contained not a single word about this incident.

Things had become so sensitive at Bimini Place, that I found myself unable to even get a normal sports story into print. Jockey Don Pierce, a specialist in come-from-behind rides, was a top jockey on the circuit and regularly rode for Charlie Whittingham in big races. Pierce had one flaw— he had trouble getting a horse out of the gate.

So I decided to interview Pierce and do a story about a guy who was incredibly successful in spite of a weakness. Word got back to The Flamingo, who told me to stop writing the story because he feared a potential lawsuit if Pierce sued *DRF* for the loss of income from as little as a single mount. I thought it was a preposterous notion.

I reasoned that Yogi Berra was one of the greatest catchers in baseball history, but what if he could not hit a curveball or a slider? Could a baseball writer not mention that? Was there even an infinitesimal chance of Berra or the New York Yankees suing a newspaper for running a story like this?

Daily Racing Form back then, with its original ownership group still intact, was nothing like it has been since a group headed by *New York Times* turf writer Steve Crist took over. There have been numerous ownership changes, but today the *Form* has a lot of competent writers and an editorial policy that allows for writers to stretch themselves when required.

Today, it would be hard to imagine that a story on the sentencing of a New York veterinarian, who switched the identities of two South American horses and cashed a big bet at a major NYRA track, would be found buried on page 57 of the *Form*. But that is how it was in 1978, when Mark Gerard was sent to prison for a year for running a ringer. He switched their identities, running a champion Uruguayan horse named Cinzano as a modest horse named Lebon.

While news reporting has never been a strong suit at *Daily Racing Form*, columnists down through the years have offered some of the best writing and analysis seen in the game.

Evan Shipman was a poet pal of Ernest Hemingway in Paris in the 1920s. When Parisian bookstore owner Sylvia Beach coined the phrase "The Lost Generation," she had Shipman and Hemingway in mind. No more gifted writer than Shipman covered the sport anywhere, and he wrote for the *Morning Telegraph* and *Daily Racing Form*.

Charles Hatton followed Shipman and is credited by some with coining the phrase "Triple Crown" for the Derby, Preakness and Belmont Stakes. Impossibly, he elevated the discipline with his unique writing style, as well as with the brilliantly detailed conformation descriptions he wrote about the champions of the day.

Alas, the venerable back-page column of the Western editions of the so-called "Bible" of the sport had fallen on hard times with the arrival of Pat Rogerson.

I got my first taste of this guy's bizarre outlook on turf writing one June afternoon in 1972 when I was working at California Thoroughbred Consultants. Rollin Baugh had just received a phone call from his only big client, a computer company whiz named Fletcher Jones.

Jones was a debonair entrepreneur with grey hair that belied the relatively youthful age of a man whose Computer Sciences Corporation was one of the first businesses of its kind on the West Coast. Jones established

Westerly Stud in the Santa Ynez Valley. This truly state-of-the-art farm and training center was rocking and rolling that season, as they were represented at the track by the great 6-year-old mare Typecast.

In mid-June of 1972, Typecast faced off against Convenience, a 4-year-old filly who was owned and bred by Chicagoan Leonard Lavin, the founder of Alberto-Culver beauty products.

Rollin asked me to read a *Daily Racing Form* column written by Pat Rogerson. The piece was about an interview Rogerson conducted with Jones in front of a burning fireplace at the computer mogul's home, and it featured extensive quotes from Jones.

"What'd you think?" asked Baugh.

I responded that it seemed like typical Rogerson fare.

"What would you say if I told you that there was no burning fire and that Rogerson had never set foot in Jones' home?" Rollin said.

I laughed and said that I would not be shocked.

"What would you say if I told you that Jones never said any of that stuff to Rogerson?" asked Rollin.

Now that got my attention. "Wow," I said. "Really?"

Rollin asked if I would call Rogerson, because I knew him, and ask him what in the hell he was thinking when he wrote the column. Rollin suggested that I demand a retraction. So I phoned Pat. Shockingly, he was totally candid about the ruse and said that he had just done it for the sake of atmosphere to enhance the column. And then he uttered an expression that I was to hear with alarming regularity over the next half-dozen years: "So I put a few words in his mouth. I do it all the time. Nobody minds as long as I spell their names correctly."

I told Pat that he was messing with the wrong guy this time and that Fletcher Jones wanted some form of correction or retraction. He said he would think about it. A few days later, in an offhand fashion, Rogerson wrote a throwaway line in one of his columns that went something like this. "You are right, J. B. from Pasadena. That was no fireside chat." That's it. End of story. No reference to the previous column. Nothing. Case closed. Next!

When I went to work as the notes columnist at the Form, Pat Rogerson sat right next to me in the press box—when he deigned showed up at all— and was my lone on-track editorial co-worker.

When I worked at The Blood-Horse and I would tell a prospective interviewee that I worked for that publication, the revelation moved me up a couple of lengths. But when I worked at DRF and mentioned it to an interviewee, it made them take one or two steps back. It was a tough nut to crack, because I always began from a position of having to make up ground.

Pat Rogerson was a tall, boyishly handsome man with a lot of wavy hair and a gift of gab that made him an instant hit with the ladies. He could give a hoot about the ladies. He was mainly interested in sipping on a Brandy Alexander and spinning yarns. Writing a daily column cramped his style. Press box habitués marveled at how Rogerson was able to hang on to his job at the Form.

In reality, he was an accident waiting to happen. One can only turn in so many late columns and put only so many words in the mouths of horsemen and owners. It caught up with him.

One afternoon he showed up late for work in the press box at Hollywood Park and knocked out a quick column on Agitate, a horse that was trained by a hard-ass character named James Jimenez. A used-car-salesman-turned-horse-trainer, Jimenez was the last guy on the backstretch you wanted to jerk around. He had had about as much of "Patsky" as he could take.

So when Rogerson phoned him from the press box, a few hours after entries were taken, to talk about Agitate's upcoming race that weekend, Jimenez knew it was time to take his revenge. Jimenez was unusually cooperative in his phone conversation with Rogerson. Finished with the column, Pat gave it to the Teletype operator Gayle Dunbar, who sent it to the Bimini Place office.

A few moments later Rogerson received a call from The Flamingo, asking him if that phone conversation with Jimenez really ever happened. For a change, Rogerson was able to assure him that it had!

The Flamingo suggested that Rogerson must be pretty high up on the trainer's shit list, because Jimenez never entered Agitate for the race. Furthermore, Rogerson was informed that Agitate had bowed a tendon, which he could easily have learned about if he had bothered to read Nat Wess' daily notes, which were located about fifteen feet from his typewriter.

Rogerson was in the midst of a long slide into some sloppy journalistic practices. He had taken to opening copies of The Blood-Horse and copying stories verbatim from the old stakes section I used to work on at the Lexington magazine.

After several weeks of this and hearing about it from friends of mine, I could no longer watch it. It was professionally embarrassing to be associated with Rogerson.

A disconnect had always existed between the home office at Bimini Place and writers working in the field. The office was equidistant from Santa Anita and Hollywood Park—a drive of perhaps half an hour to either venue. But they were worlds apart and those in charge at Bimini Place rarely knew what transpired in the press boxes of Southern California racing.

One morning while I walked my beat on the backstretch looking for news items, trainer Noble Threewitt approached me. He told me that his business had slowed down and he could use some publicity to remind owners that he was still available to train their horses. He handed me a $100 bill. I tried to give it back to him, but he would not take it. Later, I gave the C note to the trainer's close friend John Valpredo to give back to Threewitt. Valpredo was surprised that I did not keep the money. It would not have been as startling as it was if the giver of the $100 bill had been somebody else, because Threewitt was a longtime leader in the Horsemen's Benevolent and Protective Association and, by all accounts, a classy and honest gentleman of the old school. Such was the environment on the backstretch at this time and such apparently were the practices involved in getting one's name in print in the pages of *Daily Racing Form*, that a true gentleman like Mr. Threewitt had to stoop as low as he did.

So I called The Flamingo, told him to read a certain page number from *The Blood-Horse* and compare it with a recent column turned in by Rogerson. I informed Don Fleming that this plagiarism had been going on for some time. Mr. Rogerson was soon given his walking papers.

The day he was fired by The Flamingo, Pat Rogerson gathered his belongings in the press box. I told him right to his face that I was the one that had fingered him. He asked why I would do such a thing. I responded that I was sick and tired of having to spend my time defending his behavior to horsemen on the backstretch. It had become too debilitating for me.

"Geez Baresky, I would have thought I would have been the easiest guy in the world to work with," he said. And he really believed it, too. After all, he was one of the town's foremost proponents of the "live and let live" philosophy.

So two years after I wrote my first notes column, I was moved from the inside of the *Form* to the coveted back page as the featured Western Edition columnist.

CHAPTER 6

Racehorse Owner

I bought my first racehorse on June 9 at Hollywood Park's 1978 spring-summer meeting. I put a group of friends together to claim the 3-year-old filly Sari's Tobin for $35,000. That was a sizeable chunk of cash in those days, especially when one considers that the American record price for a claim was $55,000 in the mid 1970s and the present day value of $35,000 is about $105,000.

Reasons for choosing Sari's Tobin as my first runner included the fact she was relatively risk-free, having won a stakes race at two, and was nicely bred. Her bloodlines indicated she should improve on the turf.

Her owner-breeder Ellwood "Pie Man" Johnston operated Old English Rancho in Ontario, California. He was an expert breeder of horses and enjoyed sensational success using bloodlines that, in most cases, were a couple of generations removed from fashion. This was typical of breeders in California, where unraced horses and claimers with top pedigrees were used as stallions without a second thought.

I will never forget the year Old English Rancho topped all North American breeders in number of stakes winners. In December of that season, Johnston claimed a well-bred horse for $5,000 at Agua Caliente in Mexico to stand at his farm the next season.

When the red plastic claiming tag was clipped onto Sari's Tobin after she walked out of the winners' circle, "Pie Man" Johnston acted as if he had become temporarily disoriented. A short fellow with a shock of red hair standing above his head, he always reminded me of Woody Woodpecker. In the winners' circle he acted the part as well: he flitted about, poking his head in and out of conversations, trying to find out who had the audacity to claim a horse from him.

Johnston founded a highly successful company that made the first frozen pies available in California grocery stores. He was a constant talker, a real character and one reason few people claimed horses from him is that he would unmercifully harass them afterward if the horse turned out to be a profitable claim. Many folks just were not willing to incur the little fellow's wrath.

It was bad enough that I had the chutzpah to halter the old guy's horse, but what heightened the tension was the proximity of our racetrack seating, as the "Pie Man's" box was right next that of my trainer, Gary Jones. When the "Pie Man" came back up to his box, he continued his rant about losing the filly that had just won the race. Neither Gary Jones nor I spilled the beans at that juncture, nor did we so much as glance over at Johnston, who was being "cooled out" by his wife Betty.

"Pie Man" found out soon enough that the culprits were seated right next to him and he never spoke to me again, even though prior to the claim we used to chat all the time and I had interviewed him on a regular basis. I remained very friendly with Betty, who was a lovely woman, and their son Buddy Johnston, who operated Old English Rancho until he died in 2015.

My partners in my first racehorse included two Certified Public Accountants, Nick Ben-Meir and Arthur Stephens, who remain my friends to this day. Nick and I continue to race horses as partners and Art has been my company's CPA for several years.

Other partners included William (Bill) Murray and Tony Busching. Bill used to write a letter from Italy for *The New Yorker* and penned thinly-disguised mystery novels with a racing theme that allowed him to pay back a long list of the people in racing he had come to hate. Tony was an ace handicapper who specialized in producing television commercials using live animals in the days before computerization. Tony was generous with his time when I produced and hosted a racing program that I made for a couple of years on a UHF television station on Sunset Boulevard. His office was just down the road from the studio.

Sari's Tobin ran seven times for our group, winning turf races at Del Mar and Santa Anita, and placing in a stakes second time out on the California Fair Circuit. When her quality was thoroughly exposed and it became unlikely that she would win another stakes race, we sold her for $125,000 to Robert E. Sangster, the British soccer pools magnate who lived on the Isle of Man.

A month after Sari's Tobin had placed in a stakes and two months after she had provided me with my first win as an owner, I saw a *Daily Racing*

Form chart of a win at Saratoga by a 3-year-old filly named Sorcerer. She immediately caught my attention because she was by One For All, a son of Northern Dancer that I liked. She had won an $18,000 claimer.

I presented this information to Jeff Siegel, with whom I had become friends from the day we met in the press box half a dozen years earlier. Jeff had preceded me into the ranks of owners and showed me that guys like us could actually afford to racehorses if we did it in partnership.

Jeff liked what he saw. So did Nick Ben-Meir. I suggested to Jeff that we fly to New York, go to Saratoga and try to buy Sorcerer, then bring her to Del Mar, where she would be eligible for "starter" races, or non-claiming races restricted to horses that had run for low claiming values.

The Del Mar meeting had only just gotten underway. I was not only the back-page featured columnist for *Daily Racing Form*, I was responsible for writing the stakes advances on the front page. I was a very fast writer. I knocked out a couple of days' worth of stories in advance and left them with Gale Dunbar, the *DRF* Teletype operator.

Jeff and I flew from San Diego to New York, where we landed at the end of the day. We rented a car to drive approximately 4 hours from Long Island to Saratoga. The car started acting up and finally conked out in Nyack, New York, a mere thirty-two miles from the airport. We were on a tight schedule, we could not reach anybody at the rental car office, the streets in downtown Nyack had long since been rolled up and the only place we could find that was open was the police station. After explaining our situation, we were told our best chance to get to Saratoga, if we wanted to leave at that very moment, was to hire a cab.

I will never forget the fun the Pinkertons had with Jeff and me at the backstretch gate on Nelson Avenue in Saratoga, when we pulled up in a cab at first light with a meter reading of $149. The Pinkertons thought we were absolutely crazy. I will admit that it did have the feel of something out of Damon Runyon's world.

Once on the backstretch, I found the barn of Roger Laurin. I introduced myself and we chatted about Brian Sweeney, who was friendly with Laurin and his father Lucien when they all lived in Toronto, Canada.

In one of the most memorable twists and turns of the Turf, the younger Laurin had taken a private training job with The Phipps Family and gave up training for Christopher T. Chenery's Meadow Stud a week before Riva Ridge made his racing debut at two. Meadow hired Lucien on Roger's recommendation. Riva Ridge and Secretariat became the first horses to win consecutive Kentucky Derbys with the same owner, breeder, trainer and jockey. Secretariat became the first Triple Crown winner since Citation's victory twenty-five years earlier.

I told Roger that I wanted to buy Sorcerer. "Why?" was his response. He showed her to me. She was very short and small all over. I still wanted her. I did not care how small she was—she was a runner. In her claiming win, she made three different moves and won impressively. Jeff and I thought she was going to improve. So Laurin struck a deal with the owner-breeder and we bought the filly, with Nick Ben-Meir as our partner.

Right after I had struck the deal to land Sorcerer, Joe Hirsch spotted me on the Saratoga backstretch before I could alter my course. He did a double take when he saw me walking under the tall, ancient elm trees on the historic grounds of the nation's oldest racetrack. This was my first visit to Saratoga, a track that began to host races in 1863 in the midst of the Civil War.

Joe Hirsch was my supervisor. When our eyes locked, I got that same feeling a driver gets when he sees the red lights of a police car flashing in his rear view mirror. Busted!

"Barry—is that you? Barry Irwin?" he said.

"Yes. Hi Joe. How's it going?" I replied as though I was used to bumping into him on a daily basis at The Spa.

"I didn't know you were on vacation," he said.

"I'm not."

"Well what are you doing here?" he asked as politely as he could.

"I just bought a horse from Roger Laurin," I said matter-of-factly.

"A horse?"

"Yes, that's right. She won a small claimer here just the other day," I explained.

"Well whom, may I ask, is doing your work while you are back here, buying this horse, as you say?" he wanted to know.

I explained that I had already submitted all of my stories that were due, that I only flew in for the morning and that I was going back home that same afternoon.

Hirsch tried his best to make sense of my ambitious schedule, wished me luck, and walked away.

We bought Sorcerer right about the same time as the annual Saratoga yearling sale was being conducted, so we were able to get the filly on a flight from the local airport to Southern California.

I ran into H. E. "Tex" Sutton the morning Sorcerer was entered for her first start at Del Mar for our new partnership. His company had flown the filly from New York to California. A lifelong racetracker, Tex asked if he could bet. I gave him the green light. "You sure?" he said, giving me a hard look. He had been on the track since the age of 11 and had heard every story ever concocted. "Yes, bet your money, Tex!" I told him.

Future Hall of Fame jockey Chris McCarron took the mount. He had recently moved his tack from Maryland to Southern California. He and his agent Harry "The Hat" Hacek were struggling at the time.

Sorcerer, trained by young Gary Jones, won easily by four lengths. The win came two weeks after Sari's Tobin had won at Del Mar for my first score as an owner. About three weeks later, with McCarron back on board, Sorcerer won again, this time by five lengths. Tex Sutton got down again and suddenly became my public relations man, telling anybody on the backstretch that would listen that I was going places and fast!

By the time of Sorcerer's second win in nineteen days, I had already tendered my resignation as an employee of *Daily Racing Form*. Less than a year and a half after taking over the feature column, I was pretty much fed up with working for *DRF*. More columns found their way into The Flamingo's waste paper basket than onto the back cover of *Daily Racing Form*.

I tried not to take it personally. I finally concluded that the *Form* was just not for me.

There was no rule against an employee of *Daily Racing Form* owning a racehorse. A couple of *DRF* veterans, namely pedigree-buff Leon Rasmussen and chart-caller Jay Woodward, had dabbled in bloodstock for a few years. Leon had a filly that could run and Jay had a few runners, but none of them had won three races in a month at Del Mar, so the focus was squarely on me.

It was starting to get a bit uncomfortable, both around Bimini Place and upstairs, above the grandstand, in the press box. Everybody was talking about Jeff and me.

I was a popular guy when I was writing the back-page column, broadcasting two-hour long radio shows on Friday and Saturday, and starring in a television show on a UHF station in Hollywood.

But once I started competing against other owners and trainers, my popularity became a thing of the past. People who had always been friendly gradually became rivals. Jealousy reared its ugly head, not only among those seated in the owners' and trainers' box section, but also in the press box.

I had reached a point where I no longer wanted to write about racing—I wanted to participate in it. I had given writing everything I had, but working for house organs and adhering to a company line gave me no professional or personal satisfaction. I was too independent.

Working for *The Blood-Horse*, *The Thoroughbred of California* and *Daily Racing Form* provided me with a solid background in the sport and industry of Thoroughbred racing, and, more importantly, it gave me access to the top horsemen in the game.

I learned quickly enough that if I needed to interview any owner, whether it was a captain of industry, a financier or an entertainment figure, all I had to do was call. Nelson Bunker Hunt, the billionaire oil man who tried and failed to corner the silver market in the late 1970s, came out of a board meeting to chat with me about one of his horses that was in training with Charlie Whittingham.

Any time I wanted any information on anything, I had carte blanche to ask any question of any horseman in North America. Unlike, for example, a writer working in show business or on Wall Street, I could ask candid questions and expect an honest reply. I would regularly be furnished with detailed explanations of how and why a trainer, veterinarian or jockey did certain things. This was invaluable in gaining an education about how to play the game.

Racing professionals, by and large, comprise a very generous group and most are truly flattered when a writer takes a genuine interest in what they do and what they are trying to accomplish. I can only imagine the evasive responses that show biz and Wall Street types would give to writers' queries to reveal their route to success. Sports reporters are not as lucky as turf writers either, because coaches or managers keep their tactics close to the vest. Racing participants are only too glad to discuss their methods.

So the backstretch and frontside of the racetrack became my university in learning the game of horseracing and my professors were the greatest professionals of their time.

I have been asked repeatedly over the years how I taught myself to analyze horses and races, and why I have been able to build a successful life in racing.

As for learning about the conformation of a horse, I asked questions of top experts both at home and abroad all the time.

I learned a lot about looking at a horse from Rollin Baugh and Brian Sweeney. I was fortunate to be taught about this art by some of racing's finest judges. Ralph Kraft, a Fasig-Tipton employee, ran the company's California affiliate. He spent much of his time touring horse farms in North America and inspected and judged yearlings for sales in Saratoga and Del Mar. During my tenure as editor at *The Thoroughbred of California*, I talked to Ralph about horses all the time because his office was adjacent to mine and I went with him on his inspection tours a few times. Sometimes our chats would go right past my family's dinnertime.

Whenever I went to the paddock for a race, I always situated myself in a spot that allowed me to watch the horses as they walked directly toward me, so that I could judge the conformation of their front limbs.

Even before I bought Sari's Tobin and Sorcerer, I had laid the groundwork for my entry into ownership.

Through the kindness of a Southern California bloodstock agent named Fred Purner Jr., who built a career by taking advantage of his father's good name, I was able to visit England, Ireland and France as a journalist. Fred's dad was the top racetrack publicity man in the game and the press box at Santa Anita was named in his honor. Unfortunately, the apple fell many yards from the tree. Fred Jr. eventually was disgraced because of some shady financial dealings with his Catholic church in Sierra Madre.

Fred was nice to me and let me join a few of his junkets from California to Europe for free, on the understanding that I would return the favor by writing some stories about the ventures.

I came to the conclusion that the Goffs fall yearling sale in County Kildare, Ireland offered 1-year-old horses that could be bought reasonably, transported to California and sold at the annual 2-year-old in-training sales at Hollywood Park. This was not a novel idea, as Fred was already doing this. But I wanted a friend of mine to try it.

So in the fall of 1976, I floated the notion to James Mamakos, a lawyer-turned-real-estate-investor whom I had met while working as a writer. I asked Jim to consider buying a few yearlings in Ireland. Finally he agreed, with the understanding that I would have Rollin Baugh inspect anything before I bid on it for him.

I picked out two yearling fillies that I liked, bought them cheaply, never mentioned a word to Rollin Baugh, and they were sent to America. Jim wound up keeping both to race and they won three races in ten starts in California. Jim later bred from them.

By the following year in 1977, I was managing a small group of horses that were imported from England by Hollywood film producer Irving Allen, whose nickname became the "Master of Disaster" after he churned out the likes of "The Towering Inferno" and "The Poseidon Adventure." Allen is most well known for losing out on the James Bond franchise when he split with longtime friend Albert "Cubby" Broccoli and later insulted author Ian Fleming.

Allen was a dynamo of a man with a great interest in matters of the Turf. He lived in Southern California, yet he followed English racing closely. He was very good to me and involved me in a documentary project he was producing about The Beach Boys. I spent a week with The Beach Boys, interviewing them and providing Allen with plenty of material. They were pretty messed up in the mid-1970s and struggled just to get past a routine sound check, let alone put on a full concert.

I was introduced to Allen by our mutual friend Bill Miles, whose wife Tichi Wilkerson Miles operated *The Hollywood Reporter*. Allen owned the historic Derisley Wood Stud in Newmarket, England, where he stood My Swallow. A sensation that was unbeaten in seven starts, including three French Group 1 races at two, My Swallow had finished right behind Turf legends Brigadier Gerard and Mill Reef in the classic Two Thousand Guineas. When they met in the Guineas, the trio had won eighteen of nineteen races between them.

Allen wanted to import My Swallow to California and have me manage him as a stallion. He asked what he needed to do. I suggested that he send over a few offspring of My Swallow, give to them A. T. "Tommy" Doyle and try to create some buzz in Southern California.

All Hope, a son of My Swallow, was duly sent to trainer Doyle. A grand little horse, full of quality, he managed a sprint win between a pair of losses in his initial three starts in Southern California. The morning after a loss by All Hope in a six-and-a-half-furlong race down the hillside turf course at Santa Anita, Tommy Doyle pulled me aside. A taciturn individual who had grown up riding work in an English stable, where a lad's mail was routinely read to make sure that no betting secrets left the yard, Doyle was unusually gleeful and forthcoming.

"Darrel [McHargue] told me he never had a chance to really ride the colt yesterday," revealed Doyle. "Said he was clipping heels all the way down the hill. Says the race took nothing—NOTHING—out of the colt. Barry, do you think Mr. Allen would mind if I ran him back in five days and stretched him out around two turns? The thing of it is, he'll win it!"

I loaded up at the betting windows on All Hope and the My Swallow colt beat a better than average stakes field at Santa Anita, cruising home under jockey McHargue by 2 ½ lengths at odds of eight to one. I made a nice five-figure score.

I invested that money immediately in a filly named Tough Elsie. Mike Mitchell had claimed her for $25,000 from Laz Barrera, ran her twice and she broke down in the second race. He was trying to get rid of her. I offered him $10,000 and he took it. The filly had not won a race at four so her career was finished, her form had completely deteriorated, and she had an anemic pedigree that was filled with what I used to call "white type"—a contrast to the black-type that indicated that there were stakes horses present in the immediate pedigree.

Mitchell, however, did not realize the filly had won a stakes, finished second to the top-class filly Old Goat in a tough New York allowance race and, even though many of her wins came either in claiming or lightly-regarded races restricted to New York-breds, *Daily Racing Form* thought enough of her to rate her as the highest ranked 3-year-old filly sprinter of 1976. On top of it all, she had the muscular body of a Quarter Horse.

I paid for the filly, hopped on a plane and arrived in Lexington, Kentucky in the midst of Keeneland's annual November Breeding Stock Sale. I was armed with the race record, pedigree, *Daily Racing Form* handicap ranking and a photograph of Tough Elsie. I was determined to turn a quick profit.

The first guy I ran into who I knew was J. T. L. "Johnny" Jones. Also known as "Alphabet" Jones, he was a Texan who had an appreciation for speed and conformation. I showed Johnny the stuff, assured him he would love her when he laid eyes on her and he bought her sight-unseen for $25,000. Tough Elsie went on to produce a pair of stakes winners as a broodmare.

So the year before I first dipped my big toe into the ranks of owners, I was already wheeling and dealing in the horse business on several different levels.

Chapter 7

Bloodstock Agent

I quit working for *Daily Racing Form* at the close of the 1978 Del Mar summer meeting. I felt little pride in my profession of writing about horse racing because being a turf writer in Southern California in the late 1970s was embarrassing. Trying to write about my sport was frustrating because too much of what I submitted was being rejected by The Flamingo. In the end, I wanted to be a player, not a guy writing about players. It was time to move on.

I had built up some momentum with my three wins at Del Mar, I had been able to make some worthwhile contacts during my days as a writer and I knew my way around the backstretches of the major racetracks and horse auction houses in North America.

Although I knew a lot about racing and bloodstock, I knew nothing about business, so I was fortunate enough to team up with my friend Nick Ben-Meir, a record industry CPA. Nick and I formed a bloodstock agency. I worked out of a room in his office, which was on the second floor of a building on Beverly Drive, just South of Wilshire Boulevard in Beverly Hills. The plan was that I would operate the bloodstock end of things and Nick would run the business end.

Nick and I did not last long as partners, because—as I saw it—Nick wanted too much involvement in the bloodstock and racing. Nick was running a small but successful accounting practice, which specialized in managing rock 'n' roll bands, developing new artists and handling finances for concert tours. Nick had been a long time horseplayer and was a partner in my first couple of runners. He honestly thought he could help me in bloodstock, but I felt he was interfering. After a short period of time, we split up and I moved my office close to my apartment in Pasadena to operate Pacifica Thoroughbreds.

I bought a folding chair with leather trim and an Italian-made table with a nifty wooden veneer that I used as a desk. My office was on the landing of an old Pasadena home that had been turned into a suite of offices. I could only afford the landing site. The chair eventually broke and was trashed, but I still have the desk, which serves as a table in the foyer of my 220-year-old residence in Kentucky some thirty-five years later.

A bloodstock agent acts as a broker between buyer and seller in the sale of a horse. I was not a typical member of this profession, as I was more interested in being an entrepreneur than a broker, and whenever I had the chance to play an ownership role, I took it. This risky practice accounted for some major scores, some disastrous lows and an accumulation of bloodstock that eventually led to my financial demise when the market turned and I was unable to generate enough cash flow to keep the enterprise afloat.

California had a vibrant breeding industry at the height of a boom market in North America in the early 1980s. Because of my contacts and connections, I was able to use my ingenuity to import and syndicate sires and stallion prospects from Europe and Kentucky. Among those I brought to stand in California were Torsion from Kentucky and Moscow Ballet and African Sky from Ireland.

I bought African Sky from the Irish National Stud and fully syndicated him to stand in Southern California at a desert-area ranch three-quarters of the way from Los Angeles to Palm Springs. A black stallion with a lot of charisma, he had been a Group 1 winner in France for international art dealer Daniel Wildenstein and had been represented recently at Santa Anita and Hollywood Park by a sensational filly from France named Kilijaro.

On the eve of the Prix de l'Arc de Triomphe, I was at the public auction at Saint-Cloud racecourse in Paris, when Serge Fradkoff's daring gambit of opening the bidding at $400,000 caught any rivals off guard and he was able to secure Kilijaro on that one bid. When she appeared at Santa Anita a few weeks later, stretching out from a mile to a mile and a quarter to win the Grade 1 Yellow Ribbon Stakes, I cashed a large wager on her.

Fradkoff was a partner of Ed Seltzer, a transplanted Chicagoan with numerous Midwestern car dealerships who had moved to Miami, where he accumulated real estate and traded in breeding stock and racehorses. So when I asked Ed, under attractive terms and conditions for him, to fund the acquisition of African Sky, he was quite familiar with the sire and he agreed to become my partner. Ed was able to get his original investment back from the immediate syndication and we both prospered on the transaction over the next few years.

A couple of days after African Sky had arrived in the Southern California desert, I got a call from Jerry Hobbs, the manager at Three Rings Ranch, who told me the horse had been turned out in a paddock of about an acre and none of his ranch hands could catch it.

I contacted the manager of the Irish National Stud and explained the situation. He told me the stallion man who had worked with him for the last eight years would be sent to California to offer his assistance. I did not hear from the Stud or the stallion man for about ten days. One afternoon Hobbs called to say, "Your Irish man has been here sitting on a bench outside my office for two days now and he's wearing a heavy wool suit and he looks pretty hot and uncomfortable. You might want to come out here."

Rather than making their visitor feel at home, the inhospitable ranchmen opted instead to ignore and make fun of him. When I arrived, I saw that the Irishman was indeed sitting outside in near hundred-degree weather, sweating profusely from his bright red forehead. His suit was made of a heavier weight of wool than is generally used in America, as was the Irish tweed flat cap on his head.

After I introduced myself and apologized for his treatment, the fellow and I walked over to the paddock where African Sky ruled the roost. He told me that he had never ventured as far as five or six miles from his home near the Stud, let alone ever been on an airplane or a cab ride as long as the two-hour one through the desert from Los Angeles International Airport to Beaumont, California.

The little Irishman asked Hobbs what the problem seemed to be. Hobbs explained that the horse was wild, uncontrollable and unable to be caught. The Irishman confidently told Hobbs he would catch the horse, at which point perhaps twenty or so ranch hands and office staff took up positions at various vantage points along the wooden plank fence surrounding the paddock.

When the Irishman walked into the paddock and the gate closed behind him, the cowboys began to whoop and holler like they were at a rodeo. They expected the worst and actually seemed to be looking forward to the visitor getting knocked squarely on his butt.

The stallion snorted and pawed the earth, kicking back spurts of gravely dirt, lowered his head as though to narrow in on his target and seemed poised for action. Just then, the man took the cap from his head, held it in his hand and extended it in his outstretched arm as an offering to the beast. The short, overweight, overdressed and red-faced Irishman seemed like an overmatched toreador about to meet his maker.

Just like in the movies, the fire-breathing, shiny black stallion kicked up a tremendous cloud of dust and ran at full speed right at the defenseless little man. When African Sky got to within a few feet of the fellow, the horse athletically came to a sudden halt, arched his neck and lowered his head subserviently. Quick as a wink, the stud groom snapped a lead shank onto the stallion's headstall.

When the horse came to a surprising halt, all the yelling and screaming instantly stopped. When the Irishman proudly led African Sky in a circle on the end of a shank, the formerly antagonistic cowboys upped the ante of their vocal shenanigans, whooping and hollering for all they were worth, because they knew they had seen something truly special. Instead of jeering, now the boot-clad ranch hands were celebrating the horsemanship of the little magician. Not one of these he-men had demonstrated the cojones to get near the stallion, let alone walk into the beast's private paddock and confront him. And now the diminutive fellow from Ireland was handling African Sky as though he were a child's pony.

Watching that proud little fellow from County Kildare strut his stuff in the dusty dirt paddock at the ranch that morning was the most exciting thing I've ever seen in my life. The real-life drama was gut wrenching and truly unforgettable.

But the drama was far from over; Jerry Hobbs then demanded that the man lead the stallion over to the breeding shed to cover a mare, so that the ranch staff could see how to handle him in a working situation. They were scared to death to do it themselves.

Because none of the ranch hands would participate, this city-raised boy had to jump in and assist with the live covering of the broodmare. The stallion was led into the low-ceilinged wooden shed. He knew exactly why he was there and produced a large, shiny, speckled, rock-hard member. At that point, the Irishman was told to wash it off. Stallions in America are disinfected before covering a mare. Irish Stud protocol did not include this preparation.

I was given the horse's head while the Irishman proceeded to wash the erection. Steam was rising off the horse's back and sides, he snorted loudly and his eyes looked like they were popping out of their sockets as African Sky glared right down at me.

African Sky was so intent on getting down to business, he wasn't too inconvenienced by the disinfection process. We were in very tight quarters against the side of the barn, below a very low ceiling. It was scary as hell and the beast in front of me was heaving mightily in anticipation of being presented with his mare.

The Irishman took the shank, led the stallion to the middle of the shed and African Sky mounted the mare. The stallion was quite professional; he did his business, dismounted and was cleaned up before being put in a stall.

I was so unnerved by the lack of cooperation and redneck attitude shown by the ranchmen that I arranged later that very day to have the stallion picked up and transferred to another ranch.

African Sky was a popular stallion in California, even though he did not match the success he had enjoyed in Ireland. He was a mean, dangerous stallion and we later heard that he might even have killed a man in Ireland. While visiting him awhile later, I saw African Sky bite off the finger of his handler only seconds after I had warned the man to be careful. The handler told me that he and African Sky had come to an understanding, which I guess was, that if African Sky bit off any digits, he would drop them on the ground. The handler was driven to the hospital, where the finger was surgically put back in place.

During my Pacifica Thoroughbreds bloodstock days, I syndicated a few stallions that had an impact on the local and national scene, including Moscow Ballet, a stakes winner at two in Ireland for the legendary trainer Vincent O'Brien.

John Harris joined me in the purchase of this well-bred son of English Triple Crown hero Nijinsky out of a half-sister to Mill Reef, the Epsom Derby and Prix de l'Arc de Triomphe hero whose six consecutive Group 1 wins was a European record that stood for thirty years.

One of the few Californians to be invited into The Jockey Club, Harris owned Harris Ranch in central California, where, on several thousand acres, he operated the largest beef feedlot on the West Coast, which at one time housed some 150,000 head of cattle.

Moscow Ballet was bred for turf and he ran all of his races on turf in Ireland, but I was able to convince John that he was conformed like a dirt horse and his speed would work on the fast dirt tracks in California.

The muscular, compact stallion was successful as a sire in California and gave both of us the best United States-based female racehorses either of us have ever raced. With his longtime pal and partner, fellow Central California farmer and racehorse owner-breeder Don Valpredo, Harris bred Soviet Problem, best in fifteen of twenty starts. In a heartbreaking defeat, she lost the 1994 Breeders' Cup Sprint in the final stride to the colt Cherokee Run.

The Moscow Ballet filly I wound up with was named Golden Ballet. She became one of the few fillies to sweep Santa Anita's winter/spring series of stakes races that were devoted to 3-year-old fillies, including the Grade 1 Santa Anita Oaks and Grade 1 Las Virgenes Stakes. But more about her later.

Another stallion I imported to California was Kentucky-based Torsion, a reasonably successful racehorse and stallion that stood as the property of a syndicate for Brereton C. Jones at his Airdrie Stud in the Bluegrass.

This time I partnered with a Southern California Chrysler dealer named Carl Cannata, who, with his wife Olivia, operated Lakeview Thoroughbred Farm. The Cannatas had shown themselves to be honest business people and caring horse people. When I decided to relocate African Sky, it was to The Cannatas' farm that I moved him.

Torsion proved extremely popular at Lakeview. However, part way through the breeding season it was obvious that something had gone terribly wrong with him as a fertile stallion, as mares bred to him were routinely coming up empty.

Carl and Olivia were as puzzled as anybody else and could not explain why a horse that had impregnated an average of 88 percent of his mares over the last few years suddenly would be down at the 30 percent level.

A good friend of mine, veterinarian Dr. Atwood "Woody" Asbury, suggested that I contact the University of California at Davis, which provided us with a stallion reproduction specialist who drove down to analyze the situation. After just one day, the expert phoned to tell me that he had discovered the problem: "They are collecting semen from him and artificially inseminating the mares," he revealed.

Aside from violating The Jockey Club rules against the use of this practice, Lakeview Farm was getting the exact opposite results from using artificial insemination. Unlike with some breeds, such as Quarter Horses and Standardbreds, The Jockey Club's Stud Book disallows this practice with Thoroughbreds in order to limit the production of live foals from the successful union of one stallion to one mare.

A great debate has waged for many decades about whether opening up the Stud Book to embrace artificial insemination would strengthen or weaken the breed. Proponents argue that artificial insemination is cleaner and safer for both the mare and the stallion. They also say that the cream would have a better chance to rise to the top, since the best stallions would be able to produce more foals.

Opponents say that there is already entirely too much inbreeding in the modern day Thoroughbred and this would only serve to accelerate its demise. Diversity would be lost. Based on commercial considerations alone, I am against the practice.

Interestingly, what I learned from the Torsion incident was that in some instances, the lack of live covers for a stallion results in a lessening of libido and consequently a reduction in both the quantity and quality of the sperm. The vet explained to me that a live cover, in lay terms, excites a Thoroughbred and the result of this enhanced state of anticipation stimulates the reproductive system to upgrade the volume of viable sperm.

I explained the situation to Carl Cannata, who was unaware the practice was being used. He immediately took steps to cease the routine and return the stallion to live covers. The horse's fertility immediately improved and he finished up the season with his usual effectiveness.

Syndicating and standing stallions was a lucrative and worthwhile business in a good market. The one stallion deal I created that should have made the most money for me turned out to be an utter disaster.

Robert Resnick answered a tombstone advertisement I ran in *The Blood-Horse*. He invited me to his San Fernando Valley office for a chat. Like a kindred spirit named Richard Haisfield with whom I would meet for a chat a quarter century later, Bob was a businessman who had come to the realization that the Thoroughbred stallion business offered an opportunity for a sharp operator to run any number of schemes that would enrich him.

Both Resnick and Haisfield were especially fond of deals in which banks would loan money based on perceived collateral, because if any deal went south on them, they wanted the bank to go after assets and not them.

Both Resnick and Haisfield especially loved deals in which they could exploit the United States Tax Code. Stallions were used merely a tools they could exploit to create value, evade taxes while never personally being at risk.

At our meeting, Resnick explained that he wanted to pick up where Fletcher Jones had left off before he died in a plane crash. Jones was the computer company whiz who had built up a mega-million-dollar company named Computer Sciences, erected a breeding and training facility in the Santa Ynez Valley that was the finest in the history of California, and suddenly disappeared.

Physically, Resnick bore a striking resemblance to Jones. He had the same color hair, his complexion was fair and he was full of life. My automatic shit detector told me at once that Bob was basically full of hot air. But when he brought up Jones' name and dream, he piqued my curiosity.

When Resnick or Haisfield talked to me, they both did the same thing, which was to see if their conman spiel would sound credible to me. While crafting their pitch, they would watch my eyes to see if I was buying it. They knew what they were saying was bullshit, they suspected that I knew it was bullshit, yet they wanted to see if it would fly in chump land. It was absurd, but they never stopped auditioning their cons for me.

Bob told me he wanted a top stallion to stand at a farm he had bought in the Santa Ynez Valley that he had named the Flying Horse Farm. Whereas Jones had a real dream, the wherewithal to back it up and real business acumen, Resnick had a dream based on OPM (other people's money) and no short supply of cheek.

Resnick was a pharmacist by trade who had worked hard to establish a nice lifestyle. But when he found out how easy it was for him to make stacks of cash by creating questionable shelters to exploit the tax code with Thoroughbred breeding stock, the monster in him jumped out.

It's the One was a colt that Amin Saiden, a Venezuelan banker and successful horse breeder, had bought as a yearling for $46,000 and turned over to his close friend, Hall of Fame trainer Laz Barrera. The grandson of The Phipps' Family's Bold Ruler had become a Grade 1 winner by taking the Charles H. Strub Stakes in 1982. The market was in a period of hyperinflation. I was able to work out a sweetheart deal between Resnick and Saiden in which I would syndicate the horse among a group of investors, the buyer and seller would continue to race the colt in partnership and the colt eventually would enter stud at Resnick's Flying Horse Farm.

Because of the way I structured the deal, Resnick would never be out of pocket, because I raised enough cash up front to cover the initial deposit to the seller, who also granted liberal terms on an installment basis, which coincided with investors' payments for shares in the horse.

If I proved to be successful in selling enough shares in the colt to breeders, I figured to earn something in the neighborhood of $575,000. The horse was offered on the basis of about $6 million, a figure for which Bold Ruler's son Secretariat had been syndicated in the winter of 1973.

The minimum number of shares I needed to sell were duly sold and Resnick received enough cash to make the initial down payment on the purchase of his interest in It's the One. Saiden was happy, Resnick was happy and I was happy. My money would be paid out over time, but I knew it would come my way eventually.

It's the One proceeded to finish third in the Grade 1 Santa Anita Handicap to John Henry and set a new track record for a mile and a quarter when winning the Grade 2 New Orleans Handicap in his second start for our newly formed syndicate. Before he went to stud, It's the One finished 1-2-3 in twenty-five of twenty-eight starts and earned more than $1 million.

Getting the horse to stud proved to be a difficult situation. As the 1983 breeding season approached, I visited Flying Horse Farm, only to find that the proposed breeding shed had not been built and there was no grass cover in the paddocks. What pharmacist Resnick knew about farm life proved to be next to nothing. He actually thought that grass pastures were the result of Mother Nature just doing her job. Furthermore, he lacked the cash to build the barn. I put him on a deadline, which he missed.

As the one who formed the syndicate that included some of the most prominent breeders in North America, including John C. Mabee of Golden Eagle Farm (and operator of San Diego County's biggest supermarket chain) and Mrs. Benjamin Ridder of Murrieta Stud (Ben was chair of the board of Knight-Ridder publications), I felt more responsibility to them than I did to my partner Bob Resnick. Amin Saiden shared my concerns.

So, as the racing manager, I called for a syndicate meeting at the Cockatoo Inn in Hawthorne, California to take a vote that would keep It's the One in training for an additional year until Resnick had an opportunity to get his farm in shape to receive the stallion and visiting mares.

Resnick called his own syndicate meeting, which, coincidentally enough, took place in an adjacent room of the same Cockatoo Hotel, but featured finger sandwiches as a means of luring syndicate members to his suite. Resnick's wife thought those finger sandwiches were a nifty touch.

My agenda was approved, but only after Mabee made an impassioned speech on behalf of Resnick, based on the notion that Resnick deserved the benefit of the doubt since he had skin in the game and I was nothing more than a bloodstock agent.

Forget that my point of view was the correct one for the syndicate members and the horse! John tried to turn this into a referendum on Capitalism, the American Way and the free enterprise system. I explained to John that I was putting my hard-earned $575,000 in harm's way in order to do the right thing for the syndicate members and that I had generated Resnick's entire skin in the game. Later on, when Resnick revealed himself to be the boob that he was, Mabee let me know that he regretted his stance on that issue.

I received precious little financial reward for my involvement in It's the One, but there were some moments that have stuck with me. One of the shares in the horse was sold to a group of guys whom I had met at the track, including a fellow who worked in the stable area as an electrician and did everything from repairing faulty wiring to changing the occasional light bulb.

Halfway through a race in which It's the One was competing at Hollywood Park, I was sitting next to Laz Barrera in his box overlooking the finishing line. Both Laz and I became aware of the body of a man kneeling next to us. The fellow made some remark, such as "Laz, how does he look to you?"

It was the electrician, dressed in his uniform. Laz got the biggest kick out of telling this story about how Barry Irwin was such a great salesman, he even got the guy who had been changing light bulbs that morning to buy a share in It's the One by that afternoon!

CHAPTER 8

The Horse Trader

Morrie Mirkin was one of those larger-than-life characters that invariably find their way to Beverly Hills or Hollywood.

When he spoke he reminded me of Edward G. Robinson, but he had the physical presence of John Gotti. He was a big guy, always impeccably dressed and immaculately groomed.

Morrie kept a hair trimmer on the dashboard of his Bentley and, while his car warmed up, he tidied the sideburns below his fluffy, expertly coiffed grey hair.

Twenty-three years before I first met him in 1980, Morrie had founded Budget Rent a Car, as the story goes, in a storefront in downtown Los Angeles with an investment of $10,000 he used to buy 10 automobiles. With the aid of a distant relative named Jules Lederer, Mirkin was able to grow the company into an international giant that he eventually sold to Transamerica Corporation.

Morrie's genius was as a concept man—he was a constant source of innovative ideas. Some of his ideas were brilliant; some were downright nutty, as well as costly.

By locating car lots on inexpensive real estate a few blocks from airports and cutting rental fees for his cars, Mirkin put enough pressure on industry leaders Hertz and Avis to completely change the face of the rental business, when he appealed to the budget-minded consumer.

Somewhat less brilliant was an investment made during the Middle East oil crisis of the early 1970s, when Morrie shelled out $500,000 to a con man named Sam Leach, a California inventor who supposedly came up with a way to extract energy from "common tap water" that could power an automobile from a box the size of a luggage trunk.

A hardcore, bottom-line businessman, Mirkin was not usually the type of sucker to buy a machine into which a dollar bill was inserted and a fresh $20 bill emerged. But Mr. Sam Leach obviously was a step ahead of your average bloodstock agent.

I met Morrie through Gary Jones when youthful Jones trained the ill-bred Eleven Stitches to racing glory for Mirkin's wife Claudia, who was as close to being a socialite as the Golden State was capable of producing at the time. Claudia made a light industry out of marrying prominent men, among them Clement L. Hirsch, a conservative Republican, who, as a member of the so-called "kitchen cabinet," raised the money and harnessed the power to propel Ronald Reagan up the political ladder.

Morrie fell in love with racing and saw that potentially lucrative business opportunities existed within the framework of the Thoroughbred game. One of his first ideas, not so unusually, closely mirrored his greatest business success.

At a dinner attended by Gary Jones and me at the Beverly Hills home of Mr. and Mrs. Mirkin, Morrie regaled us for the umpteenth time with his latest version of how he had developed the concept of renting cars near airports. The stage was being set for Morrie to unveil his latest blockbuster idea.

Gary had clued me in on the drive to Mirkin's home. Morrie wanted to start Budget Rent a Horse. Gary said he knew I would find the idea crazy, but he wanted me to behave, pay attention, be respectful, and nod in all the appropriate places—all with the idea of indulging the promotional genius in the hope that, at some point, we could actually do some traditional business with Mirkin.

The short strokes of how Budget Rent-a-Horse would play out were so out of whack with the rules of racing that, try as I might, I found myself unable to stick to Gary's guidelines and I started to wise up Morrie. At one point, Gary kicked me so hard under the table I think I might have gasped.

Morrie and I were always very friendly. Even though I pooh-poohed his horse-rental notion, I think he tolerated me because he knew I would always give him an opinion he felt he could use.

Although we did not get off on the right foot, Morrie and I did do some business together. For all the glamour, excitement and fun racing offered, it was the prospect of making money that intrigued Morrie.

Unlike the majority of wealthy people who get involved in racing and are attracted by the trappings of the game's lifestyle, Morrie was unwilling to be a pigeon in a game loaded with poachers.

Morrie asked me how we could make some money.

I told him, "By buying and selling horses."

He asked me how much he needed to put up to make some "dough."

I responded, "A quarter-million would be a nice starting point."

Morrie invited me to his office on Doheny Drive in Beverly Hills. I wound up sitting on one of half a dozen or so chairs set in front of Morrie's big desk. There was an older fellow there who was Morrie's "bank guy," as well as a couple of other older guys with grey hair that was combed forward from the base of the skull into a sweeping wave that covered any traces of baldness and defied gravity in the process.

I later found out that Morrie used to hold court in his office every morning, usually sitting in front a few of his sycophants, go-fers and cronies. Morrie had a huge ego that constantly needed massaging and those in attendance were usually deferential to him. In exchange for their loyalty, they got to listen as Morrie conducted business from behind his huge wooden desk.

Morrie, the "bank guy" and I went to City National Bank on Wilshire Boulevard. While Morrie sat back preening in his chair, his mouthpiece stated the type and terms of a loan he wanted for his client for our horse venture.

"My client is a prime customer of this banking institution," the "bank guy" said to the loan officer, as Morrie tossed back his head and smiled toward the ceiling. "And, as such, he wants to borrow not at prime plus one, or prime plus a half, or even prime plus a quarter—he wants to borrow $200,000 at prime. Period."

Was Morrie capable of securing his own loan? You betcha. But he loved to hear himself spoken about in important, glowing tones. So whatever he had to pay the "bank guy" was worth it to Morrie to hear what a big shot he was.

With a bank loan for $200,000 in place, Morrie and I were off and running. To his credit, Morrie left every decision up to me. Our deal was that we would buy and sell for a year, then reassess.

With my buying and selling horses in Ireland, France, Argentina and the United States, Morrie and I had a lot of action during the first several months of the venture.

One of the best horses I was able to buy for us was a filly that I acquired in Argentina named Dalsenda.

Dalsenda was a Grade 2 winner in Argentina of the Premio General Luis Maria Campos. I think we gave about $110,000 for her. When she arrived in California in 1981, I decided to place her with trainer John

Russell. My idea was to get the filly up to a race and sell her immediately before or afterward.

Russell trained for several prominent, wealthy owners and had a reputation for being a classy fellow. Born in England to a father who became a trainer in the United Kingdom after emigrating from South Africa, Russell arrived stateside with an accent and demeanor that allowed him to charm his way from one good client to another.

After he won 2-year-old race after 2-year-old race in Southern California with unfashionable Florida homebreds that were owned by Fred W. Hooper and developed Susan's Girl into a champion filly, he caught the attention of the Phipps Family, for whom he went to work as a private trainer.

It did not take the blue-blooded Phipps long to realize that, when Russell was winning with Hooper's juveniles, it was J. E. "Cotton" Tinsley who deserved the credit for sending them into Hollywood Park fit and ready to win, not their new trainer.

After a few seasons, Russell was replaced by Argentine-born, French-based Angel Penna Sr., who returned the Phippses to their former racing glory and was elected to the Racing Hall of Fame.

A dark bay filly with a sleek look, Dalsenda trained extremely well and got ready for her California debut with a sparkling three-quarter breeze in 1:11 and change at Hollywood Park.

Following the workout, Russell phoned me to ask about buying the filly. I told him that I had a partner and we wanted $300,000.

"I am going to buy her from you for $165,000," he stated matter-of-factly. "I checked, I know what you paid for her and that's plenty of profit."

Taken aback by the tone and content of his response, I regained my composure and told Russell for a second time that the price was $300,000.

"No, I am going to buy the filly from you for $165,000. Come by and I'll give you a check," he said and hung up.

I didn't know whether to laugh or be concerned, so I phoned Morrie Mirkin and relayed the conversation to him. Much to my surprise, he had already received a phone call from John Russell.

"Barry, I'm sure what you tell me is correct," Mirkin said. "But maybe this guy is right. Why not just take the profit and move on?"

I explained to Morrie that the filly had trained sensationally, was even-money to win and would do so impressively, at which point we could make a big score by selling her for at least $300,000.

"The guy tells me the filly is not as good as you think she is and that we should just take the money and run," Mirkin said.

I appealed to Morrie's business acumen by saying "Morrie, do you believe this guy is more motivated to help us out—two guys who have never had a horse with him—or is he more likely to be looking out for his long-established clients and his own wallet?"

Morrie, of course, saw the logic in my argument, was singularly unimpressed and unmoved by Russell's lavish English accent and told me to handle the situation as I saw fit.

I drove to Hollywood Park that same afternoon and met with John Russell in a remote area of the grandstand.

"Listen, you don't want to tangle with me," Russell said, sounding more like the street punk that lived just below the surface of his British veneer. "You need me. These other trainers on the backside, they don't like you. They consider you to be the biggest asshole in racing. So don't fuck with me. Sell me this horse, take your money and move on."

He kept going on, but my mind was stuck on his pronunciation of the word asshole, which he intoned as "oss" hole. For some reason it struck me as funny that such a common slur would still be delivered with such a classy-sounding accent.

Russell had miscalculated, figuring that I was in some way vulnerable because a couple of years earlier I had taken many of the sport's notables to task in a story I had written for the non-racing, Los Angeles-based magazine *New West*.

Unable to get anywhere with Russell, I then went to visit the stewards on their roof perch above the grandstand at Hollywood Park.

I explained the situation to them, told them I wanted to move the horse and asked how to do it.

"Did he try to hit you?" asked one of the stewards.

I said Russell never got physical, just verbally abusive, and the steward who had asked the question said, "Good, because he's done that before."

The stewards advised me to phone Russell, find out exactly how much Morrie and I owed for the filly's expenses, and then come to the track with a cashier's check, pay the funds directly to Russell and physically remove the horse from his barn.

I was able to get the expense amount, went to City National to obtain a cashier's check and returned to the track. I called Gary Jones and told him the story. I asked if he would mind accompanying me to Russell's barn to pick up the filly. Gary wanted the filly, because he had seen her train, but he wanted no part of getting involved with John Russell in any sort of contentious situation.

Jones handed me a leather shank and wished me good luck.

I walked over to Russell's barn, found his assistant Richard Cross and told him that I was there to take the horse. With as blank a face as he could muster, the visibly uncomfortable young Englishman said, "She's not here."

Normally, I would have thought the guy was pulling my leg. But there was something sinister about the entire situation and I knew he was not kidding me.

I probed and prodded, but still no confession about the location of the suspiciously absent filly.

Once again I contacted the stewards, who told me they would call Russell to try to ascertain the whereabouts of the filly.

Surely, I thought to myself, Russell didn't really hope to get away with whatever he had planned, as he had failed to buy the horse at a cheap price from us. I just couldn't figure out what his game was.

A few hours later, I received a phone call from John Russell.

"Whom should the check be made out to for the filly?" he said.

I responded by asking, "Shouldn't we discuss the price first?"

"You told me the price—$300,000."

I informed him whom to make the check out to. He told me when to come by the barn the next day to get the check.

Morrie and I banked the check for $300,000.

When the filly appeared shortly afterward and won her North American racing debut in handsome fashion, she raced for a partnership that included Summa Stable, Nelson Bunker Hunt and Alan Landsburg.

Nelson Bunker Hunt had just squandered the fortune of arguably the richest family in the world when his bid to corner the world silver market ended in failure, and led not only to his bankruptcy, but also to his conviction for manipulating the precious metals market.

Summa Stable was the *nom de course* of Bruce McNall, a conman who idolized Hunt and joined forces with him to form partnerships for Hunt's large crop of home-bred racing prospects. McNall loved precious metals of a different kind, as he was a numismatist of some note. His own fraudulent dealings with banks and high-profile clients, such as hockey great Wayne Gretsky, landed him in a California jail for almost five years.

Alan Landsburg, a television producer of such hits as *Kate and Allie* and *That's Incredible*, survived his association with his partners to go on to head the California Horse Racing Board and the Thoroughbred Owners of California.

Morrie and I retired the loan at City National Bank, split a large sum of cash and each kept a valuable broodmare when we ended our partnership after about a year.

When I tell this story to people familiar with the characters involved, nobody believes the part about John Russell and how he hid Dalsenda. They think I made it up.

Thank goodness for the presence of Richard Cross in this tale, because without his role in the saga, I would have no credible witness. Half a dozen years later, Richard went on to train our Clover Racing Stable's English import Lizzy Hare to win the Grade 2, $150,000 Del Mar Oaks.

CHAPTER 9

Three-legged Stud

After leaving *Daily Racing Form* in the summer of 1978, I started a bloodstock business that I named Pacifica Thoroughbreds. Among the bits of business I did was acquiring stallions and stallion prospects for breeders.

In the early 1980s, one of the most aggressive farm owners seeking new stallions to stand at his farm near Atascadero, California was Wally Dollase.

A tall, handsome fellow in his late thirties, Wally was a salesman *par excellence.*

Wally not only could smell money, but also he had an unbridled confidence that allowed him to go after it, whether the amounts were small enough to buy a share in an unproven stallion for less than $10,000, or to buy a farm for more than $1 million.

The Wisconsin native tried training in San Francisco in the late 1960s, but gave it up in order to start a family with his beautiful New Zealand-born wife. Wally worked in pharmaceuticals and sold real estate before zeroing in on the lucrative possibilities of standing Thoroughbred stallions.

Owning a farm, standing stallions and marketing stallion seasons allowed Wally the luxury of keeping his burgeoning family in one locale, while also affording him the opportunity to use his salesmanship and enthusiasm to make money selling equine semen.

Even though as a real estate agent in various horsey locales between Paso Robles and Santa Barbara, Wally had earned a reputation for selling more sizzle than steak, leery horse breeders put aside their assessments of Wally's lack of ethics to participate in his ventures, because Wally's infectious enthusiasm promised even his detractors the chance to make money by joining his stallion syndicates.

Truth be told, none of Wally's stallions ever accomplished much at stud. But Wally and those who played along with him still made money, especially if the investors sold their breeding rights annually or sold the produce of the stallions at public auction. Those who opted to ride the wave as far as racing the offspring invariably got left holding the bag.

A good promoter can make money with a stallion prospect for four years before the cat is fully out of the bag and it becomes known that the offspring of a new sire are less than stellar. And nobody in the California breeding industry made more hay before the product went to the ultimate market than Wally Dollase did.

Anybody in the bloodstock business in California in the early 1980s knew that Wally was live to buy a new stallion prospect. Like me, Wally was an adventurous fellow and he was one of the few breeders who were open-minded enough to consider importing a stallion prospect from abroad.

In the summer of 1980, I presented a French colt to Wally as a promising prospect that could be raced first and placed in stud afterward. The 4-year-old was named Boitron and was owned by famed Greek shipping tycoon Stavros Niarchos.

Thoroughbreds had long fascinated Swiss resident Niarchos. While in his late forties, he bought his first horses through Fasig-Tipton's president Humphrey S. Finney, who acquired breeding stock for him. Finney bought horses from the Estate of William Woodward after that poor fellow's wife shot him dead at their Long Island estate when she mistook him for a prowler.

Niarchos, who went on to spend a record $47,850,000 for Pablo Picasso's self portrait *Yo, Picasso*, had a taste for the unique and had actually bid on the great American racehorse Nashua, who was sold by the Woodward Estate on a sealed-bid basis. Unable to secure that son of Nasrullah, Niarchos instead bought some shares in his sire and female relatives of Nashua.

In running a breeding and racing operation as a business, Niarchos always sold male horses that were not good enough to be mated with his mares, so Boitron—although nearly a champion racehorse—became available.

Four years old at the time he was offered to me, Boitron had served his purpose for the Niarchos Stable, as he had run second to Champion Irish River at 2 in a Group 1, won a Group 3 at Deauville at 3 while placing in another Group 1 behind Irish River and, in the start before we bought him, he beat Champion English Sprinter and Champion French Miler Kilijaro in a Group 2 at Deauville.

More importantly, the "honest servant" Boitron had been an indispensable workmate and barometer for Nureyev, the most famous horse bred and raced by Niarchos in that era.

I approached Wally about joining me in the purchase of Boitron. My proposal called for Wally to commit to buy half and for me to commit to buy the other half. We agreed to form a syndicate that I would manage during the racing life of the horse and that Wally would take over when Boitron went to stud at his Rio Vista farm.

If we wound up buying him, I planned to select Gary Jones to train the colt, so he and I went to France to inspect the 4-year-old. We arrived in time to see him just before the colt split champion Milers Kilijaro and Northjet in the 6 ½-furlong Group 3 Prix de Seine-et-Oise at Maisons-Laffitte racecourse near Paris.

We both loved what we saw, which was a taller than average, powerhouse of a horse with bulk so prodigious, he looked like he may have already stood a season or two at stud.

Boitron was syndicated in quick order for $900,000. My group was comprised of a bunch of fellows who I had come to know in the breeding game, including an insurance man and a veterinarian. Wally was able to get one major investor to take a large swing: Verne H. Winchell, Jr., a brilliant Pasadena businessman who developed Winchell's doughnuts and Denny's restaurants into lucrative national franchises.

Boitron became ours in the fall of 1980. In the spring of 1981, he made two starts—the only two races he would ever run in North America—at Hollywood Park. The French-bred stormed home late to win a mile conditions race and ran sixth of eleven in a stakes race three weeks later.

Shortly afterward, we decided to fly Boitron to Chicago for the Stars and Stripes Handicap, as a possible prelude to a tilt against John Henry in the Arlington Million.

Boitron had a nasty habit of kicking out with his hind legs when he was confined in a stall. Gary Jones had actually tacked rubber mats on the walls of his stall at the racetrack to protect the horse's hind legs and feet.

The Murty Brothers equine transportation company handled the flight arrangements to send Boitron to Chicago. They also owned a horse that accompanied Boitron on the flight.

Between Los Angeles and Chicago, Boitron got in a kicking match with the Murty Brothers' horse and when he arrived on the tarmac in Chicago, it was immediately apparent that Boitron had injured a hind leg. The colt had to be withdrawn from his intended race and flown home to Los Angeles.

Dr. Jack Robbins examined Boitron upon the horse's return and informed us that the colt had damaged one of his hind legs to such an extent that he recommended his retirement as a racehorse.

Boitron was vanned from Southern California to Wally Dollase's farm near Atascadero. The veterinarian wanted Boitron to be confined to a stall for 45 days before he could gradually be walked and exercised and then, after a point, he could be placed in a small corral, after which time he probably could be turned out in a small paddock.

It was a bitter pill to swallow for all involved, as the horse had shown a lot of potential in his races at Hollywood Park. But because we had bought him as a stallion prospect, we had the potential to earn income from standing him at stud.

A few weeks after Boitron had arrived at Dollase's Rio Vista farm, I got a phone call from Wally.

In previous conversations, Wally had complained about the handling and training methods Gary Jones had used with Boitron. Wally started the conversation by explaining that he had once been a trainer before he left the profession to raise his family in a stable environment

Wally proceeded to tell me how he would train Boitron if he had been at the helm. I listened to his monologue and, after what I considered to be an appropriate amount of time, said, "Wally, I hear what you are saying, but at this stage of the game, what's the point? The horse is finished. End of story."

Then he dropped a bombshell: "Not really," he replied. He went on to say that he was not only training the horse on his farm, but that he had breezed him that very morning and, as the horse's new trainer, planned to bring him back to the races.

I could tell that Wally was not kidding because Wally is not a kidder.

"Wally, that horse is supposed to be in a stall for 45 days, what in the hell are you talking about?" I said. "Besides, what do you mean you are training him? You don't even have a racetrack!"

The stallion farm owner tried to explain that he had a path around a few of his farm paddocks that he sometimes used to exercise horses and it was on this trail that he gave Boitron a workout.

I got off the phone as quickly as possible and immediately phoned Louis R. Rowan, who was not only a syndicate member, but covered Boitron through his insurance company.

Rowan, an experienced and highly successful breeder and racehorse owner (not to mention one of the only Californians who had been invited to become a member of The Jockey Club), was aghast. He said he would phone Wally at once, read him the riot act and tell him to confine the horse to his stall until he could get there. Rowan then drove from Pasadena to Atascadero to assess the damage.

Next I phoned Dr. William Stevenson, another Boitron syndicate member, who was a reproductive vet and an experienced practitioner in dealing with racehorses. Bill was located in the Santa Ynez Valley, not far from Atascadero, and he promised to drive to Rio Vista as soon as possible.

Rowan and Dr. Stevenson found Boitron to be lame in his already-injured hind leg. They ordered Wally not to try any more foolishness with the colt.

The upshot of the additional stress placed on Boitron's previously injured hind leg was that, a few years later, the stallion developed complications, as the blood supply in his lower limb had become compromised. Problems began to surface in the horse's right hind foot because of a loss of circulation.

Wally brought in equine foot specialist Dr. Ric Redden, a world-renowned veterinarian and farrier who specialized in treating laminitis.

"I took the bandage off, and his whole foot—coffin bone and everything—was in the bandage," Dr. Redden said. "It was brown and just fell off."

Dr. Redden suggested that Wally contact Dr. Barrie Grant at Washington State University, where he practiced veterinary surgery, and probe the idea of fitting Boitron with prosthesis.

A decade earlier, a New York-based sprinter named Spanish Riddle had become the most famous Thoroughbred racehorse to get a prosthetic limb, when a human surgeon replaced a damaged foot with an artificial device.

But Boitron required a much larger area of bone and sinew to be replaced, as any artificial limb would have to encompass the area from about four inches below the right hock down to the ground.

University engineers, using a steering column from an old Volkswagen found in a local junk yard, went through a long process of trial and error that required Boitron to be placed under anesthesia no less than eighteen times before coming up with a workable prosthesis for the stallion.

Boitron, who entered stud in 1982, served three seasons with the artificial hind limb before he succumbed to peritonitis in May of 1987.

Wally Dollase had compromised the health of the horse by going against orders from a veterinarian, and by training him and putting him under undue stress in order to fulfill a dream.

Like most promoters, whether they are televangelists selling a fake cure that winds up killing a believer or a real estate developer selling property under high-tension wires that cause buyers to die of leukemia, Wally did not accept responsibility for his actions.

And, like the best of promoters, he turned a negative into a positive. In order to quickly escape any possible taint from having put Boitron on the fast track toward destruction, he reinvented himself as the guy who saved the poor bastard's life by supplying him with prosthesis and giving him a new lease on life. Hail Wally, savior of equine life.

Dollase was able to generate a lot of feel-good media stories about his saving Boitron. The high point came in the mid 1980s when CBS' *60 Minutes* did a segment on the so-called "three-legged horse."

The promoter sold Rio Vista to Jheri Redding, the guy who invented crème rinse in the 1930s, gave black folks the Jheri Curl and brought the popular Redken hair products to Beverly Hills salons. Redding wanted to reinvent the horse business, but his results did not meet his expectations.

Wally went through several incarnations, first becoming a successful trainer in Southern California and later in Kentucky. He retired after suffering from some health issues and died in the bluegrass in the fall of 2015.

Some referred to him as a snake oil salesman, while others pointed to him as using a magic potion. Immediately before and after the millennium, some trainers had their winning percentages increase dramatically and saw their rate of developing champions increase.

Usage of performance enhancing drugs (PEDs) like erythropoietin and clenbuterol, thought to be common among certain trainers, was credited with changing the luck of a few horsemen who somehow were able to skirt the rules by administering these substances.

Wally Dollase was singled out regularly in private conversation by fellow horsemen as a likely user of illegal PEDs. Those who raced and bet horses wondered out loud and on Internet message boards whether Wally's background in pharmaceuticals in some way allowed him to take an edge in the sport.

In 2003, when the California Horse Racing Board decided to make the use of clenbuterol legal under certain circumstances, the Board held a meeting in Santa Anita's backstretch kitchen to educate horsemen about the change. During a question and answer session, Wally asked the CHRB veterinarian about withdrawal times for the drug.

The question was greeted by considerable laughter and snickering. One trainer in attendance verbally suggested that Wally knew far more about the subject than the veterinarian on hand.

Once tests were developed for certain PEDs, many a trainer including Wally saw their winning percentages drop precipitously.

CHAPTER 10

Broke and Fixed

As had been the case at the close of the 1960s, my life imploded and spurred me to move back to the Bluegrass in the late 1980s. In the span of about a year and a half, I became divorced, bankrupt and broke. Really broke—don't have money to buy dinner broke.

My business problems were that I owned more also-rans and hay-burners than income producers; the expenses to maintain my equine portfolio of more than 125 horses was infinitely greater than my ability to generate income from their sale; and changes in the IRS Tax Code made owning runners and breeding stock considerably less attractive than it had been earlier in the decade.

In the early 1980s, the value of racing and breeding stock experienced an unprecedented surge that was fueled by rampant inflation. When I first started borrowing money from Bank of America in Pasadena as the owner of Pacifica Thoroughbreds in the early 1980s, inflation was so rampant that banks were charging interest rates as high as 23 percent and few were complaining, because money was so easy to make. In times of inflation, I was told, people had no use for money, cash was no longer king and investors wanted to put their money into tangibles.

Horses were tangibles. So were the food they ate and the vitamins they were given because both could be expensed and written off. More importantly, horses could be used as a tool to exploit the tax code legally. Many sophisticated investors entered the market to form tax shelters and own tangibles. And I supplied the raw material to these people.

I dealt in racehorses, breeding stock, stallions and stallion shares. Times were so good that if I could not make at least $50,000 on a transaction, I would not waste my time working on the deal.

There was a time in 1982-4 where horses were bought and sold, not so much for their intrinsic value or ability to generate income, but because of the tax write-offs they provided. When the core elements of a business transaction become secondary to the tax advantage, it is not healthy for that industry. Ronald Reagan was president of the United States and he signed a new tax law that did no favors for his friends in the Bluegrass or in California, where he once had been president of the state's Thoroughbred breeders organization, and the merde hit the fan.

Although many so-called blue blood families had been involved in racing and breeding pursuits since before World War II, they made a mass exodus in the late 1980s. If the Federal Government no longer wanted to be their partner by providing attractive tax incentives, they and their tax advisors reasoned, they would close up shop. And they did so in unprecedented numbers.

An economic recession in 1987 jump-started my demise. Banks panicked, with good reason, and started calling in loans. They made the equivalent of margin calls when the value of a horse dipped below the amount of money the banks loaned to their customers to buy those horses. Many owners were stuck between a rock and a hard place because, even if they wanted to sell their horses, they would be required to pay the shortfall between what they had borrowed and the sale price. The trouble was, they were all under water. So many people simply declared bankruptcy or walked away from their commitments.

I received bad advice from advisors, caved into pressure from creditors and took the easy way out through bankruptcy. Angst from the deterioration of my second marriage impaired my ability to think clearly.

My downward slide was entirely of my own making. Because I was in the eye of the storm, however, I didn't realize this at the time.

Although the advice some lawyers and accountants gave me was bad, I was given some very good counsel from an improbable source: a lawyer who put me on the track toward a sane approach to life.

The attorney took advantage of my vulnerability by exacting from me one of the best horses I've ever owned, while simultaneously forcing me to realize that the root of my issues was not the many individual problems I was experiencing, but rather what I brought to those problems.

He pointed out, in a very kind, intelligent yet insistent manner, that I had never learned to accept responsibility for my own actions, and that I chose instead to blame others for my problems. It was hard to listen to and

I initially resisted his advice, explaining why I considered myself to be the victim of a series of calamitous events. But he was equally insistent that, as I was a man in my mid-40s, it was high time to grow up.

He was absolutely correct, of course. And bitter as I remain today at the loss of a mare that would be responsible for producing a winner of a Triple Crown race, I also am deeply grateful to him for teaching me the greatest lesson of my life. I had lacked the introspection and guidance to see my major shortcoming as a person. I hit bottom. The lawyer had waited until I had become sufficiently battered to his have this heart-to-heart talk that wound up changing my life.

Hindsight is a wonderful thing for introspection but useless in real time in terms of your ability to change the course of events. Looking back, I never should have declared bankruptcy because my assets, if sold in a rational manner, would probably have covered 75 percent of my total debt. But I was not thinking rationally.

Bankruptcy turned out to be a positive thing for me in two regards: first, losing all of my personal possessions taught me the valuable lesson that you can go on living without them and they are not nearly as important as I made them out to be; second, although I felt like an utter failure, the prospect of a fresh start gave me instant hope going forward. I gained a new perspective in a very short period of time and undertook to avoid the business mistakes I had made in the past by taking responsibility for my actions. I made a conscious effort to keep this in mind in each new endeavor.

One afternoon I got a phone call from my friend Jeff Siegel. He told me about a 3-year-old filly that was entered in a $50,000 claiming race at Santa Anita the next afternoon. He thought she had the potential to become a stakes winner. Jeff wanted to know if I would be interested in claiming her with him, Nick Ben-Meir and a few of Nick's show business pals.

I explained to Jeff that my circumstances were such that I had taken to borrowing $20 at a time from people just to be able to eat. He said that if I liked the filly, we would work something out. He invited me to his condo, which was about a five-minute drive down the road from my hillside home, to analyze a video replay of the filly's last race.

I told Jeff that my BMW had been repossessed and my only other vehicle was a 35-year-old Willys Jeepster that I stopped driving because it no longer had any brake lining and it was too scary to drive down the hill. Jeff picked me up, drove me to his condo and played the race video.

After watching the race, I told Jeff that I really liked her and thought her stride was superb and that she looked like a gifted athlete. Jeff was excited to hear that I liked her. Jeff was a complex guy. On one hand, he has a ton of confidence in himself and in his ability to analyze racing, but on the other, he wanted reassurance to avoid making mistakes. Basically, Jeff wanted me to bless the deal. My endorsement meant enough to him that he was willing to involve me in the horse.

Abrojo, the 3-year-old filly in question, won her race at Santa Anita the next day by an impressive six-length margin. Eddie Gregson, whom the partners had chosen to train the filly, walked downstairs to the area near the finish line where the racing officials dealt with claims and was surprised to run into Charlie Whittingham. Affectionately known in the racing press as The Bald Eagle, Whittingham never claimed horses, yet this time, he was down there for a "shake" of pills from a leather bottle to determine which party among those entering a claim would wind up with Abrojo. Gregson emerged with a big gorgeous smile on his actor-handsome face.

What made Abrojo a good filly was her stride. Whenever her rider was able to relax her and get her into that rhythmic stride, she was hard to beat in the races just below the top level. It was a joy to watch her run.

Abrojo made five starts while I was a member of the partnership that owned her. She won three of them, namely the California Oaks, the Pacifica Invitational and the Fleet Diver Handicap. Gregson saddled her when she ran unplaced twice in Southern California, and his Northern California affiliate Fordell Fierce saddled her for three wins in three starts in the Bay Area.

Members of the partnership were Pacifica Thoroughbreds, Jeff Siegel, Nick Ben-Meir, Marty Bregman, Bob Estrin and Marty Bauer.

Bregman had represented Woody Allen and Barbara Streisand, among others, when he was an agent, but his greatest find was Al Pacino, whose star he rode to fame as the producer of several Pacino cinematic vehicles including the cult classic *Scarface*. The Manhattan-born show biz mastermind was a good racing partner and he loved going to the track.

Bob Estrin was a film editor of note; his projects included Robert Redford's classic movie *The Candidate*. He also was a professor at the University of Southern California's famed film school.

Completing the group was Marty Bauer, as exotic a human being as I've ever met, who, by his own reckoning, visited a shrink as many as three times a week. Based on what I witnessed, I would say that amount of time was well justified. Bauer rode top client Michael J. Fox's popularity to a merger between his company and another to form UTA (United Talent Agency), which became the leader in creative management in Hollywood. He left a few years later to establish the eponymous Bauer Company.

Bauer admitted to knowing nothing about horses or horse racing, but that didn't stop him from giving his opinion on everything and manipulating the partners and trainers to effect what he wanted to see happen.

Nobody I ever met could stand being in Bauer's company because he had a terminal case of "spilkes," which is Yiddish for anxiety (literally, "ants in the pants"). Bauer couldn't tolerate anybody, including himself.

On a short car ride to the stable area to see how Abrojo came back from her victory in September of 1987 at Bay Meadows racetrack in the Bay Area, Nick Ben-Meir, Marty Bauer and I began to brainstorm about what to do next with a filly that had easily won a stakes.

Gregson trained the filly for her wins in the Bay Area, where Fordell Fierce saddled Abrojo, but when Eddie ran her in Southern California, she lost both of her races. So Bauer lobbied strongly to leave the filly with Fierce in San Francisco. Nick and I pointed out that Gregson was the trainer and Fordell was only helping him and that before any decision was made, all of the partners needed to discuss the matter at length. The three of us agreed not to mention anything about our thoughts to Fierce when we got to the barn.

No sooner had we stepped out of the car than Bauer was in Fierce's face saying that he didn't care what anybody else said, Abrojo was going to stay put with Fierce. This placed Fordell, a very mild-mannered, classy guy, in an uncomfortable position because Gregson was not only a well-respected peer, but also a good pal of Fierce's who benefited immensely from their relationship.

So incredulous was I at Bauer's irrational act of self-absorption that I snapped. For the only time in my adult life, I physically went after another human being. I grabbed Bauer by his lapels and shoved him backwards, pushing him hard against a wooden stall door. Bauer saw the look in my eye, backed off and shut his pie hole.

When I returned home, I apologized to Nick for losing my cool and instructed him to see if any of the partners wanted to buy me out. After a short period of negotiation I wound up selling my interest in Abrojo based on a total valuation of $375,000. We had paid $53,250 for her nine months earlier.

The profit from the sale and net race earnings of Abrojo, coupled with the ability to buy into the filly without having to fund it with up-front cash, provided me with a life preserver tossed my way by Jeff Siegel. I never forgot his gesture and when the time came, I repaid him many, many times over.

Later on, after it had become obvious that Jeff functioned more as a consultant than as a vitally involved partner who shared the workload, financial commitment and responsibility, people asked why I remained his partner. So I shared our history with them. Many said that I had surely repaid the debt by that time. But when it comes to friendship and somebody doing me a good turn, I don't think there needs to be a scorecard.

It is said that every time God closes a door, he opens a window. My window opened when I was at my lowest.

CHAPTER 11

Clover Racing Stable

One winter day in the late 1980s, I fielded a call at my Sierra Madre home in the Southern California foothills from a guy that talked like Humphrey Bogart. He asked for a meeting to discuss something mutually beneficial. The Bogart impression broadened when I met Dana Marchetta in person.

His complexion was swarthy, his forehead glistened from an abundance of product that had oozed down from his doo-wop hairstyle and his face was lined with creases too deep for a guy probably only in his late thirties. Yet his visage did not detract from his obvious charisma. Speaking in low tones and with a clenched upper lip most likely were studied affectations, and the package taken as a whole gave me the creeps, but it stirred my interest in hearing what the guy had to say. OK, maybe he wasn't there looking for the Maltese Falcon, but he had my rapt attention.

Marchetta, accompanied by a pair of equally shifty looking underlings, sat down and proceeded to lay out plans for a business venture he hoped to involve me in. He had spent the previous two years raising money and marketing a couple of well-bred yearlings for a stable that formed racing partnerships.

According to Marchetta, the stable's owner had come up with a viable concept in forming partnerships, but he bought bad horses, overcharged for them and never gave the investors any sort of chance to succeed.

If he could partner with an ethical horseman, Dana said, the partnership concept could be a winner because he had found a tremendous market willing to buy an interest in a racehorse. He wanted to continue to be involved in the industry, but only if he could deal with a reputable horseman.

Dana set up a productive boiler room operation to hawk the deal. It really was quite clever.

His boss would buy a yearling for about $100,000 and syndicate it for about $1 million. Even taking into consideration the inclusion of expenses, the mark up was shockingly outrageous. The yearling had been bought at public auction, Marchetta explained, but none of the investors had any idea what the horse cost, as they lacked the savvy to discover the details.

I was intrigued on many levels. How, I wondered, could a bunch of sleazy-looking guys like this sell anything if their prospective customers actually eyeballed them? Where did they find people to talk to? How much money would it take to start up a joint venture? When did they want to get started? Stuff like that.

The most fascinating of the answers emerged when Marchetta revealed some of the marketing techniques that were developed by this merry band of misfits. One of the crewmembers stationed himself at a well-known car wash on the Sunset Strip, across the street from the famous Schwab's Drug Store. He sat on a patio table bench, clocked incoming automobiles, waited until an expensive one appeared, identified the owner and sat patiently until the mark, watching their car go through the wash, passed by his headquarters.

The salesman engaged the customer in conversation, which he instantly focused on the idea of Thoroughbred ownership and how cheaply one could become involved in the Sport of Kings. Let's face it, he would say, after you've bought that trophy car, the boat and the plane, the only thing missing from the equation was the racehorse. The salesman made a good living from working that car wash.

Maître d's, hookers, valet car parkers—anybody who serviced a clientele of possible players—were engaged to provide leads for the boiler room outfit. And apparently there were plenty of takers.

The goldmine of all goldmines was a list of commodities that buyers complete with their phone numbers from the Siegel (no relation to my partner Jeff Siegel) Trading Company in Los Angeles. In 1989, this company ended up getting slammed with the biggest lawsuit in the fourteen-year history of the Commodity Futures Trading Commission for employing high-pressure tactics in marketing its services. Until that moment, I had never realized the close connection between buyers of commodities and potential buyers of racehorse partnerships. This list would prove invaluable to our venture.

After the Dana Marchetta Crime Family left my home, I sketched out details of what a joint venture might look like. My idea was to involve two friends, namely Jeff Siegel and Jamie Schloss. Jeff and I would run the horse division, Marchetta and his crew would be in charge of marketing and Jamie would use his background in accounting and law to set up and run the business end of the company. Jamie would serve as a buffer between the two divisions. The boiler room crowd would be given a 45 percent equity interest, the horsemen would be given a like amount and Jamie would get 10 percent.

Before finalizing a deal, I asked my pal Nick Ben-Meir to meet with the boiler room guys and me, both to hear what they had to say and to decide whether they were too sketchy to become partners with. We met in Nick's West Hollywood office on Doheny. I knew Nick well enough to be able to be able to judge his immediate reaction. One look at the boiler room crowd was enough for him. If I had to put his facial expression into a single phrase, it would be, "What, are you kidding me?" He later confirmed his "thumbs down" opinion based on how the boys looked and the vague, casual manner in which they glossed over complicated issues. Nothing was a problem for these guys, to hear them tell it.

I learned that the boiler room guys were survivors. What they lacked in formal education they more than made up for in street smarts. Problems that arose were solved in the most unconventional and borderline-illegal ways. Can't afford to buy a phone or make a long distance call? No problem. Tapping into their underground network of similarly minded miscreants, they came up with calling cards that they stole from major American corporations. Moving right along. ...

Jamie, Jeff and I each thought the partnership concept had merit. We were scared to death that the image and tactics of the boiler room guys could scuttle the vessel before the venture got up and running. But the prospect of somebody providing us with money to buy horses was too great a carrot for us to pass. So we decided the potential reward was worth the risk because the horse business had burned a lot of its clients and it needed new blood. We put clothespins on our noses, held our collective breath and strained our necks toward the carrot.

Right about here, I would love to be able to write, "And the rest is history." But the twists and turns I would experience in the subsequent four decades of my career as a racehorse syndicator were only just beginning.

I presented the deal to the boiler rooms guys and they accepted, mostly because they had been given an equity interest the five of them could share, and in February of 1987 we became incorporated. I came up with the name Clover Racing Stable (a clover is a symbol of luck) and designed the distinctive silks with Kelly green four-leaf clovers dotting the black jacket.

None of us had any money. I worked out of my house. So did Jeff and Jamie. God only knows where the boiler room group hung out.

Jeff and I set about looking for our first horse. We settled on an unraced, newly turned 3-year-old colt in the barn of trainer Neil Drysdale. Political Ambition was appropriately named by his breeder Brereton C. Jones, who said he was selling the colt to raise money for what turned out to be a successful campaign that year for the office of Lieutenant Governor of the State of Kentucky. Jones later became Kentucky's governor as well.

We agreed to buy the colt for $60,000 plus a 5 percent commission of $3,000 to Drysdale, as long as the Airdrie Stud owner gave us a bit of time to raise the capital. There had been a well-established history of Kentucky breeders selling horses on the cuff.

When I told Marchetta the details of our prospective first purchase, his dark complexion turned pale, as he became apoplectic when he learned of the colt's plebian pedigree. Dana was used to marketing yearlings that were bred in the purple. Political Ambition was totally lacking in pedigree, especially in the sire department. Kirtling, his sire, had been imported from Italy and, other than Brereton Jones, who stood him at his Kentucky farm, his arrival in the Bluegrass had gone entirely unnoticed.

Dana informed me that he and his sales crew would be unable to market a horse with this little parentage. In a meeting at my home, I explained to the boiler room guys that Jeff and I had discussed our game plan and decided since none of us had any money, the best use of what little capital we did have would be to buy the most gifted athlete we could afford and not a fancy catalogue page. This, I said, was especially important because, unlike their previous employer, we were actually going to have to race the horse we bought. Dana told me that I was loco in la cabeza. But he had little choice other than to jump on board.

Much to our surprise, the boiler room boys swung into action instantly. Hank Shuman, a partner in the failed venture with Marchetta's previous employer, was the first prospective participant in the new venture to inspect the colt. I met him one morning at Santa Anita at the Association stable gate and brought him to Drysdale's barn to take a gander at Political Ambition. Hank became our first buyer and raced horses with my partnerships for the next twenty racing seasons. Like Jeff and me, Hank was a "Westside Jew" so he felt comfortable with us. An engineer for Northrop-Grumman, he was also a brilliant handicapper and loved to go racing at England's Cheltenham Racecourse for steeplechase and hurdle contests each winter.

The colt was syndicated within a matter of days based on a total valuation of $100,000. We had decided to sell interests of 10 percent or less so that no one partner owned enough to throw his weight around. When it came time to pay for the colt, we needed one final sale, so we bit the bullet and agreed to sell a 25 percent interest to City of Commerce businessman

Dave Wolf, a decision that would haunt us for years to come. But, at last, Clover Racing Stable was off and running.

Political Ambition was a very special athlete. He was one of those rare animals whose ease of movement, even at a walk, made it seem as though his feet never touched the ground. Jesse Owens, the greatest American sprinter of all time, developed a style of running in which his feet touched the ground very lightly. It was almost as though he were running barefoot on hot coals. When I saw Political Ambition walk and train, I was reminded of something Owens had once said, which was that the less time the feet spend on the ground, the faster a sprinter would run. Jeff and I watched Political Ambition breeze and we were sold on him.

On May 29 of 1987, Political Ambition made his racing debut in a seven-furlong maiden race on dirt at Hollywood Park. Drysdale, Jeff and I knew the colt would eventually want to stretch out on grass, but in those days California trainers all wanted to start a horse out in a dirt sprint. The colt took hold late when the penny dropped in the final furlong and a half; he made up a lot of ground, finished in a rally to take fourth and excited the hell out of all of us.

Our 25 percent partner Dave Wolf, another member of the Hebraic persuasion, called me and said, "We've got ourselves a pferd," which in both content and meaning translated to, "We've got ourselves a bona fide racehorse."

Using the partnership's profits from the syndication of our first horse, Clover Racing Stable rented an office in Beverly Hills, a location insisted upon by the always image-conscious Dana Marchetta. Everybody was given business cards. Phones were set up in individual offices, which was an upgrade from the boiler room guys' previous situation.

I spent some, but not a lot of time at that office. The drive from Sierra Madre to Beverly Hills proved to be boring but not as tedious as observing the boiler room guys in action. I urged them to behave and not do anything to get Jeff, Jamie or me in trouble. I told them to knock off using stolen phone cards.

But they were incorrigible. The most exotic member of the menagerie was a guy, barely into his forties, who had never met a prospective customer in person, yet he arrived each day at work dressed in an elaborate costume tailored to fit his manufactured persona. His tall, lithe body was elegantly clad in an off white suit a Southern plantation owner might have worn on a particularly hot summer day. Not unlike Colonel Harland Sanders himself, this fellow had a healthy head of white hair. To tie the entire outfit together, he added a finishing touch: a wooden walking stick with a bulbous handle.

As bizarre as he looked—and believe me, he was an absolute study of sartorial splendor—the range and content of his skills as an orator trumped his aesthetic style. He was that proverbial gentleman who was capable of selling snow to an Eskimo. He specialized in taking complete and total advantage of unsophisticated folks of advanced years, getting them to perform any manner of stunts that happened to appeal to him on any particular day.

He was dazzling in action. He never wanted to know the name, pedigree, trainer or locale of a horse. All he wanted to know was its gender and syndication price. With the vocal styling of a trained actor, this fellow would lean back in his chair with his dark, laced shoes perched atop his desk and spin yarns to the lonely, bored and eager people on the other end of the line.

It turned out that this was the lucky day for the recipient of his phone call, because the salesman just happened to have the opportunity of a lifetime. Now the salesman was not at liberty to reveal the exact nature of the opportunity over the phone. Only a check in the amount of $5,000 or $10,000 (depending on how much he thought he could exact from the mark) delivered to our offices by courier the next morning would enable him to reveal the deal point. He never sent these people anything. He never told them anything.

His theory on sales was that if he couldn't get a person on the phone to show confidence in him, he considered them hopeless as a prospective customer. It was a matter of will. He was our top salesman. But what he was doing was strictly illegal and our relationship did not last very long.

Another member that the marketing crew brought on board was a woman whose age was impossible to accurately determine because she had spent so much time tanning herself in the hot Florida sun that her skin was dark as a Hershey bar. Like the others, she knew next to nothing about horses or horse racing.

Her stock-in-trade was a deep, husky voice that wealthy, elderly, lonely men of a certain type went crazy over. Her voice had a mesmerizing quality that some guys just couldn't get enough of. She would talk about everything and anything, as the fellow on the other end of the phone held out hope for a meeting with this dark-skinned vixen.

That meeting rarely, if ever, took place. After spending as much as forty-five minutes to an hour and a half talking to a gentleman, she would say something like, "You know, Harry, I'd love to be able to chat with you all day, because you are my kind of fella. But a girl does have to make a living, and unless I can sell you part of this cult we have for sale, I'm going to have to move on, darling."

Her East Coast accent was thick and her pronunciation of some words was strange to my ear, especially when she intoned the word colt like it was cult. When she eventually left the company and moved out of the office, I went through her desk. Her handwritten notes revealed that she thought the word was in fact cult instead of colt, which blew my mind. She had raised a lot of money and had little idea of what she had been talking about.

Marchetta and his crew demonstrated the ability to raise cash on a regular basis. Their unethical conduct and shady ways of skirting the law began to weigh on me. They would say anything to sell a horse. And since I had to live with the consequences, I found it increasingly difficult to deal with them.

Dana was constantly trying to tap into the cash reserves of the company by changing the deal on commissions to the salesmen, as well as by asking me to provide incentives to the salesmen, such as expensive wristwatches as a bonus for the top seller of the month. They seemed to never stop trying us for more money.

Political Ambition returned sixteen days after his debut, again racing over seven furlongs on dirt at Hollywood Park, where he stormed down the lane to win by six lengths. The winners' circle caught the attention of the press box and the horse folk seated in the box section because it looked like more than a hundred people had descended upon the enclosure. Locals were not used to seeing such numbers but they eventually got used to it as, over the next several years, anywhere from twenty-five to fifty people regularly showed up for Clover Racing Stable celebrations after a winning race.

For the partners, it was a real family affair; Hank Shuman brought his mother and Dave Wolf brought his son. Instead of embracing a new entity like our stable, rival owners and the press, acting out of jealousy, made fun of our group. Mrs. Shuman, who was quite elderly at the time, wore a heavy overcoat and carried a large bag during the summer. Jenine Sahadi, the queen of snark, said something like, "Where do they find these people? Do they just pull them off the street? Look, they even have a bag lady!"

The partners were a good group of hard-working people who bought Political Ambition from us because they wanted to be involved in racing and have some fun. Eventually, the trainers who didn't want a Clover Racing Stable horse were few and far between. Miss Sahadi herself, who wound up training Grade 1 winners for Barry Irwin and Jeff Siegel, jumped on the bandwagon.

Our clients rarely embarrassed me, but I was starting to get extremely leery of being seen in public with the Dana Marchetta Crime Family.

During the summer, Political Ambition won races back-to-back in his second and third outings on the grass, a surface for which he was bred both in his sire line and family. Neil Drysdale told us that he planned to point the colt for the Grade 1 Hollywood Derby and he thought the colt was improving enough to win it.

The thought of being thrust into the limelight alongside Dana Marchetta and his crew was something I grew increasingly uncomfortable with. So I proposed to Jeff and Jamie that we buy out our partners. The timing was right for us, because Political Ambition had just finished sixth of nine in his first race since winning two in a row at Del Mar. Those guys never believed in the longevity of any enterprise. They were fly-by-night guys who wanted to pounce, make a quick buck and leave town before they left too much of a trail of devastation behind. When we increased their commissions and gave them a bit of cash, they eagerly accepted our buyout terms.

Political Ambition became a Grade 1 winner when taking a division of the Hollywood Derby, which meant that Clover Racing Stable had been able to reach the highest level of racing with its very first syndicated runner. Jeff, Jamie and I owned 100 percent of the stock at the time.

Confirming that his Grade 1 win was not a fluke, Political Ambition came back three weeks later against seasoned older runners in the Grade 1 Hollywood Turf Cup Invitational Handicap to finish third beaten slightly more than 2 lengths when stretched out by Drysdale from nine to twelve furlongs. Then, in his first start as a 4-year-old, he scored one of the most visually impressive wins of his career when taking a Santa Anita allowance race by 4 lengths. He appeared to be on the verge of stardom.

Neil Drysdale decided to point Political Ambition for an important grass race, run on the day before the Kentucky Derby, at Churchill Downs, which had installed a grass course in the mid 1980s. Clover Racing Stable was interested in seeing if its colt could mount a national campaign. Much to everybody's surprise and disappointment, Political Ambition never ran to his three to one odds; in a lackluster performance, he checked in seventh of ten and was beaten more than eight lengths. His rider Eddie Delahoussaye attributed the poor effort to the colt's inability to get a hold of the grass, which was sand-based as opposed to the dirt-based courses in Southern California.

Back home in California, Political Ambition was brought back 3 weeks after his Louisville debacle and held on for a neck triumph in a blanket finish over ten furlongs in the Hollywood Turf Handicap. His 1:58 3/5 clocking broke the Inglewood course record and stood for five years.

On the strength of that record-breaking victory, I was able to strike a deal to sell a 50 percent interest in Political Ambition to a Japanese businessman and horse owner/breeder named Tadahiro Hotehama. I had been working through his American-based agent, a Japanese-born fellow whom I had met at Santa Anita several years earlier. He lived nearby in Pasadena and we chatted frequently. He was in the import/export business and knew a few important horse owners in Japan.

Hotehama, or as we called him "The Toddymeister," had toyed with the notion of doing something with Political Ambition for months. When the colt showed such high grit in his record-breaking performance, The Toddymeister found that he could no longer resist buying into him.

Over the years, I have sold many horses, both privately and publicly, to Japanese horsemen, all with satisfactory results. Hotehama was the notable exception. His word, both spoken and in writing, meant very little to him and served as a starting point for negotiation if results did not work out in his favor.

Instead of having Political Ambition vetted by a licensed practitioner, Hotehama showed up on the eve of the colt's next scheduled appearance, which was the Grade 1 Sunset Handicap. Drysdale and Clover Racing Stable deemed it too close to the race to subject the horse to a barrage of x-rays. Hotehama had brought along his trainer from Japan. The trainer was enthralled by the horse's effortless way of walking and running. He wanted the colt. A deal was struck.

Political Ambition finished sixth of 11 beaten about four lengths. He came out of the race lame and was diagnosed with a broken bone. Hotehama did everything he could to squirm out of the deal. So the Political Ambition partnership filed a lawsuit against Hotehama. Lawyers met for both sides. Proceedings dragged out for months.

Three months after Political Ambition was injured, I interrupted my honeymoon in Hawaii to fly with my new bride Elizabeth "Becky" Raine Irwin to Tokyo in order to renegotiate the terms of our original deal with Hotehama.

The Toddymeister tried to wear me down by either entirely skipping our meetings or making me wait for hours on end at various hotels and restaurants that he owned, all to make me anxious to complete our negotiation so that I could resume my honeymoon. Little did he realize what a honeymoon veteran he was dealing with. I held firm and doggedly stuck to my task.

I wound up signing a deal that contained the word "release," which plainly meant that, under certain conditions, Hotehama would release the long-overdue payment-in-full that he owed to us for Political Ambition. After he refused to release the funds, his lawyers argued that the wording actually said that we would release Hotehama from any further payment requirements. He attempted to resurrect the age-old gambit of distorting the difference between languages to his best advantage. The Toddymeister did very little to further the image of Japanese horse owners with their American counterparts.

Meanwhile, by some miracle, Neil Drysdale was able to completely resuscitate Political Ambition's racing career. Kept to a mile, the (by then) 5-year-old raced four times that season. He won all three of his races at Santa Anita and finished third during the summer at Hollywood Park. In the spring, he beat Steinlen to take the El Rincon. A month before the Breeders' Cup, he won the Col. F.W. Koester, the Southern California prep for the $1 million Breeders' Cup Mile, in convincing style against stable mate Sabona.

Political Ambition was the third choice on the morning line for the 1989 BC Mile. Unfortunately, he went slightly lame on an ankle. X rays did not show anything but our vet Dr. Steve Buttgenbach was convinced that the ankle was fractured. He explained that the composition of the sesamoid bones was different from that of most other bones in the equine skeletal structure, and the suspected fracture line might take as long as ten to fourteen days to appear.

I told Neil to scratch the horse before the races began.

Our 25 percent partner Dave Wolf went ballistic. He wanted to run. As the vet had been unable to diagnose an injury, he insisted on running. I explained to Wolf that we would be placing the horse's life in danger because a shattered sesamoid injury in the race would likely mean the horse would have to be euthanized. Dave was not impressed.

When Steinlen and Sabona ran first and second, Wolf only became angrier because Political Ambition had beaten them both that season. When a Clover horse won a Breeders' Cup race on the same card, it was like pouring kerosene on a burning fire. Wolf created a lot of friction between Clover Racing Stable and its clients.

Fortunately for us the fracture line on the injured sesamoid bone did surface some eleven days later and Jeff and I were off the hook. But prior to that, we had to endure several intense days in clientland.

Political Ambition retired as a winner of nine of his eighteen starts. He earned $625,555 and realized several hundred thousand additional dollars for us from our sale of 50 percent to Tadahiro Hotehama, who eventually came up with at least some of the remaining money he owed us. Political Ambition generated well over a million dollars for his partners.

Drysdale was able to find a suitable South American farm that would buy him, which added another quarter-million dollars or so for the coffers. The horse stood in South America for years and was repatriated toward the end of his breeding career to stand at Harris Farm near Coalinga in Central California.

Political Ambition was our first buy and our first Grade 1 winner. He was not Clover Racing Stable's first major winner. Lizzy Hare, a filly imported from England early in Clover's first summer of racing, earned that honor. English émigré Richard Cross was instrumental in our acquisition of the 3-year-old filly, which was trained in Newmarket by his former boss Luca Cumani. The filly spent four days in quarantine and, after just a day in the Del Mar stable area, she finished fourth in a stakes prep for her major goal, the Grade 2 Del Mar Oaks.

Lizzy Hare ran a decent race, finishing fourth beaten about six lengths. But she stepped in a hole while pulling up afterwards, dumping her 24-year-old jockey Gary Stevens and sending him to the hospital for assorted aches and pains.

Stevens was back aboard the stretch runner for the $150,000 Oaks sixteen days later. She took a bump early in the race and was relegated back to tenth in a field of eleven. Under sensitive handling by Stevens, the filly began picking up horses around the far turn and was able to find room, where she rallied into the home stretch and unleashed an eye-catching burst of speed, which got her a three-quarter length victory at odds of seven to one.

So in its very first season of racing, Clover Racing Stable won the best grass races for a 3-year-old colt and filly in Southern California, which was considered a close second to New York as North America's leading racing circuit.

We were hot, our silks were considered magical by racing fans and horseplayers alike, and our runners struck fear into the hearts and minds of our competitors.

The Beverly Hills offices of Clover Racing Stable were closed, the boiler room guys gradually were phased out in favor of more suitable personnel and Pasadena, California became the new headquarters of the operation.

CHAPTER 12

The Big 'Cap

I walked into Santa Anita Park before noon that late winter day in 1989, taking the tree-lined path from the iconic round receiving barn that would be used later in the afternoon by the horses before they headed to be saddled for the Santa Anita Handicap.

I had history on my mind. For twenty years I had read and written about the history of the Turf, its players and its horses. That day I would be part of history, as our outfit—Clover Racing Stables—had a runner in the big race, which was variously referred to through the years as the "Big 'Cap," the "Santa Anita" or the "Hundred Grander."

Initially it was called the "Hundred Grander" because it was the first race in the world with prize money of $100,000. The present day equivalent at the end of 2015 was about $1,750,000.

Run at a mile and a quarter starting from a chute to the left of the grandstand and finishing after a full trip around the oval, the Santa Anita Handicap was the centerpiece of racing in the West since its inception in 1935. It was a handicap, with weights assigned prior to the traditional annual opening the day after Christmas.

The fabled race that riveted the attention of a nation half a century earlier, when radio and newsreels chronicled Seabiscuit's quest to win the Big 'Cap in his third attempt, had a $1 million purse in 1989 and was still one of the most sought-after prizes in North American racing.

As I walked toward the large fountain that was ringed by individual plaques on which were inscribed the names of past Santa Anita Derby winners, I ran into Jude Feld, a racetracker I had known since he broke into the game as a chart taker in the press box for *Daily Racing Form*.

A jolly soul whose rosy red cheeks, round face and ho-ho-ho laugh reminded one of Santa Claus, Jude was in full bloom and throat when he said, "Hey, Baresky—what are you guys *thinking*? I know this isn't Julio's idea."

Feld had worked as a groom for Julio Canani, trainer of Martial Law, our long shot entrant in the Santa Anita Handicap. Jolly as Jude may have feigned to be, his message rang loud and clear—Jeff and I looked like we were nuts to be running our colt in the biggest handicap race of the year.

Jude was not the only scoffer to try to dampen my enthusiasm on the day. Plenty of others—guys I had worked with for up to twenty years—in their own way let it be known that we were about to be made fools of for running a horse that did not belong on the most visible racing stage of the year.

Most of these so-called "experts" not only were incredulous that we would take a horse with such modest form and run it in the storied Big 'Cap, but that we would get our partners to shell out $40,000 for the privilege.

I became very agitated because these guys treated me like I was getting my racing partners to pony up a lot of cash just so that our stable could gain visibility by having a runner in the big race.

These detractors, with their jibes and digs, were questioning my integrity. I thought I deserved the benefit of the doubt. I was incensed that these wise guys had lumped me in with the majority of owners, guys who ran horses where they did not figure based on a vague hope for success instead of a conviction based on solid horsemanship and analysis of form.

I really should not have been surprised. Our own trainer, Julio Canani, was not bullish on running the colt in the race himself. On paper, Martial Law did not figure to win. Peruvian-born Canani was a man's man, a very proud horseman and he did not want to be made to look stupid.

Jeff Siegel knew Julio better than I did, as the trainer spent a lot of time in the press box where Siegel banged out selections for his syndicate of daily newspapers, whereas I had not been a habitué of the rooftop venue since quitting my job as a columnist for *Daily Racing Form* a decade earlier.

Martial Law had not been made eligible to the Santa Anita Handicap by the time nominations had closed. The first deadline, which required a $500 fee, closed the previous August, when Clover had not yet bought the colt. December and January deadlines with payments of $2,000 and $2,500 came before Martial Law had made his first start in America. So if Clover Racing Stables wanted to run him in the Big 'Cap, the colt would have to be supplemented at a cost of $25,000, followed by an additional payment of $15,000 to get him past the entry box and into the starting gate.

A vote was taken of the seventeen partners who owned Martial Law and a majority wanted to run him in the $1 million race.

Jeff was charged with the task of getting Julio to commit to entering the colt in the race by calling the racing secretary before the 5 p.m. deadline on the Wednesday prior to the weekend race. Jeff didn't feel comfortable pushing Julio and the trainer sensed it, so Jeff was unable to get a straight answer out of him.

Pressure mounted as the clock ticked closer to 5 p.m. Jeff had not called me back, so I phoned him in the press box ten minutes before the deadline. He told me that Julio would not give him a straight answer. I had him put Julio on the phone and said to the trainer point-blank, "Are we running or what?"

Canani said, "You wanna *run?*"

I said, "*Yes,* I want to run."

Canani replied, "Okay, then we run!"

Bottom line: Julio wanted to run, but he didn't want it to look like his idea. He wanted to be pushed. Jeff couldn't push, so I did.

Like many trainers, Julio wanted to run if it looked like some dumb owner forced him to, so if the horse laid an egg on Saturday, his image would be spared. But, if the horse won, then of course it had really been Julio's idea all along. Trainers have a lot in common with tightrope walkers, but their rope is only six inches off the ground and there is foam rubber padding beneath.

So the die was cast: $40,000 would be spent to race a horse that, five months earlier, had been bought at public auction in England for only $20,000 more than the fees were to make him eligible to the Big 'Cap. Clover Racing Stable had paid somewhat more than $60,000 in December for Martial Law and had syndicated him for $100,000.

Martial Law was bred in 1985, a bit off the beaten track in Pennsylvania, because his dam Sateen had previously been booked to The Minstrel, who stood just across the state line at Windfields Farm in neighboring Maryland. For several years in that era, especially when The Minstrel's sire Northern Dancer stood at Windfields, many of the mares bred to that breed-shaping sire were housed in rural Pennsylvania at Marshall Jenny's Derry Meeting Farm.

The breeder of Martial Law was the Darley Stud of Dubai's crown prince Sheikh Mohammed bin Rashid al Maktoum, who bred horses in England, Ireland and the United States while racing almost exclusively in Britain and Europe.

Martial Law was sent, along with the rest of Sheik Mohammed's young stock, to race in England. In 10 starts—4 as a 2-year-old and 6 as a 3-year-old—the homebred colt raced with a small trainer named J. W. Watts in the North of England, winning once at two years old and twice at three.

Racing in modest company at decidedly lower-end Redcar racecourse, Martial Law had managed to win his latest start, in which the gross purse was about $8,000. The colt eked out a win going seven-eighths of a mile, but when racing between six and eight furlongs in England, the colt had no style or trip.

Martial Law probably never should have been sent abroad because he was not bred for the turf. True, his sire Mr. Leader was a wizard on the green stuff, winning the Stars and Stripes Handicap in a new course record time of 1:47 2/5 for 1 1/8 miles at Arlington Park in Chicago. But, as a sire of grass runners, Mr. Leader was virtually useless.

I knew the family of Martial Law well, as in the early 1970s, while taking about a 9-month hiatus from writing and editing *The Thoroughbred of California*, I worked in the bloodstock office of Rollin W. Baugh in Newport Beach, California. Rollin bought and managed Martial Law's second dam, a Claiborne castoff named Satin.

Satin was brilliantly fast, but had a screw loose and was basically a run-off. Trainer Gene Cleveland was able to coax several wins out of Satin, who went to the breeding shed a winner of ten races from thirty-two outings, even though a stakes victory had eluded her. She had superb credentials to become a successful broodmare, as she had an abundance of raw speed and a mouth-watering pedigree.

Tracing back to the foundation matron Coliseum, Satin was produced by Lea Moon, who foaled five stakes winners, while the next dam, Coliseum's daughter Lea Lark, produced four stakes winners, among them the Two-Year-Old Champion Filly Leallah.

Most of the production by the sire and from the family came on North American dirt tracks, which is why Jeff and I decided to take a chance on importing Martial Law, hoping that the horse would take to the dirt in California.

From the day Martial Law first set foot on the Santa Anita track, it became obvious to Julio Canani that he had a gifted runner on his hands. Without exception, each of the 4-year-old's workouts leading up to his California debut was an eye opener.

Canani brought the colt over on January 28 of 1989 for his first start in a six-furlong sprint. The trainer told jockey Martin Pedroza to let Martial Law settle and make a late run. Neither the trainer nor the owners expected to win a sprint on dirt first time out with the colt.

Taking hold late in the stretch, Martial Law finished, full of run, to wind up fourth of eight, beaten just under six lengths.

Martial Law was not overlooked in his second start when he stretched out around two turns in an allowance race contested on a muddy track. Bettors made the colt the favorite because he had finished like a blur in his local debut and he owned a pedigree made to order for a muddy strip.

In a dazzling performance in a field of nine runners, Martial Law finished with such a furious stretch kick that Santa Anita's race caller said, "And Martial Law looks like he just jumped in at the eighth pole."

Martial Law won by six lengths that afternoon.

The Big 'Cap was twenty-three days away. In the days immediately following the allowance victory, neither Jeff, nor Julio, nor I had thought about or talked about the Santa Anita Handicap.

When the horse began to train even better after the race than before it, and as the field for the $1 million race did not appear to be coming up strong, our chats began to gravitate toward considering a run in the big race.

The one thing that has always bound Jeff and me together is that we are both very optimistic when it comes to buying horses and racing them. From the early 1970s, when we made a habit of trying to buy Claiborne Farm castoffs at the Keeneland November Breeding Stock Sales in Lexington, the two of us did not focus on negatives when sizing up a horse, but on the positives. I feel that this approach has played a huge part in allowing us to achieve many of our successes, both in buying horses and in racing them so daringly.

When we feel confident about a horse, we never let so-called "conventional wisdom" stand in the way of a good idea. We both felt positive that running Martial Law in the Santa Anita Handicap was a good idea.

We did worry about what professionals and prospective clients would think of us for running a huge long shot in the biggest handicap race of the season. We decided that if we got weighted low enough, we would encourage our trainer and partners to go for the jackpot.

As is my bent, I lobbied the racing officials who had influence to give us the lowest possible weight. I used scholarship and logic to make my point and, when the weights came out, we were assigned 113 pounds, about 4 or 5 pounds more than we deserved.

Instead of handicapping the horse, the racing panel in charge of the weights handicapped us, figuring that if we were game enough to put up $40,000 to run, then we must know something they did not.

When one grows up in Southern California and is a racing fan, there is no other race on the calendar that carries the tradition, gets the media coverage or has the buzz that the Santa Anita Handicap has.

I was completely engulfed in Big 'Cap mania by the time the race was run. I was, to put it mildly, a complete nervous wreck. The pressure—of being responsible for the dreams of 17 partners, encouraging the partners to put up $40,000 for a chance to realize their ambitions, and having to endure one skeptic's jab after another for running a horse where it did not belong—had all gotten to me. I had never experienced this type of stress before.

Some of the pressure was taken off our shoulders when, earlier on that glorious Sunday afternoon, our Clover runner Galba—the longest shot on the board with a return of $63 on a $2 bet—scored an improbable upset when he won the $100,000 New Orleans Handicap at Fair Grounds for trainer Neil Drysdale.

When the starting gates opened to the roar of the 58,240 in attendance at Santa Anita on March 5, 1989 for the Santa Anita Handicap, Martial Law was sent away at odds of more than 50 to 1 in a field of 11 older horses.

Martin Pedroza rode the horse. A "speed rider" known for getting horses away from the gate fast, he was at that time a marginal rider in the colony at the major tracks, doing his best work on the five-eighths track at the local LA County Fair Meet at Pomona, where he was the daring and bold king of the bullring.

Jeff and I made a big point of letting both Martin and Julio know that the likeable young man had to be patient going a mile and a quarter against top competition. Pedroza had been instrumental in urging us to supplement the colt to the Big 'Cap. He had an amazing amount of confidence in the colt because of his spectacular morning workouts at Santa Anita.

To put the performance into better perspective, one only has to reflect on the final clocking of the mile-and-a-quarter race. His time of 1:58.80 had been bettered in the previous 54 races only once: in 1979, by Affirmed, the last horse to win the Triple Crown. Martial Law's clocking was not beaten again for a quarter of a century, when Game On Dude ran faster in 2014.

Martial Law ran only once after his Big 'Cap win. The colt was sent to contest the $400,000 Oaklawn Park Handicap 41 days after his Santa Anita race. The entire affair was a fiasco. Our trainer was more interested in continuing to hone his skills as a romantic Latin lover than in seeing to the comfort and well being of his horse. In the race itself, poor Martin Pedroza was a target of the local riders, who forced him to race very wide throughout. Every time he tried to make a move, another rider thwarted him.

Martial Law finished sixth of eight, beaten a little more than five lengths at odds of slightly less than three to one. He emerged a few days later with a bowed tendon and was retired to stud.

The Martial Law partners were a varied bunch, with a couple of owners who proved troublesome. Within a week of the partners being notified that the colt had been retired, an erroneous workout was published in *Daily Racing Form*, in which Martial Law was listed as having breezed at Santa Anita.

Things like this happen occasionally, where clockers mistakenly mix up horses that breeze in the morning. Martial Law was a plain bay and very easy to improperly identify.

Instead of phoning me to find out about the workout, two of the partners took it upon themselves to visit the Santa Anita stewards in their office at the track to report the incident. They took the position that Jeff and I, as managers of the colt, were trying in some way to pull a fast one and rip off the partners of the prize steed. It was an early lesson for both of us that owning a horse involved more emotion than intellect.

Martial Law was a flop at stud, which was not surprising given that his own sire Mr. Leader never sired a son that carried on his bloodline, and he was a light-bodied, feminine type of colt who was narrow through the chest and lacked oomph.

He was a shooting star—here today, gone tomorrow. How good was he? I don't know. But the evidence suggests that, if he had started out in America and been trained to run on dirt, he might have been one of the all-time greats. To this day, we've never had a horse train as brilliantly as he did. He showed as much talent in the Big' Cap and in his spectacular workouts as any horse we've ever owned.

PHOTOS

Author's paternal family, grandfather Moishe,
aunt Bertha (front right), grandmother
Mary and uncle Fischel (top right).

Author at age 7

Author's father practicing
start for 120 yard hurdles at
Roosevelt High School.

Clockwise, photos from the mid-1970s, the young bloodstock agent; leaning on rail at Del Mar with Nick Ben-Meir; handicapping the races at Del Mar with Jeff Siegel

Barry Irwin chats with Rafael Bejarano
in Keeneland walking ring.

Dr. Alex Harthill, Gary Capuano and Barry Irwin on Churchill
Downs backstretch during the Captain Bodgit era in 1997.

Barry Irwin interviewing Professor Gordon Jones
of the Los Angeles Herald-Examiner on set of
his weekly TV show on a UHF station.

Barry Irwin, Jeff Siegel, Jose Santos and Mark Hennig
in Arlington Million trophy presentation.

Prized (5) pulling away from Horse of the Year Sunday Silence in the 1989 Swaps Stakes in a major upset over the Kentucky Derby winner.

Barry Irwin leading in favored Captain Bodgit following
his triumph on a muddy track in the Wood Memorial.

Jockey Chris McCarron, Gary Barber and Barry Irwin are
all smiles after The Deputy won rich Santa Anita Derby.

Ipi Tombe set a race or course record in each of her wins in Dubai.

Irwin (third right) grabbing for some rope as his raucous racing
partners from Zimbabwe led in Ipi Tombe after Dubai Duty Free.

Kathleen and Barry led in Irridescence after Weichong Marwing rode South African Champion to win a Grade 2 at Newmarket.

Irridescence posed by Marwing after his absolutely brilliant ride in winning the Audemars Piguet Queen Elizabeth in Hong Kong.

Animal Kingdom made history in taking 2011 Kentucky Derby as he found another gear in the last furlong under the Twin Spires.

Animal Kingdom dominated the 2013 Dubai World Cup, which with prize money of $10 million is the richest race in the world.

Irwin on Cloud Nine after his Derby triumph.

Author relaxed with wife, Kathleen in Saratoga paddock.

CHAPTER 13

A Prize Colt

Joe Brocklebank phoned in December of 1988 to tell me about a promising 2-year-old colt in Florida named Prized. Irish-born Brocklebank had been a jockey in New York for nearly twenty years before becoming a bloodstock agent in the 1980s and developing a good opinion of a horse.

"Look, a jockey agent friend of mine, Phil Werkmeister, has been following this 2-year-old down at Calder," Brocklebank said. "Phil is no dummy and he says this colt can really run. He thinks he can be moved up, too."

I had noticed Prized's first couple of races before Joe phoned me, because Prized was sired by Kris S., a new stallion that I had some history with. Prized's owner, Meadowbrook Farm, had a reputation for being a seller, which was a positive sign, but I had heard through the grapevine that the colt would not pass the vet.

"Only one way to find out you know," Joe said. "Make an offer."

I was able to strike a deal with Barbara La Croix, whose late husband Joe was a great guy who had established Meadowbrook Farm near Ocala, Florida. Meadowbrook, like many farms in Ocala, dealt in second-tier bloodstock with pedigrees one generation removed from true quality because the business in Central Florida did not justify more extensive investment.

Upon X-raying Prized, it became immediately apparent why he had failed the vet twice: he had a spur or chip in a knee and multiple spurs on both hocks, so the horse appeared to be compromised both in his front and hind limbs.

The spurs undoubtedly had been caused by training and racing on the unique Tartan surface installed by the Minnesota Mining and

Manufacturing Company more than twenty five years earlier, when Calder racecourse was operated by retired 3M CEO William L. McKnight. His Tartan Farm operation bred and raced the all-time great runner Dr. Fager in the 1960s. Installation of the three-inch thick rubber padding around the one-mile circumference of the racing oval resulted in chronic trauma to the horses' hocks.

Many horses that were stabled at Calder during the rubber-track era developed spurs on their hind limbs because, when a horse's hind legs met the rubber, the reverberation on the legs caused reactions that resulted in changes to healthy bones of the lower limbs.

Fortunately for us, our vet advised us that the spurs should not cause the colt any problems going forward and the spur in his knee was outside the joint, making it unlikely to cause any cartilage damage.

My biggest concern was the movement of Prized's front limbs. When viewing his action on video replays from the side, he appeared to cover a lot of ground. Watching him from the head-on view, however, was an entirely different matter. He carried his head very low in an awkward manner, almost as if he were in danger of losing his balance and falling down, and he flailed his right front leg almost spastically.

In deciding whether to buy a horse in training, I first look for a good mover. Since the shortest route between two points is a straight line, I want a horse whose front legs move straight forward. Deviation to either side is undesirable because it causes wasted motion, which results in excess ground covered. I have noticed that when two horses are locked in battle down the stretch, invariably the horse with the most efficient action prevails because it is getting everything out of its stride, which the inefficient mover cannot match. Bad movers also tire earlier than good movers.

I must have watched Prized's replays dozens of times before I was able to reconcile myself to the notion that, although he may have moved awkwardly, he was worth buying because he did cover an enormous amount of ground. Also, he was a trier, he looked like he had a lot of stamina and he definitely appeared to be a horse that could be improved upon, as his trainer did not have him looking his best.

My deal with Mrs. La Croix called for Prized to be campaigned on a fifty-fifty basis in the names of both partners, with his jockey wearing Clover Racing Stables' silks, Neil Drysdale training him in Southern California and Clover acting as the manager.

Barbara lived in Southern California and maintained a residence at her farm in Ocala. She was a seasoned pro, her son David was a trainer and, to her credit, she never caused us any problems in the racing life of the horse.

She was grateful for what Clover and Drysdale accomplished with her horse, because it enhanced the value of her stallion Kris S.

In my second year as a full-time bloodstock agent in 1979, I had been the underbidder on Kris S. when he was offered as a 2-year-old at Hollywood Park in the spring of his juvenile season. This black son of Roberto moved with a grace that belied his seventeen-hand height and massive frame. He was knocked down for $140,000 to Evan S. Jackson, a former jump jockey who had moved his stable from the East Coast to Southern California. He trained for many well-established clients, including Claiborne Farm.

Evan Shipman Jackson was closely related to Evan Shipman, the aforementioned erudite writer who moved on from his literary pursuits as part of Ernest Hemingway, F. Scott Fitzgerald and James Joyce's "Lost Generation" in Paris in the 1920s to write a column for *Daily Racing Form's* sister publication *The Morning Telegraph*. Blue blood owners were comfortable dealing with Jackson because he spoke their language and seemed to be one of them. In reality, he was a very sharp trader who took no prisoners when it came to dealing in bloodstock, no matter how blue their blood was.

A cause célèbre in the winter of 1978 exposed the duplicitous nature of Jackson's motives when he unwittingly assumed that *Daily Racing* Form columnist Pat Rogerson would protect him after an interview, in which the trainer tried to deftly explain why he had not tried to win with Claiborne Farm's 3-year-old Bicker in a couple of races before letting him try to finish first. When Jackson did decide the time was right, one afternoon in the saddling paddock at Santa Anita, he slapped a pair of blinkers on the colt.

Jockey Angel Cordero Jr. knew exactly how talented Bicker was, and when he saw blinkers on the colt as Jackson gave him a leg up, he could not believe his eyes. Cordero said something like, "Boss, I thought you were going to wait on the blinkers until it was a go." Jackson brushed it off, hurriedly telling Cordero that the owners had unexpectedly flown in for the race and this was the day to let him run. Cordero couldn't hold Bicker with those blinkers on and the colt returned generous odds of more than 4 to 1 after he romped home by a dozen lengths.

When Rogerson naïvely spilled the beans about Jackson's method of "giving" a well-bred, stamina-laden newcomer a couple of races to learn the game before letting him extend himself, all hell broke loose. What horseplayers suspected for years without having actual proof had just been exposed in print in the sport's "Bible." Stewards summoned both writer and trainer to explain the meaning of the column. Jackson talked his way out of that one, but his reputation was signed, sealed and delivered on a laminated plaque for all to see.

Insiders at the 2-year-old sale who were involved in the Kris S. story told me their versions of what transpired. Following the drop of the hammer, Jackson is said to have gone back to the sales barn of Albert Yank, who was the selling agent for Kris S. at the Hollywood Park sale, and informed "Alberto Pie" that he expected a commission. The senior agent on the circuit, who cut his teeth in merchandising as a kid selling fancy fruit at his family's stand at the famed Farmers' Market in the Borscht Belt, Yank politely but firmly explained to Jackson the correct protocol. Yank said that he would be unable to accommodate the trainer, as a request of this nature must be approved *before* and not *after* the fall of the hammer.

Supposedly Jackson issued an immediate ultimatum, telling Yank that unless he got his commission, Jackson would make sure the colt failed a post-hammer inspection of the animal's throat, thereby making the transaction null and void. Yank said the colt's throat was not an issue, to which Jackson allegedly said, "It will be."

Sure enough, a vet report was generated showing an irregularity in the colt's throat and, in effect, rescinding the sale. The sales company and Jackson became embroiled in a tug of war. Had I known this, I would have moved to buy Kris S., but I only found out later from my friend Jim Sacco that he was able to get one of his own clients to step in and buy the colt.

Realizing the creative powers of the principals involved in the fiasco, I reckoned it was entirely possible that the report of this incident was either accurate or completely fabricated because Sacco was highly capable of inventing a clever pitch to sell Kris S. Either way, the tale is worth the telling because of Kris S.'s storied place in the history of the Turf.

San Diego businessman Lloyd Schunemann bought the colt, named Kris S. after his daughter. Sacco took over the horse's training. I enjoyed Sacco's company very much. He was such a sketchy character, I found it hard to trust him, but he was a wheeler-dealer and we did a lot of business together. One of the first horses I sold to him went on to perform well in stakes races for Schunemann. Ironically, we bought that stakes winner a few years before the Kris S. sale shenanigans from none other than Evan S. Jackson. And when that horse, named Antique, won the first division of the Henry P. Russell Handicap at Santa Anita for Sacco and Schunemann, the other division was won by All Hope. I managed All Hope for movie producer Irving Allen and was able to cash a big bet on him, which funded the purchase of a filly that I was able to sell for a big profit to kick start my career as a bloodstock dealer. Funny how these things play out.

A loaded gun, it is said, can be dangerous in any man's hands. So is a fast racehorse, and Jim Sacco was the wrong guy to be given a quality colt like Kris S. He lacked the tools and experience to bring out the best in a quality racehorse. Sacco knew the colt was supremely talented and had a big future, but he needlessly cranked him up to win first time out in the summer of his 2-year-old season. In a display of sheer speed, the colt won a maiden race going five and a half furlongs, clocking a blistering 1:03 3/5 in June at Hollywood Park. A seasoned horseman would have brought out the colt for a race towards the end of the year and readied him for the Triple Crown.

In a five-race career, Kris S. never made the Triple Crown, even though I thought he was good enough to win the Kentucky Derby. So did Jim Scully, a friend of mine from Lexington whose job I filled when I was hired to write for *The Blood-Horse*.

Scully was a wild man and a bit of a hero of mine, because he never let Lawrence Shropshire get under his skin. Every morning, Jim would put his feet up on his desk, sip his coffee and spend half an hour reading *Daily Racing Form* while Shropshire fumed and glared at him.

The year Bold Ruler's son Secretariat became the first colt in a quarter century to win the Triple Crown, Scully bid a record price for a yearling sold at public auction of $600,000 for another Bold Ruler colt his group of clients named Wajima. Bred and sold by Claiborne Farm, Wajima was voted Champion Colt at three in 1975, but he never won the Kentucky Derby, a race Scully desperately wanted to win.

Scully was part of the ownership group that campaigned Kris S. in his final two career outings. Kris S. easily won the Bradbury Stakes by two lengths and followed up with a fourth place finish in the San Felipe Handicap prepping for the Santa Anita Derby. He never ran again.

Prized was in the third crop of foals sired by Kris S., who sent out five stakes winners in his first crop and New York Grade 1 winner Evening Kris in his second crop. Prized was taller than average, but not as tall as his sire. Prized was more elegant than Kris S. and, while he lacked his sire's brute strength, he did not inherit the coarse head typical of the Roberto sire line. Before Clover bought into him, Prized had run four times, finishing well for second in a pair of seven-furlong races and easily winning two route races by eight and a half and eight lengths at Calder.

In an accommodation to Mrs. La Croix, who thought her trainer deserved a shot to win a stakes before Prized was taken from him, we ran the Kris S. colt for the first time on January 7 in the Tropical Park Derby at Calder. He finished third, beaten more than 7 lengths. We were not disappointed with the race and we fulfilled our obligation.

A month after Prized arrived in his Santa Anita barn, Neil Drysdale pulled me aside and said, "Barry, you have no idea how good this horse is." I replied, "You have no idea how good I think he is." Drysdale closed the subject by saying, "No matter *how* good you think he is, believe me, he is better than that!"

Exactly two months after the Tropical Park Derby, I was standing in Santa Anita's walking ring, watching Prized walk by in advance of the Bradbury Stakes, a race designed as a prep for the Grade 1 Santa Anita Derby. I could see that Prized was not walking soundly.

"Neil, this horse is lame," I said to him.

"Shush, not now," he cautioned me. "We will talk in a bit."

After the colt and the racing partners left the paddock, Neil took me aside and said "I know he's not right. It's his tibia. There's a hairline fracture there. It is not a big deal and will require a couple of months for him to get over it.

"He is going to win this race for fun," Drysdale said. "Afterwards we'll put him away for two months. Unfortunately we will miss the Triple Crown, but we will have a fantastic colt for the summer and fall. Just watch this sucker run today!"

Of course Neil was correct. The colt cantered across the finishing post, winning by 1¾ lengths without so much as drawing a deep breath.

Being forced to cool his jets during the Triple Crown was the best thing that ever happened to Prized because those three demanding races came too soon for his immature frame and constitution to survive them intact. It was a bitter pill for our partners to swallow, but Jeff and I did our best to bolster their enthusiasm during the downtime.

The 1989 Triple Crown—one of the best of all time—came and went without Prized taking part. Sunday Silence won the Derby and Preakness and lost out on the Triple Crown after finishing behind Easy Goer in the Belmont.

Jeff's disappointment in missing the Triple Crown with Prized was eased considerably when Sunday Silence won the Kentucky Derby. Years earlier, Jeff had recommended the claim for $32,000 of Sunday's Silence's dam, so he received many plaudits in the media thanks to his pals in the press box. And Jeff enjoyed a $10,000 payday as a result of a $100 bet at odds of 100 to 1 he had made 6 months earlier in Agua Caliente's Future Book on Sunday Silence to win the Derby.

When Sunday Silence returned home to California, Charlie Whittingham surprised everybody by announcing he was going to run the colt, which he owned with Arthur Hancock and Dr. Ernest Galliard, in the Swaps Stakes at Hollywood Park. Neil, Jeff and I drooled over the prospect of running a primed and fresh Prized against a hard-raced and sapped Sunday Silence.

Whittingham was Drysdale's mentor. The protégé could not figure out why The Bald Eagle wanted to run Sunday Silence back so quickly and in a race that was not a meaningful fixture on the national racing calendar.

I had my own ideas. Knowing Marge Everett's influence on Charlie and knowing Charlie's frustration over having missed out on the Triple Crown, a perfect storm came together to ensure that Sunday Silence's name would be dropped into the entry box for the 1989 Swaps Stakes. It had been forty-three days since Sunday Silence had been flown back to California after being trounced by Easy Goer in the Belmont Stakes.

Prized prepped for the Swaps in the Silver Screen Stakes and finished a nice third. For the Swaps, Prized had regular rider Eddie Delahoussaye in the saddle and Sunday Silence had Pat Valenzuela up. Sunday Silence, a fiery colt, made an early run for home. When the field turned into the stretch, Sunday Silence was in front and looked home and dry. Whittingham put his binoculars down.

Race caller Luke Kruytbosch went into what seemed like a canned spiel, announcing, "This is why he is the Champion." No sooner were those scripted words uttered than Sunday Silence reverted to his worrisome Kentucky Derby antics by weaving across the Hollywood Park track like a drunken sailor in search of a buoy. Racing fans had seen him do this before. Sunday Silence never was a totally straightforward colt.

Jockey Delahoussaye said, "At the top of the lane I figured I was running for second money, but when I saw Sunday Silence start to weave, I said to myself, 'Hey, we've got a shot to win this thing.'"

Prized simultaneously lowered his center of gravity, dropped his head in his patented manner, lengthened and quickened his stride, and reached Sunday Silence in the dying strides to score a three-quarter-length victory.

Prized managed to shock those onlookers who had assembled for a coronation. Sunday Silence was the odds-on 1 to 5 favorite over 5 to 1 Prized. Everybody in the place, it seemed, was genuinely surprised except Jeff, Neil, Delahoussaye and me.

Jay Hovdey, writing in the *Los Angeles Times*, reported, "It wasn't exactly Onion beating Secretariat. Or Upset shocking Man o' War. But on a scale of one to 10, the stunning victory by Prized, at the expense of Kentucky Derby and Preakness winner Sunday Silence, in Sunday's Swaps Stakes at Hollywood Park was easily a Richter-rattling nine."

For the second time that year, a Clover Racing Stable long shot had upset a Charlie Whittingham favorite, as Martial Law was more than fifty to one when winning the Santa Anita Handicap, in which Whittingham's Nasr el Arab was the betting choice.

We knew that we did not beat the "real" Sunday Silence. We knew that it was a mistake for Sunday Silence to have been brought back so quickly. Sunday Silence was vulnerable because of his exhaustive Triple Crown campaign against a great horse in Easy Goer. But we were nothing if not opportunists and we exploited the situation. We were proud of that, but none of us felt that we had proved Prized was in the same class as Sunday Silence.

Neil Drysdale proved again something that was true of Charlie Whittingham and himself. Given a goal, both mentor and student had a rare ability to focus on a race and bring out the best a horse had to offer. When Whittingham zeroed in on a race, it was all over but the running. He would watch that horse train. He would meet that horse back at the paddock, grab on to him and walk him back to his barn. He got inside the mind of that horse. He became one with that horse. Whittingham was perhaps the greatest in the modern era of racing in America at winning the races he wanted most, and Drysdale proved he had learned well from his mentor.

Next in Drysdale's sights was the Molson Million, a $1 million race over the same Classic mile-and-a-quarter distance of the Swaps Stakes. It was set for early September near Toronto at the expansive Woodbine racetrack.

When Neil found an out-of-town race he wanted to win, he went all out, sending Prized and plenty of staff well in advance of the race so that the Kris S. colt could acclimate to the weather and adjust to the different racing surface.

Leaving behind the comfort of his stall at Hollywood Park, Prized was flown to Toronto to prepare for the Molson Million. Prized had little difficulty in seeing off a local horse named Charlie Barley to win by half a length. His final time of 2:02 was a fifth of a second slower than he required to win the Swaps on the faster Hollywood Park track.

The Molson was a feather in our cap as it was the second million-dollar race Clover won.

Prized was dispatched at fairly low odds of 5 to 2 (still, one of the partners walked out of Woodbine with a check for more than a third of a million dollars, just from betting on the race) but he was not the favorite for the Molson Million. That role was filled by Midwest invader Clever Trevor, whose second-place finish to Easy Goer in the Travers Stakes had been preceded by a nine-length victory at Arlington in the American Derby, which encouraged bettors to drive his odds down to one to two.

Prized was then sent to contest the mile-and-a-half Grade 1 Jockey Club Gold Cup at Belmont Park, which was nicknamed "Big Sandy." We found out exactly why it had earned that sobriquet: Prized never ran a step on a dirt track that was too cuppy and broke away from him, but in this race, in which his front-leg action and anteater style of running were never more exaggerated, Prized struggled to reach the finish line and wound up fourth, beaten nearly twenty-five lengths.

To say we were deflated is to state the obvious. But Neil Drysdale was never short on plans.

"Let's run him in the Breeders' Cup Turf," Drysdale said to Jeff and me. "I can send him down early to Gulfstream Park, try him on the grass and, if he likes it, we can run in the race. It's worth $2 million you know."

So that evening, I had dinner with a bunch of the racing partners, soothed their bruised feelings as best I could and rebuilt their enthusiasm by revealing our newly formed plans for the Breeders' Cup Turf. The resiliency of a horse owner is second to none and, by the time they went off to bed, visions of Breeders' Cup trophies danced in their head.

Among American trainers, Neil Drysdale is the deepest thinker. Before any other trainers had even thought of sending their BC-bound stock to Gulfstream to prepare for the big day, Prized, Sabona and Political Ambition were ensconced at the South Florida track that would host the 1989 Cup. Few were around to observe some of the most meaningful and exciting pre-Cup workouts in history.

Prized on two occasions was pitted in team drills on the grass against two of the best older grass Milers in North America in Sabona, a consistent runner at the Grade 1 level that season, and our very own Political Ambition, a multiple Grade 1 winner. Prized blew them off the course with considerable ease. "He's much better on grass than dirt, boys," Neil said to us. "This could be a big day for you guys."

I called an English bloodstock agent whom I dealt with and asked him to bet £2000 on Prized at the best odds available. The fellow, a universally renowned rapscallion, kept stalling and feeding me misinformation, which resulted in his getting me down for £1000 at odds of thirty-three. I later learned that he hogged most of the available action at the best odds for himself.

We were convinced Political Ambition could win the Breeders' Cup Mile. Unfortunately, on the eve of the Mile, Political Ambition went lame and we scratched him.

Sabona, who was not held in the same regard as Political Ambition by the stable, ran second in the Breeders' Cup Mile. For a stamina infused 3-year-old like Prized to be able to bolt past him in two workouts confirmed our notion that Prized was indeed well placed.

In the one-and-one-half-mile Breeders' Cup Turf, Prized looked to be going nowhere at the five-sixteenths pole and the race caller said, "And

Prized is falling back." Just when that was uttered, Delahoussaye asked the colt for his best lick and Prized responded by gradually getting up to a contending position and out-gaming the French filly Sierra Roberta to win in a photo.

Jeff and I watched the race together from the grandstand. When Prized crossed the line, I grabbed Jeff and said, "Let's go." He was not convinced we had won and wanted to wait, so as not to be embarrassed in case the photo finish went the wrong way. I convinced him to go downstairs anyway.

Prized lit up the tote board as he was sent off at odds of nearly nine to 1. I was already counting the more than $55,000 I would collect on my bet with a British bookie that would help my recent bride Becky and me buy our first house in Pasadena.

The Breeders' Cup was the first victory of national significance that one of our horses had won and we reveled in the moment. Barbara Lacroix was ecstatic and she looked stunning in a stylish red jacket and matching hat over a black skirt. Dinny Phipps presented the trophy.

From a historical perspective, Prized became the first racehorse in history to win million-dollar races on dirt and turf in the same season, something that even the great and versatile Champion John Henry never accomplished. Prized became the first horse to win the Breeders' Cup Turf without ever having previously raced on the grass.

Prized should have been named Champion Turf Horse and been enshrined in the Hall of Fame, but he never got his due because the victory was treated in the press as a fluke, primarily because he had barely beaten a filly that few American turf writers had ever heard of.

The next season Prized dominated North American grass racing for the first half of the year and, after racking up victories at a mile in the Arcadia Handicap and then at a mile and a half in the San Luis Rey, he was voted the best American-based racehorse for those months in a weekly poll.

Prized improbably beat the country's best grass Milers in the Arcadia and the newly crowned world record holder Hawkster in the San Luis Rey in dominating performances. I wondered how those who had not voted for Prized a few months earlier for Champion Grass Horse felt about his newfound stature as the best young, home-grown grass horse America had seen in some time.

His only really bad race at four came when he flopped miserably as the big favorite for the Arlington Million. Neil Drysdale will tell you to this day that he thinks somebody got to his horse. I tend to dismiss stories like this, but people like English-born Drysdale who come from locales where bookies and gamblers historically have engaged in such nefarious practices invariably want to raise this issue.

Prized was injured and he missed the second half of his season at four. He was never the same horse again and raced only a few times at five before he was syndicated to stand at stud in Florida.

He was one of the most underrated horses ever to race in America and the full range of his talent was never fully explored.

Like John Henry, he could beat the best on dirt or turf and do it from 8 to 12 furlongs. He was a bit awkward in his gait and was not a beauty to behold when in full flight, but he had a tremendous desire to win and to run down horses in the stretch.

In seventeen starts, he won nine times and earned more than $2.2 million when that was a lot of money. The only races in which he failed to finish 1-2-3 came when he was fourth in the G1 Jockey Club Gold Cup, tenth in the G1 Arlington Million, and unplaced in the G1 Hollywood Gold Cup in his final outing.

When Kris S. eventually earned his way to Kentucky, he was a big hit as a stallion. His 88 stakes winners included 17 Grade 1 winners. Prized was the best of the lot in America.

As a stallion, Prized experienced only moderate success, probably because Kris S.'s quality could not overcome the lack of it in Prized's family.

Prized brought a lot of racing partners an enormous amount of pleasure and lifelong memories of glories on the Turf. Prized was euthanized in 2014 in Kentucky at the age of 28.

CHAPTER 14

Team Valor

Clover Racing Stable, for all intents and purposes, ceased doing new business in the spring of 1992. Jeff and I wanted to grow the company, which required an input of capital we both were prepared to make. Our two other partners were unwilling to do so.

So one fine day we decided to go it alone. I came up with the name Team Valor. I designed our colors. The green jacket represented the turf and the red V stood for valor, that characteristic I prized most in a Thoroughbred racehorse. On our stationery, I included these words: "Burning brightly against the lush green battlefield of the turf, the crimson flare of his nostril was terrible and spoke of valor."

Some of the racing stock was moved over to Team Valor, including Star of Cozzene, and some remained in Clover, which was allowed to play itself out over the next few racing seasons, while still under our management. All new business was conducted strictly within Team Valor.

The first horse syndicated by Team Valor exemplified what Jeff and I wanted to do in racing. We bought My Memoirs from a client of Richard Hannon, the English trainer who specialized in developing 2-year-olds. For years I had marveled how this former rock and roll drummer stocked his stable with horses bought, not on pedigree, but on conformation and quality. He trained his stock on a five-furlong uphill strip of ground covered with a combination of materials that included bits of leftover rubber casing for electrical wiring, which added a unique cushion to his surface. He had been using an all-weather track even before the first one appeared in England in 1989.

My Memoirs had won twice and finished second once in five starts at age two in England. All of his races except for his six-furlong debut came over seven furlongs. He had acquitted himself well at a certain level of form, but was found wanting both times he stepped up in class and *Timeform* commented that he was "thoroughly exposed." *Timeform* generally rated him at 89, which indicated that the colt would wind up being a handicapper and not a stakes colt.

Next season he made three starts at 3, improving incrementally in each and definitely heading in the right direction. In Listed races over a mile, he ran well to finish third, beaten less than two lengths in the Doncaster Mile in late March. Three weeks later he was beaten by nearly eight lengths in the Classic Trial at Thirsk and he improved his *Timeform* rating again.

My Memoirs scored what Jeff and I considered to be an eye-opening victory in the Dee Stakes in his third start at three. Carded at a sixteenth of a mile farther than the Classic American distance of a mile and a quarter, and run five days after the Kentucky Derby in 1992, the Dee was contested at Chester racecourse, hard on the River Dee just east of Wales. Chester, among the many venues in England, is the racecourse most like an American oval, as it is round with sharp bends and the runners turn to the left.

In buying horses from abroad starting in the mid 1970s, I developed a theory that racing in Europe and the British Isles had everything to do with class, whereas in America it was all about style. So as a believer that style trumped class, I was particularly interested in horses that had performed well at Chester.

My Memoirs ran down a colt named Profusion that garnered the lion's share of the kudos following the race, even though My Memoirs gave nearly nine pounds, as observers reckoned the runner-up had idled setting a slow pace and My Memoirs had caught him napping. Team Valor did not share this viewpoint.

Timeform ratings indicated that My Memoirs had improved sixteen pounds from his seasonal debut two months earlier, and nineteen pounds from age two to three. His immediate pedigree indicated that a mile should have been his best trip but, given that the Dee was his first opportunity to explore his stamina, My Memoirs looked like a ready-made Belmont Stakes candidate to us.

Also, based on more than twenty years of observing imported horses race, I learned that British and European horses were effective over longer distances in America than they had been at home. For example, seven-furlong runners abroad were able to successfully negotiate distance races around two turns in America. Milers from abroad were able to get a mile and a quarter in America. We had proven it ourselves with the English Miler Martial Law by winning the mile-and-a-quarter Santa Anita Handicap.

In addition to questions about My Memoirs' likelihood of seeing out the mile-and-a-half trip of the Belmont Stakes, there also was the huge question mark about the colt's ability to handle a dirt track, especially as there were few clues to be found in his pedigree. Also, since he did all his work at home on an uphill surface of unknown composition, nothing he had done in training held the possibility of enlightening us.

We loved his action. It was straight and true and he really used himself when roaring down the stretch in the Dee Stakes to see off what was potentially a very high-class animal. At the time, it was difficult to assess the quality of the stock he had raced against that spring, though the winner of his seasonal debut went on to win the Del Mar Derby later in the summer and the winner of his second start developed into a multiple Group winner including at the Royal Ascot meeting.

We bought My Memoirs based on our opinion that his style would be effective in America, so we were not concerned with his company lines. So we not only took our "best holt," as a Bayou horseman is wont to say, but we also set about convincing a group of partners to shell out an additional $50,000 to supplement him to the Belmont Stakes.

Every time over the years that we have asked our racing partners to step up to the plate, they have responded in the affirmative. We always take a vote before spending a client's money. I remember once, when we asked for $30,000 to supplement a horse to the Belmont Turf Classic, I had to approach a woman who was in the throes of a difficult divorce and she had lost her job. She also seemed to have become depressed for a few months. Before I even had an opportunity to get my spiel out, she stopped me short, saying, "Money? Who cares about money? I want action!"

We asked the My Memoirs partners to take a gamble and, as they always did, they accepted it as a sporting challenge.

To satisfy ourselves that we were indeed on the right track, so to speak, we had Richard Hannon transport the colt to Lingfield, to test him on the closest surface to dirt that British racing had to offer. With five weeks between races, My Memoirs needed a serious bit of work, so he was breezed a strong mile and a quarter at Lingfield on an all-weather surface.

We arranged to have the move videotaped. We were extremely excited and impressed with what we saw on that video. Jeff clocked the workout and generated some fractional time splits. Even if they were only partially accurate, the splits indicated that we were neither smoking our socks nor drinking our bath water. We were "in bidness."

Winning the 1992 Belmont shaped up as a formidable challenge. Favored at nearly even money was A.P. Indy, the golden boy of his generation. A Japanese owner—through an Australian bloodstock agent who was charged with finding a horse that could win the Kentucky Derby—went to $2.9 million to buy him at the Keeneland July Yearling Sale in 1990. A.P. Indy sold for the highest price of his crop because he was a phenomenal physical specimen and his parentage was purple-blooded. His sire Seattle Slew won the Triple Crown. His dam Weekend Surprise was a Saratoga stakes winner at two, she was already the dam of Preakness winner Summer Squall, and her own sire Secretariat had also won the Triple Crown.

Eddie Delahoussaye would have been our first choice to ride My Memoirs, but he was A.P. Indy's regular rider and had been aboard for his six consecutive wins since the colt had run fourth in his debut for trainer Neil Drysdale.

So we went with, in our opinion, the best jockey in New York, Jerry Bailey, a rider with whom we had enjoyed considerable success. Jerry was not only a gifted athlete, he was also a savvy rider with an understanding of race shape and the impact of pace on a race. We provided Jerry with a video of the Dee Stakes and told him everything we knew about the colt.

My Memoirs did his quarantine period and training at Aqueduct, where Hannon preferred to be because it was quiet and away from the hubbub of Triple Crown hysteria at Belmont Park, which was twenty minutes down the road. A good-sized, athletic bay with an excellent temperament, My Memoirs settled right in and never gave his handlers a moment's worry.

The only pre-race drama came at the Belmont Stakes draw, when some members of the press had a field day making light of Team Valor's entry, including how foolhardy it was to waste $50,000 to supplement a horse that had never run in a big race, had never run on dirt, had never so much as breezed on the dirt, was not bred for the distance and was trained by a guy none of them had ever heard of.

Interestingly, the press on hand had very short attention spans, as the Irish invader Go and Go had won the Belmont the year before. True, Go and Go had won on dirt the previous fall, when Dermot Weld opted to keep him in the Laurel Futurity after it had been switched from turf, but that Maryland race was run in a sea of slop, so before winning the Belmont Stakes for fun, he still had as many questions to answer as My Memoirs did.

Although too polite to verbalize it, the press truly believed American form was the best in the world. These skeptics shared the same mentality as those who scoffed twenty-one years earlier, when Canonero II came up from Venezuela to win the Kentucky Derby and followed it up with a victory in the Preakness. I knew they were sadly mistaken because I knew that second-rate Europeans regularly won races at the highest level on the American Turf. I had seen enough Royal Ascots and Prix de l'Arc de Triomphes in person to know the difference between real horses and pretenders.

My Memoirs was dismissed at odds of 18 to 1 for the Belmont., A.P. Indy started at nearly even money, Preakness hero Pine Bluff was second choice at odds of 7 to 2, Kentucky Derby and Preakness placer Casual Lies was 4 to 1, and French invader Cristofori was held at 7 to 1. Aside from these single-digit entrants, My Memoirs' odds were lower than the other six runners' in the $1,764,800third leg of the Triple Crown.

Kentucky Derby runner-up Casual Lies and Dwyer Stakes winner Agincourt alternated on the lead for a mile, setting a fast pace for the Belmont, reeling off splits of :23 1/5, :47, 1:11 4/5 and 1:36 1/5. Until the advent of phenomenon Secretariat 19 years earlier, fractions like this had rarely been witnessed.

The race began in earnest at the quarter pole. Pine Bluff had been tracking in third and moved into the lead. Casual Lies had disposed of Agincourt and was second lapped right on the leader. Delahoussaye had A. P. Indy in fourth until moving him up to third at the two-furlong pole. And Bailey had My Memoirs in fifth until he moved him up to fourth at the same juncture.

Pine Bluff maintained his narrow lead a furlong from the wire. A.P. Indy was rolling under Eddie D., they engaged the leader and finally mastered him in the final 100 yards. Approaching the finish line, A.P. Indy seemed to be home free, when suddenly the specter of My Memoirs flashed into view on the outside.

Bailey kept My Memoirs wide and away from a harsh dirt kickback, which the colt had never experienced. My Memoirs balanced himself for the stretch run and began a rally down the center of the track until a momentary lapse in mid-stretch, when he jinked. Bailey was able to regenerate the run and My Memoirs built up a powerful head of steam.

With the finishing post in sight and Delahoussaye riding A.P. Indy for all he was worth, My Memoirs surged toward him desperately. In the final few strides there seemed a chance the Team Valor colt might be able to catch the favorite. But he ran out of room, failing by three-quarters of a length. Pine Bluff hung tough and finished a neck away in third, more than thirteen lengths ahead of Sheik Mohammed's French invader Cristofori. Casual Lies was fifth.

My Memoirs did his partners, his managers and his trainer proud, rewarding our faith in him with a memorable effort. He earned $168,256, a *Timeform* rating in the mid-120s and the respect of rival horsemen. I remember The Phipps family's trainer Shug McGaughey coming up to me at B. K. Sweeney's steakhouse in Garden City the evening after the race, questioning me about where My Memoirs had come from and saying how impressed he was with him. You could see the respect in his face for our colt.

The lone sour note on the afternoon emerged from an unlikely source, as the classy rider Eddie Delahoussaye responded to questions about how much A.P. Indy had left in the tank by trotting out that cliché, "If they had gone around again, that other horse wouldn't have caught mine."

Anybody who saw the race in person knew that My Memoirs was eating A.P. Indy alive in those final desperate strides. I was very upset with Delahoussaye for making that comment as I thought it was a cheap shot. I was aware that Eddie was very proud of A.P. Indy and with good reason, as he went on to achieve Horse of the Year and Champion 3-year-old honors after winning the Breeders' Cup Classic.

Speed figures generated by Andy Beyer, which gave the winner 111 and the runner-up 110, back up my contention that A.P. Indy most likely gave everything he had to offer on the day; the 111 was a new career best for him and it was a figure he would only improve three races later when he earned a 114 in the final race of his career, the BC Classic.

A.P. Indy was worth many millions of dollars and he had been life and death to beat a lowly regarded long shot, so something had to be uttered to impart a higher shine on the winner's reputation. Such is the business, especially when riders, trainers, syndicators and farm operators are in line to benefit from earning lucrative stud fee income from breeding rights.

First and foremost, racing is a sport and not a business, so spin doctoring should not be part of the post-race comments, especially in our most important races.

It's not like A.P. Indy failed to sparkle. There was plenty to celebrate and brag about without having to gild the lilies of the Belmont garland draped around A.P. Indy's neck. His final time of 2:26 equaled Easy Goer's mark in 1989 as the second-fastest Belmont Stakes in the record books, behind only Secretariat's 1973 record of 2:24.

A.P. Indy had missed the Kentucky Derby with a quarter crack, as well as the Preakness, but in the Belmont and the Breeders' Cup Classic, he showed himself to be a colt of the absolute highest quality.

I loved A.P. Indy and supported him when he went to stud by breeding our multiple Graded stakes-winning mare Santa Catalina to him. From that mating, she produced Golden Missile in the second crop of A.P. Indy. Golden Missile earned $2,194,510 and accounted for the Grade 1 Pimlico Special before going to stud for Frank Stronach.

My Memoirs might have compromised himself when he momentarily swerved in the stretch of the Belmont. He ran once more for us, starting as the nine to five favorite for the historic Jim Dandy Stakes at Saratoga, where he turned in a subpar effort. He was retired shortly afterwards with a bowed tendon.

The shooting star that was My Memoirs did not last very long. It did, however, demonstrate once again that we were capable of sourcing top quality stock in the most unlikely places, and that our opinion of the quality and capability of a horse should not be doubted. Team Valor had come into existence less than three months earlier and everybody already knew whom we were.

CHAPTER 15

Star Attraction

Team Valor launched its first starter in 1992 when My Memoirs nearly ran down A. P. Indy in the co-second fastest Belmont Stakes on record to set the tone for the new venture.

We further defined the image of the stable by hiring Mark Hennig as our sole trainer and outfitting a barn for him at Hollywood Park. Our contract allowed Mark to train up to six horses for outside clients, so he kept a few for Texan Lee Lewis and Virginian Edward P. "Ned" Evans. Chairman of publisher MacMillan Inc., Evans was very nearly the last blue blood to follow in his father's footsteps by making a full life out of owning and breeding Thoroughbreds.

The stepson of trainer John Hennig, Mark had been steeped in horsemanship from a very young age and proved to be very effective at running one of leading trainer D. Wayne Lukas' satellite operations. I was extremely impressed with his talent, his organizational skills and his ability to communicate with my customers.

After we struck a deal, I phoned Mark to obtain his age for a press release I was composing. When he gave me his birthdate, I said "Very funny. That would make you twenty-six." When he replied that he was, in fact, twenty-six, I was shocked. It had never previously occurred to me to ask him. Based on his level of maturity and self-confidence, I had pegged his age at around thirty-three, which would have been very young. Twenty-six was stunningly young.

But Mark's age did not stop him from performing. He got off to a slow start, because training on the glib tracks in Southern California required a period of adjustment. In Florida, Kentucky and New York, the tracks were deeper and horses did not have to breeze as far or as fast to gain peak fitness as they did on the lighter surfaces in California. Most Eastern horses breeze a half-mile and rarely go past five-eighths of a mile. In Southern California, most horses go five-eighths, many go three-quarters, and seven-eighths works are commonplace. Once Mark got the hang of things after a few months, he never looked back.

One horse Mark looked forward to training was the ex-Lukas runner Star of Cozzene. He was a horse that relished soft grass and raced awkwardly on turns. With its soft grass courses and mile races contested on straightaways, France seemed to me like a perfect fit for him. But I'm getting ahead of the story.

My friend Ron Anderson, who became the most successful jockey agent of his era, placed an urgent call to me right after Star of Cozzene had broken his maiden in mid-March of his 3-year-old season at Santa Anita in his fourth career start. For transplanted French trainer Christian Doumen, he had run fourth, sprinting in his debut in a $50,000 claiming race, and following up with second-place finishes in a pair of San Francisco area mile races. In a maiden race and in the Prince Don B. Stakes, Star of Cozzene ran second to Charmonnier, a promising youngster that went on to earn $566,708, winning four stakes races including the California Cup Classic championship for horses bred in the Golden State, and placing in more than a dozen races, including Graded events in Hong Kong and at Santa Anita, Hollywood Park and Del Mar.

Video of Star of Cozzene's effort in the Bay Area stakes revealed that, had he not been forced to check and alter course in the stretch, he likely would have run out a convincing winner. Since the horse that beat him looked to have quality, this impressed us greatly. Star of Cozzene's maiden win at Santa Anita also was a special effort, as he was hemmed in and forced to change course before busting loose to win going away.

Ron Anderson was the agent for Gary Stevens, who rode Star of Cozzene in the Santa Anita maiden race, so he was able to tell us how much his jockey liked the colt. This really helped, because both Jeff and I were home sick with the flu and missed seeing the race in person.

Ron had found out the colt was for sale from Paul Assinesi, an aspiring young trainer who hustled the stable area, looking for horses to buy and sell. Assinesi immediately recognized the elite talent level of the colt and had heard that the colt's owner was under severe financial pressure. Assinesi quickly crafted a deal with trainer Doumen and wrote him a hot check for $80,000. I admired the young man's cojones and was only too happy to reward him for his chutzpah. We agreed to pay Assinesi a $45,000 profit, plus a $6,250 commission to Ron Anderson. The day after the maiden win, we wire-transferred Assinesi $125,000 to cover the rubber check he had handed to Doumen.

I wound up mining this rich vein even further a couple of weeks later. Star of Cozzene's ex-owner had another horse I wanted to buy, but he had turned down a lot of money for her after she had won her only start by more than eleven lengths because he was reluctant to part with her. I told him that if he ever changed his mind, I would always be interested. A short time later I fielded a call from the financially strapped owner telling me that if I could deliver $25,000 in cash to his office in Rancho Santa Fe, a drive of about two hours from our Pasadena office, I could buy the filly I coveted. I bought her, bred her to Cure the Blues and sold her in foal at Keeneland for a very good profit. The foal she dropped, named Rock and Roll, became a star, winning the Pennsylvania Derby and the Churchill Downs Handicap. He set a Belmont Park record of 1:39 2/5 for a mile and a sixteenth and earned $708,557.

We knew Star of Cozzene was bred to excel on grass, as his sire Cozzene had won the Breeders' Cup Mile, and Pia Star, his broodmare sire, had produced the dam of grass genius Both Ends Burning for trainer Neil Drysdale. But we opted to keep him on the main track for the time being.

Most horsemen with any sort of viable 3-year-old were banging heads with each other on the Triple Crown trail. Our plan with Star of Cozzene was to develop him through the spring and pick up some valuable prizes after the competition had knocked itself out.

We sent Star of Cozzene to Lukas' son Jeff at Belmont Park. Jeff ran him first time out for us going a mile and an eighth at Garden State Park in New Jersey for the Grade 3 Garden State Stakes. He trailed his nine rivals early, made up a lot of ground and finished in a rally, winding up third beaten 1 ½ lengths in a solid effort. We felt that we had made a great buy.

Lukas ran Star of Cozzene next in an allowance race two days after the Kentucky Derby on a dreary, wet afternoon on a sloppy track at Aqueduct. The private box area outside was deserted, with only Jeff and me braving the elements in the clubhouse, waiting for the start.

Appearing seemingly from nowhere, a legendary uniformed usher named Cliff informed Jeff that his Jordache designer jeans did not constitute proper attire for the box section and he would have to leave. One never knew if Cliff was looking for a cash tip or simply reveling in the authority given to him by his badge. We didn't know whether to register our incredulity or laugh. Jeff had no time to argue with Cliff because it was too close to post time, so he went indoors to watch the race on a monitor. I stayed put. No way was I going to watch a live race on a TV set after flying across the country. Star of Cozzene enjoyed the slop, winning as Chris Antley pleased by nine and a half lengths.

In his next few races the colt failed to distinguish himself on the main track or in his grass debut, although he did win a dirt allowance on the Belmont Stakes undercard. He took up twice in his first grass race that actually was a better effort than it looked at first blush.

Lukas' assistant Kiaran McLaughlin, who was married to Mark Hennig's sister Letty, had lofty expectations for Star of Cozzene in his second grass start. The colt made him look prescient, bolting home a six-and-a-half-length winner of the Grade 3 Choice Stakes at Monmouth. That August race began a skein of four races that Star of Cozzene employed to launch himself to a position atop the best grass colts of his crop at three.

Back to back, Star of Cozzene proceeded to beat accomplished fields going a mile on grass. He trounced other 3-year-olds in the Nureyev Stakes, leaving in his wake Fourstars Allstar, who earlier in the year had become the first American to take the classic Irish Two Thousand Guineas at The Curragh. Against older runners, Star of Cozzene scored an authoritative victory in the Grade 3 Kelso, this time finishing ahead of the consummate older grass kingpin Fourstardave on firm turf in a fast 1:33 1/5.

Jose Santos rode Star of Cozzene in both of his Belmont wins, but for the Breeders' Cup Mile at Churchill Downs he decided to ride Claiborne Farm's well-bred Scan for one of his go-to trainers, Flint "Scotty" Schulhofer. Scan finished a well-beaten eighth in the race.

Subbing for Santos was Pat Day, who dominated Churchill Downs and was the most successful jockey in the history of the Louisville track. He was the closest any modern-day rider came to mirroring Bill Shoemaker, a wisp of a jockey who was a master of position riding and elegant style in the saddle. It was said of "The Shoe" that, "he bothered a horse less than anybody." Like The Shoe, Day wanted to win without having to resort to hard riding. He wanted to win with poise.

Racetrackers referred to him as Pat "Wait All" Day. His "Pat-ented" ride was to wait as long as possible before asking his mount to run. In watching, betting and riding Pat Day over the years, I became convinced the reason he waited so long was that his dominance had led to boredom. So to challenge himself, he waited as long as possible to make his move and find out how good he really was. This little game he played drove many a captain of industry, hard-boot trainer and regular horseplayer to the brink of rage. And Pat seemed to enjoy every second of it.

We lived through a vivid example of the "Wait all Day" syndrome in that race. Star of Cozzene broke running and was allowed to drop back through the field. Turning for home, he had only two horses beat. Pat steered Star of Cozzene through the field, but he was still well back a furlong from home and appeared to be hopelessly beaten. When the colt began to pick off horses by himself, Day tepidly tapped him with his stick a couple of times, but only in the final forty yards did Day deign to ride him in earnest.

The Clover Racing Stable color bearer finished in a blur, missing second by a nose and first by a length and a quarter. Literally three or four strides past the wire he was in front in one of the most frustrating races I've ever had to watch as an owner.

When Day dismounted, he apologized, telling me that if he had any idea how much horse he had under him, he would have moved sooner, persevered more in the stretch and won the race. I believed every word he said.

Because he had not been made eligible for a fee of $500 as a foal, Star of Cozzene required a supplementary nomination of $120,000 to run in the BC, which our partners voted to pay. Pat Day did not ride our colt with the urgency of somebody who had to write that $120,000 check.

At season's end, when I decided to send Star of Cozzene to France, I chose Francois Boutin to train him. I had done a lot of business with him and he produced a lot of major winners each season. Boutin was never able to get Star of Cozzene to thrive at his yard in Lamorlaye and the colt consequently underperformed.

Star of Cozzene never was a beauty contest winner. He bore a striking resemblance about his forehead and muzzle to 1950s equine motion picture star Francis the Talking Mule. But he had always exuded health. Compared to Americans, the French feed their horses differently (e.g., black corn instead of oats), prefer to keep them lean, and have them out of their stalls during morning training sessions for a greater period of time. When I eyeballed him at Lamorlaye, he was thin, his color was poor and his coat was dry with no sheen to it.

His lack of well being also was evident in his sub-standard efforts on the racecourses of France and England. From four French starts, all in Group races at a mile, he finished third, second, fourth and fourth. He never once looked like he would win. He showed me that he was completely unsuited to the conditions. So I pulled the plug and asked Boutin to run him "off the plane" in the Arlington Million.

After a dismal ninth-place finish in the twelve-horse Million at odds of thirty-four to one, the colt was sent to Mark Hennig. From the day he returned to California, Star of Cozzene seemed rejuvenated. He literally ate like a horse. His weight quickly returned to normal once he was put back on heavy oats and alfalfa hay. And, most importantly of all, he thrived on a routine of limited time spent out of his stall. Star of Cozzene did not like to be fussed over. He wanted to be left alone. He wanted to go out, do his work, have a shower and be put back in his stall.

Ten weeks after he had arrived at Hollywood Park, Hennig sent him out for the last allowance race he would ever contest. The colt picked up right where he had left off in America and won comfortably under Gary Stevens. The pair came right back a month later to win a handicap.

Once back in the States and trained by Mark Hennig, Star of Cozzene compiled an admirable record, racing twelve times from November of 1992 through September of 1993, for eight wins and four seconds.

Star of Cozzene won his first four races once back in the US, including January renewals of the Grade 3 San Gabriel and Grade 2 San Marcos Handicaps, giving four pounds in the last named and taking the measure of subsequent Horse of the Year and Champion Turf Horse Kotashaan.

Knowing that Star of Cozzene would be sent east to contest a series of three grass races for older horses that were carded on the same weekend as the Triple Crown for 3-year-olds, Hennig gave the horse a brief respite following his San Marcos victory. He prepped nicely over a mile at Santa Anita in April and was sent back East for an epic four-race series against Claiborne Farm's mighty Champion Lure in a rivalry that captured the attention of the sport in America. Lure won the first two and Star of Cozzene won the next two.

In the Early Times Turf Classic run over a mile and an eighth on the sand-based turf course at Churchill Downs, Star of Cozzene turned in a gallant effort to finish second, beaten less than a length, by the odds-on favorite Lure. The Claiborne Farm homebred enjoyed an uncontested lead, but he gave five pounds to Star of Cozzene and won convincingly, setting a new course record of 1:46 1/5. We thought the only way we could beat Lure was if another horse softened him up a bit on the lead, the race was a little bit farther and there was some give in the ground.

Two weeks later, although the distance was the same mile and an eighth of the Churchill race, Star of Cozzene encouraged us to believe he could turn the tables, as our colt relished a mid-week breeze over the long-bladed Pimlico grass course. We were convinced that Lure, with his daisy-cutter stride and desire for firm turf, would not act as well on the Baltimore course. The day before the Early Times Dixie, the race's female counterpart, known as the Gallorette, was contested on tall grass. I salivated at the prospect of the rematch.

When I arrived at Pimlico the next day to find that the turf course has been mowed, thereby eliminating our perceived advantage, I could not believe my eyes. The grass carpet had literally been pulled from underneath our colt. This was not my first rodeo when it came to racing surfaces being altered. What often happens is that the host track, in an effort to cater to a trainer of a horse they want to run at their place, asks the trainer of the prominent runner if he has a preference for how he wants the surface treated before the race.

As a turf writer, I had seen Charlie Whittingham dictate how he wanted a track manicured before a big race. As an owner, a horse I managed wound up setting a track record after my trainer Laz Barrera told Fair Grounds Director of Racing Dr. Alex Harthill that he would only bring It's the One from Los Angeles to New Orleans if the racing surface played "like a California track." At a victory party I attended later that evening, I asked the track superintendent how long it took him to get the track like that. He said, "You didn't ask the right question. What you should have asked is how long will it take me to get it back to where it was originally. That would be about seven to nine days!"

Lure looked invincible beating Star of Cozzene in the Dixie by one and a half-lengths, once again giving him five pounds and running out a very convincing winner. Star of Cozzene ran his usual, hard race, finishing well and making up five lengths from the quarter-pole to the wire.

For the Manhattan the day after the Belmont Stakes, Lure was in line to win owner-breeder Claiborne Farm a $1 million bonus from sponsor Early Times if he swept the three-race series.

Lure faced a bigger challenge in the Manhattan, because the distance was a furlong farther than in his previous two wins in the Early Times series, rain had taken away the bounce from the hard grass course and once again Shug McGaughey's steed had to give weight (four pounds this time) to his nemesis. Still, bettors hammered the Claiborne runner down to three to five favoritism, with Star of Cozzene held at five to two.

Mark Hennig asked Jose Santos, who replaced Gary Stevens (out with a broken hand), to stay closer to Lure in the early going. "Lure had been getting away from him. Lure has been a real nightmare for this horse," Santos said.

Lure broke a step slowly but was soon pressing the pace of Solar Splendor. Fractions were tepid: basically twelve-second furlongs through a mile in 1:35 3/5. The race took shape at the quarter pole where Lure was poised to pounce on the pacesetter and Star of Cozzene was just one length away. And the race was on in earnest at the furlong grounds.

Belmont Park race announcer Tom Durkin called it this way: "They're coming to the final furlong. And Mike Smith is asking Lure for more. And Lure has the lead by a length. Star of Cozzene runs at him from the outside.

Lure and Star of Cozzene driving to the wire together. And Star of Cozzene will deprive Lure of a million dollar bonus."

When asked by Mike Smith for his best lick, Lure responded like the champion he was, increasing his margin by nearly two lengths over Star of Cozzene. When Jose Santos asked him to quicken, Star of Cozzene switched leads, lowered his body and generated an enormous amount of power to catch Lure. They raced together briefly before Star of Cozzene moved away to win by just short of a length. Final time of 1:58 4/5 was a new stakes record, accomplished with a final quarter-mile run in twenty-three seconds flat.

Final time was fast, indicating that the recent rain had most likely only taken the sting out of the hard ground. Both horses ran winning races. The four pounds might just have made the difference.

Next stop on the Lure/Star of Cozzene express was the Caesars International at Atlantic City, where racecourse owner Bob Levy had been able to engage Caesars into sponsoring a $500,000 race. Run on what some racing men and women called the best turf course ever built in the United States, the International was contested at a sixteenth of a mile shorter than the Manhattan and a sixteenth of a mile longer than the first two legs of the Early Times series.

The New York Times' distinguished sports writer Joe Durso characterized it as follows: "When Lure and Star of Cozzene took the track, they were pursuing a rivalry that brought back memories of Easy Goer and Sunday Silence in the late 1980s and maybe even Affirmed and Alydar in the late 1970s. This was the fourth straight time in two months that they had raced.

"American racing needs two things, people have been saying: stars and a story line. And it got both yesterday when Star of Cozzene ran down Lure in the homestretch to win the $500,000 Caesars International at Atlantic City Race Course and tie their sizzling rivalry at two victories apiece."

Daily Racing Form's national columnist Joe Hirsch wrote "It's the rare extravaganza that turns out to be as exciting as anticipated, but the $500,000 Caesars International at Atlantic City Sunday lived up to its advance billing as the fourth chapter in the dramatic story of racing's premier rivalry."

As reported by Hirsch, Lure set the "kind of pace his people wanted" and Star of Cozzene "overcame that edge" by staying "closer to the pace than some thought possible." Joe pointed out that Lure gave three pounds to Star of Cozzene, "but it wasn't the weight that made the difference in the Caesars."

Shug McGaughey surmised that Lure's advantage was his speed and ability to corner the sharp bends of the Atlantic City course. Star of Cozzene had difficulty cornering on regularly configured courses, but overnight rains once again took the hard edge off the fast course. Although the course officially was labeled "firm" the horses hooves went into the grass a bit, which was exactly what Star of Cozzene loved.

Lure dictated the pace, staying two lengths in front of his nearest pursuer, while Star of Cozzene mostly raced fifth of the seven runners, but only about four lengths off the pace. Lure went a half in 47 seconds and three-quarters in 1:10 4/5, racing well within himself.

In what by then had become a familiar scene, the yellow Claiborne silks flashed in front before the eighth pole two lengths clear. This time, however, Santos did not wait until the eighth pole to make his move. He had sent Star of Cozzene up early. When Star of Cozzene was asked for his effort, he instantly went into high gear, caught his rival and drove clear by one length.

Lure once again was the odds-on choice, with Star of Cozzene and Bobby Frankel's Val de Bois at five to two. The French import had finished a nose ahead of Star of Cozzene in the Breeders' Cup Mile. On this day, he could finish no closer than fourth, beaten more than half a dozen lengths.

Jose Santos was now 4 for 4 aboard Star of Cozzene and it seemed the Chilean rider had the Cozzene colt's number. He definitely knew how to get the horse to switch into a gear we had never seen before.

Lure lost nothing in defeat, as most veterans of the Turf scene realized that he was a Miler being asked to compete over trips that were just a bit too far for him. Over his best trip, he won the Breeders' Cup Mile the year before and he would take it again at season's end. But the lucrative purse structure for middle distance horses was too great to pass up, and Lure was pointed for yet another rematch with Star of Cozzene over a mile and a quarter in the Arlington Million.

The build up to the Arlington Million played out with all the melodrama of a B-movie. It had everything, from a good old-fashioned rivalry, to an infectious disease that threatened to obliterate every horse in the land. Rival Horse of the Year candidates Kotashaan and Bien Bien were stranded out West, unable to come to Chicago because of a travel ban imposed by the "inevitable" equine plague. And Lure's people initially said they would not be coming to Chicago because of the disease. There was a movement afoot from horsemen to have the race moved to a different track.

As a reporter, I had seen how immunologists exaggerated the prospects of any equine disease and I remained unfazed by the prospect of a fourteen-day post-race quarantine We sent Star of Cozzene into a makeshift stabling area in the parking lot of the racetrack, thereby saving the Arlington Million of 1993. French trainer John Hammond then decided to send the previous year's winner Dear Doctor. And owner Mark Levy spent $50,000 to supplement his hotshot local horse Evanescent. Heavy rains close to post time kept Lure in his stall, but eight runners did go post-ward. Star of Cozzene was sent away as the four-to-five choice, making him the lowest-priced favorite in the history of the race.

Star of Cozzene never looked better than on Arlington Million Day. The sky was gloomy but Star of Cozzene's sleek, dark coat shone like a highly polished boot and was set off by an outsized white sheepskin shadow roll. His compact frame seemed coiled as he pranced by the grandstand in the post parade. He had never been more ready to show what he could do.

The course was officially labeled "soft," but it actually was "heavy," with a lot of standing water on top. Star of Cozzene raced fourth most of the way down the backstretch in what seemed like an ideal trip. Approaching the far turn, the entire complexion of the race changed.

As sometimes happens when there is an unbeatable favorite, rival riders work together to put the favorite in a box. This happened to our horse. Star of Cozzene went from being a close-up fourth to having one horse beat as he raced, blocked inside along the fence around the entire final turn. He was stuck with no place to go.

"I knew the course was heavy, I could see all of the other riders moving too soon, so I waited," Santos said. "I didn't panic." When the field straightened out for the run to the wire, Santos wheeled Star of Cozzene to the far outside of the field, balanced him for the run to the wire and set his horse down in the middle of the water-logged course.

Santos knew what he was doing and what he had underneath him. As the two runners in front of him toiled in the deep going, a seemingly fresh Star of Cozzene easily caught them inside the furlong grounds and quickly pulled away to score by 3 ¼ lengths (second largest margin of victory in the history of the race). Supplementary nominee Evanescent was second, ahead of French import Johann Quatz, who was owned by our old Political Ambition partner from Japan, Tadahiro "The Toddymeister" Hotehama. His time was a slow 2:07 2/5, a fifth of a second faster than the great John Henry required to win a dozen years earlier in the inaugural Million, which was run on a similarly wet course.

Star of Cozzene was at his absolute best in the Million. In his slower paces, Star of Cozzene was hard to watch, as he ran with his head cranked to one side and moved with a clumsy, choppy action. When asked for speed, however, he morphed into a precision racing machine.

On the deep, testing going, he lowered his body and relied on his single greatest asset as a racehorse. Star of Cozzene was able to get his center of gravity very low and cock his hind leg at an angle that allowed him to generate a tremendous amount of drive power. The really great horses—runners like Frankel, Dancing Brave and Nureyev—had the rare ability to shade eleven seconds for a furlong and twenty-two seconds for a quarter. Star of Cozzene possessed the ability to summon that rare brand of explosiveness on demand.

Among the cognoscenti of the Turf, Star of Cozzene was the frontrunner, not only for Champion Turf Horse, but also for Horse of the Year. He dominated the weekly media polls, getting as many as forty-three first-place votes, while the second horse got only five. In order for him to step up and earn that award, he needed to run in the Breeders' Cup Turf. Our ownership group did not want to pony up $240,000 to do it, as we still had a bitter taste in our mouth from having spent $120,000 to make him eligible at three to run in the Breeders' Cup Mile, in which the prize money did not cover what it cost us to run him that day.

When owners race Thoroughbreds, they are to a great extent indulging themselves. It is an extravagance. When one agrees to pay a huge amount of cash to supplement a horse to a big race like the Breeders' Cup, it raises the indulgence factor to an untenable level. I remember feeling like an absolute fool when we spent $120,000 to run Star of Cozzene in the Mile.

In a post-million interview with Mark Hennig, TV host Charlsie Cantey said, "Surely they will supplement him to the Breeders' Cup." Like most members of the media, she took it for granted that shelling out almost a quarter-million dollars was a foregone conclusion. In most cases, those people worked for hundreds of dollars a week and they were "spending" our money for us—money in amounts few, if any, of them, would ever see in a lifetime. I found these remarks to be presumptuous.

We knew that not running in the BC would make us vulnerable when Eclipse Award voting took place because members of the media wanted to see the best horses go head to head, so in many instances they goaded owners of horses to pay the outlandish supplementary fees.

Prior to Star of Cozzene's final race for us, the Grade 1 Man o' War Stakes going a mile and three-eighths at Belmont Park, my old employer Rollin Baugh approached me with the idea of buying the horse for some Japanese horsemen. We struck a deal in principle beforehand and one of the prospective owners from Japan flew in for the race.

Star of Cozzene, as he had done in the Arlington Million, totally dominated the Man o' War, winning by 5½ lengths as the odds-on 4 to 5 favorite. All of the runners carried the same 126 pounds. In his wake that day was the California invader Bien Bien, who went on to compile earnings of more than $2.3 million and win seven major races before retiring to stud, as well as a pair of major French challengers: Arlington Million hero Dear Doctor and Serrant. The last named put a win streak of nine consecutive races on the line in the Man o' War.

I remember leading Star of Cozzene into the winners' circle, with the Japanese horseman standing on the other side of the horse. When we lined up to receive the magnificent trophy, tears streamed down my face; I was overcome with emotion at the thought of parting ways with our gallant horse. The best time to sell a horse is when he is on the top of his game and somebody wants to buy him. But for those of us who admire and love our horses, actually letting go is a lot easier said than done.

Our ownership group held a meeting to discuss the pros and cons of selling Star of Cozzene. On the plus side was an offer of $3 million, which, coupled with $2 million in earnings, brought the gross income to $5 million. On the opposite side of the ledger was being able to supplement to the Breeders' Cup and possibly win Horse of the Year honors. I explained to the partners that I was in favor of selling the horse because, as he had an unfashionable pedigree and lacked physical quality, he would always be worth more as a racehorse than as a stallion.

We voted on a sealed ballot, with the vast majority agreeing to sell. One hold out was John Amerman who, with his wife Jerry, later established his own stable and successfully raced several top horses with Bobby Frankel. John was a leading business executive who brought the Mattel toy company out of the doldrums as its CEO.

John and Jerry were top stock people. They knew horses and they knew dogs, as Jerry had bred and exhibited champion German Shepherds for years. John easily could have bought and raced the horse himself, but for reasons known only to him, he did not pick up the bit.

John had flown back to Atlantic City to watch Star of Cozzene win the Caesars International. He was over the moon after the race. I will never forget sitting across the aisle from him when we flew home. From the moment the plane reached 10,000 feet until its descent, he was on the Airfone calling family and friends to talk about the race. I remember wondering if he had squandered his entire portion of the prize money on the cost of those phone calls.

Frankly, I was surprised that our group voted to sell him, but the economy was not rolling at that point and several in this particular group had been met with financial setbacks so they were ready to take some cash off the table. Over the years I came to learn that my partners would invariably part with a good older horse, but rarely—if ever—with a young one.

Star of Cozzene's best Beyer that season was 117, which he ran in his Grade 1 Man o' War win at Belmont, and again when taking the Caesars International at Atlantic City. He also recorded Beyers of 116 and 115, respectively, in winning the Manhattan at Belmont and the Arlington Million.

Yet, when year-end honors were handed out, Star of Cozzene was skipped over for an Eclipse Award when voters went for the French invader Kotashaan. The pair only met twice in 1993, early in the season, when Star of Cozzene won both times. Kotashaan, unlike his rival, never left California, where he won five Grade 1 races.

Kotashaan's best career Beyer was 111, which he ran in both of his last two races. Most of his Beyer figures were in the 108 range. The difference was that Kotashaan was able not only to contest the Breeders' Cup, but also to win it by half a length.

Ultimately, because we had sold him, our ability to direct Star of Cozzene's bid for an Eclipse Award was out of our hands.

I advised Rollin Baugh not to give into temptation and run Star of Cozzene back right away in a race like the Turf Classic at Belmont, because the horse had experienced two hard races in a row on very testing ground and needed time to recover. But the new owners were headstrong and they resisted the advice.

Star of Cozzene ran back three weeks after the Man o' War and finished out of the top 3 with a 104 Beyer, his worst number since getting beat at Santa Anita in his mile prep for the Early Times series. He then was sent to run in the lucrative Japan Cup, in which he finished fifth of fifteen. His season was over. The next year he ran four times, never won, and he was retired after finishing a badly beaten twelfth of fourteen in the Arlington Million. He has been a failure at stud in Japan.

When you sell a horse for a lot of money, you want to see it do well for the new owners, not only because you like the horse, but because you want to be able to sell horses to others in the future. So we took no pleasure in seeing Star of Cozzene lose his form.

I do think Star of Cozzene could have won the Breeders' Cup Turf. However, neither Jeff nor I, nor a majority of the partners were willing to take that risk of supplementing him or turning down a big offer for the horse.

The money we earned racing and selling Star of Cozzene put our company in the black, which, for Jeff and me, was like winning a Grade 1 race of our very own. We needed that money.

CHAPTER 16

A Hundred Grand

William Murray, who gained a measure of fame as a writer of mystery novels with racing themes, spent more time at Southern California racetracks than most, yet remained an outsider.

When Murray went racing, it was not with an open mind or intellectual curiosity, but with the belief that the game was peopled by crooks and was not on the level.

He had the goods on the world to such an extent that, as the saying goes, he knew the identity of the Unknown Soldier.

I first met him in the summer of 1976 at Del Mar, where we both stayed at the Winners' Circle Lodge across the street from the racetrack. I was a columnist for *Daily Racing Form* and Bill Murray was writing a book about racing with a Del Mar background.

The book was an uneven little tome that gave him a chance to nail some of his past enemies and create new ones. Bill was very kind to me in the book, which was understandable, since I spent a lot of time guiding him through the backstretch, where he was even more of a stranger than in the clubhouse.

Bill took some really cheap shots in the book, especially with some of the denizens of the press box.

There was Smitty, an ex-hockey player from Canada who worked behind a counter serving those who spent their days working in the rooftop press box. His wife Anne worked as the secretary for the director of publicity, Dan Smith.

Smitty was a harmless guy who toiled away by steaming hot dogs, dishing up cold cuts and providing cold beverages to the writers and handicappers. I think the atmosphere of the press box replaced the camaraderie he missed from being in the locker room as a hockey player. One of the founders of Del Mar, along with Bing Crosby and Pat O'Brien, was Jimmy Durante, who was nicknamed the "old Schnozola;" unfortunately, Smitty had a proboscis as large as Durante's and as veined as that of W. C. Fields.

Murray thought a description of Smitty's nose added flavor to his little book.

One of the press box handicappers was Dushan Lazovich, a Runyonesque character who picked winners for a San Diego daily newspaper. Laz was known for wearing outlandishly colored and textured sport coats, which in his book Murray described as making him look like a jukebox.

The summer following publication of his book, Smitty gave Murray a chilly reception. Lazovich, however, wanted to take it a step further by grabbing onto the writer and throwing him out of the open-air front of the press box. Laz was restrained from completing the act and Bill Murray made himself scarce for the rest of the meeting by hiding in the upper tiers of the Del Mar plant.

Although the book purported to be non-fiction, it contained elements of fiction, because Murray never let the facts stand in the way of a good story; he would meld a few incidents into one that made for better reading—the facts or the individuals involved be damned!

Murray talked a good game in private to his pals but in print, he lacked the tackle to take on racing's heavyweights, choosing instead to write the type of thinly disguised novels that gained popularity in Hollywood.

It was the use of this ploy that found Bill getting his tit in the wringer with *Daily Racing Form* and eventually being dropped from its stable of freelance writers.

Like many writers through the ages, Murray used his sharpest pencil to even scores with his enemies. Although Bill and I had gotten off on the right foot in the mid 1970s, we eventually had a falling out.

Bill had been a partner in the first racehorse I owned, a filly named Sari's Tobin that we had claimed for $35,000 from a winning race at Hollywood Park. We did well with her, winning a few races, getting her stakes-placed and selling her for more than three times her claim price to Robert E. Sangster as a broodmare prospect. It represented the beginning in ownership for me, but was the highlight in Murray's tenure as an owner.

Bill and I fell out of sorts about ten years afterward when I sold an interest to some of his friends in a filly based in Argentina. The plan had been to race her once or twice in Buenos Aires, then import her to California. It went awry when a fence failed to yield as the filly ran into it, resulting in a leg so badly mangled that her racing career ended before it began.

Prior to the sale, Murray insisted that I guarantee to his friends that the filly would make it to California, which I reluctantly agreed to do. When the filly became useless as a racehorse, it made little sense to incur the costs to bring her to California. Murray's friends asked for their money back. I did not have the requisite amount of cash available at the time and promised to pay them back in due course, which I did.

As I had been unable to pay upon demand, Murray took this as a personal insult and accused me of selling his friends a horse that did not even exist. He never forgave me for my indiscretions, even though I produced a photograph of the filly showing the injury to the filly's forelimb.

Fast forward to the summer of 1993, some fifteen years since Bill and I met at Del Mar and stayed at the Winners' Circle Lodge. Star of Cozzene, racing for Team Valor in the Chicago suburb of Arlington Heights, had just won the Arlington Million. Not only did he finish first, earning a prize of $600,000, but his winning margin of 4 ¾ lengths was the longest in the history of the event and his odds of 2 to 5 were the shortest in the annals of the internationally prestigious race.

Additionally, Team Valor had garnered some very positive publicity, as Star of Cozzene was the first major horse to accept an invitation to the race. A highly infectious disease was prevalent at the time and Arlington required visiting horses to be stabled in temporarily facilities inside a tent on the customer parking lot, far away from the normal stabling area.

The biggest race of the Arlington Park season had been in jeopardy. Two-time Breeders' Cup Mile winner Lure was one of the big names skipping the event because of possible exposure to the virus. Jeff Siegel and I got credit from Arlington Park owner Dick Duchossois for saving the race that summer.

Star of Cozzene was an unqualified success, as he compiled earnings of more than $2 million and was sold to a Japanese owner for $3 million. He upset Lure and cost owner-breeder Claiborne Farm a $1 million bonus when reversing a pair of defeats in the Early Times and Dixie Handicaps by winning the Manhattan at Belmont Park. Later in the year he added the Man o' War Stakes on Long Island and beat Lure in the important Caesars International at Atlantic City racetrack.

A short time after the 1993 Arlington Million, Bill Murray wrote a column for *DRF* and, as was typical of his style, the article was a thinly veiled criticism of Star of Cozzene, Barry Irwin and Jeff Siegel.

In the piece, Murray referred to the two syndicators of the Arlington Million winner as "Gatsby" and "Swindle." Jeff and I were very upset with the portrayal, which implied that we were crooks. And Siegel had the chutzpah to suggest that it was he who was Gatsby and not Swindle!

Murray would like to have had readers believe that he was doing them a service by pointing out that while the Gatsbys and Swindles of the world might get lucky now and then, it didn't change the fact that, day in and day out, they were ripping people off by selling them stiffs for outrageously marked-up prices. It was Murray's position that rare wins with the likes of a Star of Cozzene served only to catch new pigeons to cheat.

The real reason Murray penned the piece was to knock yours truly off his perch. Barry Irwin's winning a race or two here and there was one thing, but for him to win a nationally-televised event like the Arlington Million cast doubt on Murray's stories to his cronies that Irwin was nothing but a phony. The truth needed to be brought to light.

Dollar amounts for the cost and eventual syndication price cited by Murray in the *Daily Racing Form* piece were grossly exaggerated. At that time, we were civil whenever we ran into each other at the track, so I phoned him the morning the story appeared in print.

At first Murray tried to be cute, pretending that he did not know what I was talking about, that he had written nothing about Team Valor or its horse Star of Cozzene. It was all just hypothetical.

We got over that nonsense in a hurry.

I told Bill in no uncertain terms that I wanted him to correct his story. I said that his numbers were false and I invited him to come to my office, where I said I would open our books to him to show him: the bill of sale for the purchase of the horse, the syndication agreement with the price at which we sold the horse to our partners and the cancelled checks. He indicated he would like to see them.

At the same time, I phoned Bill Dow of *Daily Racing Form*, enlightened him about the facts behind the piece and asked for a retraction. Bill told me he did not think he could help me, as the ball was in Murray's court.

Murray never availed himself of the opportunity to examine the documentation that, if made public, would have made his story the big lie it was.

A little investigation on my part revealed that Murray had attended a party on Labor Day weekend at the Del Mar condo of former college track coach Nick Giovinazzo. Also at the party was Paul Assenisi, the guy with whom Team Valor had worked in buying Star of Cozzene.

Paul Assinesi, a struggling young trainer, understandably went through the gamut of emotions after watching a horse that he had had his hands on, and could have kept for a relatively small amount, pop up and win a $1 million race. A win like that for Assinesi would have made his career as a trainer.

After a few drinks, Assinesi began recounting the sale. A combination of alcohol and the passage of a year and half conspired to make Assinesi distort the story to make it more entertaining for the benefit of the racing fraternity at the beachfront gathering.

Whereas we had purchased the colt for $131,250 and syndicated him for $235,000, Assinesi lowered the acquisition price to $75,000 and upped the syndication price to $350,000.

Bill Murray most likely realized the numbers were askew, but he had a source and he had a vendetta. Murray was about to nail an old enemy and make himself a saint in the process. So, as was his bent, Murray went to work, melding a few incidents into one and adding his own little twist.

Daily Racing Form tried to get Murray to write a retraction, but he would not. The *Form* tried to appease me by having some other writer do a puff piece about Team Valor. We declined.

So we hired a lawyer and sued Bill Murray and *Daily Racing Form*.

The case never went to trial because, after a few days of depositions, it became apparent to racing's self-anointed "Turf Authority" that Bill Murray would not make a good witness on the stand.

Settlement talks began immediately and I was satisfied with what we came away with, although Jeff Siegel and our lawyer wanted to take the case to trial, as they both envisioned a much bigger payday down the road.

As for me, I will always look fondly upon Bill Murray, because he enriched my life financially.

Bill Murray also taught me a lesson I have never forgotten, which is that people lie under oath. One afternoon, Murray perjured himself during the depositions. When we both headed to the bathroom at the lawyer's office, I confronted him about lying while we both were peeing at the urinal. "So sue me," he responded. For Bill Murray, the end justified the means.

Chapter 17

The Captain

Jeff Siegel wanted to be in the horse business. He was tired of being in the syndication business. Team Valor, though it dealt in horses, was actually in the entertainment business. Jeff wanted to race and trade horses for profit. He wanted to deal with professionals in the racing industry, not neophyte owners.

Team Valor was in the business of providing a vehicle for newcomers to become involved in the excitement of horse racing. The profit from Team Valor came from the mark-up between the wholesale purchase price and the retail syndication price, as well as an incentive bonus if a runner made its partners a profit.

Although Jeff and I were equal partners in the business, I earned more from Team Valor than he did because it was my full time job. Jeff acted more as a consultant. If there were any profits, we split them, but as the chief executive officer my salary was substantially higher than what Jeff received for his role.

Understandably, Jeff was eager for the prospect of making more money and being involved in the traditional aspects of the horse business, such as claiming, buying and selling horses. Even after the considerable success we had experienced, Jeff found it difficult to embrace Team Valor's business model. He never really wanted to "babysit" neophytes. If a horse ran a big race and was capable of being sold for a profit, Jeff's instinct was to take it, not to have his hands tied because a newcomer wanted to indulge himself by continuing to race it.

He wanted to be able to wheel and deal in horseflesh. Team Valor was on the opposite end of the spectrum, providing horses for end users. Our customers wanted to live the experience and consume the product and they did not join a syndicate primarily to turn a profit. Jeff, towards the end of 1995, was no longer interested in this activity.

As the cruise director of the S. S. Team Valor, I enjoyed all aspects of operating a partnership. I had the personality, the style and the communication skills to involve people in our enterprise. I was an optimist. In the days before e-mail usage and the Internet dominated the communication landscape, I churned out letters, video tapes, produced a daily audio report and made sure our sales force spoke with each client at least once a week. At our office in Pasadena, we even set up a mini theatre where our clients could watch live racing.

I nicknamed Jeff "Vice-President/Good News." If one of our horses ran well, Jeff could beat the press box elevator to the ground floor to revel in a big win and chat up the partners. He was a much better winner than I. But if a horse ran poorly, Jeff tended to stay in the ivory tower.

I, on the other hand, had the ability and patience to deal with the partners' disappointment. It takes a brave soul to face an owner after a terrible race, because as a merchant of dreams, I had the responsibility of keeping alive the long-held fantasies of my customers. A lawyer who had given me the most sage advice I had ever received once asked me what I thought my job was. After I failed at several attempts to provide an adequate answer, the lawyer said it was "to not drop the hot potato." That pretty much sums up the life of an entrepreneur and it was especially true in my case.

Because I was optimistic, our customers usually responded positively to my post-race analyses and departed the racetrack feeling better than if they had been ignored. I was always more skilled in situations that required an explanation to the partners than I was following wins. I have never been one to go overboard following a victory. People who don't know me are surprised or even skeptical to learn that I actually have a difficult time accepting congratulations in person or on the phone.

Team Valor in 1993 experienced a banner year that firmly established our brand. Our stable stats were glittering and the sporting challenges we undertook were creative, unique and daring.

With only 27 horses, Team Valor was second in North America in number of stakes wins with 21, behind only John Franks' stable, which won 32 black-type races; however, he campaigned 2 ½ times the number of horses. With our runners winning or placing in 53 stakes, we averaged a stakes win or placing for every week of the year. Underlining the quality of our stock, 1 in every 4 wins that season came in a stakes race.

With seasonal prize earnings of $3,331,891, the haul of Team Valor ranked ahead of all owners in North America with the exception of John

Franks ($5,549,703) and Paul Mellon's Rokeby Stable ($3,596,335). Mellon's booty included a $1 million bonus in the Triple Crown for the exploits of Sea Hero. Franks' horses ran 1,022 times, whereas Team Valor horses ran 186 times.

Numbers aside, Team Valor set tongues wagging with some of its moves.

Kirov Premiere, an Irish-based filly by a new stallion named Sadler's Wells (who went on to break every sire record in the books in Great Britain and Europe), had never so much as run in a stakes race. But Team Valor bought her and shipped her over to The Meadowlands to run under the lights. She dazzled her jockey Pat Day and trainer Mark Hennig by not only winning the Grade 3 Rutgers Stakes, but by also beating colts and geldings in the bargain.

Lady Blessington, an import from France (where she won the Group 3 Prix Minerve for Team Valor going 1 ½ miles), dropped precipitously in trip for the Capital Holding Mile at Churchill Downs and set a new course record when taking a notable scalp. She beat Grade 1 winner You'd Be Surprised in a photo finish, much to the surprise of Paul Mellon and trainer Mack Miller, who came back a race later to win the Kentucky Derby with Sea Hero.

Star of Cozzene could have stayed put in California to mine a rich vein of lucrative grass races in Southern California, but Team Valor bravely sent him across the country to do battle with Lure in what would develop into one of the greatest rivalries of the 1990s.

There was plenty written in newspapers and trade journals about Team Valor's being entitled to consideration for an Eclipse Award as owner of the year, but nothing came of it. Interestingly, during the first half dozen racing seasons for Jeff and me, Team Valor uniquely evolved to become a "handicapping factor." Form analysts, turf writers and horseplayers regularly included the ownership factor as part of their consideration. Our brand name had taken on a patina rarely seen in the sport.

Our stable continued to roll along in 1994 and into 1995, when we won several more stakes races, the majority of them Graded events. It was not enough to satisfy Jeff. We were an artistic success, but aside from my being able to earn a good living, our company had difficulty showing a profit that could throw off significant income to Jeff. Even when we sold Star of Cozzene, we were not exactly rolling in cash. So Jeff wanted to pull the plug.

He came up with the idea of ceasing the syndication business, raising millions of dollars in the private placement format and operating in a new entity to buy and sell horses for a profit. I was not in favor of quitting the syndication business because it provided me with my livelihood, I enjoyed it and it allowed me to use many of my creative skills.

But Jeff had been one of my closest friends for twenty-five years, we had been business partners for a long time and he had thrown me a lifeline when I really needed help. So I agreed to do it. A lot of my relationship with Jeff was based on his coming up with ideas and my following through to bring them to fruition. So I was not the least bit surprised when it was I who had to hit the road with my top salesman Jim Barrack to raise money for the new venture.

We were only able to raise slightly more than half of the $3 million we sought for the first private placement, so our buying plans would not be nearly as robust as we had hoped. We bought some horses, they developed issues and the partnership ran out of money towards the end of its first year in existence.

Jeff had become completely discouraged. There were still some Team Valor horses under management, but the private partnership was virtually in the tank. One day Jeff told me that he was done with Team Valor and that I could have it.

Since we were kaput in the syndication platform and had spent all of the private placement money, I began operating as a bloodstock agent temporarily. In my search for viable horses to market, I became increasingly impressed with a Maryland-based 2-year-old named Captain Bodgit. The name "Bodgit' is a slang word used in England. Bodgitting is handyman speak for using unconventional materials and methods to fix something around the house. This Bodgit provided a fix for Team Valor's lapsed syndication business.

Captain Bodgit developed into a very accomplished 2-year-old on the Maryland circuit under the tutelage of young Gary Capuano, the lesser-known brother of leading Mid-Atlantic claiming trainer Dale Capuano. Dale had an outgoing personality and the drive to maneuver his clientele through the treacherous waters of the claiming game. Gary was a quieter, more reserved young man of 33 who did things in a methodical manner that belied his youth.

After finishing third first time out in a July sprint at Laurel, Captain Bodgit reeled off five successive wins. Being ridden by a little known jockey named Frankie Douglas and trained at the dilapidated barn area across the street from what once was Bowie racetrack did not stop Captain Bodgit from developing into a big time horse.

In his final outing at two, Captain Bodgit roared home in a sub 12-second final furlong to win the Laurel Futurity, running a mile and an eighth in 1:49 2/5, which was excellent time for a 2-year-old on a deep track in his first try around two turns. He only won by three-quarters of a length, but the colt he beat named Concerto was held in the highest regard by his savvy trainer John J. Tammaro III. Racing for New York Yankees owner George Steinbrenner, Concerto put a nice shine on the Laurel Futurity by winning the Grade 3 Kentucky Jockey Club Stakes at Churchill Downs, where five months later he would enter the starting gate for the Kentucky Derby riding a five-race winning streak.

Captain Bodgit ran a 101 Beyer speed figure and a 6 ½ on the Ragozin Sheets, which were sensational figures for a youngster going a mile and an eighth over a deep-surfaced racing strip. Like my peers, I had heard rumors that the colt had bowed a tendon and would not pass the vet.

Through my bloodstock agent, I made an offer well into seven figures, but the colt's owner Phyllis Susini was a well-seasoned veteran with forty years of ownership experience and her deceased first husband had been a hard-knocking Maryland trainer. Mrs. Susini knew exactly what she had and she turned down the offer.

I must have watched the video replays of Captain Bodgit dozens of times in the next couple of months. I could not get the horse out of my mind. He was an absolute beast of a horse and he had already done enough to convince me he could be a Kentucky Derby horse. I wanted him.

Capuano knew what he had as well, so he took Captain Bodgit south to Florida to spend the winter in a warmer climate as he continued to train the colt for the First Saturday in May. Ten weeks after the bay colt had stamped himself as a Classic hopeful in the Laurel Futurity, Capuano sent him post ward for the Grade 3 Holy Bull, Gulfstream Park's first two-turn race of the season for the Classic generation.

Captain Bodgit made an imposing appearance in the Gulfstream Park paddock and was bet down from 10 to 1 to 3 to 1, with 8 to 5 favoritism going to the Breeders' Cup Juvenile runner-up Acceptable. The last-named, like Concerto, was owned by his breeder George Steinbrenner.

Streaking speed horse Arthur L., with John Velasquez up, won easily, with Acceptable second and Captain Bodgit third beaten 6 ½ lengths. He broke in a tangle, lurching out of the gate with his head positioned at an awkward angle. A slow pace hurt his chances. He tried to mount a bid around the stretch curve, but it was short-lived and he looked particularly in need of the exercise as he was hard-pressed to hold on to third.

I called my agent Don Brauer. "Offer Phyllis Susini $500,000 for Captain Bodgit."

Don said "No way. I am not going to do that after she turned down our offer last year for all that money. It's insulting."

I said "Don, there is every chance this race scared the hell out of her. Did you see how lousy he looked coming down the stretch? Look, this horse already injured a tendon. This woman was married to a trainer. She knows how fragile these things are. A race like this might just jolt her back to reality. She just might jump at this offer. Just call her, for Chrissakes."

When Don Brauer phoned me back he said, "Hey, we just might be live here. She's definitely thinking about it."

I quickly swung into action, crafting a deal to give the seller $500,000 plus a one-time $50,000 bonus for a Grade 1 either at 3 or 4. This time she took the offer.

Facing me were two dilemmas: where was I going to get the money to pay for the horse and who could I get to vet a horse with a suspected problem?

The prospect of raising money has rarely, if ever, proved daunting to me. But finding a vet who had the talent and experience to look past the obvious and make a comprehensive decision that required an accurate assessment of the risk was very nearly impossible. There was Dr. Jack Robbins in California and in Kentucky there was Dr. Alex Harthill.

Harthill was widely recognized as the best racetrack vet in America. I only knew him to say "hello." The only time I had used him as a vet was when I brought an X-ray of a horse's knee from Churchill Downs' backstretch across 4th Street to Doc's office. "There's supposed to be a chip in there, but the trainer tells me it's old and been there a long time," I said. Harthill snapped the film to his light box, held a magnifying glass up to the X-ray and said in the best deadpan voice he could muster, "Well, I see that chip all right. See, there it is right there. But I cannot find a date on it!" Nobody got a bigger kick from his humor than did Doc himself. He cracked himself up.

Stories of larceny, skullduggery and fixing races were part and parcel of the Harthill legend, both on the backstretches of America and among visitors to Churchill Downs for the Kentucky Derby, a race Harthill most likely had impacted (both legally and illegally) across six different decades. When I was between marriages, I shared a condo with a former exercise rider for Charlie Whittingham. Her best friend came west from Louisville to spend a couple of weeks with us, after she had broken up with Harthill. The vet secretly trained his own small string at Churchill Downs, where he usually had a talented horsewoman act as his "program" trainer and he invariably slept with her.

The stories this young woman regaled us with about Harthill's deeds and misdeeds were the most amazing tales I have heard to this day. Harthill was a genius with horses, but he had larceny in his veins and loved nothing more than pulling off an artistic stroke. But he was always ahead of any other vet in racing, as he kept up to date on human medicine and new human drugs, always looking for things that could work with horses. He was the first vet to scope and use Lasix on a horse, and he had been taught the ways drugs made horses run faster or slower from his own veterinarian father.

I once turned down a horse on the Arlington Park backstretch because I did not like the vet report. When I walked out of the barn, Dr. Harthill was waiting for me. "Look, don't let that so-called vet talk you off of buying this filly," he said. "He's an idiot. I know this filly and there's not a goddamn thing wrong with her." Based on all the stories I had been told, I chose not to trust Harthill and it turned out to be a costly lesson, as the filly went on to win half a dozen races in a row including some stakes.

Half a dozen years before the advent of Captain Bodgit in my life, I managed to get a signed contract to buy an ill-bred, silly-named 2-year-old colt called Lil E Tee. My vet turned down the colt, but Harthill okayed him for another owner in line behind me. At three, Lil E Tee went on to win the Kentucky Derby. That was enough for me. I vowed then and there that if another complicated vetting were required, I would contact Dr. Alex Harthill.

So I decided on Dr. Harthill because of the uniqueness of the tendon story. I needed somebody who had seen it all and Dr. Harthill was that man. I was game myself, but as a syndicator it behooved me to be as careful as possible in assessing risk on behalf of my clients. I needed The Pope to bless this deal and The Pope was Doc Harthill.

Harthill asked, "Do you think he's the real deal?"

I replied, "Yes, no question about it."

"All right then, I know you've got a good opinion and I love to be involved with a top horse," he said. "I'll go down there and vet him for you."

It was the dead of winter in Louisville and Harthill had been on enough wild goose chases in his career, so he brought in Dr. Jerry Johnson, who was spending the winter in Miami, to X-ray the colt's joints and scan his tendon. Dr. Johnson's report was encouraging enough for Harthill to board a plane to Miami.

Harthill had been hired for two days, but wound up staying four, the last two days on his own dime. Like Harthill, I did not want to fly across the country for nothing, so I phoned the vet for a progress report.

"Tell me about how he got that tendon," Harthill asked.

I relayed both of the stories I had been told. The first one went like this: in March of his 2-year-old season, the vet who owned him noticed a swelling in the tendon and attributed it to the colt's banging the leg against the side of his stall. The vet said he considered it to be of little or no consequence. "I scan everything," the vet said, "but this was so minor, I never even thought to ultrasound it."

The second story went like this: while training as a 2-year-old at Ocala Stud in Central Florida, Captain Bodgit was cooling out on an electric hotwalker one morning and he reared up, catching a front leg over a metal part of the machine. In an effort to free himself, he put a crease in the tendon."

I told Harthill that I disregarded the first story as blatant merchandising, but I gave a lot of credence to the second version.

Harthill said, "I believe it, because this does not look like a racetrack bow to me. It had to be some sort of freak accident like you mentioned."

I asked Harthill what he thought of the tendon.

"The tendon is very ugly. It is definitely very ugly," Harthill said.

I asked, "Is it an automatic throw out?"

"No, I wouldn't say that," Harthill replied. "I like this colt a lot. Come on down here."

Harthill and I watched the colt train on the vet's third morning at Hialeah. When Captain Bodgit came around for a third time to complete his morning spin, he seemed to be breezing. Doc and I looked at each other and almost simultaneously asked Capuano if he did that every day.

"Every day, just like that," Capuano said matter-of-factly. Capuano added that the colt galloped a full mile before his breezes, "just to take the edge off him."

After we left Capuano, Harthill whispered, "I haven't seen a horse train like this for a long, long time. I am totally intrigued by him. As a matter of routine, he jogs a mile, gallops 2 miles and finishes up faster than a 2-minute lick. First time I saw it, I thought for sure he was breezing. I don't know a horse in training that could stand that gaff. This horse is a throwback.

"Barry, he is a man. He goes out there and trains like a locomotive, comes back and doesn't take a deep breath or as much as a sip of water. I really like this colt."

It was hard not to like the colt in person. I could not believe the depth of his shoulder, chest and especially his girth. He was a true monster.

As for the tendon, I asked Harthill if he had ever seen anything like this—a horse injuring a tendon before he had ever raced, never being taken out of training, running as early as July of his juvenile year and racing at the highest level.

"No, I haven't," said Harthill. "I have seen horses heal and go on and do things like this, but never one that was kept in full training and went on to heal."

I came to the conclusion that whatever tendon damage occurred could not have been related to stress, but to an external blow. Otherwise the whole thing didn't make any sense. It defied logic.

Having all but made up my mind to buy the colt, I asked Dr. Harthill if among horsemen I would look like an idiot.

"Yes, yes you would," he said. After a pause he added, "But so will I."

Dr. Harthill dictated and filed a vet report that, in part, read as follows: "At your request I traveled to Hialeah to meet the most challenging pre-purchase evaluation in fifty years of veterinary equine practice.

"The clinical appearance of the left fore superficial flexor tendon is rather unsightly from two different angles. At other angles it is hard to see at all. On palpation it is void of inflammation and without pain from mashing on it.

"Ultra-sonic picture revealed two old lesions—one medial and one lateral—that are rapidly filling in with healthy fibers. I personally went to the track on two consecutive days and observed a strenuous exercise program. On each occasion, he grew stronger at the end of his 2-mile gallops. I check him an hour after exercise each day. The conformation and integrity of the tendon never changed.

"We all know how fragile horses are and some misfortune can come at any time, but I sincerely believe that this horse is as sound as almost any horse I have seen. In spite of the way his tendon looks."

The Pope had blessed him. Say hallelujah.

I had planned to turn the colt over to Mark Hennig to train. Doc planted the thought in my head to consider keeping the colt with Gary Capuano.

"Nothing against Mark, you understand," Harthill said. "His record with you speaks for itself. But you and I both know what is going to happen if you give this colt to another trainer. They are going to take one look at that leg and they are not going to train him as hard as this young man will.

"Gary has the confidence to train him hard and this colt's hole card is his ability to train hard and get a lot out of it. This is a lot of horse."

He was right, of course, because a new trainer would look at that tendon every morning, pussy foot and try to reinvent the wheel. If Captain Bodgit was going to make the starting gate under the Twin Spires on the first Saturday in May, he needed to be trained with total confidence.

Before flying from Los Angeles to Miami, I contacted 104 folks I considered likely to want to race a Kentucky Derby candidate. I explained what I knew about the tendon prior to Harthill's evaluation and prepared them to move quickly. I did this in advance because I needed to gauge how strong my investors were since I had not offered a new horse in a year, and

I wanted to see where the money would come from as it was due just a few days later.

As it turned out, I had absolutely nothing to worry about. I could have sold the horse twice. In fact, the horse sold out so fast that my best client from the previous five years got shut out and wound up never speaking to me again. I offered the colt on a first-come, first-served basis. We closed with a record number of thirty-two partners. I broke the partnership into points, with partners being able to buy as little as 1 point and as many as twenty-five. One fellow bought twenty-five points, while several bought one or two.

Before I called my lawyer to discuss the syndicate agreement, I phoned half a dozen of my biggest-spending, long-tenured clients and discussed my compensation on the deal. I was more interested in getting the horse than in making money. I just wanted to swing back into action with a live Triple Crown runner.

The consensus among my partners was that I should not charge a markup. They did not feel comfortable paying a markup. They thought I was being too greedy. They said they would rather pay more on the back end if the horse turned out to be successful. So, at their suggestion, I took one point for putting the deal together and managing the racing career of the colt. I added two incentives: a 5 percent commission for reselling the colt if the partnership was in the black, and a 20 percent bonus of any profit after all monies in and out had been taken into consideration. It was the first time I ever did a deal like that and it would be the last, because in the end, I made more money than the horse originally cost the partners. But more about that later.

Although I decided to retain Gary Capuano to train the colt, we did switch riders from Maryland journeyman Frankie Douglas to California-based Alex Solis. Captain Bodgit needed a strong rider and Alex Solis rode and was built in the same mold as Laffit Pincay Jr.

In his first start for our partnership, Captain Bodgit ran in the Grade 2 Fountain of Youth, which, at a mile and a sixteenth, was the traditional prep for the Grade 1 Florida Derby. Solis had a rough week —he was dumped from a horse one day and injured his hand another day. But he made it out for the February 22 Triple Crown prep.

Pulpit was even money to win the Fountain of Youth Stakes. Bred and owned by Claiborne Farm, he was an extraordinarily well-bred son of A.P. Indy out of Mr. Prospector's Grade 1 Frizette Stakes winner Preach. He was unraced at two and he had won both of his starts at three at Gulfstream Park for Frank Brothers. He won his 7-furlong debut by 7 ½ lengths and his 1 1/16-mile first allowance condition a month later by 6 ¾. Brothers uncharacteristically brought him back in fourteen days for the Grade 2 stakes.

Third choice Captain Bodgit, said Capuano, acted "nasty in the gate" and "an assistant starter grabbed his ears and nose" and then literally "manhandled him in the gate." The Captain broke to his left and was slowly into stride. At one point in the run down the backstretch, Captain Bodgit trailed the leaders by more than 22 lengths.

Fortunately for Captain Bodgit, the pace was exceptionally fast, with a tailwind on the backstretch aiding a sensationally-fast half in :45 3/5 and three-quarters in 1:09 3/5. Pulpit rated in third, came wide into the stretch, managed to gain command in the final furlong and won without being hard pressed by 1 ½ lengths.

As impressive as Pulpit had been, the talking horse out of the Fountain of Youth was Captain Bodgit. I had never owned nor ever seen a horse come around the stretch curve with the sheer power Captain Bodgit displayed that afternoon. The power he put on display was actually frightening to behold. He looked like he could have run through a series of brick walls. So fast did Captain Bodgit come around the turn that his momentum carried him wide. Yet he still managed to make up an enormous amount of ground. At the wire, Captain Bodgit was lapped on runner-up Acceptable, who had only half a length to spare over him.

I had not experienced a feeling like this since My Memoirs almost ran down Pulpit's sire A.P. Indy in the 1992 Belmont Stakes. I remember wondering after that race if we would ever be lucky enough to get another horse with a finish like his again. Then we developed Star of Cozzene into a dizzying finisher that gave me goose bumps. Now from out of the blue, we had Captain Bodgit.

Horses that can cover enormous amounts of ground and demonstrate rapid turnover at the same time are the rarest gems in racing. The power that Captain Bodgit exuded when he turned on the afterburners in the stretch was otherworldly in its scope.

Captain Bodgit was 20 lengths back at the half-mile pole, 21 ½ lengths back at the three-eighths pole, 9 ½ lengths back at the quarter pole and 4 lengths back at the furlong pole. He tossed in an unbelievable :21 3/5 third quarter and still had enough oomph to shade 6 seconds for his furious final sixteenth of a mile. He also gave 5 pounds to Pulpit in the Fountain of Youth.

Sportswriters who covered the Triple Crown but did not follow the Turf sport on a regular basis fawned over Pulpit, who was installed as the 7-to-2 favorite for the Kentucky Derby. Seasoned racing professionals and career turf writers, however, were blown away with Captain Bodgit's explosiveness and began looking his way for the Kentucky Derby.

Captain Bodgit bettered his juvenile top of 6 ½ on the Ragozin Sheets by half a point. Len Friedman, who oversaw the day-to-day operations at the lower Manhattan-based company, said, "This tells me your horse is ready to run a 4. That puts him right in there with past Kentucky Derby winners. You've got a shot."

When lists appeared in *The New York Times* and *Daily Racing Form* with Captain Bodgit second only to Pulpit, Kentucky Derby fever gripped Team Valor and our racing partners. Voicing their support, in what would turn out to be a chorus of those selecting Captain Bodgit to win the Kentucky Derby, were NYRA race caller Tom Durkin and *DRF* Derby beat writer Steve Haskin.

Jeff Siegel and I had not spoken for months, ever since he walked away from the company. One day he mustered the energy to call me, which took a lot of guts. Many of his press box pals and friends apparently had been asking him questions about Captain Bodgit and he could not answer them without looking uninvolved.

"Look, obviously I am sorry for what I did," he began. "Obviously I was wrong in what I said. I totally get it and realize that racing a horse like this in the partnership format makes sense. Tell me what I have to do to be involved in any way and I will do it."

Being the fair-minded individual that I am, I accepted at face value what Jeff said and told him he was back on board, but that I did not want any interference on Captain Bodgit. He was very thankful and very agreeable.

CHAPTER 18

Near Miss Derby

Captain Bodgit lost his first two races at three, running third in both the Grade 3 Holy Bull and Grade 2 Fountain of Youth. Most Kentucky Derby aspirants that fail to win in their first couple of races at 3 pose two unanswered questions for their connections, but this was not the case with Captain Bodgit.

Most owners do not know in advance of the Run for the Roses if their horse can get the mile and a quarter. The Captain showed us that, not only would he see out the searching mile and a quarter of the Derby, but that he would relish it.

He also showed us he could stand the gaff of tough training and racing, which is what causes the high rate of attrition among the ranks of contenders each year.

I knew we had the goods. My biggest concern was not the Derby itself, but the best way to peak on the first Saturday in May.

In a report to my partners, I characterized the situation as follows:

"As we stand right now, nothing is set in concrete and every option is open to us. All I am concerned about right now is not peaking too soon.

"No other good horse we have ever owned could run a race this hard and be able to come back as good or better in three weeks and this concerns me. So we will watch the colt at least a week to ten days before making a firm decision."

In an ideal world, Gary Capuano would want to run Captain Bodgit back in the Florida Derby, the $500,000 race run three weeks after the Fountain of Youth, going a mile and an eighth. The trouble was that Captain Bodgit did not seem comfortable racing at Gulfstream Park. Also he would have to face Pulpit, who was being mentioned in the same breath as Secretariat.

Washington Post turf scribe Andy Beyer summed up the situation when he wrote, "The swooping move that Captain Bodgit made will not win many races on the speed-favoring Gulfstream track, but it is the type of move that often wins the Kentucky Derby."

No horse that had not raced at two had won the Kentucky Derby since Apollo turned the trick 115 years earlier. Pulpit did not race at 2. But no horse in memory had burst onto the scene this late in his career and made such a favorable impression as Pulpit. I had a healthy respect for his talents and pegged him as the one to beat in the Florida Derby. However, as he was lightly raced and had already been asked to come back in two weeks for the Fountain of Youth, I expected it to eventually catch up with him because he lacked the foundation that racing at two would have given him. I thought he would prove vulnerable sooner rather than later.

Capuano went so far as to say that he had run the best horse in the Fountain of Youth and looked forward to racing Pulpit again, no matter that the unbeaten Claiborne color bearer would be a strong odds-on choice.

When Captain Bodgit trained like a fresh horse for the Florida Derby, the die was cast and Capuano announced that the Florida Derby would be The Captain's next start. Pulpit was bet down from 3 to 5 to an unbelievable 2 to 5, with Captain Bodgit nearly 4 to 1 ahead of 9-to-2 Acceptable. All carried 122 pounds.

Gulfstream Park was as guilty as any racetrack in the country when it came to souping up the racing surface on the afternoons of big races. So Pulpit's trainer Frankie Brothers and jockey Shane Sellers expected their colt to bust out of the gate and set the pace. But, according to the jockey, Pulpit seemed flat on the day and never sought the lead.

Pulpit got a good trip, saving ground all the way and moving in on the leaders at the quarter pole after following reasonable fractions of :23 1/5, :47 3/5 and 1:12. Although the budding superstar had not taken the field to the stretch, he nonetheless seemed poised to pounce and run to victory.

Captain Bodgit, racing 8 lengths off the pace much of the way, began his run earlier this time. Solis said he asked The Captain a little bit at the five-sixteenths pole and he got a much bigger response than he thought he would. Captain Bodgit swooped dramatically into contention just outside the quarter pole and came with such a rush that he did not allow Pulpit to complete a move to get outside of the pacesetters for the run to the wire. The race was won by Captain Bodgit and lost by Pulpit at that instant.

The strong run of Captain Bodgit down the stretch not only forced Pulpit to fashion his rally along the rail, it also discouraged him when he could not keep up. Captain Bodgit ran on to score by 2 ½ lengths and Pulpit was hard pressed to finish a neck ahead of the pace-pressing 68 to 1 Frisk Me Now.

As often happens when a seemingly invincible horse is beaten, sportswriters are lost at sea. Most of the beat writers were unfazed that Captain Bodgit had turned the tables on Pulpit. Award-winning Miami sports columnist Ed Pope could abide neither the dethroning of Pulpit as the golden colt of his crop, nor my arrogance at the post-race debriefing in expecting a win that to Pope seemed so unlikely. He confidently stated that Pulpit would turn the tables and restore the rightful order of the Turf in the immediate future.

Looking down the Kentucky Derby trail, I wanted to get Captain Bodgit to the bluegrass as quickly as possible. Taking a horse out of the hot and humid climate of Miami in March and getting it to the cool and crisp environs of Kentucky always could be counted on to provide a tonic to a budding racehorse in the spring of the year. My idea was to run Captain Bodgit in the Blue Grass Stakes at Keeneland as his final prep for the Derby.

Capuano instead wanted to take Captain Bodgit back home to Bowie racetrack in Maryland and use the Wood Memorial at Aqueduct in New York as the final race before the Derby. "I don't like those tight turns at Keeneland, which can be a speed-favoring track," Capuano said. "I know he likes to train at Bowie. I also know there is a great belief that getting to Kentucky early is the thing to do, but the weather in Maryland isn't that much different from Kentucky's, we are familiar with Maryland and we will feel comfortable there."

Certainly, another motivating factor for Capuano was the chance to avoid scrutiny and the press' hounding him in Kentucky. He had enjoyed being out of the limelight while stabled at Hialeah instead of Gulfstream, where the media would have interfered with his daily routine.

Gary dug in his heels and refused to send the colt to the Bluegrass because of adverse weather reports. As it turned out, it was a stroke of luck that the colt was not sent to Kentucky because we learned from Keeneland that Captain Bodgit was not eligible for the Blue Grass. It seemed that the racing office had never received his nomination form.

My wife Becky made the front page of *Daily Racing Form*. "I don't know what happened," she said. "We faxed a nomination to Turfway Park the same day for the Jim Beam and they received it. Either Keeneland lost the paperwork or our fax never went through."

If anybody was at fault, it was not Becky, who is honest as the day is long, but Howard Battle, whose job as the racing secretary at Keeneland was to line up the best field possible for the racing association's signature race.

Battle was quoted as saying he could have kicked himself for not reaching out to me after the Fountain of Youth at Gulfstream, where he had gone to hustle nominations for the Blue Grass. When somebody in his position fails to get a nomination from one of the top two or three favorites for the Kentucky Derby, something is not right.

"God only knows the last Kentucky Derby favorite that trained at Bowie," *Los Angeles Times* turf writer Bill Christine said to me before researching the matter to find that thirty-one years earlier Kauai King had won a pair of prep races at Bowie. Once a popular train stop where horseplayers from Baltimore could catch a WB & A Railroad car every five minutes for a round-trip fare of 65 cents, Bowie ceased carding races a dozen years earlier when the addition of racetracks in the mid-Atlantic drastically cut into its business.

But neither Bowie's run-down stable area, which was right out of the Great Depression, nor its old-fashioned training track, which had an abandoned grandstand as its backdrop, stopped Captain Bodgit from moving forward. He turned in a sparkling :46 1/5 half over the slow, deep training surface.

Rain was in the forecast for the Wood Memorial. Gary Capuano worried about a heavy or drying-out track that might put too much pressure on Captain Bodgit's suspicious tendon. In a pre-race interview earlier in the week, I put horseplayers on notice by saying "I wouldn't be surprised if we lost." A fan, concerned that we would not be trying with the colt, reported my comment to the Aqueduct stewards, who contacted me for an explanation. I filed that one under "Only in America!"

Captain Bodgit was vanned to Aqueduct the day before the April 12 Wood Memorial. A threat of rain was literally the only thing dampening the prospect of running the Kentucky Derby favorite. Capuano said that if the track were wet, it would not stop him from running the colt, but that if it were holding, he would probably scratch him. So we spent most of the afternoon watching the skies, talking to riders after they came back from riding on the track and speaking to everybody we could to learn more about the condition of the track.

Fortunately for us, Alex Solis rode a winner for Capuano's brother Dale in a race prior to the Wood and told Gary the track still was fast and it would not pull on their colt. But our colt still needed to deal with a severe track bias in order to win the $500,000 Derby trial.

"Coming from off the pace against the grain of a sloppy and speed-conducive track, Team Valor's Captain Bodgit accelerated when asked and easily won by 2 lengths, running the third-fastest Wood on record," wrote *Daily Racing Form* reporter and handicapper Dave Litfin.

Solis said, "It was such an easy race. I had a perfect position. At the five-sixteenths pole I asked him and he threw me into the back seat!"

As the colt approached the wire, race caller Tom Durkin intoned, "And Barry Irwin is going to the Kentucky Derby!"

On the same afternoon, Pulpit completely restored the burnish to his Golden Boy image with a commanding performance in the Blue Grass Stakes at Keeneland, where as the 2 to 5 favorite he glided to a 3 ½-length triumph. A rematch between Pulpit and Captain Bodgit was now in the offing for the Derby. "Now we'll find out who's best," Pulpit's trainer Frankie Brothers told Jay Privman of *Daily Racing Form*.

When asked whom he would make the favorite for the Run for the Roses, Churchill Downs' morning line maker Mike Battaglia told *Baltimore Sun* turf writer Tom Keyser that it would be a tough call between Pulpit and Captain Bodgit. "I want to sit back and look at the two races again," Battaglia said. "Captain Bodgit was so impressive. But I'm leaning toward Pulpit because he was the 2-to-5 favorite in the Blue Grass. He's only had one loss, so I think he's got a slight edge."

Trainers of horses finishing behind The Captain in the Wood came away with a different take, including Shug McGaughey, a sometime Claiborne Farm conditioner and trainer of the Wood runner-up, who said, "Both the winners of the Blue Grass and Arkansas Derby ran good, but I'm not sure they ran as good as Captain Bodgit."

William Nack in *Sports Illustrated* wrote "Just two months ago the man was fretting that his peers might view him as an idiot for buying the colt with the unsightly leg. Today, he is the sage of Team Valor."

Yes, Captain Bodgit looked like he did improve again. But I feared at this point that no horse could continue improving forever without a regression somewhere along the way. I hoped that he had not peaked. Pulpit, on the other hand, was lightly raced, he had already experienced a regression, he was back on track once again and I thought he had more of a right to improve than did Captain Bodgit.

Capuano was not intellectually or emotionally ready to head to Louisville, as he wanted to return to his home base at Bowie, train the colt in familiar surroundings and not show up to Churchill Downs until the Tuesday before the Run for the Roses. I was able to convince Gary that it was in the best interest of the horse and the partnership to take advantage of a direct flight from New Jersey to Louisville and get Captain Bodgit on the grounds at Churchill Downs to acclimate himself to the track's unique surface. He reluctantly agreed. The colt bounced out of the race in splendid condition, showing no signs of tiredness or post-race sluggishness. The next day, he was flown to Louisville.

Dr. Alex Harthill was the type of person for whom there was no such thing as too much attention. As if to shine the brightest of lights on himself for Kentucky Derby number 123, Harthill convinced Capuano to stable Captain Bodgit in one of the stalls in his barn, where Alex and his staff could keep an eye on him and keep strangers away.

Truth be told, Gary was more worried about Harthill than about any stranger and he made it abundantly clear to the legendary Derby Doctor that his horse ran bute and Lasix-free, his horse ran clean and his horse did not need any sort of help whatsoever. Gary may have been the last Boy Scout in racing and he was deadly serious about Harthill's not interfering in any way with his horse.

In order to show how serious he was about keeping strangers away, Harthill went the extra mile to erect what amounted to an additional door onto the front of the horse's stall. The extension protruded about 9 to 12 inches farther than the usual opening of the stall. The white-painted wood made the door even more noticeable.

Interestingly, onlookers had different takes on the purpose of the stall addition. Some thought it was a brilliant touch to make the horse more secure. Some thought it was added so that Harthill could perform his magic easier. One thing was for sure: the security door made people more, not less, interested in peeking inside to see what was behind it. So the door caused more problems than it was supposed to solve.

Capuano had nothing to fear from Harthill because Doc loved him, had total respect for him and for the horse, and simply wanted to be part of the Team.

Since I had been part of the press corps that had covered the Kentucky Derby, I cautioned Gary Capuano about the pitfalls that he would soon face.

Sure enough, no sooner had Gary arrived at the barn than *Louisville Courier Journal* columnist Rick Bozich showed up with paper and pencil in hand. Bozich would not be the first writer to arrive for an interview with the story he wanted to write already firmly formed in his mind. He just needed Capuano to add a few nods and say just a couple of words for him to complete his column.

Bozich, however, had met a different type of person in young Mr. Gary Capuano. Bozich wanted to write that Capuano had grown up dreaming about winning the Kentucky Derby and, more specifically, had thought about seeing the iconic Twin Spires in person. "Gary, when you first drove in here and saw those Twin Spires, it was something that you had always dreamed about, right?" asked Bozich. "Not really," Capuano answered.

Gary and I traded glances at each other during Bozich's faux interview and occasionally raised an eyebrow at each other. My point was well made by Bozich and well taken by Capuano.

A favorite topic among members of the press centered on favoritism for the Derby—not so much who the favorite would be, but the jinx that had formed around that dubious distinction. No favorite had taken the Derby since Spectacular Bid's win eighteen years earlier.

I was not as concerned about whether The Captain would start favored so much as I was about how the colt would take to Churchill Downs' track surface. In those days, the racing strip was not like it would become a few years later when Monarchos ran the second-fastest time in history.

Up until 2000, Churchill Downs' track was like no other. It tended to be cuppy. Many horses, especially those from California, had difficulty getting a hold of the track because it broke away from them. It was a track that required a period of adjustment.

Captain Bodgit took to the Churchill Downs racing surface to the great relief of his trainer and manager. A week before the Derby, he turned in a bullet half-mile in :47 1/5, up five-eighths in less than a minute. As usual, he galloped between breezes like the monster he was.

I had stayed home in Pasadena before heading to New York for the Wood because I wanted to size up the competition from the Grade 1 Santa Anita Derby, which was run a week before the Wood. Silver Charm got beat by Free House but I came away with more respect for the runner-up because he had run dizzying splits of :22, :45 and 1:09 to put away the brilliant colt-sized filly Sharp Cat. Silver Charm was passed in deep stretch by Free House, yet came right back at him to just miss. I told my wife that Silver Charm was the horse to beat in the Kentucky Derby because he not only was talented, he was also as game as they come.

The week of the Kentucky Derby was like nothing I had ever experienced in terms of the media crush, the needs of my partners and the unending demands on my time. I had thirty-two partners with unrealistic requests for Derby day perks. Amazingly, by networking with hotel doormen, bellhops, hookers, maître d's, ticket scalpers and my Kentucky based acquaintances and friends, I was able to obtain ninety-eight seats for my clients and their families on Derby day.

George Steinbrenner stopped me on Derby day as I walked the clubhouse, shook my hand and said, "Congratulations!"

I said "For what? For having a Florida-bred in the Derby?" He was very active in the Florida Breeders' Association.

Steinbrenner said, "No, I mean for successfully dealing with thirty-two partners! Anybody can come up with a Derby horse, but nobody can satisfy that many partners. You know, I started the first racing partnership, the Kinsman partnership, so I fully appreciate what you have done."

Then he gave me a playful glancing, jab-like fist to the chin and said, "Go get 'em, champ."

A few years later I bought a half-interest in Illusioned from George. We raced it in partnership, he let me manage it and the colt broke a track record in winning the Grade 3 Ack Ack Stakes at Churchill Downs. I always found him to be a sportsman and a very reasonable guy to deal with.

Steinbrenner knew of what he spoke. On Derby eve Team Valor hosted a party at a local eatery on Fourth Street near the University of Louisville. Most of the partners were in attendance. At one point during the evening, I asked for everybody's attention and said that we would be dividing the perks on race day because they had been limited by the track. I explained that some would be able to go to the walking ring and some would be able to go to the winner's circle, but not both.

By and large, they understood and agreed to go along with the program. There was one exception: a couple who were lawyers. Using some self-serving, convoluted reasoning, they argued that since they had different last names and filed their income taxes separately, they should be treated as individuals and each given a perk.

During that week, I tried to make myself as accessible as possible to the media. I had agreed to allow an ESPN crew from the *Outside the Lines* program to follow me and videotape me while I interacted with people in various situations. A lot of footage was shot of me but when the program aired after the Derby, it became apparent that Kenny Mayne, the producer, was not playing fair with me. He discarded the staged bits and used mostly outtakes that the crew had convinced me would be off the record.

When the lawyers started to insist on receiving both perks, I became irate and said, "Thanks for fucking up my day." Taking advantage of my generous invitation to the party, Kenny Mayne and his crew included that dust-up on the telecast.

ABC had developed a helmet camera to use on Alex Solis so that a unique angle could be shown on the Kentucky Derby telecast. I allowed them to do this in order to be as cooperative as possible. I quickly learned a few things about the TV crowd: you could not trust them, they had no guilt about monopolizing all your time and they wanted to turn you into an actor for their scripts.

Churchill Downs did little in those days to discourage unauthorized visits to the backstretch. Groupies developed that had no affiliation to Derby connections who merely wanted to hang out and soak in the rich pre-race atmosphere. People came from across the country just to sip coffee in close proximity of the trainers and get a glimpse of the horses.

Harthill's glaring white stall screen was a magnet for those afflicted by Derby lunacy. One fellow took a photo of Captain Bodgit using a flash bulb. I told him he was free to take photographs, but not to use the flash. I asked him to disable the flash. A short time later he took another shot, accompanied once again by a flash. I asked to see the camera. It was one of those inexpensive disposable models. Reverting to my time as a Little League pitcher, I did a full windup and threw that camera as far as I could. It failed, only marginally, to clear the chain-link backstretch fence.

Although I did not see this with my own two eyes, a couple of partners, who were situated at the gap from the stable area to the track, told me that, as the horses passed between rows of visitors, people grabbed onto horse's tails and plucked out souvenirs, which upset the horses to no end as they came onto the racetrack.

Rain fell during the Derby eve party and continued overnight. When Becky and I arrived early at Churchill Downs on the morning of the Derby, it was wet, blustery and about 40 degrees. She put on the brand new white hat that she had bought for the occasion. So strong was the wind that morning that it blew off the hat, which went flying and landed upside down in a puddle, leaving a pancake-sized blotch. When you own horses, you take everything as an omen, so this only heightened our anxiety level.

Halfway through the Kentucky Derby day card, I excused myself and walked to the executive offices to ask the customer relations liaison if there was some place I could lie down for an hour or so. I had an umbilical hernia and occasionally it would pop out and cause considerable discomfort. I was given permission to use the jockey's room and I was directed into a darkened room where the riders sometimes rested or took catnaps. I took off my coat, loosened my necktie and rested on my back and, after about an hour, I became relaxed enough for the tummy to come back into proper alignment.

Mike Battaglia, no doubt influenced by residing in the incestuous environs of horse country, duly made Pulpit his 2 to 1 favorite over 5 to 2 Captain Bodgit. At post time, Captain Bodgit was a clear favorite at odds of 3 to 1 and Pulpit was not even the second choice, as his odds of nearly 5 to 1 put him behind 4 to 1 Silver Charm.

Pulpit's odds were a direct reflection of the state of the going. The surface gradually dried out during the afternoon and the track was officially rated as "good," so speed did not figure to be as effective as it would have been on a fast track.

Free-running California invader Free House was allowed to use his speed early when the gates sprung open for Kentucky Derby 123, as he was drawn on the outside in the field of thirteen—a field which was considered to be so contentious that it had drawn the smallest number of entries since 1979, when Spectacular Bid ran among only ten horses.

Free House held the lead to the turn, when Pulpit took over after breaking well in the middle of the field.

Pulpit set a measured pace, with a quarter in :23 2/4 and a half in :47 2/5, just inside of Free House. Silver Charm raced a close-up fourth, as Gary Stevens was able to maneuver him into a ground-saving position when in tight going into the first turn. This move turned out to be both crucial and beneficial to Silver Charm. Captain Bodgit raced in about eighth or ninth position down the backstretch, about 8 lengths off the leaders, saving ground inside.

As the field rounded the far turn, heading towards the quarter pole, Shane Sellers had to start riding Pulpit, while David Flores was sitting chilly on Free House, Gary Stevens was maneuvering Silver Charm into position just outside of Free House, and Alex Solis had Captain Bodgit in high gear making an impression just behind the leaders. It looked like anybody's race.

Pulpit was done, but to his credit he kept on fighting until inside the eighth pole. Free House had taken command and Silver Charm was bearing down on him. Captain Bodgit, who took the turn just outside of Silver Charm, was ready to engage the leaders.

When Silver Charm took command and was challenged shortly afterwards by Captain Bodgit, Free House could not withstand the pressure any longer, he switched leads and was no longer able to keep up. Captain Bodgit, to the naked eye, loomed up outside of Silver Charm, seemed to have the energy to get by him, but Silver Charm fought back as he had done in the Santa Anita Derby and held Captain Bodgit safe by a head.

I turned to Becky and said, "See what I mean. You don't just run by this horse." I was not surprised that Silver Charm beat us, even though I really did think our colt had the energy to get by him in deep stretch.

In watching the head-on replay of the race, it became immediately apparent that the crucial point of the race came at the sixteenth pole. As Captain Bodgit came to Silver Charm's flank, Gary Stevens—in a move that had been turned into an art form by Bill Shoemaker—continued whipping with his right hand as his left hand ever so slightly steered Silver Charm to the right towards Captain Bodgit.

Silver Charm took a portion of Captain Bodgit's path, causing Captain Bodgit to lose enough momentum to cost him the race. The "race riding" gambit forced Solis to momentarily steady Captain Bodgit and made it impossible for him to continue using his whip to encourage our colt.

I learned in that split second the difference between a good rider and a great rider. Alex Solis was a good rider; a very good rider. But he rode in the moment. Gary Stevens was a great rider, because he rode like a chess player, thinking several moves in advance. I think we ran the best horse and the deserving winner, but a master in the saddle of Silver Charm outrode us.

My notion that we had run the best horse was bolstered two weeks later in the Preakness Stakes, when bettors made Captain Bodgit the 2 to 1 favorite over 5 to 2 Free House, with Silver Charm the 3 to 1 third choice.

Leaving Churchill Downs that evening I walked out next to Bernie Hettel, a steward in the stand. I asked him why no inquiry had been called to review the stretch run. "Barry, c'mon, this is the Kentucky Derby," he said. "A lot more than that has to happen for a horse to be taken down than that. We looked at it. We saw it. But we didn't think it was enough to warrant a disqualification."

Captain Bodgit lost nothing in defeat in terms of his stature and standing as a racehorse. He had run a great race in one of the most talent-laden and contentious Derbys of all time. The first two home ran a 115 Beyer figure, 10 points better than the 105 top The Captain had achieved in winning the Wood Memorial.

The next morning, when we asked to see Captain Bodgit out of his stall, I was mortified to see how knocked out he was. It was immediately apparent to me that we had finally gotten to the bottom of The Captain's reserves. He looked like a boxer the day after a 15-round heavyweight world title bout.

Camped at the barn was Joe De Francis, who had spent the morning working on Gary Capuano to make sure local hero Captain Bodgit would run in the Preakness two weeks later. I knew Gary would want to run in the Preakness for several reasons, not the least of which was its location in his backyard. I did not care one whit about any of that. My consideration first and foremost was the well being of our horse.

Looking at Captain Bodgit in the flesh, I was certain that running him back in two weeks was a bad idea and I told Capuano not to commit to anything without getting the green light from me. I made it abundantly clear to De Francis and the media that no decision would be made about the Preakness for a few days until we had an opportunity to evaluate how our horse had come out of the race.

Andy Beyer's 115 rating served only to heighten my anxiety about running the colt back in two weeks. Under most ordinary circumstances, the colt should be a candidate to regress in his next race. But the history books told a different story, because horses that performed heroically in the Kentucky Derby invariably had been able to return in two weeks and do well in the Preakness.

The real challenge would be coming back three weeks after the Preakness for the Belmont Stakes. My position was that since we were not going to be going for a Triple Crown win, why not skip the Preakness and point for the Belmont. Because if any one of the Triple Crown races was made for our colt, it was the Belmont; Captain Bodgit was all about stamina and figured to love the mile and a half, and having an extra three weeks would also benefit him.

Captain Bodgit was sent back to the Bowie Training Center. I was still taking a wait-and-see attitude toward the Preakness. Tuesday before the race, he blew out sharply and Gary told me that he was tearing the barn down the next day. So we put his name in the box and entered him for the Preakness.

Captain Bodgit drew the 9 hole in a field of 10. The start was held up several minutes when 54 to 1 long shot Cryp Too proved difficult to load. Captain Bodgit left the gate in good order, but the field ran away from him and well into the first turn he was dead last. Cryp Too set fast fractions of :22 4/5 and :46 2/5.

Free House was full of beans and assumed command by a full length halfway down the backstretch, with Silver Charm right behind him after the pacesetter faded. The 6 furlongs was run in a fast 1:10 2/5.

Turning into the stretch, Free House held only a narrow advantage over his nemesis Silver Charm. Free House responded to Kent Desormeaux and pulled 1 length clear again. Silver Charm, however, was not vanquished and he came back on to be on even terms with Free House. Another California invader, newcomer Touch Gold, had moved into a contending position inside, just 1 length behind the leaders.

Captain Bodgit made up substantial ground from the three-eighths to the quarter pole, where he arrived with a wall of horses in front of him. He bulled his way for a run between horses, was carried a bit wide by his momentum and finally settled down to business in the final furlong and a half. Riding for all he was worth, Solis managed to extract a huge run from his mount and Captain Bodgit closed furiously. He made up a lot of ground, flew past Touch Gold, was lapped on the top two with just a few strides remaining and surged to finish third, beaten a short neck for all the money. It was a thoroughly gallant and genuine effort that only a great horse could have mustered.

In a poll conducted by *The Blood-Horse*, readers voted the 1997 Preakness Stakes the race of the 1990s. The top three finishers earned a 118 Beyer figure.

Silver Charm won by a bob of the head. He missed in a bid to win the Triple Crown by less than a length when second to Touch Gold in the

Belmont, with Free House in third. Silver Charm went on to win seven of his next fifteen races and to amass earnings of more than $6 million.

Two days after the Preakness, Captain Bodgit was discovered to have some swelling in a tendon different from the one he had injured as an unraced 2-year-old. With the colt's medical history in mind, I decided to retire him to stud.

Captain Bodgit was a gift to my operation on many levels. First and foremost, he put us back right where we had left off: as a racing syndicate with the top stable of runners. Secondly, it redefined my relationship with Jeff Siegel, which allowed me more freedom to stretch myself creatively as a horseman. Most importantly we had brought a new level of excitement to our loyal racing partners. And last, but not least, it provided us with a financial boon.

Captain Bodgit was syndicated as a stallion on the basis of $2.5 million. He earned more than $878,000 for our partnership. Based on the original syndicate agreement with my partners, Team Valor received $125,000 for a 5 percent commission for the sale to the new syndicate, as well as an additional $500,000 for its bonus, based on 20 percent of net profits. From just those two sources, we earned more than the entire cost of the horse.

During a business period spanning four decades, I have experimented with every conceivable form of compensation for my endeavors as a syndicator. When the dust settled this time, several of the Captain Bodgit partners approached me with hat in hand, admitting that the formula they themselves had devised—to compensate my company with the 25 percent bonus and sales commission—was not as brilliant an idea as they had originally thought.

My company's earning more than the cost of the horse is not something they had envisioned. There are always going to be some investors who resent paying a markup, who want to be in on the ground floor and reward a manager based only on performance. But these same folks do not want him to make too much. That is exactly what happened with my management of Captain Bodgit.

I had some partners who were very happy with my performance on the track, but less so in their bank accounts. So what was there to do? Moving forward, they asked me not to tell them what I had paid for a horse in the future. They asked me to be fair with them and charge a fair markup, plus a more reasonable back-end bonus. So that is exactly how we have conducted our business ever since. We marked up our horses based on how well or poorly we were able to buy them. Sometimes we mark them up 50 percent. Sometimes we do not mark them up at all. I would say we average between a 25 and 33 1/3 percent markup. We receive a bonus of 10 percent for any net profits and a 5 percent sales commission. This has worked out well.

I am convinced that Captain Bodgit strained the tendon in his valiant effort to reach Silver Charm and Free House. He must have overextended himself when he hurtled his body at those other two horses.

We have never owned a horse quite like Captain Bodgit before or since. The depth of his body was matched only by the depth of his courage. He was not the prettiest mover we ever campaigned, but he got more out of his God-given tools than any horse we have ever owned.

Only one horse we would ever own was blessed with the cardiovascular gifts of Captain Bodgit. Dr. Harthill summed it up best when he first watched him train. He was a man.

CHAPTER 19

Where Are The Girls

In the first week of the new millennium, my eyes were opened by Horse Chestnut when he scored a powerful victory in the Broward Handicap at Gulfstream Park, in what was not only his American debut, but also his first start on a dirt track.

I had developed an ambivalent attitude about South African form. I remembered a time when Hawaii came from South Africa to become an American Champion, winning our best grass races along the Eastern Seaboard in the late 1960s. And I certainly recalled a time when horses that had been imported from the tip of the African continent came to California and won our best races. Horses like Colorado King in 1960 and Bold Tropic in the 1980s rose to the top of their division against top-class competition in Southern California.

But in the twenty years between Bold Tropic and Horse Chestnut, South African horses did not make a lot of noise on the international scene.

As a bloodstock agent, the only time I ever heard South Africa mentioned occurred when somebody needed to off-load a marginal stallion and, in due course, the name of South Africa was invariably invoked. It seemed like a last resort locale or dumping ground for unwanted bloodstock.

I would also note that Group 3 horses from Europe would occasionally win Grade 1 races in South Africa. So I developed a belief that "third world" South African racing was two full cuts below the level where I competed.

A year before the advent of Horse Chestnut, the filly Spook Express, another South African import, won well in Florida. She later went on to earn more than $1 million, become a multiple Graded stakes winner in America and finish second in the Breeders' Cup Filly & Mare Turf.

But it was Horse Chestnut who really captured my imagination and brought the Dark Continent into the light for me. I thought he had Horse of the Year potential.

Horse Chestnut and Spook Express had been developed into top-class horses in South Africa by a training wizard named Mike de Kock. Towards the end of 2000, I was offered a horse in South Africa named Delta Form that was trained by de Kock. Instead of immediately casting aside information about Delta Form as I had done with other South African horses in previous years, this time I examined the materials closely. I also phoned de Kock to hear what he had to say about the horse's remarkable turnaround since joining his stable.

Delta Form was a gelding. My racing partners had never expressed much interest in racing geldings. In fact, when I offered one of my biggest racing partners an interest in one, his response was, "What in the hell am I going to do with a worthless gelding?" It is true that a colt of the same racing quality and class is always worth more than a comparable gelding, but the real reason my partners do not want a gelding is because they are buying into a dream, not a horse. And the dream is to win a race big enough so that their horse can go to stud and earn millions of dollars in stud fees for them. It is about that fantasy and not much else.

The gelding that my racing partner had rejected out of hand was an ex-$25,000 claimer bred off the beaten path in Texas. He was one of the ugliest horses I had ever bought. I spent every bit of forty-five minutes looking at him from every conceivable angle before I could convince myself he would do.

Named Thomas Jo, he won three stakes and finished third in the Grade 1 Belmont Stakes in his initial four starts for Team Valor. Because I could not fully syndicate him, I sold half of him to Manhattan real estate tycoon Earle I. Mack, which turned out to be a fortunate circumstance because "The Earle of Mack" was able to sell the horse to a Saudi for a hefty sum. Between his earnings and his sale price, Thomas Jo realized well over $1 million for our partnership.

Even with the success of Thomas Jo, I still found myself unable to enthuse my racing partners enough to fully syndicate another gelding. Knowing this when Delta Form had been offered to me, I decided to present the gelding to Hollywood motion picture producer Gary Barber, who not only was an émigré from South Africa, but was game enough to buy any horse that could run, regardless of its gender or reproductive status.

As I was unfamiliar with dealing in South Africa, I also enlisted Gary's aid to work out any kinks on the business end of the transaction. Gary started his professional life as an accountant in South Africa, so he knew the ropes and, if he did not, he had plenty of friends in the Republic who could help us.

Delta Form, prior to joining de Kock's stable, had been a moderate performer, winning just twice in fifteen starts, with a minor stakes placing in the boondocks. Taken over by de Kock, he won all four of his starts, capping the run with a smashing score in the Summer Handicap, which at the time was the richest race run in South Africa. De Kock attributed Delta Form's improvement to a difference in training style.

Gary bought half of Delta Form. As I feared, I was only able to sell half of the 50 percent I had committed to buy, so I became a major owner along with Barber. The Australian-born, South African-developed gelding raced with success for our partnership, winning the $250,000 Grade 2 Del Mar Handicap and the Listed Henry P. Russell Handicap, while placing in the Grade 1 Hollywood Turf Cup in California and Grade 1 Belmont Turf Classic in New York en route to earning $342,811 for our group.

I had always felt that a good horse could come from anywhere. Ever since I began following racing as a fan, then as a journalist and eventually as a dealer in bloodstock, I was attracted to foreign horses and racing. If I could get the very best from a substandard locale, I would consider buying it because, when a horse is dominating a minor circuit, nobody knows for sure where that horse will level off.

In August of 2002, a couple of weeks before Delta Form won the Del Mar Handicap in new course record time, I was offered the highly accomplished South African filly Ipi Tombe. My English agent Gordian Troeller had been approached by South African agent Robin Bruss with the idea of buying the filly, which was owned by a group of racing partners from Zimbabwe.

In her most recent outing a month earlier, Ipi Tombe overcame the 15 post position, in a field of 18 mostly older male runners, by using a devastating turn of foot to win the Durban July, the most important race on the South African racing calendar.

In the process, Ipi Tombe became the first 3-year-old filly to win the 11-furlong all-aged classic in forty-five years. The victory was the filly's eighth from ten starts and she ran second, with legitimate excuses in the other two races, such as when her rider apparently gave her a race in Zimbabwe and when de Kock ran her at altitude in Johannesburg before she had been acclimatized in her first outing for him.

Robin Bruss, a deal maker extraordinaire with a global outlook and great skills as a negotiator, had been born in Zimbabwe, so he could relate to the racing partners of Ipi Tombe. Among the terms of the deal were the following requirements: that it must include the current partners who wished to remain in the partnership, that the filly be sent to race in Dubai over the winter and that she stay in training with De Kock. The $750,000 price tag was the highest ever for a Team Valor filly, but it seemed fair to me. I knew my partners would never support the purchase of 100 percent of an expensive South African filly that would race first in Dubai; it was too exotic for their taste. So I set out to find a racing partner who would take a 50-percent swing.

Naturally, the first person I talked to about buying Ipi Tombe with me was Gary Barber. After pals of his back home in South Africa said the purchase price was way out of line, Barber declined the offer. At that time, South African horsemen were extremely provincial in their thinking. They had little faith in their own horses and did not consider them to be players on the world stage.

Next I contacted Elliott Walden, who was training for WinStar Farm, which was owned by Texas-based partners Kenny Troutt and Bill Casner. Elliott had told me that, if I ever found a good horse anywhere, I had to let him have the first crack at it. So I met with Elliott one afternoon in the box section at Saratoga racetrack with Kenny Troutt, a dynamic businessman who, less than fifteen years earlier, had developed a long-distance telephone company named Excel, which he took public in 1996 and later merged with Teleglobe in a $3.5-billion deal.

Troutt listened intently to my presentation, but was not really interested in buying a grass filly from the middle of nowhere and having to race it in the desert with unknown partners before it ever came to America.

Walden was able to sell Kenny on the deal based on Elliott's selling my track record with foreign fillies.

When I spoke with Mike de Kock about the racing program's going forward, I told him my group would agree to race the filly in Dubai but we wanted a fresh horse for American racing, so he could not over-race her in the Gulf. De Kock was dealing with a chaotic group of Zimbabweans. They wanted to win the Dubai World Cup, the richest race in the world, run over 1¼ miles on the dirt. So we ran into a bump in the road well after the sellers had been paid.

When I found out early in 2003 that de Kock had entered the filly in a dirt race, I phoned him directly and, in no uncertain terms, told him that he would have to scratch her because my ass was on the line with Kenny Troutt and I did not want this filly chewed up racing on dirt. There was absolutely no evidence the filly could act on dirt. De Kock agreed, but the withdrawal of the filly did not sit well with the Zimbabweans, some of whom had already flown from South Africa to Dubai for the race.

Some of the sellers were upset but in the end the incident proved fruitful because they soon learned their true position in the order of command with regard to the management of Ipi Tombe. Having ridden the crest of a wave rarely experienced by any racing man, let alone one from a small, troubled country like Zimbabwe, the sellers had gotten used to calling the shots. It took a bit of adjustment but they soon learned that they had to turn over the reins to me.

Ipi Tombe ran three times in Dubai, each race a new jewel in her crown. She had been very good racing in Zimbabwe. She became great racing in South Africa. In Dubai she moved into that rarified air breathed only by the gods of racing. She would leave Dubai as the Horse of the Year and as the most popular horse ever to race in the desert community. The crowds absolutely adored her.

Ipi Tombe was nothing special to look at. She was nicely balanced but she exhibited neither a particularly deep girth nor extraordinary bone below the knee, nor did her head denote an undeniable look of quality—nothing stood out or struck a seasoned observer as being out of the ordinary. She did have a wonderful disposition—she was very sweet and loving—but as a horseman would put it, she was plain.

In full flight, however, it was a different story. Ipi Tombe was able to deliver an instant burst of energy that swept all before her, even when victory seemed completely out of her grasp.

What made Ipi Tombe a Champion could not be seen on the outside. One of fifty-five yearlings bred on a farm in Zimbabwe during the height of a treacherous period of national upheaval, when white-owned farms were routinely taken over by blacks with approval from the government of Robert Mugabe, Ipi Tombe was one of about twenty yearlings that went missing one day after all the yearlings had been set loose from their paddocks. Miraculously she was found two days later, after fending for herself in the wild. Her breeder said that the courage she displayed to survive the ordeal provided a glimpse into the depth of her racing heart. Other than a bruised foot, she was fine. She was sold later that year for the equivalent of $100.

Ipi Tombe made her first Dubai start in February facing nine males over about a mile in the Listed Al Fahidi Fort. De Kock told me he had her 85 percent ready and expected her to run a big race anyway because he felt she had improved since leaving South Africa. Leaving her previous form well behind, the bay filly was stuck inside and behind horses, but when an opening appeared along the rail she employed her customary turn of foot to wrap up the race early in the straight. She won being eased down in the last 50 meters by more than 2 lengths. In her wake was Trademark, South Africa's Champion Older Horse of the previous year who went on to win the Graded Bernard Baruch and Graded Fourstardave Handicaps back to back at Saratoga in 2003. Ipi Tombe shattered the stakes record by more than 2 seconds and chopped more than a second off the course record at Nad al Sheba.

I called Kevin Greeley, a Kentuckian who was working in the racing office at Nad al Sheba, and asked him what he thought of the race. "It was just a cakewalk for her," he said. "You know, this was no hollow field. Although it is just a Listed race, it is a Group 2 in quality. Wow, was she impressive."

Another report from the Gulf noted that, "These were quality horses chasing her and yet she won with absolute contempt."

Yet another report from the racing association characterized the race as being one of the "best trials seen for the Dubai Duty Free in years."

Timeform agreed, assigning her a rating of 124 after giving weight all around to seasoned and quality males. It was obvious that the filly had improved by leaps and bounds from her previous form.

One month after her desert debut, Ipi Tombe stepped up in the Jebel Hatta to the 9-furlong distance of the Grade 1 Dubai Duty Free, her main goal that she would contest three weeks later. Carrying top weight of 128 pounds because of a Grade 1 penalty, she conceded 3 pounds to nine male rivals. Once again, Ipi Tombe outran her previous form in scoring by nearly 4 lengths. Rated early, she moved inside for a clearer run from sixth place with 3 furlongs remaining, quickly wrested command, opened up a sizeable advantage 300 meters from the wire and was eased in the stretch.

Her clocking of 1:48.62 broke the stakes record and was comparable to the winners' times of the previous two renewals of the Duty Free.

Timeform rated this effort with a mark of 126, an improvement of 2 pounds over her Al Fahidi Fort performance. Ipi Tombe "more than confirmed the impression she made on her UAE debut in a Listed race here last month" and "will take plenty of beating in the Dubai Duty Free," read the publication's comments on her Jebel Hatta run.

As well as she ran in winning her next two starts, Ipi Tombe probably was right at her peak for the Jebel Hatta, because her turn of foot was at its freshest and her domination was thorough. The sight of her being eased with such a big lead and winning over a tough field by more than 3 lengths was something special to behold.

Ipi Tombe became the darling of racegoers and horse folk alike during the winter of 2003. When she came to the paddock, walked out on the track, drew off to win and was led back to the paddock after the win, denizens in the crowd chanted in unison, "Ipi" followed by, "Tombe."

Watching the Duty Free from ground level in the paddock at Nad al Sheba, I could make out Ipi Tombe as the field ran down the stretch. She was languishing in about eighth place, some 8 lengths off the pace. Her chances of impacting the race appeared slim. She looked to be going nowhere in the middle of the course. I started calculating what fourth place was worth from the $2-million purse because I thought it was all she figured to get.

Suddenly, as if a light had been switched on, Ipi Tombe emerged from the pack, accelerated very quickly down the center of the course and found one new gear after another as she began to pick off her opposition. When she hit the front half a furlong from the wire, she had built up such a head of steam that jockey Kevin Shea merely had to steer her towards the finishing post. Even though Shea did not persevere in the final stages, Ipi Tombe drew off to win by 3 lengths in 1:47.61, yet another course record at Nad al Sheba.

Ipi Tombe did not have to improve to win the Duty Free. Royal Tryst, the Godolphin runner that had been second to her in her desert debut, ran third beaten 4 lengths. In second, between the pair, was the German older horse Paolini, who won the Duty Free in a dead-heat the following season in a career that saw him become a multiple Group 1 winner, place in many of the world's top races, including the Arlington Million, and amass earnings in excess of $4 million.

When Ipi Tombe launched her bid, she came over a bit on Paolini, whose jockey lodged an objection. Somebody asked me if I had any idea why the objection had been made and I said, "The only impact our filly had on him was that she went by him so fast, the wind she created might have altered his stride!" The objection was quickly dismissed.

"Ipi Tombe, Ipi Tombe, Ipi Tombe," the crowd chanted, as they stamped their feet and clapped their hands in a raucous celebration that was both exciting and a bit unnerving. Our group assembled on the dirt track past the finish line to greet our heroine. I was unfamiliar with the post-race victory routine, so I just followed my partners.

The look on their faces said it all. They registered the shock of a dream fully realized, intensified by the manner in which it had unfolded. Ipi Tombe seemed headed for an ignoble defeat, only to instantly bolt through the crowded pack from nowhere and not only win, but also obliterate her opposition. Their expressions erupted in amazement. Their eyes danced with delight. These folks knew they had a good filly, but even they were stunned by this performance.

The Zimbabweans were a resilient and hardy bunch, all real racing men. The leader Rob Davenport was a great owner, but another partner named Henk Leyenaar was the international embodiment of the Mr. Big

Shot syndrome. He was a heavyset man and he liked to throw his weight around, both physically and behaviorally. There he was on the track, front and center, cigar stub clenched firmly between his teeth, grabbing onto one end of a rope used to lead in the filly in.

I really didn't know where to stand or where to go until Rob Davenport handed the rope on the right side of the filly to me and made me grab on to it. "Don't let him push you around," Rob advised. Mike de Kock walked next to me on the rope for a while, then turned back to stand next to the jockey so he could talk to him. I remember, when walking side by side with de Kock, how much energy he exuded. It felt like what I imaged being in the middle of a rugby crush must be like. De Kock really got worked up over this race. He was actually roaring as he marched down the home stretch. I had never seen anybody with this much drive in racing before.

Ipi Tombe was voted Horse of the Year over Godolphin's own World Cup winner Moon Ballad. Her earnings of $1.2 million brought our Winter Carnival haul to $1,314,345. The filly was well into the black and her value as a racehorse and broodmare both increased significantly.

At year's end on the 2003 International Classification generated by the International Federation of Horseracing Authorities, Ipi Tombe was the highest rated middle-distance female turf runner in the world.

Ipi Tombe was flown to Kentucky and turned over to Elliott Walden, who raced her once in the Grade 3 Locust Grove Stakes at Churchill Downs. With Pat Day in the saddle, the filly proved the coziest of winners by a half-length, to push her fourteen-race career record to twelve wins and two seconds. Her record for our partnership was four wins in four starts. Sadly, the great filly suffered a bowed tendon and was retired.

What Ipi Tombe lacked in pedigree she made up for in racing talent. We sent her to be covered in Ireland by Sadler's Wells and offered her at the Tattersalls December Sales, which she topped on a bid of 850,000 guineas ($1,702,154) from an agent representing NetJets founder Richard Santulli and *Thoroughbred Daily News* publisher Barry Weisbord. Weisbord had talked us into spending a considerable sum to advertise the mare in the *TDN* and wound up selling himself with his own promotional idea. That was the biggest bang we ever got for our advertising dollar.

When all was said and done, her racetrack earnings of $1,416,273 for us and her sale price of $1,702,154 combined for gross receipts of $3,118,427, which was a fabulous return on an initial investment of $750,000.

Ipi Tombe helped put Mike de Kock's operation on top of the foreign trainers who were raiding Dubai, catapulted South African bloodstock into the consciousness of international racehorse buyers, and established Team Valor's brand name around the world as one of the leading prospectors of racing talent.

CHAPTER 20

The African Ladies

In the Xhosa language, *Ipi Tombe* means, "Where are the girls?" The answer was South Africa. Ipi Tombe served as the portal to an exciting new battlefield on the international Turf for my racing enterprise.

While Ipi Tombe was rewriting the record books in Dubai, I reached out for a second filly in the Republic. I offered a half-interest first to Gary Barber and, once again, he declined. One of his South African pals advised him, in no uncertain terms, to not buy the filly and went so far as to tell him that if he ignored his advice, the fellow would never talk horses with Gary again. He was adamant and made it personal.

There was a time in South African racing, before I became involved, when local horsemen had absolutely no faith in their homegrown product. Racing season after racing season, they had seen horses imported from Australia, South America, Great Britain and Europe dominate their homebreds. So it was not entirely shocking that they were down on their own stock.

A gorgeous filly named Crimson Palace, who was left with a crook in her neck after running into a stationary pole, had not let her injury prevent her from achieving stardom. She won three of her first four starts, including triumphs against older fillies and mares, during the equivalent of May in her 3-year-old season. Despite competing under weight-for-age conditions, she won a Graded race, run over 9 furlongs at the major racing venue in Cape Town, in course-record time.

She proved difficult to syndicate, especially after Los Angeles businessman Richard Masson decided against buying a 35-percent share. Once again I had to retain a large portion of her, which turned out to be another blessing in disguise. Getting stuck with large portions of animals that my racing partners had considered dubious on form was proving to be a financial boon to my operation.

Although Mike de Kock himself did not think much of the purchase initially, he revealed to me at the time of her debut in Dubai that Crimson Palace might be just as good as Ipi Tombe, who we had raced there the previous year. Frankly I did not know what to make of this. Could this really happen twice and in the span of a year?

In a lone start for us in January of 2004, Crimson Palace broke Ipi Tombe's course record for 9 furlongs when she won in a common gallop by nearly 5 lengths. A son of Sheik Mohammed wanted her desperately and de Kock was anxious to get a top Arab client. We were fully aware of how good she was and what she was capable of achieving. When we were offered a sum just shy of $2 million, it became too difficult to retain her. We took the money and ran.

Crimson Palace went on to become the first South African horse to win a Group race in England and the first South African horse to win a Grade 1 race in America when she triumphed in the $750,000 Beverly D Stakes at Arlington Park.

I was very happy to see her work out for Godolphin racing stable because it was a feather in our caps as sellers. We had a satisfied client in Sheik Mohammed and the achievement confirmed my faith in South African racehorses.

Crimson Palace had been let go by successful South African breeder and auction company owner Lionel Cohen. A few seasons later, when his filly Sun Classique began to show promise on the racecourses of South Africa, I tried to buy her. Cohen, like many owners in South African had gone to school on me. This time he refused to sell. Based on what I had proved with Crimson Palace, Cohen had gained the confidence to go on the road himself. Sun Classique duly raced against males to win the $5-million Sheema Classic in Dubai.

A year later, in a matter of a fortnight, I made further inroads into the South African market that would have a lasting positive influence on Team Valor and South Africa's racing and breeding industry.

Two days before Irridescence contested the Grade 1 SA Fillies Classic at Turffontein racecourse in Johannesburg, I struck a deal to buy the 3-year-old from Mike de Kock and two of his clients. After a dissatisfied buyer returned her when he discovered she was a cribber—a horse that bites a piece of wood in its stall and sucks in air—they were able to buy her cheaply at a yearling sale. She excited her partners early on when she won three races in a row, disappointed them by finishing sixth and seventh when highly tried in a pair of Cape Town Grade 1 races in very large fields, and managed to resuscitate her form a bit when she was a nice second in the Grade 2 Guineas back in Johannesburg.

Irridescence was extremely immature for a filly that was in the autumn of her 3-year-old season so she struck me as one to improve by leaps and bounds as she matured. I made a higher offer to de Kock than I had paid for Crimson Palace, who was a Grade 1 winner at the time, and I added a $65,000 bonus in the event that she won a Grade 1 for me. He grabbed it. I told de Kock that I wouldn't be able to pay him until the following week and he was fine with that. The filly would run for Team Valor in the Grade 1 on Saturday, with prize money going to the sellers.

I knew that offering her the day before she ran would make it impossible for me to sell enough shares ahead of time to cover the cost of the filly, but I had little choice. I offered her at a price of $375,000 on April Fools' Day and assured my clients that Irridescence was far from being a joke as a racehorse. I did not press anybody to participate.

When only 28 percent of the filly was sold prior to the race, Jeff Siegel was distraught. He told me that I was crazy and questioned why I would take such an unnecessary gamble. I told him that I had a good feeling about Irridescence in my gut.

Irridescence went off as the 3-to-1 second choice to odds-on Royal Approval, the filly that beat her in the Guineas and later won the South African Oaks. Irridescence easily handled her nemesis to win by more than 2 lengths. It was nearly 10 lengths back to the third horse.

It took me quite a while before I built up the nerve to call Mike de Kock and I told him so. "No, no, don't be silly," de Kock said. "Hey, my attitude is that whatever is good for my clients is good for me. I am a trainer with kids to feed and send to college. I know how owners feel when they sell a horse that wins a good race and they have left money on the table. But I am a trainer. I think differently. If you and your team are happy, then Mike de Kock is happy."

Irridescence proved to be a win-win situation, as de Kock and partners received an excellent price for the filly, they got to keep the prize money for the race and they earned a $65,000 bonus for winning a Grade 1. Team Valor got a filly that was worth a fortune and was easy to syndicate. Richard Masson and his wife Sue, having earlier changed their minds about buying into Crimson Palace, had seen enough to make them feel comfortable this time and they bought 35 percent of Irridescence at a somewhat higher price than the original Team Valor partners paid before she won the Grade 1. Everybody seemed happy.

On the same card at Turffontein, a 2-year-old gelding named Carnadore, which Mike de Kock advised us to buy earlier in the week, easily won the Grade 3 Protea Stakes for a partnership comprised of Team Valor, Gary Barber and his South African friend Larry Nestadt.

Carnadore (Champion Male at two) and Irridescence (Champion Filly at three) went on that season to win Equus Awards as the top members of their divisions.

A few weeks after Irridescence won the Grade 1, I traveled to South Africa to attend the National Yearling Sale for the first time. While in Johannesburg, my girlfriend/secretary Kathleen Jones and I were fortunate enough to be on hand to watch Irridescence easily account for the Grade 2 Gerald Rosenberg Memorial Stakes at Newmarket racecourse with a "pocket-sized" rider named Weichong Marwing in the tack.

I bought four fillies at the National Yearling Sale. As is my policy, I had Kathleen carry the catalogue while I looked at the horses without knowing or wanting to know their pedigrees. If I found something I liked, I reviewed its pedigree later in the evening back in our hotel room. My thought was that most of the pedigrees were unfashionable based on international commercial standards and, since I was only interested in buying athletes, I based my own standards on how they moved and looked.

A yearling I bought named Little Miss Magic went on to upset older fillies and mares at three to win the Grade 1 Empress Club Stakes at Turffontein for trainer Mike de Kock. Another yearling I bought named Sally Bowles missed by a nose in the Grade 1 Allan Robertson Fillies Championship Stakes at two, but she won multiple features, including the Grade 2 Guineas in Durban. Robin Bruss' brother Neil, a Zimbabwean émigré, trained Sally Bowles.

Irridescence added a win in the Grade 1 Woolavington Stakes later in her 3-year-old season and, in a career that saw her race in six different countries, went on to blaze a new trail for South African fillies around the world.

In the desert, Irridescence easily won the Balanchine Stakes in her prep for the Grade 1 Dubai Duty Free, which featured an increase in prize money from $2 to $5 million. Mike de Kock told my Chicago-based racing partner Ed Weil and me that he fully expected the filly to win the Duty Free because she had been training unbelievably well. In the paddock before the race, in which she was second favorite with the British bookies, the filly began to act up a bit. "When did she start doing this?" de Kock asked his wife and assistant trainer Diane, who said, "Last time."

Already flighty, Irridescence got spooked by something and she jinked toward the metal railing that enclosed the paddock, hitting it with her stifle and going lame in her right hind limb. Desperate to run the filly, de Kock grabbed her by the shank, took her onto the track, jogged her back and forth, and tried to show the racing officials that she was sound; nevertheless, the stewards had no choice but to scratch her. Thankfully, the racing association refunded our $50,000 entry fee. This incident was unquestionably the most frustrating experience of my career because, not only had Ed Weil, his wife Dia and I flown from the United States to Dubai, but we were also confident that Irridescence was really live to win a $3-million first prize.

By the following month, De Kock was able to get the filly going perfectly again and he sent her to Hong Kong for the Group 1 Audemars Piguet Queen Elizabeth II Cup, going a mile and a quarter on grass at the magnificent Sha Tin racecourse. Once again, Irridescence proved to be a handful, causing Weichong Marwing fits in the expansive paddock. Long Island racing partner Steve Karlin, who represented our ownership group, said, "She got so close to kicking the fence on the way out of the paddock, I told my wife Cynthee, 'Hey, let's just get the hell out of here. I can't take another one of these.'"

Employing enterprising tactics, Marwing sent Irridescence immediately to the front. Using a long, rhythmic stride, the tall, dark-coated filly bowled along in front on easy fractions of :26 2/5, :51 2/5 and 1:16 1/5. Marwing, a gifted athlete and jockey in the Bill Shoemaker/Pat Day mold, had a light hold as the filly tugged him along while she skimmed the rail. Shoemaker and Day had a knack of letting a front-runner feel as though they were running off, while they were, in fact, under control.

Turning into the stretch, Marwing purposely allowed the filly to drift a couple of paths so that he would not be stuck against the rail. Irridescence was running well within herself, her ears pricked, until Marwing set her down just before the furlong grounds. Although she set all the fractions, the filly ran each quarter-mile faster than the last with a one-tenth of a second difference between the second and third quarter, finishing her last two in :23 2/5 and :22 2/5.

Irridescence dug in for the fight, racing with her ears flat against her head, and managed to hold on to score by a nose over New Zealand import Best Gift, with English invader and race favorite Ouija Board another nose away in third. One step past the wire, Irridescence was second; a step later, she was third.

The filly provided her connections with a fabulous international victory and a brilliant career credential. In all honesty, the $1,030,000 first prize from the $1.8-million purse was not enough to make us forget the pain of missing the $5-million Dubai Duty Free. The APQE2 was a tour de force by Weichong Marwing, who created the win with an inspired, flawlessly timed ride.

Irridescence beat two terrific international racehorses: Best Gift, an earner of more than $2.5 million, was a top older horse in Hong Kong; and Ouija Board was one of the all-time greats of international racing. After winning the Oaks in both England and Ireland, she toured the world, winning two Breeders' Cups, the Vase in Hong Kong, the Prince of Wales's Stakes at Royal Ascot and the Nassau Stakes in England. She gained placings along the way, including in the Japan Cup (the richest race in Japan), the Sheema Classic (a $5-million race in Dubai) and the Prix de l'Arc de Triomphe (the richest race in Europe), for career earnings of $6.3 million. Her Galileo son Australia won the English and Irish Derbys in 2014.

Irridescence became unmanageable in France for John Hammond and failed in another Duty Free Bid for de Kock. But she closed out her career by becoming the first South African horse to earn black-type in a Group 1 race in England when she was third in the Falmouth Stakes, and she just missed winning the $750,000 Grade 1 Beverly D. Stakes in a photo finish.

After the Beverly D. Stakes, Richard Masson bought out Team Valor and partners to gain sole possession of the filly, who eventually joined his broodmare band in Kentucky. Between her earnings and what she sold for, her gross receipts totaled nearly $3.5 million, almost ten times her initial purchase price.

The same year I bought Crimson Palace, I also bought a group of mature racing fillies that were exported directly from South Africa to New York, where they spent sixty days in quarantine. Tara's Touch won the Grade 3 Royal North Stakes at Woodbine and the $100,000 Stravinsky Stakes at Keeneland. A few days after she was retired and sent to the farm, we received a call informing us that she broke a leg in a paddock and would have to be euthanized. Kathleen and I had bonded with the filly in a special way and her demise was a bitter pill to swallow.

Another in that South African draft was Secret Heart. A big mare standing 16 hands and 2 inches, with a deep girth and correct front limbs, she had been good enough to win a Listed race and place in several Grade 1 stakes at two and three. She was past her prime when she raced for us but, as a broodmare, she hit the heights before being found dead in her stall one morning from a coronary thrombosis.

We kept Pluck, the first foal out of Secret Heart, for racing. Todd Pletcher developed him into a top grass colt at 2, when he came into his own to win the Graded Summer Stakes over a mile at Woodbine, which qualified him for the $1-million Breeders' Cup Juvenile Turf. Leading up to that race at Churchill Downs Pluck did not train with a lot of enthusiasm. In his final workout, a filly, which was by his same sire More Than Ready, easily outpointed him. I was depressed. Pletcher told me not to read too much into it, as the filly More Than Real was an exceptional work horse. The day before Pluck contested the BC Juvenile Turf, More Than Real won the Breeders' Cup Juvenile Fillies by two lengths in a dominating performance.

I watched the Breeders' Cup Juvenile Turf at ground level on the track, not far from the starting gate. In what I consider to be the single most amazing instance of overcoming adversity in a race by any horse, let alone one of mine, Pluck—from his outside draw in the 12 hole—stumbled at the start, touching his nose on the ground and nearly dropping to his knees. By the time Garrett Gomez straightened him up, Pluck was last, fully five lengths behind the next-to-last runner in the twelve-horse field.

Rounding the first bend, a 32-to-1 shot named Rough Sailing slipped and slid across the course. Pluck had to swerve to avoid clipping Rosie Napravnik, the fallen rider. I threw my hands up in the air, signaling that I had given up. Less than twenty seconds into the race, Pluck already had his forward progress impeded twice. Following tepid, even, twelve-second furlongs through a half-mile that was run in slightly less than forty-eight seconds, Pluck was still last and still about five lengths behind the penultimate runner.

I could not tell by looking at the way Gomez was positioned in the saddle if he had given up and was going to ease him. Pluck continued to race with a big gap between himself and the last horse in the pack. Curving for home, Pluck suddenly caught up to the pack. He still had not passed a horse and he was still last at the quarter pole. But he was rolling.

I remember saying out loud, "Is this for real? Is something like this even possible?"

Gomez steered Pluck through a gap nearing the furlong pole, got into a strong rhythm with his mount and swung his right hand in circles to motivate the colt. Midway down the stretch, Pluck lifted and switched into hyper-speed, dashing by the field, striking the front and winning, geared down. With all of the incredulity he could muster, race caller Trevor Denman shouted, "And Pluck from last to first, winning it in a canter."

Secret Heart produced another successful homebred racehorse for Team Valor named Three Hearts, a daughter of Hat Trick, a Sunday Silence stallion that I bought in Japan. Three Hearts became a Graded stakes winner at Del Mar in 2014, the same year we lost her dam.

The year after my first visit to the National Yearling Sale, where I bought Grade 1 winner Little Miss Magic and near Group 1 winner Sally Bowles, I returned to the Germiston sales grounds and bought five more fillies. Among them were Stately, a subsequent Grade 3 winner at two, and Captain's Lover, a promising maiden winner at two. I thought Captain's Lover was something special, so I found her dam Sunshine Lover and bought her with a filly at her side, which I named Ebony Flyer.

Captain's Lover was a beautifully balanced bay that cost the equivalent of $27,000. Trained by young Justin Snaith, she won six of eight starts in South Africa, most notably the Grade 1 Cape Fillies Guineas, and was voted Champion Filly at three. As she matured, she became ornery. Leaving the paddock for the Guineas, she lashed out and cut a hind leg on a thorny rose bush. That was the start of her cantankerous behavior.

Sent to AndreFabre in France, Captain's Lover saw off a field of males in the Group 3 Prix du Pin, going seven furlongs. André told me that he thought she could be a Breeders' Cup Mile prospect, so he brought her back to Longchamp for the Group 1 Prix de la Forêt over the same seven furlongs. Winner Paco Boy crossed over in front of her at the break and she did well to be beaten a head for third. Fabre lost interest in bringing her to California for the Breeders' Cup after the Forêt.

It was decided to point Captain's Lover for the Grade 1 Matriarch Stakes at Hollywood Park. Her prep was supposed to be the Group 3 Prix Perth at Saint-Cloud, but there she found something to spook at in the pre-parade ring, flipped over backwards and injured her back. She had to be scratched.

Captain's Lover made it to America, but never recaptured her top form. Her best race was on a sloppy track at Monmouth, where Pletcher suggested that we keep her in the off-the-turf Matchmaker Stakes, which she won easily. She was retired as a broodmare in Kentucky as a major winner on three continents. We sold a half-interest in the champion to Gaynor Rupert of Drakenstein Stud in South Africa and bred her on Southern Hemisphere time to Giant's Causeway. After being sent back to South Africa, Captain's Lover had her foal, a filly named Song of Happiness, which sold for 3 million rand ($295,000), a record price in the Republic for a yearling filly sold at public auction.

Gaynor Rupert had good reason for buying half of Captain's Lover: she became involved in her half-sister Ebony Flyer, who had been a suckling when I bought her at her mother's side.

Probably the tallest horse Team Valor has ever owned is Ebony Flyer, who stood 17 hands and 2 inches. She had the big stride of a tall horse, but also the quickness of her sixteen-hand half-sister Captain's Lover. When she made her racing debut, in what was the North American equivalent of the late fall of her season at two, I was on hand. She ran five furlongs up the straight at Kenilworth.

The sight of this tall filly out-breaking her field and winning, eased up by more than 3 lengths, was hard to process because it just did not seem normal. That afternoon she beat Covenant, who already had a race under her girth and went on to become the best female sprinter of her generation, with wins in the 5-furlong Grade 2 Southern Cross Stakes, the 6-furlong Grade 2 Sceptre Stakes, and the Grade 1 Majorca Stakes going a mile. It was fun to follow her career since she was a half-sister to Secret Heart, the dam of Pluck and Three Hearts.

Ebony Flyer ran once more at two, easily taking a Listed race in Port Elizabeth. She was put away for a few months with the Grade 1 Cape Fillies Guineas in December as her goal. Snaith prepped her for the Guineas in the Grade 2 Odessa Stud Fillies Championship going 7 furlongs. It was the best performance of her career. She began from the unfavorable outside stall at Kenilworth in a field of thirteen. Bernard Fayd'herbe kept her three wide. When allowed to run, she slipped her field in the blink of an eye. She won eased up during the last half-furlong by five and a half lengths.

"I threw the reins at her entering the straight," Fayd'herbe said, "to get her to relax. Then I picked her up and squeezed on her just a little bit. She dropped low, accelerated and took off with me. What a feeling! Barry, I never call owners, but I had to tell you that I could have won by a city block. This filly is just unbelievable. She is a champion."

In an unprecedented move, the official handicapper for The Jockey Club raised her Merit Rating twenty-one points in one fell swoop. He rated her five pounds clear of the next filly on the list and only three pounds below the top-rated colt.

Charles Faull, an all-around racing and breeding genius if there ever was one, contacted me about buying into Ebony Flyer. His client was Mrs. Gaynor Rupert, who had invested substantial capital into developing a broodmare band, and stocked her fabulously well-appointed Drakenstein Stud with top stallions, including ex-Florida sire Trippi. But she had not yet managed to race a top-class runner.

Faull wanted Gaynor to have any part of Ebony Flyer that we were willing to sell because he truly believed that she was a horse the likes of which South Africa had not seen in years. And Faull was perhaps more familiar with the history of the South African Turf than anybody alive. Snaith wanted Gaynor to be involved because he thought Ebony Flyer could sweep all before her and he felt Gaynor should be a part of it. And she, like everybody else who had seen the Guineas trial, realized Ebony Flyer provided a gilt-edged opportunity to own a surefire classic winner.

Our partnership agreed, somewhat reluctantly, to take some money off the table while still controlling Ebony Flyer's destiny. Gaynor bought a third of the horse at a record price for a filly sold in training in South Africa. Gaynor and her husband Johann Rupert were extraordinarily wealthy and Gaynor was particularly discreet and careful about not being perceived as ostentatious in her spending habits. Her only concern in buying the filly was what others might think of the cost of this purchase.

As these things sometimes happen, Mike de Kock at the same time came up with a brilliant filly that trained 5,000 feet above sea level at a training center outside Johannesburg. Named Igugu, the Australian-born daughter of the Galileo, the world's most exciting young sire, won her first three starts and had a legitimate excuse when she was finally beaten. She finished second in a lucrative sales stakes to Hollywoodboulevard. which in a four-race skein won three features, including Grade 3 events going seven and a half and eight furlongs.

De Kock blamed a rushed preparation for Igugu's loss and vowed to have her spot-on for the Grade 1 Guineas. She was sent off at odds of 8to 5. The overwhelming choice, at odds of less than 1to 2, was Cape Town heroine Ebony Flyer.

In her previous start, Ebony Flyer ran seven furlongs on a course with a short stretch. For the mile Guineas, the course with the long stretch was used. Ebony Flyer raced fourth for much of the way, three wide, with Igugu right outside her.

Igugu was the first off the bridle. When Fayd'herbe niggled Ebony Flyer halfway down the long stretch, she surprised her rider by cutting with him and putting in her best move earlier than he had desired. Igugu was caught flat-footed and could not match Ebony Flyer's instant acceleration. The favorite opened up a three-and-a-half to four-length advantage and was never in danger of losing. Igugu was able to cut into her margin and finished a length and a quarter behind Ebony Flyer at the wire.

De Kock, who believed Igugu could be the best filly he ever trained, dressed down jockey Anthony Delpech and then blamed the long van ride from Johannesburg to Cape Town for Igugu's loss. De Kock had correctly sized up Igugu and she went on to prove it in spades, winning the rest of her seven South African starts, including four Grade 1s, among them the J & B Met. But on the day of the Guineas, his filly was caught for speed and could not cope with Ebony Flyer. They were two of the most talented fillies ever to race in South Africa.

After the race, connections and fans of Igugu were bloodied but unbowed and expected to exact revenge. The two never met again, although Igugu's connections never stopped trying to egg Justin Snaith and me into a rematch.

The Guineas was a great day for the racing partners of Ebony Flyer. Leading the horse in were: Anant and Vanashree Singh, long-time South African racing partners with Team Valor, who became my good friends; Gaynor Rupert, winning her first South African classic race; and Frank Michelsen, a Team Valor partner in Sunshine Lover and ace handicapper from Massachusetts. Justin Snaith, who had won the race for the third time in the last four years, joined in the celebration, as did his brother, stable manager Jono, and their dad, ex-leading trainer Chris.

Ebony Flyer gave her Team Valor-owned broodmare Sunshine Lover a second Grade 1 Cape Fillies Guineas winner, and pedigree pundits scratched their heads to come up with any other mare in the history of racing whose first two foals were classic winners of the same race. The syndicated producer was voted Broodmare of the Year for her feat.

Considerable discussion in the press, on Internet message boards and among the principals and their advisors about Ebony Flyer's next start, centered around which trip would prove most effective for the filly. I thought seven-eighths of a mile, while Snaith and Faull both reckoned a mile and a quarter would suit her and Gaynor remained undecided.

There were plenty of traditional races available to the filly, such as the Grade 1 Paddock Stakes and the Grade 1 Majorca Stakes, but I opted for the historic Queen's Plate, which took place a month after the Guineas over the same course and against all-aged runners. No 3-year-old filly had turned the trick.

I decided that Ebony Flyer had the talent to compete at the highest level in Europe and I planned to send her to Andre Fabre in Chantilly.

If I had owned 100 percent of Ebony Flyer, I would never have run her again in South Africa. But my two biggest partners were South Africans. When I first started racing with Anant Singh, he told me that a man of color had never won the biggest races in South Africa and he wanted to be the first. Gaynor had invested a substantial amount in order to gain some traction in South Africa with a headline horse.

Since The Ruperts, through their fine wine brand L'Ormarins, sponsored the Queen's Plate and the 150th running of the race was scheduled exactly a month after the Guineas, I decided to have Ebony Flyer run for the last time in South Africa in Gaynor's race. It was the least I could do.

Run over the course and distance of the Guineas, the Grade 1 fixture was contested under weight-for-age conditions. If successful, Ebony Flyer would become the first 3-year-old filly to win the race throughout its 150 editions. In fact, only a couple of 3-year-old fillies had ever managed to finish in the top three.

Once again, Ebony Flyer had popped a very disadvantageous draw, landing the twelve in a field of fourteen. This was the third time, in as many starts at 3 that she drew outside on a course that was heavily biased in favor of low draws. It was as if God himself wanted to see how good the filly was by testing her with wide draws. Who knew he had so much interest in horseracing!

Heading the field for the race was Pocket Power, who was the most accomplished horse ever to race in the Republic and sought an unprecedented fifth win in the race; Mother Russia, who was a champion older filly trained by Mike de Kock and sought her fourth Grade 1 win; and Past Master, who was the "now" horse. Interestingly, Ebony Flyer, Pocket Power and Past Master all were sired by Jet Master.

After having to be used early to overcome her wide draw, Ebony Flyer never landed a blow, stalling midway down the stretch after race winner Mother Russia momentarily intimidated her. She was able to muster a good finish for third place and she missed second by a fast-diminishing, three-quarters of a length. In total she was beaten three lengths. As disappointing as it was to not see the filly compete for the win, her performance was still one for the ages. Behind her, she had multiple Horse of the Year-winner Pocket Power and next-time-out Grade 1 J & B Met winner Past Master.

Ebony Flyer accomplished something no other filly had been able to do in recent memory. In the previous decade, Team Valor had owned all of the best internationally performed fillies from South Africa except one. None of them compared with Ebony Flyer and that included Ipi Tombe, which is something I never expected to be able to say.

After the race, Fayd'herbe told us the filly had made a whistling noise while pulling up. I had South Africa's leading vet John McVeigh scope her and he discovered that the filly suffered from a partially paralyzed vocal cord. She had not been getting all of her air. In retrospect, this explained why Ebony Flyer had slowed down perceptibly in the Guineas and why she did not run to my expectations in the Queen's Plate.

The taller the horse, the longer the vocal cord and the more prone it is toward paralysis. I have seen horses that were completely sound in the wind one day become compromised the next. When Gaynor had the filly vetted for purchase, her throat was normal. Six weeks later, it was not normal. We canceled our foreign plans. Ebony Flyer underwent two operations to open her airway.

When Ebony Flyer came back to the races, she once again showed her brilliance. In eight races, she won four times and was second twice. She added Grade 1 wins in the Majorca over a mile and in the SA Fillies Sprint over six furlongs. For as much brilliance as she showed in these Grade 1 races, it paled in comparison to the race she ran when winning the seven-furlong Odessa Stud Stakes. On that day and in that race, she was at her absolute best. If she had been sound of wind and been able to develop from there, she would have had a chance to become an international legend. As it was, when not 100 percent, she was still good enough to win a classic race over one of South Africa's greatest racehorses in Igugu. I consider Ebony Flyer to be the best filly we ever had our hands on.

CHAPTER 21

Looking Abroad

My interest in international racing, both human and equine, was born from a love of the Olympics. Foreign runners with exotic names like Paavo Nurmi and Emil Zatopek, complete with handles like "The Flying Finn" and "The Czech Locomotive," running in faraway sounding places like Antwerp and Amsterdam, captured my imagination as a youth.

The simple fact that they were foreign made them interesting to me. When a foreign runner of prominence, such as Australian Miler John Landy, would come to Los Angeles to race, I made sure my dad took me to the Coliseum to watch him run.

At the same time that TV began to embrace the mile run after Roger Bannister broke the four-minute barrier in 1954, TV also brought horseracing to American households. My mom and dad were none too happy when Santa Anita and Hollywood Park telecasts made it so easy for their son to gain familiarity with local horses.

Just as I had done with track runners, I gravitated toward horses from distant lands. And instead of only being able to read historical reportage about the Irish import Noor beating Citation or the Argentine import Kayak II challenging Seabiscuit, I was able to watch horses like English import St. Vincent develop into a champion grass horse in Southern California on our own television.

My favorite horse was Swaps, who in 1955 and 1956 set many American and world records on dirt in Southern California. But I liked watching turf racing better than racing on dirt.

Racing on the turf produces more exciting exhibitions of raw speed. Dirt racing is all about power; grass racing is about speed. Like a jumbo-sized passenger jet as it gradually builds up momentum to reach a speed fast enough to take off, a horse that races on dirt powers through the track. Like a Formula 1 car that streaks from zero to sixty in 1.9 seconds, a horse that races on grass uses instant acceleration to skim across the top of the turf.

As an old-time trainer later explained it to me, horses have to run *through* dirt, but they run on top of turf. I developed a real taste for the turn of foot displayed by top foreign grass horses when they exploded in the stretch.

In Argentina, this brand of finishing speed is called *brio*, appropriated from the Italian word meaning verve or energy. Nothing is more prized in an Argentine horse than *brio*. No runners in the world produce *brio* quite like the Europeans and, more specifically, the French.

I loved to see a horse like St. Vincent come from England to dominate American runners on the grass at Santa Anita. I was, it must be said, just as enthralled, during this era of St. Vincent and Swaps, to read about the exploits of Ribot, the Italian wonder horse that won all sixteen of his lifetime starts including back-to-back renewals of the Prix de l'Arc de Triomphe.

In the immediately ensuing years, I followed grass and foreign racing. I followed with rapt attention when Ogden Phipps experimented with Buckpasser on the grass. I thought a lot about what Swaps, Dr. Fager and Secretariat might have been able to do if they had been trained and raced exclusively in Europe, since each won their only grass start in such a captivating manner. I kept up with the career of Sea-Bird in France. I followed the exploits of Sir Ivor in Europe. And when I first started writing about the Turf professionally, I remember being bowled over by the performances of the great grass fillies Allez France and Dahlia. My first foreign report for *The Blood-Horse* was about Nijinsky, the North American-bred that became the first Triple Crown winner in England since Bahram 35 years earlier. With rare exceptions, grass runners trained in America did not show this same brand of finishing speed.

When I was in a position to go abroad and see how horses were trained at Ballydoyle by Vincent O'Brien, at The Curragh by Dermot Weld, in Chantilly by Alec Head and in Lamorlaye by Francois Boutin, I learned that their training had everything to do with why these foreign-based horses were able to perform better on turf than our American-trained horses. I soon came to believe that, all things being equal, any horse trained in Great Britain or Europe would outperform its peer in America. I have never had reason to change my mind.

Halfway through the year 2007, I decided to buy out my longtime friend and partner Jeff Siegel. When I took sole ownership of Team Valor, I added International to the name to signify a shift in focus to acquiring more racing stock abroad, as well as occasionally racing horses in their country of origin. In the case of South Africa, a permanent base was established.

I had sensed that the world was going "flat" with the revolution of the Internet and I had always been more interested in prospecting talent abroad rather than locally because of the variety of horses available in other countries.

By 2007, doing business in foreign lands had become much easier. Dealing in foreign horses certainly was nothing new to either Jeff or me, but there had been an increasing divide between Jeff's vision for the company and my own.

Jeff wanted to concentrate on America and I wanted to concentrate abroad. Jeff wanted a large, locally based stable full of "everyday" horses that could provide a steady stream of action and could be turned over if they did not work out. I wanted more of a boutique stable filled with potential stars.

The pressure of trying to prospect, buy, syndicate, develop and race future stars put too much pressure on Jeff. I was getting weary of the protracted discussions on the subject. My choice was to either disband the stable, which I came close to doing, or to buy out Jeff. I chose the latter, even though at the time it was difficult to justify financially.

In the initial six months after I bought out Jeff, Team Valor International caught fire, winning eleven stakes races before year's end. Tellingly, eight of them were with horses that either were racing abroad or had been bought in a foreign country.

South African runners accounted for six of the stakes wins, both abroad and at home. Captain's Lover became Team Valor's first South African classic winner in the Grade 1 Cape Fillies Guineas. Jazzy had been a top female sprinter in South Africa, but her career was compromised by bleeding. Lasix figured to help extend her career in America. I was also anxious to try her on the main track because she was by a Mr. Prospector grandson out of a Halo-line mare that cried out for dirt. She easily transferred her turf form to dirt, winning the Grade 2 Gallant Bloom Stakes sprinting at Belmont Park.

Domestic highlights in 2008 were provided by a $4,000 yearling that Captain Bodgit's trainer Gary Capuano selected for a Maryland client. We bought Unbridled Belle after she won her debut and, in 2008, campaigned her to victories in the Grade 1 Beldame Stakes at Belmont Park and the $1-million Delaware Handicap. She earned nearly $2 million before retirement.

The next six years were more of the same, with a mix of foreign and domestic horses winning major races for our "international" stable. Each year, however, the number of domestically acquired stakes winners was dwarfed by that of those acquired abroad.

In 2008, TVI won fourteen stakes, eight of which were won by horses we bought in America.

In 2009, TVI won nineteen stakes, seven of which were won by domestic horses.

In 2010, TVI won eighteen stakes, with only four won by horses we bought domestically.

In 2011, TVI won seventeen stakes, with six won by horses bought domestically.

Then in 2012 and 2013, TVI won eleven and ten stakes, with only a single horse having been bought domestically.

In 2008, the first full year of operating the stable on my own, Team Valor won four Grade 1 races. In the United States, 3-year-old Visionaire won the Grade 1 King's Bishop Stakes at Saratoga. I exported him to stand in South Africa because I liked his conformation and wanted to breed mares to him there. He was a champion first-season sire based on progeny earnings and winners in the 2014-2015 season.

In that same 2008 season in South Africa, we won Grade 1 races with the privately bought Jet Master filly Stratos. National Yearling Sale buy On Her Toes took the Grade 1 Allan Robertson Filly Championship. Privately bought Russian Sage took the Grade 1 Daily News 2000 for our group and was voted Champion Colt at three at season's end.

The year 2008 showed the breadth of the stable's reach, as South African Captain's Lover went to France and beat males, sprinting at Longchamp in the Group 3 Prix du Pin, and South African Alexandra Rose ventured to Los Angeles to take the Grade 3 Monrovia Handicap, sprinting at Santa Anita.

In the late fall of 2008, I was captivated by the rhythmic action that the 2-year-old English-based colt Gitano Hernando displayed at Wolverhampton on the all-weather track. Horses that move really well usually have difficulty producing a beautiful action on a synthetic surface. I became obsessed with him, but was getting nowhere in trying to buy him through my usual channels.

Gitano Hernando's owner Walther Jacobs had recently died. One would have expected the colt to be buyable, but Jacobs' widow was reluctant to part with him. I had become friendly with her stepson, Andreas Jacobs, whose father had developed German-based Gestüt Fährhof into a leading stud farm and later extended his holdings to include Newsells Park Stud in England. At public auctions of breeding stock, both in Kentucky and England, Walther Jacobs had acquired several of Team Valor's retired racing fillies for his broodmare band. It seems as though we shared a similar taste in horses.

I called Andreas and asked if he could help me buy Gitano Hernando. I cheekily suggested that his stepmother probably should be selling the colt, rather than racing it, in order to put the estate of her husband in order. Nothing happened for a while, but after several weeks had passed, Andreas Jacobs advised me to get back in touch with Newsells. We struck a deal immediately. I wanted the horse badly and I overpaid for him based on what he had done so far. But I felt comfortable with the deal. I left the colt in England with his young trainer Marco Botti, who hailed from a prominent Italian racing family.

Gitano Hernando developed quickly into a world-class racehorse. I sized him up as a potential World Cup runner in Dubai because the spectacular new Meydan racecourse had installed a synthetic track.

In the fall of the colt's season at three, I asked Botti to prepare him to run at Santa Anita in a $300,000 Grade 1 against older runners, going nine furlongs on a synthetic track. The colt arrived from England in peak condition, thanks in great part to administering an electrolyte protocol developed by our veterinary consultant Dr. Rob Holland. On the same weekend as the Grade 1 Goodwood Stakes, there was a Grade 2 race on the grass that Botti was more interested in for the colt. Botti lacked confidence in the colt and wanted the easier option. He prevailed upon a young Team Valor employee named Aron Wellman to talk me into running in the easier race. I held my ground as I was convinced Gitano Hernando would be a freak on synthetic tracks.

Kieren Fallon had been back riding for less than a month after being reinstated following an 18-month ban for substance abuse. I gave him the call. Three-year-old Gitano Hernando saw off by a neck the highly accomplished 4-year-old Colonel John, who a year earlier had won the Grade 1 Travers and Grade 1 Santa Anita Derby. Kentucky Derby winner Mine That Bird also was in his wake. Much to his credit, Botti admitted that I had made the right decision. He expressed his gratitude to me. *Timeform* wrote that Gitano Hernando "rewarded Team Valor's have-a-go attitude with a determined success" and provided "his trainer with his most high-profile win and his rider with his biggest success since returning in September."

When the controversial Chechen Republic leader Ramzan Kadyrov offered about $3 million, we decided to sell the horse. Gitano Hernando subsequently scored a lucrative victory in the $3-million Singapore Airlines Gold Cup, earning back nearly half of his purchase price and making for a very happy customer. Star of Cozzene embarrassingly had flopped for his new owners, so when Crimson Palace and Gitano Hernando won Grade 1 races we took this as good news, because it showed buyers of expensive horses that they could receive good value from a horse bought from Team Valor.

Gitano Hernando was owned in part by Gary Barber, who was a willing participant in many of my foreign adventures. Although a couple of his South African pals had talked him out of buying Ipi Tombe and Crimson Palace, Gary and I campaigned some terrific foreign-bought horses in other locales. including bringing several to America. Interestingly, one of the fellows who had put Gary off of buying Ipi Tombe subsequently became a silent partner with Gary in several Team Valor horses.

Impressed with what Team Valor had done importing fillies from Europe and winning well with them in Southern California, Gary asked our mutual trainer Jenine Sahadi if he could partner with us on some horses. Among the very first we raced together was The Deputy. It took the colt four starts to break his maiden as a 2-year-old in England, but when he did win, going seven furlongs at Epsom, he looked promising. Five days later, when he was brought back in a lucrative stakes sponsored by a sales company, he demonstrated *brio* by flashing home, seemingly from nowhere, to miss by a couple of noses. He looked like Nureyev did when he sliced through the English Two Thousand Guineas field.

I arrived a few days later at his stable in Lambourn, England. I inspected him for less than three minutes. He looked like an American horse. He was well balanced, with a beautiful profile, clean limbs, an athletic walk and great presence. He was a very easy horse to buy.

In what seemed like déjà vu, The Deputy from his very first workout trained like he had been in America all of his life and acted out a scenario first fashioned a dozen years earlier by Martial Law. His first breeze was an eye-opener and each breeze thereafter was a treat to behold.

When I realized how good The Deputy was, I located his dam and persuaded Steve Johnson and Dr. Ira Mersack of Margaux Farm to buy her for about $60,000 and give me a third for my part in identifying the quality of The Deputy and finding the mare. We bred this Shadwell Stud cull Manfath to Kingmambo and sold her that same year at Keeneland in November for $650,000. The foal she was carrying, named King Kamehameha, won the Japan Derby, was syndicated for a record $20.5 million and became a leading stallion in Japan.

The Deputy was part of a gifted group of 3-year-olds that raced in the Southern California in 2000 and won three of his four starts, losing only the Grade 2 San Felipe to subsequent Kentucky Derby winner Fusaichi Pegasus. We knew he loved the dirt, but we started him first on grass because of the scheduling and he beat an exceptionally promising Bobby Frankel-trained colt named Promontory Gold in the Hill Rise Stakes.

Switched to dirt, The Deputy wired his field to win the Grade 2 Santa Catalina Stakes beating High Yield, which went on in March to win the Grade 1 Fountain of Youth at Gulfstream Park and in April to win the Grade 1 Blue Grass Stakes at Keeneland, and Captain Steve, which went on that season to win the Grade 1 Swaps Stakes and retire with earnings of more than $6.6 million after winning the Grade 1 Dubai World Cup.

The Deputy ran Fusaichi Pegasus to three-quarters of a length in the Grade 2 San Felipe and rebounded to take the Grade 1 Santa Anita Derby over War Chant, which won the Grade 1 Breeders' Cup Mile. The Deputy achieved a career-best 109 Beyer speed figure in the Santa Anita Derby.

On the tote board for the Kentucky Derby, The Deputy sat as the nine-to-two second choice to five-to-two Fusaichi Pegasus. Coming up the escalator from the walking ring to the box section at Churchill Downs I told my Chicago racing partner Ed Weil that The Deputy had "melted away."

In the days leading up to the Run for the Roses, Jenine Sahadi understandably had her focus diverted from the task at hand by a media hungry for content about the tall, confident, attractive University of Southern California graduate's quest to become the first female to train a Kentucky Derby winner. Dr. Alex Harthill, who kept his hands off of Captain Bodgit, couldn't comply this time, as he thought Jenine had lost her way. God only knows what Harthill did to The Deputy.

The Deputy never ran a step in the Derby, finishing fourteenth of nineteen. He never ran again, due to a bowed tendon. He was syndicated, stood without any success at Margaux Farm and eventually wound up way off the beaten trail at a small farm in Iowa. Jenine Sahadi, no doubt aided in her development of the colt by his jockey and morning exercise partner Chris McCarron, did a masterful job with The Deputy until just a few days before the Derby and she deserved a better finish to his career. She was totally in tune with the colt and nobody could have achieved more with him.

Another foreign horse Gary Barber and Team Valor raced in partnership named Sweet Stream caught my attention at two by winning an Italian conditions race going seven furlongs by an astounding fourteen lengths. When she tested positive for the tick-borne blood disease Equine Piroplasmosis, we treated her medically, but the drugs began to take its toll on her health and we stopped it.

Since the filly was barred from import to the United States, I offered my racing partners their money back. All of them took it except for four guys. Gary, who owned half of the filly, asked if the buy-back gesture included him and I said no, pointing out that he was my partner not a client. So we turned the filly over to English-born John Hammond, a Chantilly-based trainer who gave the filly a lot of time to recover.

Sweet Stream returned to racing in August, required four starts to win a small race and took hold in a Listed event at Saint-Cloud at the close of the flat campaign in France by winning in a manner that inspired a turf writer to dub her "The Frightening Finishing Machine."

Hammond, a conservative, well-read and highly intelligent fellow, phoned me one day in the fall and said he wanted to run the filly in the Group 1 Prix Vermeille, which is the most important trial for sophomore fillies preparing for the Prix de l'Arc de Triomphe. Sweet Stream had only won a pair of Listed races and had a single Group placing, which she achieved in her most recent start when a 50 to 1 long shot, so the idea seemed outlandish. When Hammond phoned back two days before the race and told me that I should consider flying to France for the race, I very nearly did so, given his ultra-conservative nature.

This was the same John Hammond that once phoned me from the tarmac of a French airport saying he had second thoughts about sending our colt Dive for Cover to Ireland for the Derby. I quashed that notion and the colt ran a bang-up fourth. But it demonstrated beyond a shadow of a doubt that he was very conservative and did not like taking shots in important races.

I should have listened to John about the Prix Vermeille, because Sweet Stream at odds of thirty to one rallied the length of the Longchamp stretch up the rail to score a huge upset over two-time German staying champion Royal Fantasy and Pride. The last-named filly would go on to amass earnings of just under $4 million, win the Group 1 Champion Stakes in England, the Group 1 Hong Kong Cup and the Group 1 Grand Prix de Saint-Cloud, while falling only a neck shy of beating Rail Link when second in the Arc de Triomphe.

Hammond personally delivered the rose-gold plate from the Vermeille to me in Kentucky and embarrassingly revealed that he had dropped it, causing a scar on the surface of the trophy. We sent the trophy to a specialist in Cincinnati to restore it to its original state and it took nearly a year for them to match the gold. When we picked it up, we noticed that we could still see signs of the insult. But when I occasionally eyeball that plate, the dimple brings a smile to my lips, as it serves to remind me of what a great guy John Hammond is and how he won the Prix Vermeille for us.

Sweet Stream came back the next season to win the Group 2 Park Hill Stakes, a race known in England as the "Fillies St. Leger." She was a convincing length-and-a-half winner of the Doncaster race contested over fourteen and a half furlongs. At season's end, Sweet Stream was accorded championship honors as the highest weighted older staying filly or mare in England in 2006.

The Group 1-winning champion may have lacked quality in her pedigree in both her male and female lineage; however, she was a stunning beauty, with true quality. She gave one the impression that she was capable of producing a classic winner if mated properly. We bred Sweet Stream to my favorite European stallion Monsun, consigned her to Tattersalls' December Sale in England and she was knocked down on a bid equivalent to $2.3 million. Her sale price and earnings of more than $625,000 realized gross receipts of slightly under $3 million. The foal she was carrying at the time she was sold became the highest-weighted staying filly of her generation in Germany.

Gary and I, having experienced good fortune racing an Italian horse, bought another one in 2002 in Becrux (pronounced Beck Rucks), named after the second-brightest star in the Southern Cross constellation. He won his first three starts at two by wide margins, employing a very athletic action that led me to believe he might be the right tool to win the rich United Arab Emirates Derby. We sent him to Mike de Kock in Dubai.

In his first four outings for us—three in Dubai and one in New York—he ran dismally, except for a wide-margin allowance win on dirt at Nad al Sheba. When de Kock sent him to Kiaran McLaughlin in New York, it was with this comment "Barry, he's not what you think he is," clearly meaning the colt lacked quality. After a terrible race in New York, Becrux underwent a myectomy to cure a problem of displacing his soft palate and he was flown to Del Mar to contest the Oceanside Stakes. Kiaran and Neil Drysdale both trained for Shadwell Stud, so Kiaran sent the colt to him for this race.

Becrux proved a handy winner of the Oceanside. We were so happy to have the horse in California and running well that we made a difficult decision and left him with Neil Drysdale, much to the disappointment of Kiaran McLaughlin.

Becrux turned out to be a handful to train. Neil Drysdale never met a colt he didn't want to geld unless it was A.P. Indy, his Horse of the Year, and during my years with him he tried, sometimes successfully, to get me to agree to castrate a lot of them. I once told him when he died and arrived at the pearly gates that St. Peter would give him a choice—"Submit to castration and enter; or remain whole and go straight to hell!"

In all my years in racing as an owner-manager, I have agreed to castrate many colts, none with any discernible degree of improvement. Horses generally are "cut" in hopes that the elimination of male hormones will change their behavior, attitude, weight and over-muscling.

On the other hand, I ordered two horses cut and it turned around their careers. I am not pointing this out to make myself look smart, but to illustrate that when most trainers ask for a horse to be gelded it is to make their jobs easier and not necessarily as a last resort to cure a problem. When I had the two horses in question cut, it was to address an actual problem. One colt's testicles hung too low and interfered with his movement. After being cut he went on to win a Grade 3 and place in a Grade 1 at three. The other was Becrux.

Becrux was gelded because his behavior was worsening and his locomotion was in jeopardy because his neck started to become too thick and cresty like a breeding stallion. He had been a Champion Colt at 2 and a stakes winner in America, but I gelded him anyway because I thought he would never fulfill his potential unless he could keep his mind on business and move his body freely.

The collaborative teamwork that is essential in a successful racing enterprise was never more in evidence than with Becrux in 2006. My decision as the racing manager to geld the colt, Drysdale's vision in training him and his jockey's brilliance in riding him combined for the biggest day in the life of Becrux. The attitude adjustment was evident when in his first three races after being gelded, Becrux had two wins and a close second.

Charlie Whittingham's genius as a trainer shone brightest when he honed in on a goal with a horse. Neil Drysdale was his most gifted student. Neil reckoned that Becrux could win the $1-million Woodbine Mile. So after Becrux won the Wickerr Stakes in his comeback at Del Mar, Drysdale sent him up early to Canada, prepping him in the Grade 2 Play the King Stakes going seven furlongs and Becrux showed a real liking for the Woodbine course when second beaten a half-length.

A couple of days before the Sunday renewal of the $1-million Mile, which fell between the end of Del Mar and the beginning of Santa Anita, Corey Nakatani's agent begged off the mount, saying his rider had injured a collar bone, an occurrence that did not stop him from calling a local golf course to request a tee time for the following day. This same agent, without missing a beat, recommended his other rider Patrick Valenzuela as a substitute, even though P. Val had not ridden in a race in exactly two months.

Barber did not want to ride P. Val under any circumstances because of the rider's rap sheet for substance abuse, Drysdale wanted to ride Victor Espinoza and Team Valor wanted to ride P. Val. With Espinoza out of contact, P. Val got the nod and, in what must have been an unprecedented circumstance, the California stewards did not stand in the way of Valenzuela obtaining a license to ride in Canada, even though the jockey was barred from riding in California because he had failed to comply with documentation that his body was clear of drugs at the time.

In communicating with my partners, I expressed my position on riding P. Val as follows: "We know he is absolutely nuts, but if you are ever going to ride the guy, now is the time, while he is fresh, healthy and motivated. Can you imagine how hard he is going to try to win this race? We'd be nuts ourselves if we didn't avail ourselves of this opportunity."

Before the race when I went to the jocks' room adjacent to Woodbine's administrative offices below the ground level of the racetrack to meet Valenzuela, I was relieved to see him physically present, which was never a given with him. Secondly, I was pleased to see how fit, coherent and vibrant he appeared.

P. Val had only recently emerged from detox at a famous private residential rehab facility in Pasadena, where California racing officials tried to obtain urine and hair follicle samples to test for drugs. I was shocked to see that P. Val had no facial or scalp hair, other than the tiniest tuft of hair with a thin band around it protruding from the base of his otherwise shaved skull.

Drysdale had walked the course and informed P. Val that it was soft near the rail. I told P. Val that we chose him because he was such a good position rider, that the course was playing for speed and to lay as close as possible without using his horse. I suggested that he wait as long as possible to cut his mount loose.

P. Val, as the great athletes do, rose to the occasion and gave Becrux the ride of his life, positioning him beautifully, getting him to the front by a head within the shadow of the wire and, having saved just a little bit extra, lifting him across the line to score by a neck.

Gary and I have owned and raced a lot of good horses together and won a lot of good races, but I don't think I ever saw him happier than when we walked on either side of Becrux and led him into the winners' circle after winning the Woodbine Mile.

In addition to Gary Barber, other clients of trainer Jenine Sahadi that showed interest in racing foreign horses with us were Richard Masson and his wife Sue Ann. The Massons' best horse raced in partnership with Team Valor was the South African Champion Irridescence, but she was not the only one.

River Belle had won her first two starts as a 2-year-old in England. She burst home with a rush to win her debut very impressively by three and a half lengths. She came back in two weeks to take the Group 3 Princess Margaret at Ascot under Kieren Fallon. Team Valor bought River Belle in partnership with The Massons and Texans Bill and Corrine Heiligbrodt. In a pair of Group 1 races in England, River Belle failed to hit the board for her new connections.

River Belle cleared U. S. quarantine in a depleted state, so I sent her to Dr. Barry Eisaman's Ocala training center with instructions to fatten her up and send her in when she was ready to resume serious training. When Todd Pletcher ran her at Saratoga in August at three it was her first start in eleven months.

River Belle ran well in her first three outings for Pletcher, winning an allowance race at The Spa, running a close third in the Grade 3 Boiling Springs at Monmouth Park and putting up a gritty display of courage when beaten a length into third for the Grade 1 Queen Elizabeth II Challenge Cup at Keeneland.

I did not feel that the filly was getting the right kind of ride. She was a difficult filly to handle, she was quirky and Kieren Fallon obviously knew what it took to make her win. In the late fall of 2004, Churchill Downs encountered a jockey strike over insurance issues. I thought our filly could win the Grade 2 Mrs. Revere Stakes, but since top jockeys had trouble riding her, I feared the worst if she had to be piloted by one of the strike-breakers, a motley crew consisting of exercise riders, has-beens and never-will-bes. So I called Fallon and asked for a favor.

Fallon not only was leading rider that season in England, he was rapidly closing in on 200 wins and he would have to give up some prize rides over that weekend near the end of the flat season. But the six-time British champion jockey did me a solid by agreeing to come to Kentucky for the weekend.

In what I count as one of the very best rides one of our horses ever received, Fallon put the nose of River Belle squarely on the wire first. He virtually carried her to the line and positioned her head for the picture of the filly's racing life. One step before and one step after the line, the filly was a loser, but right on the line itself—on that thin, elegant span of wire—River Belle was a winner. And so was Fallon in every sense of the word.

I will never forget the winners' circle, as there were so many "suits" from the Churchill Downs' executive offices on hand, it looked like a board meeting. I thought the head honcho Tom Meeker was going to kiss me he was so happy that we had managed to save his weekend of racing and to do it with an internationally famous rider.

Gypsy's Warning was another top-class filly Team Valor raced in partnership with the Massons. A beautifully molded filly that simply dripped with class, the granddaughter of Storm Cat had won the Grade 1 Thekwini, South Africa's season-ending mile race that invariably crowns the champion filly at two.

In her case, she was overlooked for honors as her win was considered a fluke. I thought her Thekwini victory was absolutely sensational, as she employed an Ipi Tombe-like turn of foot to come from last to win by a neck.

She beat two runners that Mike de Kock would later win importantly with in Zirconeum, who was best at three in the Grade 1 Woolavington Stakes, and Mother Russia, who was a winner of four Grade 1 races including the Queen's Plate over males.

The only reason Gypsy's Warning did not win an Equus Award at two was that her owner and trainer were not well known. Once again, the owners did not want to sell, but Robin Bruss and I crafted a deal that appealed to them. They were not wealthy people, but they enjoyed their racing. So we allowed them to share in a percentage of the filly's earnings during her 3-year-old season without having to pay any expenses and we put their names on the racing program. They went to her races at three and they had a ball.

Racing under the tutelage of the no-nonsense veteran Ormond Ferraris, who was Mike de Kock's mentor, Gypsy's Warning ran six times for our group in South Africa, never being worse than third, winning half of her starts and winning or placing in three Grade 1 races, including a win going nine furlongs in the Grade 1 SA Fillies Classic.

Transferred to Graham Motion in America, Gypsy's Warning ran five times for our group in 2010, capping her season with a Grade 1 victory when dropped from a mile and a quarter to a mile for the prestigious Matriarch Stakes at Hollywood Park.

It was a great victory for the filly, for our racing partners and for the South African breeding and racing industry. And it made up in part for what happened the month before at Santa Anita in the Grade 1 Yellow Ribbon Stakes in which she was backed down to favoritism at odds of two to one.

In the previous race on the card, Mike Smith had ridden Zenyatta to an amazing nineteenth victory without defeat. The post-race celebration was both lengthy and emotional. In the walking ring before the Yellow Ribbon, Smith understandably was still reveling in the victory. My employee Aron Wellman, a big Zenyatta fan, spent his time in the walking ring reliving the race, instead of representing the interests of Gypsy's Warning's owners by getting Smith to focus on the task at hand.

So for the only time in her twenty-one-race career, Gypsy's Warning set the pace. When she was challenged she bravely fought back, but lacked the reserve energy she had always been taught to save for the final drive, as she had wasted it by making the pace. I did not blame Smith, but I did blame Aron Wellman, because he did not act in a professional manner on what should have been a big day for our filly. Wellman should have talked strategy with the preoccupied jockey and focused his mind on the task at hand.

We sold Gypsy's Warning at the Keeneland November Breeding Stock Sale for $1,050,000 to The Niarchos Family's Flaxman Holdings company. Coulda, shoulda been a lot more.

CHAPTER 22

Foreign Blood

A new wrinkle moving into the next millennium was the emergence of international stakes winners resulting from mares and stallions bought or imported by Team Valor International.

Prior to forming racing partnerships, I dealt in breeding stock, especially stallions. Among the first ones I bought and syndicated was the American-bred Moscow Ballet, who was a purple-blooded son of Nijinsky out of a half-sister to Mill Reef. In four starts for Vincent O'Brien, the Irish-based colt won the Railway Stakes at two and ran only once at three, when I bought him. I sold half to Central California rancher John Harris, whose horse division was adjacent to his cattle feedlot, which was the largest west of the Mississippi with a herd numbering more than 100,000 head.

Jeff Siegel was impressed enough with a Moscow Ballet runner that broke her maiden at Hollywood Park in the Nursery Stakes that I flew out from my new digs in Central Kentucky to inspect her at Santa Anita. Built like a fully developed clone of Secretariat, the gleaming chestnut took my breath away, as I literally gasped when I saw her.

Golden Ballet joined all-time leading money-earning distaffer Serena's Song as the only filly to sweep Santa Anita's winter/spring series of 3-year-old filly stakes when she took the Grade 2 Santa Ynez, Grade 1 Las Virgenes and the Grade 1 Santa Anita Oaks after we transferred her to Jenine Sahadi. In the Oaks she dominated a field that included Bobby Frankel-trained, Juddmonte Stable-owned Flute, who came right back to win the Grade 1 Kentucky Oaks and, later, the Grade 1 Alabama Stakes.

Golden Ballet stumbled at the start of the Grade 2 Railbird Stakes at Hollywood Park, which resulted in a career-ending tendon injury, but she gutted out the win for Team Valor and our racing partners Bill and Corinne Heiligbrodt. We sold Golden Ballet for $1.6 million at Keeneland at the end of her season at three to Aaron and Marie Jones, for whom she produced Drosselmeyer, whose career included victories in the classic Grade 1 Belmont Stakes and the Grade 1 Breeders' Cup Classic.

One of the early imports for Gary Barber and me was the English-based, 2-year-old filly Piña Colada, who was a winner from three starts when trained in England by Richard Hannon. She placed in a pair of Graded stakes and became a black-type winner for us in America. As I sometimes do when I like an unexposed European import, I buy its dam, hoping to cash in if the runner is successful. It is a form of insider trading, but one that is strictly legal and ethical. Piña Colada's dam was Drei, a daughter of the diminutive but ultra-classy Lyphard, which had become one of my favorite sires, especially of broodmares. We gave $50,000 for Drei and later sold a Monsun colt out of her at Tattersalls auction in England for the U. S. equivalent of about $400,000.

Gary and I retained the next Monsun colt out of the mare and named it Triple Threat. Racing out of leading French trainer Andre Fabre's yard in Chantilly, the black-coated colt was a promising winner at two. He left the gate awkwardly and slowly debuting at three, but overcame the miscue and finished brilliantly down the long straight at Longchamp to take the Group 3 Prix La Force. In his next start, he remained in the gate for every bit of five seconds, again roaring down the lane with incredible energy, but this time he could finish no better than third because he had given away 10 lengths at the break.

We were convinced we would have a legitimate French Derby candidate if Triple Threat's gate issues could be figured out. Andre Fabre first used the local equine psychologist in Chantilly. The colt failed to improve. Then I pulled an ace from my deck of cards and contacted the world's most famous "horse whisperer" Monty Roberts, with whom I had a relationship going back to the early 1970s when I edited *The Thoroughbred of California* magazine. A decade prior to the situation with Triple Threat, Monty had straightened out a psycho animal for me named Spirit o' War and I was awed by his commitment and success with the horse.

In one respect, Monty was much like Harthill: if he had a chance to work on a top horse, he would drop everything and go to the ends of the Earth. So Monty set up camp at the Dolce Hotel in Chantilly and devoted two and half weeks of his life to getting Triple Threat over his issues in the gate. He correctly diagnosed the puzzling problem as a sensitivity of the colt's skin over his stifle joints whenever he touched the metal sides of the starting gate. Employing a special blanket of his own design, Monty got the colt used to going in and out of the gate, demonstrating to the colt that his skin was now desensitized. After Triple Threat got over that hurdle, Monty then popped the colt out of the gate time after time after time, for several days on end.

We missed the French Derby, because Triple Threat had become exhausted from the repetitive gate drills. He did, however, come back in July to win the Group 2 Prix Eugene Adam. Triple Threat, before departing France to race in America, amassed earnings, breeders awards and owners premiums for Gary and me that totaled to about $475,000

My relationship with Andre Fabre, France's greatest trainer of the modern era, came about in a curious manner. I had imported a filly named Banyu Dewi, who was Group-placed at two in Germany. Between the time I bought her and the time of her arrival in America, Banyu Dewi became a stakes winner without having to race. Say what?

In a glorious bit of serendipity, it turned out that a colt that had beaten her in a Listed race had been disqualified for a drug violation so Banyu Dewi had been moved up to first place. My elation over that gift turned to depression a short time later, when I was informed that Banyu Dewi had bowed a tendon while breezing three furlongs. When I sent the filly to her American trainer, I stressed to him that she had been out of training and needed to be started from scratch. But a visiting German representative of the previous owner chanced to meet my American trainer at Belmont Park and assured him the filly was ready to breeze. I was, to say the least, flabbergasted that the trainer would value this fellow's word over mine.

I will never forget the first time I laid eyes on Banyu Dewi after she got off the van in America. Small, unbalanced, dumpy and carrying her neck in an erect manner, she looked more like a llama than a Thoroughbred. But what she lacked in beauty, she more than made up for in heart and desire. When she won an allowance race for us at Saratoga, she became the first and only horse in my nearly half-century of racing to win a non-claiming race after returning to the races from a bowed tendon. She further enhanced her broodmare credentials by placing in the Grade 3 Glens Falls at Saratoga and the Grade 3 Long Island at Aqueduct.

Banyu Dewi was bred to Gulch, offered at the Keeneland November Breeding Stock Sale and hammered down for $100,000. In the immediate aftermath, the successful bidder was lost in the crush of the crowd in the busy area behind the sales pavilion.

I walked to the back of the pavilion to find out who had bought Banyu Dewi and I met Denali Stud owner Craig Bandoroff, who had consigned the mare to the sale as the agent for Team Valor. Craig said the auctioneer could no longer find the buyer. Our options were to run the mare back through the sale or try to locate the buyer. When I asked the bid spotter about the identity of the buyer, he began describing her and suddenly spotted her in the crowd. I did not recognize the woman. I pointed her out to Craig and asked if he knew her.

"Of course I know her," he said. "She is a client of mine. That's Elisabeth Fabre, Andre Fabre's wife. There's no way it's her."

I egged on Craig to at least broach the subject with Mme. Fabre. Craig came back and sheepishly said, "Yeah, well, it *was* her. She raised her hand, didn't expect to get the filly and then had second thoughts. What do you want me to do?"

Craig was caught between a rock and a hard place, because he fully understood his role as my agent and did not want to piss me off, yet he did not want Elisabeth or Andre Fabre to become upset with him either.

"Ask her if she likes the mare," I said. "If she does, tell her we will sell it for $75,000. Or see if she wants to be partners, since we both keep mares at Denali."

Craig went one better. In a moment of sheer entrepreneurial inspiration, Craig crafted a deal that called for Mme. Fabre to buy half the mare in ownership with Team Valor, paying no expenses in Kentucky except half of any stud fees and shipping invoices going forward, in exchange for Andre Fabre to train all of the mare's foals at no cost. It was absolutely brilliant.

By the time the Gulch foal, Banerji, was ready to run for Fabre, Banyu Dewi had a Cozzene colt on the ground and the mare was back in foal to Grand Slam. Andre Fabre was unimpressed by Banerji, who won a small race, and Elisabeth decided that we should sell the mare and end the partnership. It was a shame that we did not wait for the second foal, the Cozzene chestnut that Mrs. Fabre had named Brigantin, to run.

Racing from two through five for Andre Fabre and at six and seven for Chris Waller in Australia, Brigantin became one of the best stayers of his generation in France, winning the Group 2 Prix Vicomtesse Vigier and the Group 3 Prix de Lutèce, while hitting the board in Group 1 events in England (Ascot Gold Cup), France (Prix du Cadran) and Australia (Sydney Cup). He earned more than $650,000.

South African mares that I put into production in Kentucky also began to bear fruit. The best broodmare prospect that I imported to Kentucky from South Africa was Secret Heart, a Listed winner who had placed in several Grade 1 races. She gave us Graded winners Pluck and Three Hearts before dying prematurely.

Another South African import was Ginger Sea. She was a high-priced yearling when Robin Bruss and a friend bought the daughter of Western Winter. She managed to win a race, but trainer Neil Bruss could not control her bleeding. I bought a third of her, based on a total value of $100,000 and brought her to be trained on Lasix in America. She was such a bad bleeder that she gushed while jogging in the shedrow.

Ginger Sea had a weak family, so my two partners gave up their interests to me because they did not want to breed her in America. I kept her because she was the best looking broodmare I had ever owned. Her first foal Badleroibrown was by the same sire and from the same crop as Animal Kingdom. Robby Albarado rode both of them a week apart when they were two. When I asked him which one was better, the colt that had won at Keeneland named Animal Kingdom or the one that just got touched off when second at Churchill Downs, he said, "What, are you kidding me? That other colt ([Animal Kingdom] isn't even a Thoroughbred compared to this one. He's got gears!"

Badleroibrown developed a paralyzed vocal cord so he underwent tie-back surgery; he managed to win a race, but he never was able to realize his potential. He was such a talented horse that the Animal Kingdom partnership leased him as a work mate.

Ginger Sea's second foal resembled her in conformation and quality. I bred her to Hat Trick, a son of Sunday Silence that Robin Bruss spotted in Japan. I bought the horse, owned him for a week and turned him over for a profit to Walmac Farm, which syndicated him to stand in Kentucky. He sired the Grade 3 winner Three Hearts, out of one of my South African mares, and, mated with Ginger Sea, he sired a colt that favored the mare greatly, which was a good thing. I named the colt Howe Great, combining the hockey reference in the sire's name and famed hockey player Gordie Howe's name for a bit of wordplay. Howe Great became a Grade 3 winner for us in the Palm Beach Stakes at Gulfstream Park, and has earned about $570,000.

Of all the foreign fillies I have imported, none has had quite the impact on our program, or on my life, as the German-bred Dalicia. In a *TDN* (*Thoroughbred Daily News*) story in 2006, I learned that she was being offered at auction near Baden-Baden as part of a dispersal of stock owned by Isle of Jersey breeders Don and Erika Bass. Dalicia intrigued me after reading that two months earlier she had defeated the previous season's Horse of the Year, Soldier Hollow, going a mile and a quarter in a Group 3 at Baden-Baden racecourse. She was by a leading stallion in Acatenango from a top German family.

I contacted a second-generation German bloodstock agent whom I trusted named Dirk Eisler to ask him a lot of questions about the filly, and I decided to bid on her after Dirk told me what a sensational physical specimen she was. Dirk bid by taking my cues on the phone and we were successful in outlasting a persistent rival on a final nod of €400,000. It was a record price for a German filly or mare sold at public auction. When I chatted with Andreas Jacobs later, he revealed he had been the underbidder. I asked why he stopped and he said that €400,000 was pushing it, he admitted to bidding on her for sentimental reasons since his father's Gestut Fahrhof developed the bloodline and said he still had plenty of mares from the family in production at the stud.

Dalicia's purchase price, including taxes and commissions, came out to about €445,000, or $532,000. I added my customary 25 percent on auction purchases for a Team Valor racing partnership. The LLC we formed to race Dalcia had a value of $664,400. We ran her immediately after the sale in Europe and she failed to sparkle, so I sent her to be trained by Neil Drysdale in Southern California.

I had a healthy respect for German racing and breeding stock. Although a lot of the horses were coarse, heavy and lacked speed, German stock commanded my attention because Germans bred to race, so their selection of bloodlines and physical specimens was based on having to use the offspring of their producers. If they could not run or could not stand the rigors of training they had nothing to show for their endeavors. And to show how dedicated they were in producing tough, hardy and classy stock, they did not allow the use of race-day drugs and they placed strict eligibility restrictions in their breeding programs on stock imported from locales where drugs were allowed. Rules also were in place regarding horses that bled. Most serious breeders in England, Ireland and France had at least some German mares in their broodmare bands as a way of introducing a hardier and tougher strain into their bloodlines.

What really interested me about German breeding was the emphasis on toughness at the direct expense of fashion, as well as the breeders' conscious effort to develop sire lines that provided an outcross to the overused speed bloodlines of Mr. Prospector, which had taken over American pedigrees, and the concentration of Northern Dancer blood that was difficult to avoid in Europe.

Dalicia had run just once at the back end of her season at two and did not break her maiden until the seventh start of her career, when she won going a mile and a quarter in mid-August of her 3-year-old season. She was not ordinary, as she broke her maiden in a $75,000 national Listed race that counted for black-type in German auction catalogues. Earlier in the season, she had been highly tried, taking her chances in the Group 1 German Oaks after running second in a Listed race that qualified for black-type in international sales catalogues. In that Oaks prep, she split Saldentigerin, who wound up as the Champion Filly at three, and Vallera, which became a Group 3 winner later in the campaign.

This was very good form and I was quite familiar with it, since, during that same season, Team Valor had raced the top filly La Ina, which was touched off by a nose in the Group 1 German Oaks, finishing ahead of Saldentigerin.

Dalicia hit her best stride in the summer and fall of her season at four, running fourth in a pair of Group 2 races in France and Germany, and placing third in a German Group 3 and a French Listed race, before famously taking a notable scalp in Soldier Hollow at Baden-Baden in the Group 3 Preis der Sparkassen-Finanzgruppe. Soldier Hollow was a tough customer, a quality that he would underline internationally the following season, when he ran a close third in the Grade 1 Arlington Million in Chicago. Soldier Hollow gave Dalicia eleven pounds in the Group 3, yet *Timeform* labeled her a "smart performer," a plaudit that carried a lot weight in the offices of Team Valor.

Neil Drysdale had his hands on many top horses from Europe and specifically Germany, but he reckoned he had something special once he started breezing Dalicia. She trained better than any European horse Team Valor had ever imported. In addition to his involvement in Team Valor, Jeff Siegel also had a stake in the publication *Handicapper's Report*, which provided horseplayers with helpful information like workout reports that were generated by its private clocker. One of the Dalicia partners, Mike Jarvis from Southern California, was an avid reader of the report and, every time Dalicia was entered, he called to wax enthusiastic about the mare's chances.

The reports were accurate. Dalicia breezed brilliantly, but she always worked hard against the bridle, she was never allowed to fully extend herself and she gave the distinct impression that, if given her head, she would open up a dozen lengths in the time it took to utter, "Did you see that?"

But Dalicia never reproduced her morning form in the afternoon in five races for Team Valor. She ran much better than average. She just never followed through with her run the way she had promised to in the morning. In her initial four outings, from March to June, she ran second, first, third and fourth. In every race, she generated a run that promised to make her a winner, but she only followed through with her run once, and even on that day, she seemed to be "straight as a string" to prevail by a neck.

I hypothesized to Drysdale that the mare might not be getting her air because she was displacing her soft palate, whether from the stress of the approaching finishing line or because of some structural deficiency. So, after looking all over a winner a furlong from home in the Grade 2 Beverly Hills

Handicap, she faded to finish fourth. Subsequently, the mare underwent a tenectomy, which involved severing a muscle below her to jaw to stop her palate from displacing.

Given a few weeks to recover from the throat surgery, Dalicia returned to training for Drysdale at Del Mar and seemed to have improved. She was scheduled to run during the first week of August in a stakes race, for which she proved difficult to saddle. Neil moved her inside to saddle her away from the crowd. At some point the mare reared up and came down on a dolly that had been inappropriately placed and she sustained a severe gash to a hind leg.

Rushed immediately by van to the Helen C. Woodward Equine Clinic six miles down the road, Dalicia was found to have severed a sesamoidal ligament. Surgery was performed to address the insult and to stop the blood leakage. After four days in the clinic, the mare was vanned to the Santa Ynez Valley to receive several treatments in an oxygen-rich hyperbaric chamber to improve blood flow in the injured leg.

The surgeon who operated on Dalicia informed us that each hind ankle had two sesamoidal ligaments. Only one was required for support, so the mare could race again. Dalicia did make it back to the races the following season at Santa Anita, where she never lifted a hoof and ran unplaced. I retired her and had her flown to Kentucky, where she was prepared for the breeding season at Denali Stud.

My research indicated that the best stallion to cover Dalicia was Kingmambo and the mare was booked to him for the 2007 breeding season, which had commenced the day before her final career outing. Less than a week after Dalcia was booked to Kingmambo I received what turned out to be the first in a series of communiqués from Lane's End Farm informing me that, although the Mr. Prospector stallion had successfully bred five mares, maiden mares would only be accepted if they were small to medium sized; furthermore, the handlers had to be able to have them stand quietly and be willing to place them in a lowered area where their hind legs would be covered in a Polytrack surface to keep them from moving around too much. Denali assured me that, even though Dalicia was a tall mare, they would work something out.

Six days later, Lane's End sent out another update advising me that Kingmambo had been taken out of service again. Kingmambo suffered from a neurological issue in his neck that prevented him from being able to rise up to mount a mare. Mares had to be lowered for him so that he could perform his duties as a stallion. Denali Stud kept in close contact with Lane's End and we were all hopeful that the prize stallion would be able to cover our mare.

Denali farm manager Gary Bush asked office staffer Amy Tindell on April 18 to phone Lane's End and book Dalicia to be covered the next day. Lane's End said that Kingmambo was still "off-line" and would be unavailable. Craig Bandoroff phoned me with the bad news. I was driving down a country road in the Bluegrass and I told Craig I would get a hold of Richard Haisfield, a part owner of the mare, to see if any of the stallions he owned interests in might be available on such short notice because we did not want to miss covering Dalicia on this breeding cycle.

"How about Leroi?" were the first words out of Haisfield's mouth. "I would love to have that mare covered by Leroi."

I knew that Haisfield would push for Leroidesanimaux, but my plan for the mare was to breed her well enough to attract international buyers at public auction in England. Leroi did not even come close to fitting that profile.

I told Richard that breeding to Leroi would be fine with me if we were breeding to race, but commercially, a drop from Kingmambo to Leroidesanimaux represented one that undoubtedly would be viewed as being too precipitous for our group to embrace. I told him that I would call him right back and, as was his style, he urged me to get the job done.

When I got off the phone with Haisfield, I phoned my office and had my assistant generate a hypothetical pedigree on the "Pedigree Query" website, showing what a Leroidesanimaux foal out of Dalicia would look like. I had her read me the names in the pedigree and I asked her a lot of questions about names and position of stallions in the pedigree. I was satisfied that the mating was adequate and I especially liked the inbreeding to Lyphard, one of my all-time favorite sires. Breeding a speedy Miler to a 10-furlong mare summed up my notion of an ideal mating. I also liked the idea of giving a mare of this quality to Leroidesanimaux. And I loved the prospect of getting "stuck" with the foal to race.

I called back Bandoroff to tell him what Haisfield said and Craig became upset. Understandably, Craig was concerned on two levels: he worried that our substantial investment in Dalicia would be jeopardized by breeding her to an unproven, non-commercial stallion with an unfashionable pedigree; and he considered Haisfield to be toxic because his questionable business practices were, by that time, well-known and Craig feared that further involvement with Haisfield would taint the mare and us.

My position, I told Craig, was that we were up the creek without a paddle; it was past the middle of April and the mare needed to be covered. I said that we should be grateful to Haisfield for making room in Leroi's book. I argued that we could breed her to Leroi, get a foal, then breed her back to a fashionable stallion and sell her a year later than we had originally planned. But time was of the essence. Craig saw the logic and agreed with the decision, so I phoned Richard back to tell him the mare would be arriving at Stonewall Farm the next morning to be covered by Leroidesanimaux. Dalicia was bred to Leroidesanimaux on April 19 and was impregnated on a single cover.

I first came into contact with Richard Haisfield through a referral from trainer Dale Romans, who told me that a banker friend of his said that Haisfield was looking to expand his equine interests. I met him for lunch in the old Dudley's Restaurant on Mill Street in Lexington. He looked and acted just like another conman I had met some twenty years earlier named Robert Resnick. They shared a business model that had, at its core, the use of perceived equity in real estate to borrow millions of dollars from banks without much of a conviction in repaying the loans. To them, horses were tools to get their hands on enormous amounts of capital, and they used the IRS tax code to keep as much of it as possible. If they could screw a few people along the way for entertainment, so much the better.

At Haisfield's request, I explained my business model to him. He asked me if he could make money participating in my racing partnerships. I told him that it was unlikely. He told me that his interest was in breeding, specifically in developing stallions, and that he had little to no interest in racing because of the risk to capital.

After we had sized each other up, we got down to basics. Haisfield asked if I would work for "semen," meaning that if I found stallion prospects for him, he would not remunerate me with cash, but in breeding rights. I was in the process of getting divorced and I was concerned at the time with generating capital to fund my teenage daughter Chloë's future college education, so I told Richard that working for semen was fine with me because I could sell my breeding rights for cash each year. Haisfield liked that and said he wanted me to find him some horses to stand at stud. He told me that, if I were successful, he would return the favor by occasionally investing in one of my racing partnerships. Dalicia was one of those instances.

The first horse I secured for Haisfield was Medaglia d'Oro. Most people knew he was there for the taking, but being able to do a deal with his trainer Bobby Frankel and his owner Ed Gann was a hurdle no breeder had been able to clear. Throughout my years of covering Frankel as a journalist, doing deals with him as a bloodstock agent and using him as a trainer, I had had my ups and downs with him.

I had not spoken to Frankel in several years. He had prevented one of our horses from getting into the body of the Hollywood Derby by entering a horse with the specific purpose of keeping my horse out. He entered the horse, informed the media that he had no intention of running the horse, and had only entered it to keep my horse out of the race because it was a contender that he feared.

Frankel was a great trainer. He divorced his first wife. They had a child named Bethenny, who has become a pop icon, known best perhaps for her Skinnygirl Cocktails. She was raised by her stepfather, a rival New York trainer named John Parisella. Somebody once asked a horseman how good a trainer Frankel was and the guy replied, "How good? Are you kidding me? He's so good he got his wife claimed!"

I was the first person to take Frankel to Europe. He wound up buying seven horses on our trip to France and my net commission from him, after his clients spent several hundred thousand dollars, was an insulting $2,500.

But I needed to do a deal on Medaglia d'Oro, so I swallowed my pride and asked my friend Ron Anderson to pave the way for me to talk directly with Frankel. When it came to doing deals and making money, Frankel could be extremely well mannered. Over the next several months, Bobby was so nice it almost made me think he had softened his hard-shelled, brash New Yorker exterior. But I found him impossible to warm up to. The negotiations to buy Medaglia d'Oro went smoothly and without a hitch. Haisfield paid $10.5-million for the horse and MDO was sent to Kentucky and installed at stud at Hill 'n' Dale Farm.

Another horse I bought for Haisfield was Lawyer Ron. He had won the Grade 2 Arkansas Derby. He did not have a fashionable pedigree, but when I inspected him at Churchill Downs, I was very impressed with him physically and thought he had the temperament to develop into a top horse. He was a horse I really pushed Haisfield to buy.

Lawyer Ron was not for sale. However, he raced for the estate of a recently deceased owner-breeder who had named him for his Kentucky-based attorney Ron Bamburger. I drove out to visit the lawyer at his office. Bamburger was a difficult character with hidden agendas. On one hand, he professed to be interested in what was best for the estate, but on the other hand, he clearly had his ego involved because the colt had been named for him.

I knew that Bamburger would have to come to grips sooner or later with selling the colt. And he realized that I was well aware of it. It became apparent that Bamburger was not going to let go of a live Kentucky Derby candidate that carried his own name. On the other side of the table was the equally duplicitous Richard Haisfield, who professed to have no ego involvement in his equine investments and not a single drop of sporting blood.

But the more I talked to each of these liars, the more I realized that the lure of the Kentucky Derby was preventing Bamburger from being a willing seller and encouraging Haisfield to be a willing buyer. In the end, I was able to structure a deal by persuading Bamburger to satisfy his obligation to the estate by taking some cash off the table and convincing Haisfield that Laywer Ron could bring him a lot of attention.

Lawyer Ron finished twelfth of twenty, beaten more than twenty lengths in the Kentucky Derby.

The partnership was complicated and contained very specific deal points that had to be addressed in a timely and equitable manner, which was something Haisfield had historically failed to do. Lawsuits followed. Bamburger was no pushover and Haisfield had pissed off an adversary who was well up to the task of matching his legal shenanigans.

Transferred from his original trainer Bob Holthus to Todd Pletcher, Lawyer Ron developed into one of most impressive older horses in memory, breaking Saratoga's nine-furlong track record with a 1:46 4/5 clocking in his Grade 1 Whitney win; he followed it with a victory by more than eight lengths in the Grade 1 Woodward Stakes, which earned him an Eclipse Award for the best older male in training at four. Lawyer Ron died during this second season at stud, which was a shame because he had sired some excellent runners in his first crop of foals and looked a cinch to become a very successful stallion.

Another important stallion acquisition I arranged for Haisfield to buy was Leroidesanimaux, who also was trained by Bobby Frankel. I asked Frankel about the horse and Bobby put me in direct contact with its owner, Brazilian businessman and owner-breeder Goncalo Torrealba. I had previously developed a nice relationship with Goncalo and was surprised when he showed some interest in selling the horse. He explained to me that if he did sell the horse, he would not sell the entire animal, because he wanted to continue to race him and eventually breed mares to him.

Torrealba, whose family eventually bought a majority stake in the well-known Kentucky establishment Three Chimneys Farm, was thoroughly versed in every aspect of the horse industry and raced internationally at the highest level. We became friendly when we both campaigned horses with Mike de Kock in Dubai and used to compare notes.

I was very apprehensive about vouching for Haisfield as a potential business partner and I cautioned Richard about ruining my relationship with Goncalo. Haisfield, of course, lied and told me that he would do nothing to put my friendship with Torrealba at risk. Later on, as with most deals in which Haisfield was involved, he failed in one way or another to follow through with his obligations and his relationship with Goncalo became yet another casualty. The only deal Haisfield failed to screw up was Medaglia d'Oro because he had to buy him outright with no terms or conditions.

Haisfield bought a majority interest in Leroi. He had been bred and initially raced in Brazil, where he had a win and a Grade 1 second in three starts, with a lone loss in his only career dirt race, in which he was beaten more than twenty-three lengths. He finished fourth, sprinting in his Santa Anita debut, then proceeded to reel off six wins in a row, stalking or setting the pace. His first five wins came in Southern California. In the start immediately before Haisfield got involved, the horse "wired" his field in the Grade 2 Fourstardave Handicap at Saratoga.

A deal was struck for the Never Tell Stable of Haisfield's wife Audrey and Torrealba's TNT Stud to race Leroi in partnership just before the renewal of the Grade 1 Atto Mile, a $1-million race he won in the most swashbuckling style, dashing his way down the stretch to win by nearly eight lengths and record a huge 115 Beyer speed figure.

Word that Leroidesanimaux had compromised a front hoof did not stop bettors from making him a near even-money favorite for the Breeders' Cup Mile at Belmont Park. He was not at his best that day, as his season low 108 Beyer indicated, but he was gallant in failing by less than a length of holding off Artie Schiller. He was retired to stud right afterward.

Leroidesanimaux brought to the stud a truly remarkable race record. He got beat in his first and last American starts, in between reeling off eight consecutive victories that featured a Hollywood Park course record of 1:38 2/5 for a mile and a sixteenth in the Grade 3 Inglewood Handicap, as well as three Grade 1 victories. His winning performance in the Atto Mile was considered by seasoned observers of the Turf to be among the most impressive grass victories in North America in a long time. He even won a sprint stakes down the hill at Santa Anita with a sensationally fast clocking of 1:11 3/5.

Physically, Leroi stood close to 16 hands. He was built low to the ground for speed, with a big chest, excellent overall balance and strong hindquarters. His left front leg toed in, which was a bit of a concern, but not enough to stop anybody from breeding to him if they otherwise liked him.

The real concern about Leroidesanimaux at stud was his pedigree, which was too international for most Kentucky breeders to relate to commercially. Candy Stripes, his sire, was born in Kentucky, ran second in the Group 1 French Two Thousand Guineas and became a sensation at stud in Argentina. Taylor Made Farm brought him up to stand him in Kentucky, but after three seasons, Candy Stripes was sent back to South America.

From 159 North American foals, he sired only half a dozen stakes winners; he flopped commercially as well. Candy Stripes picked up right where he had left off in South America, siring international superstar Invasor, who was the best racehorse in the world in 2006. One of Candy Stripes' daughters produced Candy Ride, a great racehorse in Argentina and America. Candy Ride has been one of the best stallions at stud in the United States. Unfortunately, most Kentucky breeders only remembered how poorly they had fared with Candy Stripes when they bred to him in the Bluegrass, so a son of his held little intrigue.

Leroidesanimaux, who came from one of Juddmonte Farm's best families, had half-brothers win Grade 1 and Grade 3 stakes before he emerged as an American Champion. But the half-brothers won in Brazil, which geographically has about as much relevance to a Kentucky breeder as Jupiter or Saturn. And his broodmare sire is the foreign-sounding British stallion Ahoonora, whose obscure bloodline few local breeders could figure out how to use with their mares. Most of the people who were charged with booking mares to stallions in Kentucky never got past the first dam, which is unfortunate because the second dam features such household names as Banks Hill and Dansili among six international Champions, eight Grade 1 winners, five American Grade 1 winners, two Breeders' Cup winners, three Breeders' Cup-placed runners and seventeen individual stakes winners.

When requests for breeding services to Leroi came in slower than anticipated, I suggested to Haisfield that he offer free breedings to qualified Grade 1 winners or producers. Haisfield took it a step further, giving away freebies to any Graded winner or producer without qualifying them, so Leroi's book became adulterated with a lot of substandard mares. Commercially, Leroi went from being behind the eight ball to being placed in the trash bin.

CHAPTER 23

Enter the Kingdom

Residents of Central Kentucky's bluegrass region divide their passion between horses and wildcats. The horses are Thoroughbreds and the wildcats are players on the University of Kentucky basketball team.

Fans who follow the round ball sport in the Bluegrass, where they are collectively known as "The Big Blue Nation," found themselves in a deep blue funk by mid-afternoon on March 20, 2008. After their eleventh-seeded Wildcats fell apart in the final 22 seconds of a match with sixth-seeded Marquette, they got knocked out of the South regional in the first round of the National Collegiate Athletic Association tournament, aka "March Madness."

My wife Kathleen and I are UK basketball diehards, so it was a bitter pill to swallow. By evening, though, our spirits were buoyed by news that Dalicia had foaled a colt by Leroidesanimaux at Denali Stud. Gary Bush said the chestnut weighed in at 118 pounds and stood 40 ¼ inches tall. He was born at 6:58 p.m., stood about an hour later and began nursing half an hour after that.

A week after the colt, which would be named Animal Kingdom, was born, he was discovered to have fractured two ribs, most likely as a result of the strenuous birthing process. He had to spend an additional week in a stall until the farm vet deemed him to be sufficiently recovered that he could be turned out in a paddock.

As a foal, Animal Kingdom had an exquisite head, excellent bone, good balance and a frame large enough to grow into as a yearling, although he was not particularly strong behind.

Commercial farms in Kentucky routinely x-ray specific points of a foal's skeletal structure in the winter of their first year in order to identify any issues that might need to be surgically addressed before a yearling is prepared for the summer and fall sales.

Animal Kingdom was discovered to have OCD (Osteochondritis Dissecans) lesions in both stifles and a small OCD fragment in his left hind ankle. Dr. Larry Bramlage surgically debrided and removed the undesirable bones. The surgeon treated the joints at the Rood and Riddle Equine Clinic in Lexington and sent the colt back to Denali early in January of 2009.

OCD lesions occur in as many as one of four horses across all breeds, and are most commonly caused by nutritional imbalances in the diet and rapid growth spurts. Lesions routinely appear in otherwise normal joints and undermine the cartilage, causing bony flaps that tend to break off and lead to chronic arthritis. Removal in racing prospects is common and generally ends the problem.

Animal Kingdom developed nicely from being a foal to a yearling. His ample frame and height held out the promise of considerable further physical development. He did not look like any sort of prospect for 2-year-old racing. He resembled his dam rather than his sire when he headed to the Keeneland yearling sale in mid-September as part of Denali's consignment.

I bid on Animal Kingdom from the ring and had him knocked down to me for $100,000, which met his reserve set before the sale. Our plan before the sale was to accept $100,000 for him if anybody bid that much and, if not, to take him home. Dalicia was scheduled to sell at public auction in December and we did not want the sales record to reflect a low price for her first foal.

As I invariably do, I gave any partners who did not want to race the colt an escape hatch by offering to buy them out. I told them I valued the colt at $20,000 and would pay based on $25,000. Twenty Leroidesanimaux yearlings sold that year for an average price of $21,703, a figure inflated by our colt's ring price of $100,000, which was far and away the highest price for a Leroi yearling in 2009. Two fellows took me up on the offer. I then offered the remaining Dalicia partners the opportunity to buy these interests. When nobody responded in the affirmative, I increased my personal stake in Animal Kingdom to about 20 percent and was pleased to do so because I liked him.

Animal Kingdom, along with my homebred Leroidesanimaux colt Badleroibrown, was sent immediately after the sale to be broken and initially trained by former D. Wayne Lukas assistant Randy Bradshaw, who had leased a barn from Frank Stronach at his Adena Springs training complex near Ocala, Florida.

In November, I came up with the name Animal Kingdom for the Leroi colt out of Dalicia and submitted it to The Jockey Club, which summarily rejected it, probably because there was a theme park of the same name that was part of the Walt Disney Resort in Florida. I had never heard of the Animal Kingdom park and I sent an e-mail to Rick Bailey of The Jockey Club asking him to reconsider my name, explaining that Leroidesanimaux was French for "King of the Animals." I always found Rick to be very reasonable and he did not disappoint me.

Interestingly, when I named the other Leroidesanimaux colt, I submitted the name Badbadleroibrown. The Jockey Club rejected it. I was prepared for this rejection. My pal Nick Ben-Meir, a recording industry manager, had obtained a signed affidavit that gave me permission to name the colt after the tune of writer and singer Jim Croce from his widow. Bailey told me that the song had become so popular that it transcended private rights and had become part of the American culture. This concept was so without merit that I found myself temporarily unable to respond. Rick must have realized how absurd that explanation sounded once it came out of his pie hole and he came up with the idea of dropping the first "bad." So to avoid having to take the case all the way to the Supreme Court, I agreed to settle for Badleroibrown.

Dalicia, which was in foal to Mr. Greeley, was sold early in December at the Tattersalls sale in Newmarket for about $400,000. The buyer was the Yoshida Family from Japan. Over the years they had done very well acquiring breeding stock from me, including buying the dams of their Japan Derby winner and sire King Kamehameha and Grade 1 American Oaks winner Cesario, whose son Epiphaneia won the $4-million Japan Cup and was the top-ranked long distance runner of 2014 in the world.

Randy Bradshaw told me at the end of the year that Animal Kingdom was improving in his hind-end strength and that he was a big colt who was definitely "worth trying." In three months of training in Ocala, Animal Kingdom had not yet been asked to show any speed over the rich, dark dirt track at Adena Springs.

I inspected him at the end of January in Ocala and noted that he had grown about a full inch. He was becoming quite tall and rangy. He was fulfilling the promise he had given us four months earlier. Even though he was going through a growth spurt, I could see that he had the tools to develop into a grand looking 3-year-old. Being able to get him to the races at two, however, seemed highly unlikely.

All Randy Bradshaw wanted to talk about that entire winter well into spring was Badleroibrown, Badleroibrown and more Badleroibrown. He was completely enthralled by the colt. Then, in the first week of April, Bradshaw called to say that Animal Kingdom had actually breezed a faster quarter than the "talking horse." He said, "Both of these freaking Lerois are well above average. This one [Animal Kingdom] wants to gawk at everything on the track and I may try blinkers on him next. He goes plenty fast. He just needs to learn to focus a bit more. He is a very big colt and should do well on Polytrack or grass going long. Very nice prospect here."

I had decided by late spring to send both Leroidesanimaux colts to Wayne Catalano at Arlington Park. Animal Kingdom progressed from a quarter-mile in April, to three-eighths of a mile in May to a half-mile in June. Bradshaw sent him up to Chicagoland in late June, saying, "There's nothing more I can do with him here. He's ready. It's time for him to go to the big track. He will need two turns and grass."

Animal Kingdom turned in a mind-boggling work in mid-August that was officially listed as 1:00, but some time later I learned it was :58 2/5. He worked in company with an unscheduled work mate, which he proceeded to blow off the track by some 15 lengths. "Wow, how sweet was that?" Catalano said to me on the apron at Arlington Park. "What a long stride on this sucker, huh?"

Bob Marcocchio, a 53-year veteran of the racing wars as a clocker, owner, breeder and racing manager based at Arlington Park and Woodbine, said, "I saw Animal Kingdom breeze many times as a 2-year-old and he's as good as I ever saw."

Animal Kingdom surprised me, he surprised Randy Bradshaw and he surprised Wayne Catalano by how quickly he came to hand once he began training in earnest. In a matter of weeks, he had gone from a colt that was trying to figure it all out to an eager, dedicated pupil.

At the end of August, I decided to try to buy out Richard Haisfield, who, by then, had gotten into serious financial difficulties. Over a period of a couple of weeks, I managed to get him to accept an offer of $27,500 for his 25-percent interest in Animal Kingdom. I was able to wrap up the deal and pay him three days before the colt made his racing debut on September 18, 2010.

Wayne entered Animal Kingdom in a maiden grass race around two turns for September 18. When rain softened the grass, racing officials switched the race to the Polytrack and lengthened the distance from a mile to a mile and a sixteenth. Even though they had a chute that allowed them to run the race at the "book" distance of a mile, racing officials, to their credit, kept their implicit promise to offer horsemen a two-turn race by adding an extra half-furlong to the race. Animal Kingdom drew the 9 stall in a 10-horse field, meaning that he would have to overcome a wide draw in his debut.

In spite of his outside post position and the presence in the field of some well-regarded horses, including the Mike Stidham-trained "talking horse" Willcox Inn, Animal Kingdom was installed as the 3-to-1 favorite. Bet down to 5-to-2 favoritism, the tall chestnut broke sluggishly and immediately was taken to the rail by leading rider Junior Alvarado as he went past the stands for the first time trailing his nine rivals.

Kept along the rail to the end of the backstretch, Animal Kingdom saved a lot of ground. When Alvarado wanted him to begin a rally going into the far turn, the jockey on Willcox Inn moved over, taking our colt's path and forcing Alvarado to take up sharply.

Alvarado was able to gather and balance his mount again. Coming into the stretch in the middle of the field, Alvarado had a choice between staying behind a wall of horses, hoping for an opening, or going wide.

In a classic, ill-conceived move, Alvarado yanked the colt's head to the right, jumped a couple of lanes and went outside seeking running room. Going wide on grass or synthetic tracks is not the most effective strategy. The greatest North American grass rider of all time, Fernando Toro from Chile, once explained to me the most effective way to ride the grass.

The way to play it, Toro said, is to remain inside and hope for an opening because, if one materializes, your chances of winning are good. Going outside rarely works. So, even if you stay inside and the hole never appears, it is no big deal because the horse was not going to win anyway.

While Alvarado was fashioning his move, Wilcox Inn scampered away to an insurmountable lead. AK cut into the margin by a length in the final furlong, but Willcox Inn won by nearly 3 lengths. It was obvious after the race that Willcox Inn was out of the ordinary for an Arlington Park maiden winner, which he went on to prove in a career that saw him become a multiple Graded stakes winner and amass earnings of more than $1 million.

Animal Kingdom exited his debut to rave reviews. I never received more e-mails about a young horse in my life. The length of his stride and the explosiveness of his move for such a tall colt had caught the attention of many racing folk.

Mark Belling, the Milwaukee-based radio talk-show host who regularly fills in for Rush Limbaugh, had gone racing at Arlington Park for years. An astute analyst of form and a seasoned racehorse owner, Mark said, "Very few horses at the Arlington Park meeting closed with such a rush or such sheer determination. With that short stretch run, horses just don't close that much ground as this horse did. The winner obviously is a very nice horse, but what kind of horse is this Animal Kingdom? That's what I want to know."

Wayne Catalano was pumped. He told me right after the race that Animal Kingdom might be a "Champion in the making."

My immediate thought in contemplating AK's next race was another Polytrack maiden at Keeneland but I told my partners that I would not rule out a stakes start because I thought he could hold his own in top company right away. He had displayed an inordinate amount of natural talent and he had a fantastic temperament and a real desire to compete. I could not wait for his next start.

Animal Kingdom was transferred to Keeneland, where he began breezing like an animal possessed. Wayne told me that he had decided to take it easy for a while with the colt because he had lost some weight from his hard-run first effort. Shortly thereafter, the colt reeled off three consecutive five-eighths drills on the Polytrack in 1:00, :59 and an unnerving :58 3/5 from the gate.

Trainer Greg Fox, a friend of mine, had a young horse that he wanted some company for in the gate and when he approached Catalano, Wayne said, "I might have a maiden." Fox was stunned when that red-coated maiden busted a :45 and change half and galloped out in :58 3/5. When Greg found out the colt was a once-raced juvenile pointing for a two-turn Keeneland maiden a week later, he said to Catalano, "Why would you do something like that?" Wayne shrugged his shoulders and said, "You got to train them to get them ready, right?"

Animal Kingdom was being trained more like a 5-year-old for the Metropolitan Mile than like a 2-year-old for a middle-distance maiden race. It was disconcerting. When I questioned why he went so fast out of the gate just a week before his next start going a mile and an eighth, Catalano told me, "What can I say, he's ready to rumble!"

Willcox Inn put a high shine on the form two weeks before AK's Keeneland race, when he placed in the Grade 1 Breeders' Futurity over the Keeneland Polytrack. What was unknown at the time was that two weeks after AK's Keeneland maiden race, Willcox Inn would place behind Team Valor's Pluck in the $1-million Breeders' Cup Juvenile Turf.

Horseplayers made Animal Kingdom the odds-on 7-to-10 favorite for an October 23 maiden race at Keeneland going nine furlongs on Polytrack. The track was playing in favor of inside speed and horses were not getting passed in the stretch. Catalano and I talked about it and told Robby Albarado to let the colt show his speed early in order to get a good position. Since he just worked fast from the gate, we were confident that this strategy would work.

Breaking from the 3 hole, Animal Kingdom got rolling early. Into the turn, a D. Wayne Lukas-trained colt went up on his outside and stayed about half a length ahead of Animal Kingdom. Splits were fast, with opening fractions of :23 2/5 and :47-flat. The Lukas colt, with the jockey obviously riding to instructions, tried to put pressure on our colt. The rival jockey made a premature run and cut with his mount turning for home. He was hard-ridden and managed to maintain his advantage to the top of the stretch.

Albarado had been biding his time. He asked Animal Kingdom for his best lick coming off the stretch corner. When most horses are asked to run, they either quicken or lengthen their strides, but not both. Animal Kingdom both increased the tempo and reached out for additional ground, putting 3 ¼ lengths on his rival through a final furlong run in 12 1/5 seconds to reach the line, after a mile and an eighth in 1:49. Two-year-olds that race with the pace and go fast early rarely finish faster than they began, but Animal Kingdom showed he could do it.

"He knows absolutely nothing about racing," Catalano said. "He was just getting into his stride when the race was over. Hey, that was not only a great effort by the colt, but a nice little gut check and he come through it with flying colors. I was very proud of what he did out there today. Pretty exciting!"

Prior to the race, public clocker Bruno de Julio e-mailed that he had tabbed Animal Kingdom as a potential Kentucky Derby colt based on his Arlington race. After the Keeneland race he followed up in another e-mail with profuse praise for our homebred. "He has all the tools," said de Julio, who specialized in clocking youngsters, especially at the 2-year-old sales. *Daily Racing Form* columnist Marty McGee wrote that Animal Kingdom looked like something special in his Keeneland win and appeared to be just getting warmed up when the race was over.

Andy Beyer gave AK an 84 speed figure and Ragozin gave him a 9, which is a huge number for a 2-year-old running a mile and an eighth in October.

During this period, Team Valor was on a roll. We had a well-stocked international stable but I was not happy with the type of communication, or lack thereof, that I was receiving from some of my trainers. Many of them were professional and straight shooters, many were not. Early in the summer, I began to get frustrated when I found out what some trainers had concealed from me.

Graham Motion was doing very well training for us out of barns at Fair Hill Training Center in the northeast part of Maryland, which was just across the Delaware State border. Evidence was mounting that horses responded better to the rigors of training in this country-like setting than in cramped and polluted urban backstretches. I had seen what Graham had been able to do in this environment with a close relative to Animal Kingdom named Daveron.

I bought Daveron as a yearling from the national sale in Germany a year after I had bought Dalicia, who was a full sister to Daveron's dam. Bred by Andreas Jacobs' Gestüt Fährhof, Daveron developed into a minor stakes winner abroad and won her United States debut with a strong 95 Beyer number in a Belmont Park allowance. But she was so high-strung that she was unmanageable in the traditional American racetrack environment. She was completely turned around by Motion, who trained her on grass gallops, rarely breezed her on the Tapeta track and turned her out in a paddock in the afternoon. She blossomed and I was totally impressed.

I had reached a crossroads that fall of 2009 and seriously considered shutting down my business and contracting my involvement in the industry. I was worn out from trying to figure out which trainers to trust.

Finally, after much soul searching, I decided to give it one more try. I made a drastic decision: if I was going to stay in racing, I wanted the horses trained in a setting of my own choosing with one man at the helm who would keep me informed. For various reasons that made sense to me, I had always felt that horses would perform better if trained off-site instead of at a racetrack.

I had never been able to get any traction because the vast majority of trainers liked the camaraderie of the backstretch and wanted to be at a racetrack. I decided I wanted to buy a barn at Fair Hill and hire a private trainer. I began to interview likely candidates, but none of them would leave the racetrack.

Earlier that year, I had asked Graham Motion if he would consider training privately for me. He told me that his experiments with being exclusive had taught him it was not a good fit for him. But in the late fall of 2010, I approached him again and, this time, he was receptive to my overture. In a meeting in Doc Harthill's old private office, across the street from Churchill Downs during the week of Pluck's win in the Breeders' Cup, we struck a deal: I would supply a barn and he would train the horses. He would continue to train his other horses, but he would train all of my horses. He tapped Irish-born Dave Rock, one of his two chief assistants, to train out of our barn at Fair Hill.

I put together a group of investors, we bought a forty-stall barn from ex-leading Delaware Park jockey Mike McCarthy, and we began preparing it to house our horses the following spring, when the runners returned from winter quarters in Florida.

Pluck won the Breeders' Cup Juvenile Turf that fall at Churchill Downs, we sold a half-interest in him and paid a commission to Todd Pletcher because he trained the colt when the sale was consummated and he was going to lose the colt. Pluck was duly sent to Florida. I explained to

Todd why I had decided to buy the barn and hire one trainer and he was very understanding about the move.

Eight days after Animal Kingdom roared down the Keeneland stretch, Badleroibrown debuted at Churchill Downs, going a mile on grass for Catalano and Robby Albarado. He ran a big race and finished second, beaten a neck. When I asked Albarado which one of the two Leroi colts he thought was best, he did not hesitate to tell me, unequivocally, that it was Badleroibrown.

When I informed Wayne Catalano that I had restructured my operation and planned to place all the horses under one trainer at Fair Hill, he was gravely disappointed but he took it like a professional. It was a very hard phone call for me to make.

Animal Kingdom had not eaten up and had lost some condition as a result of the hard race he had at Keeneland. I decided to send him to Randy Bradshaw's place in Ocala for a break before sending him on to Graham Motion at Palm Meadows in Florida because I thought he could use a freshener after those super-fast works and even faster races. It turned out to be the best thing for the colt.

I wrote to my Animal Kingdom partners, telling them that, if Team Valor has a Triple Crown prospect for 2011 at this stage of the game, "Animal Kingdom could be the one."

A month of paddock turnout and light racetrack exercise ignited a growth spurt in Animal Kingdom. He morphed from an elegant European-looking colt to the equine embodiment of The Incredible Hulk. His body didn't turn green, but his rib cage sprung, his hindquarters filled out and his hip broadened. He did not grow any taller; he simply bulled up. He became an imposing individual, surpassing in quality even the best physical gifts of his sire and dam. The transformation from a gawky, narrow yearling to a fully realized racing machine had been completed. I was there every step of the way and I was as amazed as anybody.

In order to figure out whether we were "smoking our socks or drinking our bath water" in considering a Derby campaign, my original idea was to rely on Randy Bradshaw, who had assisted Kentucky Derby specialist D. Wayne Lukas for many years. Because Randy had trained Animal Kingdom before, I reckoned he could train him a bit over that winter and be able to tell us whether we were being realistic about our aspirations for the Classics.

Graham Motion, however, was anxious to get the colt to his barn at Palm Meadows, so after about a month we altered the plans.

Animal Kingdom returned to training on December 10. His winter home was Palm Meadows' training center, located 10 miles inland from the ocean in western Boynton Beach, Florida. Shortly after the start of the year, he had his first breeze—an easy half-mile for Dave Rock. Graham Motion traveled from Fair Hill in order to be on hand for his next breeze, which was the first of what would be several team drills for Animal Kingdom and Pluck.

Pluck was pointing for an historic invasion of The Curragh in Ireland, where he had the Two Thousand Guineas on his dance card. Graham and I had devised a plan to emulate New York-bred Fourstars Allstar's successful Atlantic crossing in 1991, when he became the first American-trained runner to win the Irish classic.

Animal Kingdom's plans were not fully formulated, but Motion wanted to point him for an allowance race on grass, while keeping the Blue Grass Stakes at Keeneland on the back burner.

Motion liked the luxury of having two classy horses working together towards their goals because other work mates would not have to be found or sacrificed. Many a nice horse has been ruined over the years when it could not keep up with a talented work mate. But this way, both colts were able to get a lot more out of their morning trials since they both had quality.

Over the next two months, Animal Kingdom and Pluck breezed once a week on the grass, culminating in a February 25 team drill going five-eighths around the pylon cones in 1:04.

In some of the works, Animal Kingdom looked to have more in hand, yet in others, Pluck seemed to have the upper hand and to gallop out better. In point of actual fact, as the Irish love to say when they are about to reveal a truth, both colts were notoriously lazy. Pluck had been embarrassingly outworked by a filly in his final Breeders' Cup morning trial and, later in life, Animal Kingdom required workmates to be placed at various points around the track to engage his interest.

A week before Animal Kingdom's 3-year-old debut, Team Valor debuted a new player, when Crimson China was sent out by Graham Motion to win an allowance on the grass. It was his first start since he broke his maiden the previous November on the synthetic track at Wolverhampton in England.

Animal Kingdom made his first start at 3 on March 3 in a race that, at a mile, we knew was too short for him. To make matters worse, the colt drew the ten hole in a field of eleven on a course that featured a very short run to the first turn. I talked to Graham Motion about scratching and running instead in the Grade 3 Palm Beach Stakes, but the position on the calendar of the March 3 allowance race was better for our plans because it afforded the possibility of a start in Turfway Park's Rushaway if we needed that race to beef up his earnings to gain a position in the starting gate for the Blue Grass Stakes.

Animal Kingdom left the gate awkwardly as the 5 to 2 second choice. Favored Powhatan County, a colt with terrific grass form, used his ample speed to make the pace without any pressure through a quarter in :23 and a half in :47. He cut the corner into the stretch and spurted to a 2 ½-length lead a furlong from home.

Animal Kingdom, who had moved up to fourth about 5 lengths off the lead at the midway point in the race, had to be hustled along prematurely to cut the margin to about a length at the quarter pole. He was still green in his third lifetime start and wound up floating himself out to the middle of the course when coming off the bend.

Animal Kingdom was able to gather himself and get into his best stride. He flew home late, missing by a head to the favorite. He probably ran his last furlong in a sensational :11-flat. A step past the wire, he was well in front and a few strides later, he was 4 lengths in front.

The mile had been run in a lively 1:34 3/5 with a :23 4/5 final quarter. Powhatan County at two had been bothered by Pluck in the Continental Mile at Monmouth Park or he might have won it and he improved next time as the runner-up in the With Anticipation Stakes. That Saratoga Grade 3 was won by Soldat, which the following February at Gulfstream Park won the Grade 2 Fountain of Youth Stakes on the dirt. The form was solid and current.

It was a good news/bad news result. The good news, of course, was that our colt showed us he was for real in terms of quality and that a mile and a quarter, whether on the first Saturday in May or later in the summer for the Grade 1 Secretariat Stakes, would suit him best. He had enough quality to run a high-class specialist Miler to a head while still green and in need of the race.

The bad news was that he needed the money from the win to get into a race that might qualify him for a run in the Kentucky Derby. We had more viable 3-year-olds than ever before and we needed to place them where they each had their best chance to move forward without getting in one another's way.

The plan with Animal Kingdom had always been to run him in the Blue Grass because of the timing and value of the race and the fact that it was contested on a track that he had demonstrated an ability to act on. So it was decided to point him for the Rushaway, a $100,000 stakes on the Spiral Stakes undercard. Crimson China would use the Spiral as his entry card for the Kentucky Derby.

Before they were vanned to Keeneland, their spring base, Animal Kingdom and Crimson China breezed five-eighths in company at Palm Meadows. Dave Rock said it was both horses' best move of the entire winter.

In the lead up to the Spiral and Rushaway Stakes, Graham Motion was questioned about the two colts. He said, "Our original idea was to run Crimson China in the Spiral and Animal Kingdom in the Rushaway. But those plans may have to flip. Crimson China is currently fifteenth in the career earnings metric used for the Spiral for horses that haven't won stakes events.

"My original plan had nothing to do with ability," said Motion, who had won Turfway Park's signature event with Adriano in 2008. "We feel that Crimson China is just a little more seasoned and ready to jump up against these kinds of horses. They're both very much on a par, though. I think we'll just have to let the cards fall as they do."

Crimson China failed to draw into the Spiral and Animal Kingdom qualified so their entries were switched. Horseplayers sent Animal Kingdom post ward at odds of 3 to 1. Alan Garcia got Animal Kingdom out of the gate with his field. He was outrun and dropped back going past the stands the first time. The colt ran up on another horse's heels going into the first turn, forcing Garcia to sit on his mount and drop back a bit. A debris-laden dust cloud from the kickback of the horses ahead of him caused Animal Kingdom to veer away from it and go wide as he dropped farther back while navigating around the first bend.

Garcia had a difficult time getting Animal Kingdom into a good rhythm around the clubhouse turn. After completing the first turn, however, Animal Kingdom rode the rails the entire length of the backstretch. Garcia said, "I stayed on the rail because I had a feeling everybody would try and go wide. I figured if he was good enough, he would make a move and he did."

Leaving the backstretch, Garcia really had Animal Kingdom rolling and, approaching the stretch bend, he angled the big chestnut wide as he swallowed up the runners in front of him, including Decisive Moment, whose rider took a cheap shot by aggressively floating Animal Kingdom out to the middle of the track.

Animal Kingdom took being packed out with the equanimity of a horse that has a superior temperament. He returned the favor by carrying his rival back towards the rail and then responded to right-handed encouragement by drawing off to win by nearly 3 lengths. He carved almost all the winning margin in the last few strides. Once again, he made a mile and an eighth appear too short for his prodigious stamina.

Motion said, "Today it seemed you couldn't afford to get too far out of it but that just makes his race all the more impressive."

The victory was convincing and no rivals could muster an excuse. The press, however, snickered at the slow time of 1:52 3/5, not taking into consideration the condition of the track. That seemingly slow race earned a 94 Beyer figure and a new career Ragozin topper for Animal Kingdom of 8 ¾.

Animal Kingdom had been under a drive, well in advance of the half-mile pole and probably from the five-eighths pole. In the history of my syndicated runners, few of them had a run as long as a quarter-mile and precious few could produce a drive of three-eighths of a mile. Only Captain Bodgit and Prized had demonstrated the ability to sustain a drive for as long as a half-mile. So, in just his fourth career outing, Animal Kingdom showed that he was already in rarefied company.

The $285,000 share of the $500,000 purse guaranteed Animal Kingdom a berth in the starting gate for the Kentucky Derby.

Just to have a little fun with the Animal Kingdom partners on hand at Turfway, who were already salivating at the chance to run their colt in the Kentucky Derby, I said in my best deadpan fashion, "You know, this colt is probably more suited to the Epsom Derby than the Kentucky Derby." Because of Team Valor's adventurous nature, few could tell if I was serious; so the utterance was met with silence, accompanied by some dropped jaws and raised eyebrows, until I let it be known that I was just kidding.

"Wherever they want to go with this horse, I want to be there," said an exuberant Alan Garcia, who flashed that beaming headlight of a smile of his. However, shortly afterward, he switched agents to my longtime pal and business associate Ron Anderson. As it happened, instead of listening to the jockey, the agent took his hot-riding Peruvian rider in a different direction.

Crimson China ran second as the 6-to-5 favorite in the Rushaway Stakes, beaten 2 lengths. He made it into the Grade 1 Blue Grass Stakes at Keeneland, where he finished fifth beaten 3 ½ lengths, thereby bringing his partnership's Kentucky Derby dream to a screeching halt. He went on to win the Lamplighter Stakes at Monmouth that summer and turned out to be moderate afterwards.

Pluck disappointed as the odds-on 3 to 10 favorite in a mile allowance race at Tampa Bay Downs, and flopped badly again when he came in seventh, beaten 8 ½ lengths, as the favorite for the Grade 3 Transylvania Stakes at Keeneland in what ended up being his last start. We gave up the ghost on the Irish Guineas venture. Just hours before Pluck's projected return at Churchill Downs over the Breeders' Cup weekend, I received a call that he had been stricken with a violent attack of colic. En route to a clinic to be treated, he got down in the van, barely made it to the hospital and was lucky to be saved for stud. We sold out our remaining interest in him to our Australian partners and he entered stud down there.

While at Turfway Park for the Spiral Stakes, I was fortunate enough to watch the 3-year-old filly Summer Soiree win the Grade 3 Bourbonette

Stakes in very taking style. She employed a particularly long and fast stride on the Polytrack to win in stunning fashion by nearly 11 lengths.

Summer Soiree was owned in partnership by former Kentucky Governor Brereton C. Jones, the fellow from whom I had bought our first partnership-owned racehorse, Political Ambition. His partners were his son Brett and the Wahoo Partners, headed by bloodstock agent Debbie Easter. After getting in touch with Brett, we were able to strike a deal to buy the filly for $1 million.

Trained by Graham Motion, Summer Soiree went on to score a convincing 8 ½-length win the Grade 3 Boiling Spring Stakes at Monmouth and a hard-fought victory in the Grade 1 Del Mar Oaks. After placing in separate renewals of the Grade 1 Matriarch Stakes at Hollywood Park, she increased her earnings for us to $384,500. We sold her as a broodmare for $1.7 million.

Spiral Day turned out to be very productive for Team Valor International.

CHAPTER 24

The Derby Build-up

In the immediate aftermath of Animal Kingdom's Kentucky Derby victory, people wanted to know if I had bet the horse, because of his generous odds of nearly 21 to 1, or why I acted so surprised to see my colt win.

There is a silly little game engaged in by fans, media, owners and trainers after the Derby.

Some fans take the position that, if you did not bet your horse, it meant you had no faith in him, and if you were surprised your horse won, it meant you didn't know he was going to win. The point of both queries is to lessen the importance of the accomplishment by showing the owner simply got lucky.

The media, in theory, simply want a story, but in fact, many in the media bet on races, develop loyalties and ask questions that will substantiate a point of view that they bring to the story. Sadly, in what passes for modern journalism, the only thing these scriveners want is an owner or trainer to confirm the story they already have in their minds.

Owners feel that if they don't say they bet their horses, they will be perceived as having lacked faith or confidence in their steed. So they become reluctant participants in this little game by providing disingenuous answers.

Trainers never want to look weak or wrong, so they assume a posture that they knew all along the colt was a Derby winner because, God forbid, if the horse "ran in on them," it would mean they didn't know they had a Derby winner in their barn; this, apparently, is the biggest sin of which a trainer can be guilty.

Such were the twists and turns of Animal Kingdom's rollercoaster ride—from winning a late fall maiden race at Keeneland to wearing the garland of roses across his withers after the Kentucky Derby—that nobody associated with the horse went into the race with complete confidence. All were hopeful, but too many things happened in too short a span of time to allow the luxury of that impostor known as confidence.

Animal Kingdom exited the Spiral with a lot of mucous in his throat that Dr. Rob Holland treated with an antibiotic. Graham Motion surprised me by saying that he did not want to run Animal Kingdom again before the Derby. As a student of the history of the Run for the Roses, I knew this flew in the face of conventional wisdom. I pointed out to Graham that no Derby winner since Needles in 1956 had won the Derby off a six-week layoff. Recently both Barbaro, which was a Fair Hill trainee, and Big Brown, which won the Florida Derby, had been inactive five weeks before their Derby wins.

Motion was unfazed by the recitation of historical facts. He was confident he could produce the colt at his best on May 7.

The six weeks of inactivity was only one of the challenges Animal Kingdom had to overcome in order to flaunt history and win the Derby. In the 136-year annals of the Louisville Classic, only 2008 winner Big Brown had won the Derby with fewer starts—three to AK's four. Before 2009, one had to hark back to legendary WW1-era gelding Exterminator in 1918 to find a runner that had been able to pull off a Derby win in only his fifth start like AK would try to accomplish.

Another hurdle for Animal Kingdom to leap was that no Spiral winner besides Lil E. Tee in 1992, ever impacted the Kentucky Derby in any form off Turfway's signature race, which was first run in 1972 and became a more serious Derby prep ten years later.

No Derby winner had been produced by a mare imported from a foreign country in the last sixty-two editions.

And, perhaps most significantly of all, no horse that won the Kentucky Derby had done so without first having raced on a dirt surface. For seasoned Derby watchers, this presented them with their biggest stumbling block toward embracing AK's bid for Derby glory.

Ironically, I had faced the opposite dilemma in the 1989 Breeders' Cup Turf with Prized, which had never run on grass before winning the $2-million fixture. So I was trying to make history of a similar nature for a second time on a major international stage.

The plan was to give the colt plenty of time to recover from the Spiral, not breeze him for three weeks and put three timed workouts in him before the Derby. Motion planned to stable and train the colt at Keeneland, which had a synthetic surface, breeze him once over the Polytrack, and give him his last two breezes over the dirt at Churchill Downs.

Privately to my wife and office staff, in conversations with Graham Motion, publicly to media representatives and to anybody who asked me, I said that Animal Kingdom's participation in Kentucky Derby number 137 was solely dependent on how well he handled the dirt surface at Churchill Downs.

We knew we had one of the top prospects in America on the grass and I, for one, was not going to sacrifice my homebred at the altar of the Kentucky Derby unless it was demonstrated to me that he would be able to act on the main dirt track under the Twin Spires.

When it comes to running horses in the Kentucky Derby, I am unique among syndicate managers and among a very small group of racing men and women in that I will not run a horse in the Derby unless I feel it has a viable chance to succeed. A lot of people will mouth these same words, but I showed that I not only talked the talk, but walked the walk; in 2007, much to the chagrin of my racing partners, I refused to enter King of the Roxy for the Run for the Roses, even though he came within a half-length of winning the Grade 1 Santa Anita Derby while finishing well clear of the remainder, over a distance only one furlong short of the Kentucky Derby trip. I thought the mile and a quarter of the Kentucky Derby was beyond the limits of his stamina.

I take my role as a racing manager very seriously, so much so that I took umbrage with *Daily Racing Form* turf writer Jay Privman, with whom I had always been friendly, when he cryptically suggested in print that I might be falling victim to that emotional malady known as "Derby Fever." I felt professionally slighted and complained to the *DRF* editorial chief. Jay became irate and did not speak to me for a couple of years. We patched it up when I apologized and Jay accepted. Obviously, I was way too touchy but that's how much not being pigeonholed as just another boob meant to me.

So when I hinged a Derby run on Churchill Downs dirt works, most people in the know took me at my word.

Alan Garcia told us after the Spiral that he wanted to go wherever Animal Kingdom went. But his new agent Ron Anderson did a lot of business with Kiaran McLaughlin, whose good 3-year-old Soldat had won the Fountain of Youth with Garcia aboard. When Soldat ran poorly a week after the Spiral in the Florida Derby, Ron told us there was every chance McLaughlin would convince his owners to skip the Derby in favor of the Preakness. Trainers who are able to talk owners out of a Derby run have not been born yet, so we were left riderless as of April 10, less than a month before the Run for the Roses.

In chats about a potential Derby rider, I sided with Robby Albarado because he had ridden Animal Kingdom at two, he was based at Churchill Downs and he was very strong.

In the last few days before his first scheduled breeze in advance of the Run for the Roses, Animal Kingdom became a monster. He became the physical embodiment of what his sire Leroidesanimaux's name means. He was "King of the Beasts." The Spiral really ignited something in the colt. I kept thinking of the line in the movie *Dune,* in which the burgeoning powers of the young hero Paul Atreides moved him to yell out in full-throated fashion, "The sleeper has awakened!"

The prodigious strength with which Animal Kingdom galloped had become problematic for his exercise rider. Well aware of his strength, the colt had started to get, as Motion described it, "a bit cheeky," meaning he would try to take advantage of his handlers. He refused to round the turns and instead, he would occasionally go straight. He would not exert himself. In essence, he was playing the part of a rambunctious teenager and Motion was becoming a bit concerned.

When Animal Kingdom galloped alone, he could act like a jerk. In company, he generally behaved himself. Motion experimented and he discovered that a set of blinkers helped him to focus when he trained without company.

Animal Kingdom had his first breeze for the Kentucky Derby three weeks before the May 7 race and the work tab showed that his :59 1/5 was the second-fastest move of the morning at Keeneland. As with everything involving Animal Kingdom's preparation for the Run for the Roses, that was just part of the tale.

Graham Motion orchestrated a team breeze. Graham normally is the coolest customer on the track, but his countenance became so distorted as his plans went awry, I found myself looking at his face as much as I did the work. I had never seen him flustered before.

The workmate was already a football field ahead of Animal Kingdom on the backstretch and ready to break off, while Animal Kingdom was still on the turn in the middle of the track, giving his rider absolute fits. Once the rider managed to get the golden boy's attention, he had to ride him to catch up to his mate. When AK reached the other horse, his rider then had to slow him down to avoid overrunning the other horse.

Animal Kingdom broke off a length behind and finished 2 lengths clear at the finishing pole. He then galloped out 7 lengths clear after going six furlongs in 1:11 2/5. He let up through another furlong, by which time he was 14 lengths in front after a sensational 7 furlongs in 1:24. And then he pulled up a mile in 1:38 and change. It was astonishing. It was the best work one of our horses had turned in since Martial Law was preparing to win the Grade 1 Santa Anita Handicap more than twenty years earlier.

Prior to the work, I had been anxious that Animal Kingdom might be given too much time between races with too little to do, so when he turned in this huge work I was happy, as long as it did not seem to knock him out. We soon learned the move did not appear to faze him.

Meanwhile, morning line-maker Mike Battaglia, who had called the running of the Spiral at Turfway, put Animal Kingdom at 15 to 1 for the Derby, making him the co-eighth choice. Triple Crownologist Steve Haskin had Animal Kingdom breaking into his "Derby Dozen" in *The Blood-Horse* at number twelve. Number three was Toby's Corner, who the week before had upset long-time Kentucky Derby winter book favorite Uncle Mo by winning the Grade 1 Wood Memorial Stakes for our trainer, Graham Motion.

Animal Kingdom came out of his fast work on April 16 in good shape. He was scheduled to breeze the following two Saturdays at Churchill Downs. When I saw that the forecast called for heavy rains both in Louisville and Lexington, I suggested to Graham that he abort the planned trip to Louisville for the first Churchill Downs work and breeze the colt instead over the Polytrack, which absorbed water well and would provide a safe surface for his scheduled weekend breeze. Churchill Downs' track superintendent sealed the track on Friday, ending any change in plans for AK, as neither Motion nor I wanted to subject our colt to a work over a paved highway.

Graham could not have been happier. Left up to him, Animal Kingdom would have stayed at Keeneland for all of his preparations and shown up to the Churchill Downs stable area as late as the rules allowed. Graham liked training for the Derby under the radar, away from the limelight and the glare of camera flashes or video lights. He hated scrutiny. If he had his total choice, he might just have brought Animal Kingdom up to train over the winter at Fair Hill as he had done with his Wood Memorial winner.

I never understood Graham's reluctance to be in Louisville for the build up to the Derby. Every trainer alive understands that training over the surface where a horse will race gives the horse a better chance to win. Generators of speed figures like the Ragozin Sheets recognize that only a race over the track is considered to be more important than a breeze over the track. Of course, the media crush of Derby week can become tiresome, but it is a small price to pay for your horse being able to train over the track.

Precisely what scrutiny Graham was worried about also puzzled me. What he had to worry about from the public was a mystery, because Graham Motion may be the most articulate spokesman in American racing. He is intelligent, his demeanor is soothing to both to man and beast, he is very thoughtful, he is a thinker with a lot to say, he looks like a movie star and people love and admire him. What the heck he was worried about was beyond my ken.

Summer Soiree took to the track first for her pre-Kentucky Oaks breeze. Working more brilliantly than any Team Valor horse in history, and in a move I have only ever seen bettered by J. O. Tobin in Southern California, the War Front filly easily smoked through three-quarters of a mile on the rain-infused Polytrack in an unbelievable 1:09 1/5.

Half an hour later, Animal Kingdom appeared for his 6-furlong work. *The Courier-Journal* reporter Jennie Rees wrote, "On a soggy day when one almost expected to see the animals coming in two-by-two, Kentucky Derby hopeful Animal Kingdom worked over the Keeneland Polytrack." Our recent Gulfstream Park maiden winner Meistersinger was tapped to provide a lead, but it was painfully obvious as he led Animal Kingdom through a first quarter in the harness-horse time of 30 seconds that the pacemaker could not act on the Polytrack.

Animal Kingdom's rider took matters into his own hands and set sail on the big red colt, who ran down the lane in a stunning :22 3/5; but it was too little too late, as his 6-furlong clocking of 1:16 was about 4 or 5 seconds slower than what had been expected. Clockers gave him 1:02 4/5 for five-eighths, a work that ranked nineteenth on a work tab of twenty.

All I could do was close my eyes and shake my head. In his previous work, he had gone too far too fast and in this one, he had gone too short and way too slowly. Several thoughts ran through my mind. I tried to process what I had just seen in an attempt to make sense of it all and to put it into context based on all the Derby scenarios I had seen play out over the years.

After what surely must have been one of the slowest Derby works on record, I reasoned that Animal Kingdom probably had done too much the week before, so this lightening of his load actually was a good prescription to keep him fresh. Lord knows he had to be fit enough by then. Also, I thought to myself, AK gets an awful lot out of his gallops when his mind is on the job and that should ensure that he maintains his fitness up to the Derby. I composed my thoughts and reconciled myself to the notion that it was all just fine. Everything would be fine, I thought to myself. I was, in fact, giving myself a pep talk. I am an upbeat sort of guy and I was working on keeping myself positive in spite of the obvious cock-up to which I had just borne witness.

I also consoled myself by reasoning that none of the other horses training in Louisville had gained any ground on us. Animal Kingdom was in a better position to maintain his fitness, because the Derby candidates stabled at Churchill Downs were dealing with tracks that were exposed to serious weather; rain had swelled the banks of the Ohio River to record levels and had risen about 25 feet during the week, with no clear end in sight.

Asked by Jennie Rees if horsemen could get too caught up in the specifics of workouts at this time of year, Graham Motion replied, "Absolutely. I mean, I never worry about it until you guys are here, then you stress about it. If it was at home, I'd be like, 'It's fine. We'll deal with it.' And I understand it because there's so much analyzing and what have you. But to be honest, that is the beauty of Fair Hill because there's nobody there to critique you and you kind of don't get out of your game plan."

By midweek, ten days before the Run for the Roses, Animal Kingdom was still ensconced at Keeneland. Here is what I wrote in the Team Valor newsletter that Wednesday:

"If anybody thinks that training for the classics is easy, they should spend a few mornings at the track this spring, watching as each trainer assumes the role of a field commander, planning maneuvers that they hope will allow their charges to arrive under the Twin Spires in the best condition possible on the First Saturday in May, as they battle with unprecedented bouts of severe weather in hopes of garnering the most coveted floral wreath in all of American sports in the Run for the Roses.

"The lone constant in the last month in Central Kentucky has been the position of the jet stream, as it ushers one dangerous thunderstorm after another and the prospect of deadly tornadoes through the heart of horse country. Last Friday evening and early Saturday morning before Animal Kingdom was set to breeze, a few tornadoes touched down, including one in Versailles (just a few miles from Keeneland) and one in Lawrenceburg (where Barry and Kathleen Irwin lived). High winds recorded at more than 100 miles per hour caused windows to blow out in a popular downtown Lexington eatery."

On that Wednesday, ten days before the Kentucky Derby, the lone bone of contention emerged between Graham and me. It did not last long and Graham never got heavy handed, because that is not his style. Graham, unsurprisingly, made a play to keep Animal Kingdom at Keeneland for his final work and to not take him over to Churchill Downs. The botched work had set him on edge because it confirmed his worst fears that the media would scrutinize it for all they were worth, especially since TVG would be airing the final workouts. He also honestly believed that AK could be adequately prepared for the Kentucky Derby right where he was stabled at Keeneland.

When Graham and I were together, he only hinted at this subject. But he prevailed upon my assistant, Aron Wellman, who had worked as a lawyer before joining Team Valor, to present the case to me. I listened as I rolled my eyes, feigned exasperation, shook my head up and down and raised my eyebrows while my eyes were closed—all of which were my classic signs that I was bored with the topic.

Following Martin Luther King's advice to keep one's eye on the prize, I knew what I had to do to ensure that Animal Kingdom would be given his best chance to win the Kentucky Derby: I had to insist that our colt be vanned to Churchill Downs for a breeze over the track. Graham, in my opinion, had already pushed the envelope as far as one could reasonably expect by racing the colt only on grass and Polytrack and not racing him in the six weeks between the Spiral and the first Saturday in May. And I embraced his reasoning for both. But not allowing the colt to get a feel of the track by breezing over it because he wanted to avoid the scrutiny of the press was where I had to draw the line.

I will never forget what happened to Smarty Jones before the Belmont Stakes that would have given him a well-deserved Triple Crown. His trainer, another guy who wanted to train at home and away from the scrutiny of the media, sacrificed his colt's best chance to become a Triple Crown winner by putting his interests before those of his colt. He did not work his colt over Belmont's unique racing surface, which is nicknamed "Big Sandy" for a reason.

Here is what I wrote in the Team Valor newsletter:

"I insisted that Animal Kingdom train and breeze up to the Kentucky Derby under the Twin Spires, as the colt has not trained on dirt since he was a 2-year-old at Adena Springs South in Ocala and he has never raced on the dirt.

"So before we send him out for what undoubtedly will be the most difficult challenge he is likely to face in his entire career, it makes sense for us to find out if he can act on the dirt. I still want to send him over to Churchill Downs to breeze and gallop him on the main track and I would like Robby Albarado to be in the saddle, so that we can get the best opinion available on whether the colt likes the dirt.

"However, we have to balance that with the fact that this colt is rapidly improving and turning into a physical powerhouse. He is telling us he wants a bigger challenge and that he is ready for one. All we want to see right now is a sign from the colt that he can transfer his form from Poly and turf to dirt. His pedigree says no, but his racing style and physique say yes. But until he breezes over it, we are all just guessing. We do have faith in our colt and we would like to see him take part in the race. Especially this race, this year. Because if he can run on dirt, he can win the Kentucky Derby."

Earlier in the week, a fan posted online at the *Paulick Report* the following comment: "I really doubt Team Valor will skip the Derby. Call me jaded but this on-going suggestion of him going based upon a workout is a bit of fluff to keep them in the press IMHO. Does anyone really think a racing partnership is going to skip on the biggest TV publicity opportunity when their horse is already proven to be a worthy contender?"

I responded, "FYI, we skipped the Kentucky Derby with King of the Roxy when he just ran second, beaten half a length, in the G1 Santa Anita Derby. I am sorry that you find it difficult to take me at my word. We will not make a decision about running in the Derby until we are satisfied he can transfer his form to the dirt. All of my partners are on the same page and they have been very understanding. Just because we run a partnership, it doesn't necessarily follow that we are going to do stoopid things in order to gain publicity or a larger share of the limelight. Perhaps you have my stable confused with another outfit that does stuff like you suggest all of the time."

I elaborated my thoughts on the Derby saying, "I have a theory about why so many horses that do not belong in the Kentucky Derby are entered. I attribute it to Americans' reaction to the attacks on September 11. My theory is that Americans sensed their own mortality that day and ever since they act like they have five minutes to live.

"So instead of taking a long range approach to life, they want to check off their bucket list items as quickly as possible. Hence full fields for the Derby.

"When I grew up in the sport, peer pressure kept owners from running suspect horses in the Derby. Not anymore. I may be the last guy on earth with a qualified Derby candidate that was held out for horsemanship reasons. Morgan Freeman and Jack Nicholson just may be the only two guys that don't have the Kentucky Derby on their 'Bucket List.'"

So Animal Kingdom was duly vanned the hour and a half up the road from Keeneland to Churchill Downs on Thursday afternoon. He galloped on Friday morning and was set to breeze on Saturday morning with Robby Albarado in the saddle. Arrived at last, arrived at last. Thank God almighty we have arrived at Churchill Downs at last!

It turned out to be fortunate that I had arranged for a friend of mine to videotape the breeze for my analysis afterwards. Graham Motion flew in for the breeze that was scheduled just after the 8:30 a.m. renovation break. *Thoroughbred Times* writer Jeff Lowe picks it up from there in this report:

"Animal Kingdom seemed to take to the dirt just fine in a six-furlong workout on Saturday morning at Churchill Downs for the Kentucky

Derby, at least as much as Barry Irwin could see. Irwin, the principal of owner-breeder Team Valor International, was detained from seeing the workout in its entirety because of the marathon that snarls traffic in and around Churchill every year on the Saturday before the Derby. Irwin, an indoor track aficionado, took the disruption in stride, even though the move was considered fairly crucial for Animal Kingdom's dirt debut in the Derby. The Spiral Stakes winner covered six furlongs with jockey Robby Albarado in 1:13 in company with stable mate Meistersinger, who was clocked in 1:14.60.

"'We couldn't get in here because of the marathon, so when we saw it, we saw it at the end of the stretch and coming toward us, then we saw him make the turn and gallop out,' Irwin said. I'm not the right guy to ask, unfortunately,' Irwin said. 'They seemed happy. Robby is happy, the trainer [Graham Motion] is happy. Apparently he liked the dirt.

"'He worked on the dirt when Randy Bradshaw had him [in his early training] at Adena Springs, so we knew he could go on it, but we wanted to see him now as a little bit of an older horse to see whether he looked like he could transfer that form to the dirt.'"

"Animal Kingdom broke off a few lengths behind the workmate and finished five or six lengths in front, posting fractions of :12.40, :24.80, :37.20, and :49.20. He galloped seven furlongs in 1:26.40.

"Albarado proclaimed, 'You might be looking at a Derby winner, boys,' back at the barn. 'I rode him as a 2-year-old in the fall and he took the worst of it that day and still won, so I thought that day he was a very nice horse. Obviously he's grown up and proved himself. He felt great today. You can't really get a good line in the mornings [going from a synthetic surface to dirt]. It's not just the feel of the surface, its the sand that will be kicking back at him, and he's probably going to come off the pace, so you have to put all that in the angles. I think he's a nice horse and the good ones seem to overcome a lot.'"

When we all got back to the barn, we were swarmed by a full-on media crush that, in racing, only occurs on the Churchill Downs backstretch before the Kentucky Derby. Graham's face told it all—the lines in his face were totally relaxed, yet he couldn't keep a smile from dancing on his lips.

Jay Privman literally ran up to me and was more effusive than I had ever seen him as he questioned me about the work. I could tell from his excitement that the work had been a revelation to the denizens of the press box. He acted as though the Derby was now squarely in our grasp.

"Congratulations," he said, as though we had just won a race. "Did you know this horse was this good?" he said, as if, until the breeze, the colt was an unknown quantity. "When did you know this horse was this good?" He was incredulous that the colt could have flown so far under the radar until the dirt breeze.

But Privman responded to the work as part of an annual ritual that Derby aficionados go through in hopes of spotting the one colt that takes to the unique Churchill Downs surface like no other and stamps himself as the likely winner. Animal Kingdom anointed himself as the official buzz horse of Derby 137 with his stunning move.

Privman was not the only one to take notice. Bob Baffert, blown away by the move, told Steve Haskin "that's the one" and promptly announced that the Derby would be won by a Jew, more specifically Nehro, owned by Ahmed Zayat, or Irwin's colt Animal Kingdom.

Graham Motion said, "As disappointed as I was with how things turned out last week, I couldn't have been happier this week. Last week everything did not go perfectly. Today, everything went perfectly. Just cut and dried, really.

"I told Robby I wanted to go three-quarters. In an ideal world, I'd like the horses to work together, but I said, if you turn for home and you've got plenty of horse, you need to make him work out and get something out of it. That's exactly what he did."

In response to the question on the tip of everybody's tongue, Graham emphatically answered, "Knock on wood, if he's all right physically, yes, absolutely." Animal Kingdom had been given the green light by our team.

Although I had brokered the deal to buy the sire, bought and imported his dam and had managed Animal Kingdom's racing career, if I had made no contribution other than insist he breeze that Saturday a week before the Derby at Churchill Downs, it would have been enough for me because it gave the colt the his best chance to win the Kentucky Derby and change all of our lives forever.

All the right people began jumping on Animal Kingdom's bandwagon following the dirt breeze, with *The Blood-Horse* writer Steve Haskin leading the way. "The good news is that his work was exceptional. He was able to make a couple of moves to put himself where the rider wanted and leveled off beautifully after having a single cross thrown on him. And best of all was his strong gallop-out. He certainly seemed to move over the dirt well. What we like about this horse is his ability to quicken, but unlike some horses who can give that big burst for an eighth of a mile, he quickens and then just keeps going."

I thought Haskin came close to hitting the nail on the head. I think the Spiral's importance was that it gave Animal Kingdom a prep under conditions that prepared him ideally for the Kentucky Derby. Even though the Spiral was run on a synthetic track, the severe kickback, the fast, unrelenting fractions, the large field size and the crowded circumstances all combined to prepare Animal Kingdom for his Derby experience. And, best of all, he seemed to be just getting warmed up at the finish, after a sustained drive of more than a half-mile.

Before the Saturday dirt breeze, I had expressed my apprehension to a racetrack clocker about Animal Kingdom's screwed up workout pattern as he headed for a possible Derby try.

"Don't worry about conventional wisdom," he counseled. "Starting with Giacomo's upset win in 2005, it seems conventional wisdom has been thrown right out the window. I believe the race for the Graded earnings has changed the parameters of the Kentucky Derby.

"It intensifies pressure on the trainer to get a horse not only ready, but eligible. One thing you got going for you is your horse is fresh. He has not been taxed. And even though his works have been odd, it is no fault of the colt. You have the right horse, you just have to get lucky."

Animal Kingdom's eye-opening work over the hallowed ground beneath the Twin Spires allowed us to finally relax and enjoy the exciting week ahead, as the rollercoaster nature of the Triple Crown trail had worked out in our favor. All that remained was the draw.

The post position draw was set for the Wednesday evening before the Kentucky Derby. In a $10,000 claiming race run on Wednesday afternoon, Robby Albarado was thrown by a gelding, who compounded the injury by stepping on the rider's face, causing a broken nose and other assorted facial insults.

Later that evening, Albarado was named to ride Animal Kingdom in the Run for the Roses. The Team Valor homebred wound up towards the outside in post position number 16. After Big Brown had won from the 20, and Pluck had won from the outside after going to his nose from an outside draw in the Breeders' Cup, I didn't worry much about post position anymore, unless a runner drew the rail. The Grade 1 Arkansas Derby hero Archarcharch, which provided an unfortunate example of what can go wrong from that inside stall, drew this time the rail.

Florida Derby winner Dialed In was a lukewarm 4 to 1 choice over 9 to 2 Uncle Mo, the previous year's champion, which drew wide in the 18 slot. It was universally gossiped about that Uncle Mo would remain in his stable instead of running in the Derby because of a mysterious illness. In yet another twist of fate, Toby's Corner injured a hind leg a day before the draw and was not entered by Motion for the Derby.

When Robby Albarado took off his mounts on Thursday, Graham and I began to talk about whether a change in rider was going to be necessary or advisable. I had been the one who wanted Robby in the first place. He had recently undergone an unpleasant and well-publicized domestic dispute. Some in our group were not happy with my choice to begin with. Now they smelled blood and lobbied for a change. Graham mentioned the possibility that John Velasquez, who had been named to ride Uncle Mo, might become available.

Although Graham and I talked over the possibilities at length and exhausted every angle of the situation, the final decision was mine. Robby took off riding on the day after the spill. My position was that, if Robby rode on Friday, we would stick with him. I had seen many professional athletes, among them Tiger Woods and Michael Jordan, rise to the occasion when they played hurt or ill, so I had no trouble riding Robby on Animal Kingdom if he was up to the effort.

We kept in close contact with Robby's agent Lennie Pike, and Graham did the same with Johnny's agent Angel Cordero Jr. Graham did push for Johnny, who not only was the most successful rider in the country, but a close personal friend. Graham never became insistent, which was to his complete credit. After all, a Kentucky Derby triumph was the lone missing career credential in Velasquez' otherwise flawless resume.

When Robby took off all of his mounts including in the Kentucky Oaks on Friday, that was enough for me to replace him with Johnny. Robby insisted that he was only taking Friday off to give himself his best chance to recover for Saturday, but I reasoned that a viable jockey would not pass up the important stakes races on the day of the Kentucky Oaks.

Once again the rollercoaster nature of this particular Kentucky Derby had provided our group with yet another ride on Ups and Downs; our horse would be ridden by a jockey who had never so much as sat on his back.

So when the fans and press run their post-race games and ask about levels of surprise and confidence, they might be better served to ask what it takes to be successful in the hardest horse race to win in America.

CHAPTER 25

The Heavens Align

Friday before the Derby is Oaks day in Louisville, where the filly version of the Kentucky Derby is run over a distance a furlong shorter than its male counterpart. It is the most sought-after prize for a filly in American racing.

The day before the 2011 Run for the Roses, the filly with the lilies draped across her withers was Plum Pretty. She did not overwhelm her opposition as Rachel Alexandra had two years earlier, when skipping clear by an astounding 20 ¼ lengths, but Plum Pretty, like Rachel Alexandra, was sired by Medaglia d'Oro, the first stallion I had bought for Richard Haisfield. As racing folk are wont to do, I took it as an omen.

On Derby day, Team Valor had its 6-year-old mare Daveron in the Grade 3 Beaugay Stakes at Belmont Park. Neither my assistant Aron Wellman nor I could find a TV monitor at the track that showed races other than those run at Churchill Downs. So I took Aron with me to the executive offices behind the Derby Museum to ask media supremo John Asher if we could find a place to watch the New York race.

John invited us into his office, made a few calls and found the correct channel just in time to watch the start. Daveron stalked to the stretch, opened a daylight advantage and held on to win by a neck, with my pleading for her to "please hold on." I turned to Asher and said, "This could turn out to be a very lucrative day."

In a twist of fate, Daveron was ridden by Eddie Castro, who only became available when Toby's Corner went wrong a few days earlier and was scratched from the Derby.

This was the first Graded score for Daveron, who went on to win a Grade 2 at Saratoga, retire with earnings of $500,000 and sell at Keeneland for

$750,000. She cost $128,000 and generated income totaling $1.25 million. I bought her in Germany as a yearling the year after I acquired Animal Kingdom's dam Dalicia. Daveron and Animal Kingdom were produced by full sisters. The timing of Daveron's Derby Day win was exquisite. I took the Beaugay win as yet another omen.

Over the last several years, Derby owners developed a tradition of walking over with their horses to the paddock. In the beginning, only a few owners took the trek from the stable area, walking through the deep dirt around the clubhouse turn, waving at fans in the clubhouse like they were in the Rose Parade, and making their way to the gap, where a tunnel led underneath the grandstand to the paddock. After a few years, the walk became *de rigueur*.

By 2011, with the emergence of syndicate-owned Derby entrants, the number of individuals making the walk over had grown to a point where even people with the most tangential affiliation to the horses swelled the roll count to what seemed like more than 100 per entrant.

Such was the throng of people associated with number 13, Mucho Macho Man, that a bottleneck developed at the entrance to the paddock, forcing number 16, Animal Kingdom, to have to wait in the tunnel, and the entrants behind him to wait outside the gap on the racetrack.

I become annoyed when human indulgence supersedes what is best for a horse and I was frustrated to see my colt, which had been honed to a sharp edge, forced to cool his jets in claustrophobic conditions while Churchill Downs allowed the situation to get out of control. It was a dangerous scenario for finely tuned racehorses and their human connections to be in such close quarters.

The teeming throng of owners, hangers-on, B-list celebrities, bloodstock agents, jockeys' wives and media that filled the paddock was so great that some of the crowd spilled over from the grass, onto the rubberized walking ring reserved for the horses. The crush intensified as the riders were given a leg up because people felt an urge to move closer to the action.

I tend to become somewhat of a mother hen in the paddock, so I tried to protect my horse and began pushing people back onto the lawn. Animal Kingdom looked ready to roll. I was very happy to see the runners finally file out of the paddock. I stayed behind until they all cleared out.

One of the few people remaining, in a corner of the paddock, was Terry Meyocks, onetime chief executive offer of the New York Racing Association and, later, head of the Jockeys' Guild. I vented to Terry about what a challenge it had become to run a horse in the Derby, citing the pressure that owners exert on their own horses by clogging up the tunnel and the walking ring, the lack of customer service from Churchill Downs in accommodating the owners, and the hassle of devising ways to beat the system to gain entrance to the winners' circle should your horse win, as the track limited numbers. One year Mike Pegram, realizing that network TV was on a tight deadline, held up the winners' circle for several minutes until staff members from some of his McDonald's restaurants were finally allowed into the hallowed enclosure. That was a breakthrough moment for racing syndicates.

I had spent that morning at the executive offices trying to upgrade the seating Churchill had sold to some of my racing partners, which, in one instance, consisted of a folding chair behind a wall that blocked a view of the stretch run until the final 100 yards. The price of that seating was startlingly expensive.

"Man, sometimes I wonder if this whole thing is worth the trouble," I said to Terry. "I don't know if I want to do this again. What in the hell any of this three-ring circus has to do with horseracing is beyond me. It's tough enough to find a horse, get it qualified and bring it up to the race in top shape. You throw in all this other nonsense and it puts it over the top for me."

Standing with my wife Kathleen next to me in the box section beneath the Twin Spires, amongst some of my nineteen partners, I was ready for the Derby. A strange calm came over me, which was not normal before a big race. I usually get keyed up before an important race. But Animal Kingdom's appearance in the Run for the Roses did not spur any anxiety. He was being loaded in the gate. We had done our job: putting him in a position that, if he was good enough and had racing luck, could make him a Kentucky Derby winner.

I liked the horse, I bred him, I bought his sire and dam. I named him. I liked him going into the race to a certain extent, but I never thought he would win it. He had a lot to overcome. If he won, he was going to have to make a lot of history, which does not happen that often in the Derby.

Guys like me who live in the trenches, digging for Derby talent, and have seen as many Derbys as I have, do not think they are ever going to be one of those lucky bastards that win it. It just seemed too elusive, like trying to catch a cloud in a jar. So you gird yourself against disappointment. I think that's what I did. I didn't allow myself the fantasy of believing we could win it.

When the starting bell rang and a great roar burst forth from the record crowd of 164,858, Animal Kingdom left the starting gate at odds of nearly 21 to1. In spite of all the buzz from insiders, our colt was still a long shot.

Animal Kingdom broke half a step slow. Johnny Velazquez soon had him traveling at the back of the first phalanx of a dozen horses going past the stands for the first time and around the clubhouse turn. He was positioned in twelfth place, only half a dozen lengths from the clear leader Shackleford.

Velazquez kept Animal Kingdom in the center of the field in the run down the backstretch, keeping the colt well in hand as Shackleford doled out moderate fractions, including a tepid three-quarters in 1:13 2/5.

Animal Kingdom was allowed to creep up going into the far turn. Halfway around the turn, Velazquez got him going and, just before the five-sixteenths pole, about a football field away from the quarter pole, the rider spotted an opening. John Velazquez, seeking the first Kentucky Derby victory of his fabled career, sent the Team Valor colt between Soldat on his right and Santiva on his left in a move that ultimately won the race for him.

Velazquez knew his mount was in full flight and he allowed him to drift out a bit to the center of the track as he entered the homestretch to prevent Animal Kingdom's momentum from being stalled.

Then, as the field turned for home, I thought I saw him, but I wasn't sure because some guy wearing a big hat blocked my view. When the field entered the stretch. my wife started going crazy and she doesn't go crazy that often. I focused as best I could and, as AK got closer and closer to me, I started thinking, "This might even be possible. It's unrealistic, but it might be possible."

The winning rider asked his mount for his best stuff with about a furlong left in the race. Pace-setting Shackleford still had something in reserve after being allowed to get away with setting soft fractions and he still was in front a furlong from the wire.

Time stopped for me. I see the horse making this move, he becomes larger and larger, and I say to myself "Yes, that's him, I know it's him, but I don't *believe* it's him."

Animal Kingdom blew past Shackleford to take command, seemed to hesitate a bit after he got in front and then got back down to business, scooting 2 ¾ clear in the final 50 yards, just as he had done in the Spiral. He was strongest at the end and looked to have plenty left.

Ahmed Zayat's Nehro made a prophet out of Bob Baffert by completing the exacta, with Mucho Macho Man finishing well, but late, for third in a very good effort. Shackleford kept to his task and hung in there for fourth, beaten a length by the runner-up in a gutsy performance.

So came the moment that I had dreamed about as a kid, read about as a teenager, saw as a young man in my twenties and as an adult into my sixties. I had visualized winning the Derby many, many, many times. I had come close to actually realizing my dream when Captain Bodgit came within a few inches of glory.

So now, as my wife and I hugged each other and shared a kiss on the elevated presentation stand in front of the Churchill Downs grandstand and clubhouse, I compared how real life stacked up to my visualizations. I thought of the comment my wife made to me when I first met her: "It is amazing how real reality sometimes can be." I finally had an inkling of what in the hell she was talking about!

The realization of actually experiencing this special dream seemed nothing if not surreal. I guess when one subconsciously hopes for a dream to come true and it actually does, the reality of achieving it is very difficult to process consciously and to accept.

I told Graham Motion that I did not believe in fate, but the way things had systematically come about, I found that I could no longer discount the possibility of something or somebody having a hand in it. Too many things had fallen into place, in too fast a way. As a writer, I place a lot of stock in plausibility and I no longer found it plausible that all of the disparate pieces just happened to fit together as they did.

That evening, at a party for jockeys in the Galt House that Johnny Velazquez brought us to, Terry Meyocks walked up to me with that Cheshire cat grin of his. Instead of giving him an opportunity to mention my pre-Derby remarks, I quickly said, "Yeah, yeah, I know. Winning the race is definitely worth putting up with all of the bullshit."

And it was worth it, especially for my racing partners, who not only enjoyed the day itself, but also carried forward with a new layer to their lives. Most notably were the instances in which wives, who had been opposed to their husbands' involvement in racing, were now firmly on board and ready to buy their own horses to race with Team Valor. These women's acceptance of their husbands' passion was as gratifying to me as winning a Grade 1.

I knew the import of what we had accomplished. I was thrilled for Graham Motion and I was very happy for Johnny Velazquez. I showed my appreciation to assistant trainer Dave Rock by gifting him the commemorative gold wristwatch given to me by Longines, and Graham followed suit by giving his gold Kentucky Derby watch to his other assistant Adrian Rolls.

John Velazquez and the Animal Kingdom racing partnership teamed up to present jockey Robby Albarado with a sizeable check to ease the disappointment of having missed the Kentucky Derby ride.

The Animal Kingdom racing partnership donated to our company's designated charity, The Race for Education, a percent of the $1,411,800 winning purse and Team Valor matched it. Furthermore, Team Valor established a scholarship in the name of John Velazquez to be presented annually to an Hispanic college student. This scholarship joined the annual award for African American students that I named after the great nineteenth-century rider Isaac Murphy.

According to Steve Haskin in *The Blood-Horse*, although the pace had been slow, only Secretariat, in his track-record-breaking performance thirty-eight years earlier behind faster fractions, had run a faster last half-mile in Derby history than Animal Kingdom's :47 1/5.

Some Monday morning quarterbacks, trying to explain how a horse bred for the grass became the first horse in history to win the Derby without a race on dirt, said that AK won because the Derby was run like a grass race. They said the Derby was slow early and fast late. This theory, in fact, flew in the face of basic handicapping principles, as the speed horses would not have backed up and the closers would not have been able to make up ground. If anything, Animal Kingdom was due extra credit for being able to run down the leaders in a race with the slowest early fractions for the half-mile and three-quarters since 1947.

Racing has always been my preferred sport because it has something many other sports lack: a finish line. Whichever competitor arrives first at the line, barring an infraction of the rules, is the winner. The elegance of the finish line in horseracing, however, in many cases is not as clear-cut as one would like because of the many excuses offered by the losers. The reason is that in horseracing people gamble on the outcome. There are more stories in racing about the big fish that got away than there are in fishing.

In a race that historically and notoriously has been characterized as a rodeo because of rough riding tactics and shot taking, Kentucky Derby 137 was remarkable for the lack of untoward incidents in the running.

It is very nearly impossible in horseracing to gain complete satisfaction from winning a race. This Kentucky Derby not only provided us with a pristine victory, but one in which nobody had a legitimate platform to knock us down a peg. That is hard to come by and I savored every moment of it.

So, for the first time since the mighty Citation won the Kentucky Derby in 1948, the winner was produced by a mare imported to the United States. Calumet Farm had transported Hydroplane by ship in 1941 during World War II.

For the first time in history, the Derby winner was sired by a horse from Brazil.

For the first time in history, the Derby winner was foaled by a mare from Germany.

For the first time in history, the Derby winner was produced by a sire and dam from different continents.

Professionally, I took pride in having sold to a client the sires of both the Derby and Oaks winners in the same season.

Following so closely on the Breeders' Cup victory of Pluck, which I had bred from a mare I imported from South Africa, some industry watchers noticed a trend. Bloodlines authority Sid Fernando, writing in *Thoroughbred Times*, wrote, "Barry Irwin's Team Valor International has done the unthinkable for many U.S. breeders: race a homebred Kentucky Derby winner from a German-bred mare. Irwin, judging by the fallout from his post-Derby comments about unscrupulous trainers, is about as popular as the bloodlines of his Derby winner, but like him or not, he's breeding horses against the grain of the speed-oriented commercial culture here, and he's reaped the highest reward with one of them."

Daily Racing Form's bluegrass industry veteran Glenye Cain Oakford, at the end of her post-Derby piece entitled "Irwin wins Kentucky Derby the maverick way," posed the question, "But will Animal Kingdom's Derby win prove an inspirational game-changer for American breeding?"

I responded as follows: "For people who breed to race, I think it might mean a little something to them. But people that breed to sell, I think they're just shaking their heads and saying we got lucky or it was a bad group of horses or any other kind of crazy comment you want to make that doesn't take into account what actually happened."

As has become the case in modern-day journalism, post Derby stories by and large were a reflection of what the writers themselves brought to the task. It seems that every writer nowadays has an agenda and a point of view.

Because of my outspokenness on various racing topics, especially on the overuse of drugs, I became a lightning rod for controversy. So, some stories made Team Valor and me their leads, some made Graham Motion the focal point and others zeroed in on Johnny Velazquez winning his first Derby as the most newsworthy aspect of Derby 137. Some referenced Team Valor once. Some never mentioned the name Barry Irwin at all.

Some writers hailed me for my creative approach in using foreign bloodlines to win the most American of all races, while others could not get over my remarks about moving all of my horses to Motion because some previous trainers had lied to me.

One Animal Kingdom racing partner, Dave Dillion from Chicago, said, "The other partners and I have discussed this numerous times and all agree it was a cheap shot by the network. The context in which you were asked the question, after winning the Derby and trying to get through the crowds to meet Animal Kingdom and getting pulled aside and asked a question in the heat of the moment that required an extensive and thought-out response, was an obvious attempt to get a sound bite."

I received a lot of praise from those supporting my remarks and a lot of guff from those supporting the trainers. One Texas-based writer named

Gary West went so far as to say in print (even I was embarrassed for him) that he could not root for Animal Kingdom to win the Triple Crown because of what I had said. And this guy gets paid for covering Thoroughbred racing.

In the days immediately following the Derby, I found myself besieged with congratulatory e-mails. There were literally thousands of them. I started to answer a few, from longtime friends and colleagues, and then came up with a nutty notion that if somebody had taken the time to write them, the least I could do was answer them. That turned out to be a crazy exercise, as I wound up being cloistered in my home office for about three or four days in a row doing nothing but answering e-mails! By the way, it is a task I do not recommend trying.

I heard from people and family whom I had not been in contact with for decades. I was moved by the outpouring of letters and e-mails, especially those from folks against whom I had competed, as well as those whom I had nurtured in the business and become close with, going all the way back to my youth.

The first to contact me was Steve Robbins, my old buddy with whom I ran track starting in junior high school and went to the horse races with in high school. He pretty much summed up a lot of the reaction in an e-mail that read, "Well, I guess we know what the first line of your obituary is going to read."

Perhaps the most meaningful congratulatory note came from Mike Levy, a Kentucky-based farm owner, equine insurance executive and leader with the Breeders' Cup and the Thoroughbred Owners and Breeders' Association, who wrote, "You have never worried about what others think, and I admire your independence. You trusted the knowledge and experience gained over a lifetime and made your decisions with no uncertainty based on the welfare of the horse. I am very happy to have become an associate, a partner, and more importantly a friend."

When asked what winning the Kentucky Derby meant to me, I explained that when people found out what I did for a living, the first question they asked was whether I had won the Kentucky Derby. It was deflating, after all I had accomplished, to be dismissed out of hand by having to answer "no."

I looked forward to being able to answer "yes," especially at my high school reunion later that summer. But it seems that before we won the Derby, the question came up a lot. Since winning the race, it seems to come up a lot less than it used to.

Funnily enough, most of the time when the subject does come up these days, I avoid revealing that our horse won the race because having to accept accolades is just not something I have ever felt comfortable with. *I* know we won the Derby. That is sufficient for me.

Following Animal Kingdom's Kentucky Derby victory, there was more Triple Crown chat than normal because the colt's win was so emphatic, he was still a fresh and lightly raced horse, and he seemed ideally suited to staying the trip in the Belmont Stakes.

As was his wont, Graham Motion decided to send the colt to Fair Hill instead of training him at Pimlico where the Preakness Stakes was run. It was obvious to me that the old bugaboo of scrutiny was at the root of Graham's reluctance to stable the horse in Baltimore. Motion is a smart guy and he was able to provide any number of reasons for sending AK to his new home base in Maryland.

"It's just a better environment. It's more laid-back. He can eat grass. It's quieter, a lot less hubbub," Motion told a reporter. "It's a lot less intense compared with being at the racetrack. I think it's just nice to be in our own environment and not be on the road, basically. It's nice for the equine and the humans." The word "humans" said it all.

Since Animal Kingdom had never been to Fair Hill, it was not like he was going to gain an edge by returning to familiar surroundings. In fact, whatever was to be gained by the horse or his trainer or his staff in being at Fair Hill did not make up for the horse being unable to get a feel for the Pimlico racing surface. Especially the racing surface as it was fashioned the week of the 2011 Preakness.

The trade-off of adjusting to the Pimlico racing surface in favor of training at Fair Hill was not without its benefits. Animal Kingdom was able to get in full gallops on a safe surface at Fair Hill on days when the dirt track was wet. The colt had the track to himself when he went out to train. And Graham Motion had the option to get creative in order to capture his horse's attention. This was important because Animal Kingdom liked to test his handlers in the morning.

Monday of Preakness week, he galloped over a muddy dirt track and looked as good as I had ever seen him. On Tuesday, he made a routine gallop look exciting. And on Wednesday, he turned in as uniquely orchestrated a morning move as one is ever likely to witness in America.

Chronicling the Derby winner's every move since Animal Kingdom's arrival at Fair Hill, Joe Clancy wrote in *Steeplechase Times*, "And then the Kentucky Derby winner did what horses do, bucking and kicking out as his gallop ended on the turn past the wire before pulling up to a jog. The acrobatics probably didn't do much for the resting heartbeats of [rider David] Nava, trainer Graham Motion or Team Valor's Barry Irwin but they have to be a good sign. Eight days after the Derby, six days before the

Preakness, the chestnut colt feels good enough to goof off and have some fun. 'We wish he'd stop doing that, because it's a lot of twisting on him, but it does make you think he's feeling good,' said Irwin, who has been in Fair Hill for the last few days."

Graham Motion, in a moment of true inspiration, designed a morning gallop that showed exactly how creative he could be. In order to keep AK's focus, Graham placed nine horses at different positions around the track and AK picked them off one by one, in a work that could not have been duplicated at Pimlico, or any other racetrack I have ever been to.

Baltimore Sun reporter Kevin Van Valkenburg wrote, "Barry Irwin, who runs the Team Valor partnership that owns Animal Kingdom, said he was really pleased with what he saw. 'You know, the first couple days he was here, he was running around like a teenager,' Irwin said. 'He'd come past the stands, and duck and dive and just be a jerk. Since then, Graham has given him some targets. There were nine horses out there, and he went after them. As long as he can follow somebody, he's fine. He was very strong throughout, and at the end, he did an open gallop. He was smoking. I think we're looking good.'"

Philadelphia Eagles football coach Andy Reid stopped by to eyeball the Derby winner on Tuesday. United States Congressman Andy Harris showed up Wednesday for a photo op with Animal Kingdom, which tried to bite him. Maryland Governor Martin O'Malley came by the barn for a visit on Friday. Saturday morning, Animal Kingdom was loaded onto a van early in the morning and enjoyed a smooth ride from Fair Hill to the Pimlico stable area, thanks to a police escort arranged by Animal Kingdom racing partner Bruce Zoldan. Dave Rock led him off the van and, when the colt was ready, he was placed in stall number 40, which Pimlico traditionally reserved for the Derby winner before the Preakness Stakes.

As he would be in all but one of his next seven races, Animal Kingdom was favored, with players making him the 5-to-2 favorite for the Preakness Stakes. Once again, Animal Kingdom was drawn toward the outside, set to break from the 11 stall in a field of fourteen.

Animal Kingdom finished second in the Preakness, beaten half a length by Derby pacesetter Shackleford, with the promising newcomer Astrology in third. Derby favorite Dialed In, the 9-to-2 second choice for the Preakness ahead of 5-to-1 third choice Mucho Macho Man, came from last to finish fourth, just ahead of Mucho Macho Man.

The Team Valor colt had only two horses beat turning for home at the quarter pole and ran past the remainder save one, the flashy chestnut Shackleford, who proved to be a deserving winner by pressing fast fractions, taking over in the stretch and holding on determinedly.

Animal Kingdom was unable to overcome three hurdles: trouble at the break, severe kickback and getting too far back. Gigantic Mucho Macho Man, who reportedly lost a shoe for a second time in his last three starts, bumped Dialed In toward Animal Kingdom. By breaking half a step slow, Animal Kingdom set up his own downfall because he created space for Dialed In to cross over into his path.

Johnny Velazquez spoke to me about the race in detail, saying, "We got so far back, it was unbelievable. When the kickback started hitting my colt in the face, he wasn't used to it at all. It kind of startled him. When he ran in the Derby, the kickback was only hitting him chest high, but in the Preakness it was different. It was coming into his face and eyes and I think it was stinging him. He sort of lost his focus for a while.

"By the time he was on the backstretch, the colt wasn't bothered by the kickback at all and he was getting into the race. The problem is that there were so many horses in the race, I couldn't find any room from the half-mile pole to the middle of the turn. I had to take him wide to find my clearest path. He fired big, every bit as big as he had at Churchill. But he was so far back, it was difficult for him to close the gap. He fell just short. It was heartbreaking for me. I really feel we should have won this race. But I couldn't be prouder of the colt. He is the real deal. You got a champion here, boss."

Much has been made of Animal Kingdom's uncharacteristic beginning in the Preakness, where he fell back too far off the pace. In all of his previous races, the colt showed some early interest. Graham and I are convinced that the sluggish beginning had everything to do with Pimlico's adding loose soil to the dirt earlier in the week. Also, on race day, the trucks that water the track did so too far in advance of the race and when the Preakness began, the going was cuppy and loose. Animal Kingdom did not handle the going. Could he have adjusted had he been trained on the track in the week of the race? Nobody knows the answer, but when a horse gets beat half a length it certainly was something to be considered.

I spoke with Graham Motion a couple of days after the Preakness and told him that I wanted to run next in the Belmont Stakes, because a win would ensure him an Eclipse Award as champion colt at three. Then I explained my theory about what happened to Smarty Jones when his trainer hid out from the media, did not train his horse over the tricky Belmont track and lost the Triple Crown. I told Graham point blank that if he brought the horse to train over the Belmont track, I would love to run, but if he planned to keep him at Fair Hill, I would rather skip the race.

Surprisingly, Graham revealed that Johnny Velazquez had been over for dinner and gave him the same advice, so he was amenable. That was a big weight off of my shoulders.

Even though the Animal Kingdom partnership consisted of 20 fractional owners, our more than 300 other racing partners felt every bit a part of the AK team because I kept them apprised of the plans for the colt in our biweekly online newsletter. I let them know for the first time that my goal was to win the $10-million World Cup in Dubai.

"We don't want to hammer this horse," I wrote. "We've asked him to do a helluva lot in a very short period of time. It would behoove us to back off after the Belmont and start planning for both the Breeders' Cup and the World Cup in Dubai. I don't want to pile up the dirt races on him after the Triple Crown.

"He is amazingly versatile, so we might as well take advantage of his proclivity for all-weather surfaces and grass, because it will be a lot less stressful on him.

"As always, we will play it one race at a time. I know that this type of program irritates a lot of people who are used to making plans but I have always been a one-race-at-a-time type of guy and I don't see myself changing any time soon. It has served our stable well over the years.

"The long term goal with Animal Kingdom is to make him as attractive as possible as a stallion prospect because, as a Kentucky Derby winner and possible Eclipse Award winner, he would have considerable appeal worldwide as a future sire, especially given the outcross nature of his bloodlines."

Ten days before the Belmont, Animal Kingdom was up to his old tricks, as he tested both the horsemanship and emotional stability of his trainer. After completing a mile of a scheduled mile-and-a-half gallop, AK stuck his toes in the ground at about the point where the gallop began and he tossed his rider David Nava. Fortunately, Nava hung onto the reins and Animal Kingdom did not try to run off.

Animal Kingdom more or less behaved well after that incident. The Sunday before the Saturday Belmont, he was vanned very early in the morning from Fair Hill to Belmont, where at 9 a.m. he took to the main track and galloped once around.

I had not seen him in a week and I marveled at how well he looked, more specifically how much condition he still carried after the grueling and hard-fought first two legs of the Triple Crown. He did look a bit fitter behind the saddle, but his girth was prodigious and he still looked like he was not yet dead fit. "What a specimen," I thought to myself. He struck me as still looking like a fresh horse.

Animal Kingdom breezed Monday morning, barely lifting his hooves off the ground, like a grass horse with his daisy-cutter action. His :47 3/5 half was a bullet work among thirty-two on the tab. After he hit the finishing post, he just kept on going and went out five-eighths in a minute flat. It was breathtaking. Graham Motion said, "He went super. I thought he might go a tick slower, but I'm not surprised he did what he did. I'm not familiar with this track, but they tend to work a little quick on this track.

"He hasn't changed at all throughout the Triple Crown; he's remarkable. He has taken everything in stride and hasn't gotten worked up about it. Physically, he's handled everything great. Johnny said he did it all on his own, and he didn't even ask him to gallop out."

A group of media types gathered at Animal Kingdom's temporary digs on the expansive Belmont backstretch in the barn of Motion's pal David Donk and they wanted to chat. I said, "He looked like he went in :50, not :47. I think he still has a lot of energy left, that's the key. He doesn't look like a tired horse to me or anything." I was never more convinced that one of my horses would win a Grade 1 than Animal Kingdom in the Belmont Stakes. I was feeling upbeat and frisky. When the reporters started to interview Velazquez, I took Jennie Rees' tape recorder, held it front of Johnny's mouth and mocked the reporters, saying something silly like, "Johnny, uh, when exactly did you know for sure that Animal Kingdom would win the Belmont Stakes?" It drew a lot of laughs.

The next day at a press conference arranged by NYRA to promote the Belmont Stakes, I commented as follows: "I'm not worried about Shackleford, by the way. I'm worried about Mucho Macho Man. I think he's the horse to beat." It was just my opinion and was based on pedigree and observation. I meant absolutely no disrespect to anybody. Under normal circumstances, nobody would have batted an eyelash. But in light of my post-Derby remarks about lying trainers, the media was on heightened alert and proceeded to create yet another *cause célèbre* over this innocuous trifling.

The press turned the media event into a World Wrestling Federation-style trash-talking session. Obviously, it was a slow news day. Merely for saying that Shackleford did not figure to see out the trip, I was accused of badmouthing and dissing him. Shackleford failed to stay in the Belmont. Dropped back in trip to a mile the following season for the Grade 1 Metropolitan Handicap, Shackleford ran the fastest race of his career when he earned a 115 Beyer number in winning around one turn.

Team Valor had experienced mixed results with its four previous runners in the Belmont Stakes, finishing second with My Memoirs, third with Thomas Jo, fifth with Oh So Awesome and last with Dr. Greenfield.

Horseplayers made Animal Kingdom the 5-to-2 favorite for the Belmont Stakes. Derby runner-up Nehro was second choice at 5 to 1, with long-fused Master of Hounds 6 to 1 and Shackleford about 6 ½ to 1.

Animal Kingdom lost all chance half a dozen strides out of the gate in a chain-reaction bumping incident. He fell back to last, trailed by as many as 18 lengths at one stage and finished sixth, beaten 9 ¼ lengths.

Johnny Velazquez told me that, if it had not been the Belmont Stakes, he would have pulled up the colt, but he decided to let AK determine for himself if he wanted to continue or not. Halfway through the race, he trailed the field by some 15 lengths.

Animal Kingdom did give racegoers a bit of excitement, as 4 furlongs from home he put in a sustained run that carried him from last to a position about 3 lengths behind the leaders, only to run out of gas from having used too much energy in playing catch up.

Dave Grening wrote in *Daily Racing Form*, "John Velazquez said he believes that jockey Rajiv Maragh was careless in his handling of Isn't He Perfect shortly after the start of Saturday's Belmont Stakes, causing Velazquez to nearly become unseated from Animal Kingdom in the early stages of the race. Animal Kingdom, the Kentucky Derby winner and Preakness runner-up, eventually finished sixth as the 5-2 favorite in the Belmont.

"Further, Velazquez said he thinks Maragh may have deliberately taken a left-hand turn aboard Isn't He Perfect to impede Mucho Macho Man, a horse Maragh had been taken off after riding him in the Kentucky Derby and Preakness. Mucho Macho Man, under Ramon Dominguez, broke from post 10, in between Animal Kingdom and Isn't He Perfect.

"'That's what I think,' Velazquez said in a conference call with reporters Sunday morning. 'That's why I was so frustrated. Things happen in a race. If it would have happened right out of the gate I wouldn't have been so frustrated because things happen right from the start. But this happened three or four jumps after the start so that's why I was frustrated. It shouldn't happen. He should not be playing something like that in a race like this. It's stupidity and it shouldn't happen.'"

Velazquez and Animal Kingdom got bumped by Mucho Macho Man several strides out of the gate. The colt then clipped heels with Monzon. Velazquez got catapulted forward and his left foot came out of the irons. It took about a sixteenth of a mile for Velazquez to get his foot back in the stirrups. Animal Kingdom was last going into the first turn and Velazquez knew his chances to win were eliminated.

Plenty of people said Maragh deliberately hung a left-hand turn on his horse as revenge, after he had been taken off of him following rides in the

Kentucky Derby and Preakness. Racing officials suspended him for a week for failing to maintain a straight course.

"At best, it was careless," said Carmine Donofrio, the steward for the New York State Racing and Wagering Board.

It was the second serious riding incident involving Maragh in the last ten days. The track stewards convened a meeting to discuss rough riding with all of the Belmont jockeys, putting them on notice that the careless riding needed to stop.

Rather than blame Maragh, I put the blame squarely on Isn't He Perfect's connections, especially the trainer because, based on form, I thought the colt had no business being in the race. I posted on Facebook that, "the Classics are no place for amateurs."

The incident resulted in Animal Kingdom sustaining a slab fracture of a hind leg, which required surgery by Dean Richardson at the University of Pennsylvania's New Bolton Research Center. The horse was finished racing for the rest of the season.

Mike Watchmaker, who rates America's top horses weekly throughout the season in *Daily Racing Form*, summed up the debate for Eclipse Award voting in the category of 3-year-old male as follows:

"I concede that it is surprising, because he [Animal Kingdom] was ripe for a takedown over five months ago when his season ended, but I lean toward Animal Kingdom in this division.

"Animal Kingdom's victory in the Kentucky Derby, if an upset, was also thoroughly decisive, as was his prior win in the Spiral. He followed with a near miss in the Preakness, and a sixth in the Belmont Stakes, in which he suffered a ridiculously awful trip, and a season-ending injury.

"Shackleford and Ruler On Ice, the upset winners of the Preakness and Belmont in performances that weren't nearly as decisive as Animal Kingdom's Derby, never won again. Stay Thirsty and Coil, who emerged over the summer, proved unable to sustain their runs. And Uncle Mo couldn't follow through with his late-season Hail Mary.

"In the end, the Kentucky Derby, always the biggest 3-year-old race of the year, for me this year proved to be the definitive race in the 3yo male division."

Although Animal Kingdom was unable to race in the second half of the season, he had done enough for voters to crown him with an Eclipse Award as the champion colt of his generation at three. Chicago-based partner Mark Polivka accepted the trophy on our behalf in Los Angeles as I was unable to attend due to illness. The award capped an incredible year.

CHAPTER 26

Motion's Gambit

Champion Animal Kingdom was kept in training at four in 2012 with his goal being the $10-million World Cup, which was run late in March over the Kentucky Derby distance of a mile and a quarter on a Tapeta surface similar to the one he trained on at Fair Hill.

Daily Racing Form national columnist Jay Hovdey wrote, "This is very good news. There has not been a Derby winner with testicles attached answer the bell for a 4-year-old season since Giacomo, in 2006. Barbaro had an excuse, but it was only economics that kept Super Saver, Street Sense, and Big Brown from continuing their racing careers past their Derby year."

Interest in standing Animal Kingdom at stud had come from breeders in Kentucky and Newmarket. I never gave it much serious thought because I felt he still had plenty of racing left in him and I, for one, really wanted to find out exactly what this horse was capable of.

When Animal Kingdom returned to training, he weighed in at a noteworthy 1,314 pounds, making him the heaviest horse ever trained by Graham Motion at Fair Hill. The chestnut had grown taller with age and considerably heavier with inactivity because of his confinement to a stall during his initial rehabilitation. Naturally, Motion was concerned about his substantial girth but knew he was on a tight schedule to make the World Cup, so he pressed onward and gave AK the same workload as any horse on the comeback trail. He told me that he would be careful and back off if the colt showed a need for more considerate handling.

Animal Kingdom became the favorite with bookies for the World Cup as early as the second week in January, when Japanese Triple Crown winner Orfevre was withdrawn from consideration. Japanese horses had riveted the attention of internationalists since finishing one-two in the World Cup a year earlier.

The Eclipse Award winner turned in a spectacular breeze at Palm Meadows early in February, when he signaled his readiness by becoming the first horse to outwork Badleroibrown. Generating a final quarter-mile in :22 4/5, AK made up a 5-length deficit in the blink of an eye while cruising past his stable mate, and added another 8 lengths on his rival to go out three-quarters in 1:11 4/5. He galloped out seven-eighths in a stunning 1:24 and change.

We announced a race three weeks later at Tampa Bay Downs as the comeback spot for Animal Kingdom but, in actuality, Gulfstream Park racing officials put up an allowance race they promised to do their best to fill so that AK would not have to van from one Florida coast to the other. We used the Tampa Bay race as a diversion so as not to scare off entries for the Gulfstream race but were prepared to run there if the allowance was not used.

Gulfstream Park came through thanks to trainer George Weaver, who gallantly entered veteran campaigner Monument Hill to make the race go. Six horses went post-ward in mid-February, six weeks before the World Cup. As usual, Animal Kingdom began slowly from his outside slot, trailed while wide around the first turn, moved up to third on his own with a nice move on the backstretch, came wide for his run into the stretch and responded to vigorous hand riding from Johnny Velazquez to repel Monument Hill's early stretch challenge and kick clear with his very long strides.

It was invigorating to have the big guy back in action. On display was the one feature that set him apart as a racehorse—namely, how far underneath himself he reached with his hind legs. When Animal Kingdom wanted to generate speed, he would reach extremely far forward with his hind legs and it not only propelled him, it also allowed for coverage of an enormous amount of ground.

Viewing his stride from the head on, his action was as true as ever with his front limbs. His agility in handling the tight course was impressive for such a big horse. One could tell that the horse was very happy to be back racing.

Thoroughbred Times, with a headline that read, "Derby winner Animal Kingdom dazzles in long-awaited return," covered the race as follows:

"With all of the excitement swirling around the return of 2011 Kentucky Derby Presented by Yum! Brands (G1) winner Animal Kingdom, it seemed unlikely that the 2011 champion 3-year-old male would be able to live up to expectations. Instead, he exceeded them on Saturday at Gulfstream Park in his first start since being injured in the Belmont Stakes (G1).

"Animal Kingdom swept into the stretch from three wide and lengthened stride, accelerating explosively when switching leads to dispatch a challenge from Monument Hill for a dominant two-length win.

"'They went slow enough where he just pulled me into contention all on his own,' Velazquez said. 'I let him do what he wanted as opposed to wrangling him back behind horses. The second I started kissing at him in the stretch, he picked it right up and took off. It was a great feeling today and great to have him back. He felt as good as ever.'"

In what was scheduled to serve as his penultimate breeze before being flown to Dubai ten days later, Animal Kingdom breezed five furlongs in his first work since winning his comeback race. He emerged from the workout exhibiting soreness in his hind end. The stable vet thought he located a fracture in the same hind leg AK had injured in the Belmont Stakes and e-mailed digital images to Dr. Dean Richardson, who had operated on the hock a year earlier.

Dr. Richardson discounted the purported fracture as an artifact—an unexplained defect that occasionally crops up on x-rays. Dean ordered a nuclear scan, which clearly showed uptake in the ilium area of the pelvic bone. Digital x-rays of the area showed that Animal Kingdom was suffering from the beginnings of a stress fracture. Dean told me to imagine a bubble inside a bone: if the bubble had burst, there would be a fracture. This bubble preceded a fracture that did not materialize. "If anything was going to happen to this horse, this would be about as good a result as one could hope for," he said.

I immediately announced my intention of pointing Animal Kingdom for the 2013 Dubai World Cup. Dr. Richardson prescribed thirty days of stall rest, followed by sixty days of hand walking. We decided to keep the horse at Fair Hill for his rehab, which included walking on a water treadmill at Bruce Jackson's facility a few hundred yards from our barn.

My plan was to give the colt until September to indicate whether bringing him back at the same high level of racing was a probability or a pipe dream. If he could go on, we would race him; if not, I would follow up with interested parties and place him at stud. By this time he was actually more popular and valuable than he had been during the Triple Crown. There was serious interest in standing him from Japan, England and Kentucky.

I asked Dr. Richardson if the two injuries were connected.

"Well, the first injury was an accident," said the surgeon. "The second is a result of stress. They are unrelated as far as I am concerned. The good news is that, unlike soft tissue, bones actually are stronger after they heal from injury, so the pelvic area is unlikely to be a problem again. As for the hock injury, that surgical repair looks great and is holding just fine with no problems."

Dr. Richardson added that Animal Kingdom's only vulnerability in terms of future injury might emerge from the colt's overloading his left hind leg.

"As you stated, what makes him such an effective racehorse is his ability to get so far underneath him with his hind legs," the vet said. "And, with some top horses, they exert more pressure than other horses. Horses really don't reach maturity until they are five years old. So as Animal Kingdom ages, his skeletal structure will continue to strengthen and this will help him overcome the rigors of racing."

When my knee-jerk reaction was to point for the World Cup a year later, Graham Motion thought I had temporarily misplaced my few remaining marbles. But Graham himself came up with an idea that, as far as I was concerned, trumped mine to win the battle of the crazies. He proposed to point the colt for the Breeders' Cup Mile. Such was the level of ability shown by Animal Kingdom that he inspired us to consider the implausible.

Animal Kingdom ran a mile and an eighth when he broke his maiden at two and the only time he ran a mile, he could not get up to win an allowance race at three. So running a mile against the best in the world seemed like an incredible stretch. Graham reckoned, and correctly so, that if AK could make an impression at a mile in a race as important as the Breeders' Cup on grass, it would serve to elevate him in the eyes of stallion masters throughout the world. I agreed to the plan, but suggested that we keep it between ourselves until shortly before the race.

The rehabilitation went without a hitch. Animal Kingdom was back galloping a mile by June and he was up to a mile and a half by July. Taking full advantage of the Fair Hill grass course across the road from our barn that had been used since 1939 for steeplechase racing, Graham fashioned a series of race-like workouts. These impromptu little trials revealed that Animal Kingdom had actually improved once again.

Reporters wanted to know what Animal Kingdom's plans were for his comeback race. We told them we had a race in mind and we would reveal it in due course. After much speculation in the press, the mystery race was revealed in an announcement a month prior to the Breeders' Cup.

Exercise rider David Nava warned Motion that if he really planned to have the horse race-fit in a little more than three weeks, he was going to have to think outside the box. Motion responded by orchestrating a serious workout, in which AK set off fifteen lengths behind an Italian Group 3 winner that was preparing for the Laurel Turf Cup two weeks hence, as well as an Italian maiden winner of good quality. Overcoming the huge deficit, AK finished strongly; yet he managed to make it look easy, as he stretched over the yielding ground while running uphill on the undulating course. Nava said the stiff, six-furlong move was just what the horse needed.

Team Valor's *Insiders' Bulletin* reported as follows:

"Graham Motion may be defying conventional wisdom with the ambitious plan to bring Animal Kingdom back in the Breeders Cup Mile, but the Kentucky Derby winner continues to show that he is no conventional horse. Animal Kingdom inspired double takes on Wednesday with a wicked turn of foot that allowed him to bridge what looked like an insurmountable gap between him and two stable mates on the turf at Fair Hill. Barry Irwin was so awed that he sent the video link to his old partner, Jeff Siegel, to ask if he had ever seen anything like it. Siegel cracked that the video must have been trick photography."

Responding to a reporter's query about what made him confident in bringing Animal Kingdom back off the layup in the Breeders' Cup, Motion said, "The quality of the horse and his sensible nature inspired confidence despite the challenge. I'd be afraid to do it with some horses, but he's got such a remarkable attitude. I think physically, he's much more imposing (than when he won the Derby). He was always a big, strong horse, but now he's even bigger and stronger. I wouldn't say he's changed a huge amount, but mentally and physically he's definitely grown up like you'd expect him to. I'm surprised, actually, that he hasn't become more of a handful. He's always had a pretty good attitude. He's a pretty kind horse to be around for a 4-year-old stallion."

As the Breeders' Cup drew near, Motion began to second-guess himself a bit because of the magnitude of the task at hand. I counseled him not to over-think it. I knew how Graham processed these things and I figured he was worried, not about the horse under performing as much as what people might think of him if the plot failed.

News of the unorthodox undertaking inspired some outlandish comments before the race, including one from a well-known veteran observer of the Turf who said that it was unfair to take a cripple and subject him to this sort of ordeal on such a big stage because it could turn out to be a disaster that would be bad for racing.

It was obvious to me that Graham had utter confidence in the horse and his fitness level, so I reassured him that he was doing the right thing. "This is a no-lose situation," I explained. "It is like getting a free pass. Nobody—absolutely nobody—expects you to be able to get this horse ready for this race, so if he doesn't run up to snuff, nobody is going to hold it against you. And if he exceeds their expectations, then you will reap the benefits."

It was nothing if not ironic that, while I was in Australia hoping to see our homebred stayer Brigantin get a run in the Melbourne Cup, Australia's leading stallion master John Messara was in Los Angeles for the Breeders' Cup. A couple of days before the race, John inspected AK at Santa Anita. In another bit of irony, I had actually been dealing to sell him Animal Kingdom's sire a couple of years earlier.

Although I did not actually meet Messara in person until we got together in Dubai the following year, I had formed a relationship with him thanks to my South African pal Robin Bruss. I kept a mare named Alexandra Rose at Messara's famed Arrowfield Stud and we crafted a deal, in which we foal shared and sold yearlings out of my mare.

Messara is renowned in bloodstock circles as the developer of two of the world's most important and successful stallions in Danehill and his son Redoute's Choice. John is one of those larger-than-life characters of considerable intellect and charisma that envisions a concept and uses his managerial skills to reach his goal. Like me, he is not bound by conventional wisdom. He imported to Australia a horse from such a faraway land as Chile that became a top stallion.

John Messara liked what he saw in Animal Kingdom when the horse was walked for him at Santa Anita and he really liked what he saw in the Breeders' Cup Mile.

My first Australian trip turned out to be a bust, as Brigantin came out of his prep race with a badly torn ligament and failed by a place or two to draw into the Melbourne Cup. So Kathleen and I were relegated to watching the Breeders' Cup Mile on TV in our Melbourne hotel room.

Animal Kingdom was the 10 to 1 fifth choice for the $2-million Mile in a field that was reduced to only nine runners, owing to the presence of both the local 8-furlong specialist Obviously and, more importantly, the heavy favorite Wise Dan. Andy Beyer, writing in the *Washington Post*, dismissed AK as "certain to be the most over-bet horse in the Breeders Cup; he's never displayed the talent or turf ability to win at this level."

Southern California-based jockey Rafael Bejarano got Animal Kingdom to break with his field, which was a pleasant change, and took him immediately to the rail, where he raced around the first turn, saving ground, only six lengths off an opening quarter of :23 1/5. Lone speed Obviously backed up the pace and the field contracted, racing in a tight pack. Once settled for the run down the backstretch, Animal Kingdom was interfered with by the brilliant French filly Moonlight Cloud, who inexplicably came over and bumped him three furlongs into the race. Animal Kingdom fell back a few lengths after the erratic and unexpected interference.

Animal Kingdom gradually crept back into the race and entered the homestretch, still on the rail, with the entire field—save one straggler—in front him. He was forced to steady off heels momentarily. Bejarano appeared to have a lot of horse under him and Animal Kingdom promised to fire if he could find room.

Finally, in the closing stages, AK was able to get a seam. "Animal Kingdom, like a rocket, will be in a photo with Obviously and Excelebration," shouted race caller Trevor Denman, as the colt knifed his way between horses to emerge as a late threat in the closing stages.

Animal Kingdom finished so fast that the photo did not involve him, but rather Obviously and Excelebration for third. Animal Kingdom moved a half-length away from the other two. AK, alas, came too late, as Wise Dan won by 1 ½ lengths, with AK second ahead of Obviously, which had a nose to spare over British invader Excelebration. Final time, in spite of a pace slower than expected, was a new course record of 1:31.78.

Trakus, which digitally times each horse from a chip placed in the saddle, credited Animal Kingdom with the fastest quarter of the race, when he flew home in :22 2/5, which consisted of back-to-back furlongs in :11 1/5. "He exploded out of the pack and the finish was phenomenal for the way the race was run," Hall of Fame jockey Gary Stevens said on NBC Sports.

Several onlookers wondered aloud and in print if the best horse had run second. In a Sirius Radio interview with Steve Byk, New York Racing Association analyst Andy Serling did a 180-degree spin, saying, "I think Animal Kingdom ran the best race of anybody. I say that as someone who thought they were out of their minds to even run him in this race. I thought it was an absolute joke when he was 5 or 6 to 1. I wouldn't have bet him at 50 to 1. You watch that race, he steadied a good length or length and a half on the backstretch, he couldn't get through, and you could see he was turning his head.

"Granted, he saved ground, which mattered, but I'm not sure if he hadn't been able to swing clear three-wide on that turn he wouldn't have won that race. I'm sorry, and I have a lot of respect for Wise Dan—I think he's a terrific racehorse and I'm not trying to take anything away from him, but he had a perfect post and worked out a perfect trip."

ESPN.com columnist Bill Finley characterized Animal Kingdom's trip as the worst of the entire two-day Breeders' Cup. "Watch the race," he said. "As good as Wise Dan was, Animal Kingdom wins the Mile if he doesn't have a horrible trip."

Others chimed in as well. Jay Privman, *DRF* columnist and NBC analyst, said, "He might have been best." Fellow NBC analyst Randy Moss said, "I'm not willing to say with conviction that Animal Kingdom would've gotten past Wise Dan with a clean trip, but I won't argue with those who insist it."

Steve Haskin in *The Blood-Horse* wrote that Animal Kingdom "left me in awe of the horse's ability" as he burst down the lane, and he labeled his stretch run heroics as the "single most memorable moment of the Breeders' Cup." In an e-mail, Steve told me, "I thought he'd run huge, but his performance was off the charts. He is truly a great horse in my mind. You and Graham should be extremely proud of him."

It was no wonder that, when he returned to be unsaddled after the race, the beaten yet unbowed Team Valor colorbearer received a standing and sustained ovation from those attending the Breeders' Cup at Santa Anita.

Just as Animal Kingdom caught the racing world by surprise with his stunning turn of foot, he shocked me too, as we had never seen it before in the afternoon over so short a trip. Other than Frankel, the most gifted racehorse the world had witnessed since Secretariat, I had not seen anything in years that approached Animal Kingdom's dash down the lane at Santa Anita. The move cast him in a new light and significantly changed people's view of him. Possessing Miler speed to go along with his Classic credentials made Animal Kingdom truly one of the world's most versatile racehorses.

Motion's gambit had borne fruit; I reckoned Animal Kingdom's value doubled after his brilliant display because he showed that under slightly better circumstances, he had the tools to beat a runner in Wise Dan that was ranked by the International Federation of Horseracing Authorities 4 pounds clear of any Thoroughbred to have raced in America in 2012.

On Mike Penna's Lexington-based radio show, in response to his question about how my trainer had come up with the idea to run in the Breeders' Cup, I said, "I'll tell you this, every generation it seems there's a trainer who sees stuff that other people don't and has a vision and figures out a way to get there. Charlie Whittingham was a guy like that, Dermot Weld is a guy like that in Ireland, and Graham is like that here. You have to give him full credit."

On that same radio program, I expounded on a couple of other things I had on my mind regarding the Breeders' Cup: "When we announced we were going to run this horse in the Breeders' Cup Mile, you should have seen some of the stuff people wrote, stuff online or was sent to me or our partners. Why are we doing this to this poor horse, he can barely stand training, and this is too short, too tough, what is wrong with Team Valor, you're just doing this to get attention and new clients, that kind of crap," I said. "Since then, we have basically rendered those people silent. That race was so phenomenal that you can't say anything negative about the horse. He's knock proof.

"Here's a race where you had the likely Horse of the Year, Wise Dan, who is a throwback to I don't even know what, who is as versatile as any horse you'll see and is a brute of a horse—tough, sound—and for Animal Kingdom to be in the same league as him and to now have the same kind of a profile, where he apparently can now run almost any distance on any surface, it's amazing. For the two of them to be racing at the same time, we're pretty lucky as a sport right now."

After the Breeders' Cup, I was finally in position to realize my goals with Animal Kingdom. I had three goals: I wanted to continue to race the horse, I wanted to stand him at a top farm and I wanted our group to be allowed to retain a significant interest in him. Few and far between were the candidates who were agreeable to such a program.

I explained to my partners that, strictly as a stallion, Animal Kingdom at that point was worth about half of what he was worth as a racehorse. I told them I wanted to find somebody to agree to a sale based on his racehorse value, not just his stud value. Furthermore, I wanted to find somebody who would agree to race the horse in partnership through the Dubai World Cup and beyond, if the horse maintained his form.

Shortly after the Breeders' Cup, John Messara and I struck a deal that encompassed all of my priorities. In John Messara, I found the perfect partner. Our partnership not only was allowed to continue racing Animal Kingdom into the next year, but we were also able to secure his future with a top stud farm in a location where his offspring figured to flourish.

The deal was a win-win situation. The price John and I agreed upon met my mark, and the upside available for to John, if the horse continued to race effectively, ensured that he had a chance to profit significantly. We decided to leave until later the valuable North American breeding rights, which had the potential to outweigh those of the Southern Hemisphere. As things worked out, Arrowfield Stud and Team Valor International benefited mightily from the transaction.

Because of John's experience and savvy, I needed to make sure that my deal was enticing enough for him to make financial sense and provide him with incentives. The carrots I held out to John were the Dubai World Cup, with total prize money of $10 million, and a race at Royal Ascot, a venue prized by Australian breeders as no other in the world of racing.

We moved forward into the new year with a table set for the Royal Families of Dubai and Great Britain.

CHAPTER 27

Richest Horse Race

Animal Kingdom, because he was required to commence Australian stud duty in September, would only be able to run a few times for his new partnership.

The main goal in 2013 was the $10-million World Cup in Dubai on March 30. A trip to Royal Ascot was likely. There also was the possibility of one more race before AK was flown to Oz.

Based on my participation and observation, the trick in preparing an invading horse for World Cup night was to have it both fit and fresh, with an emphasis on fresh.

The challenge for a horseman was getting a horse fit enough to face the most elite company in international racing, while maintaining its freshness, both physically and mentally.

For horses training on the grounds in Dubai, fitness counted more than freshness, because local horses did not have to deal with travel issues, so they could be trained hard and rely more on fitness than freshness. But imported horses needed to be fresh so the rigors of the excursion did not tax their reserves.

Graham Motion narrowed his choices to either not running Animal Kingdom before the World Cup, or prepping him in the Grade 1 Gulfstream Park Turf Handicap. He chose the latter because it gave the horse three months between the Breeders' Cup and the GPTH, which was set a week shy of two months before the World Cup. Had Graham elected to run cold turkey, AK would have had a gap of nearly five months between races. Having just run second under somewhat similar circumstances in the Breeders' Cup, it was understandable why Graham went with the prep race, even though AK ran a winning-caliber race in the BC Mile. Having to get a horse ready to win off a lengthy respite required the athlete to be trained harder than if it could rely on a race to advance it toward race fitness.

Animal Kingdom had been flown to Palm Meadows after the Breeders' Cup. Graham returned him to the work tab five weeks after the BC Mile and scheduled eight breezes leading up to the Gulfstream Park race on February 9. AK went a half three times, followed by a pair of five-eighths works, after which he went three-quarters and seven-eighths and finished up with a five-furlong blowout five days before the Grade 1 race.

For the first time since Animal Kingdom was a 3-year-old preparing for the Triple Crown, Graham Motion had him in peak condition. The horse had exited the BC Mile in excellent shape both physically and mentally, so Graham did not have to grind on him to get him ready for his 2013 debut. AK's well being was evident in his demeanor as well.

"He's been very good down here, very sensible, which is nice," Motion told a reporter. "He's settled into a routine and he's been very straightforward since we've been down here. Maybe he's kind of mellowed some, but that's been more of a gradual process than just happening after the Breeders' Cup. He has his moments, though. He can still catch you off guard. He's been very good 95 percent of the time."

A month before the GPTH, Animal Kingdom worked a sharp five-eighths, kicking home in :23 2/5 to best Badleroibrown without being asked for much. He was carrying a bit too much weight but he had plenty of time to shed the excess poundage. Graham decided he wanted to ride Ramon Dominguez in the Gulfstream race. Johnny Velazquez, who was our first choice, gave the call to Point of Entry because he had a commitment to ride first call for his trainer Shug McGaughey.

Point of Entry was the first major long-distance grass horse of note developed by the brilliant McGaughey, who saddled him for consecutive Grade 1 victories in the Sword Dancer, Joe Hirsch and Man o' War Stakes. He was an unlucky second in the Breeders' Cup Turf going a mile and a half.

A half-interest in the well-bred son of leading sire Dynaformer had been sold to Frank Stronach to stand at his Adena Springs Farm in Kentucky. The GPTH, which was slated to be contested at Stronach's flagship East Coast track of Gulfstream Park, would be the first start for POE's new partnership between Dinny Phipps and Stronach. There was plenty of speculation in the press about POE's being under consideration for either the World Cup (mile and a quarter on Tapeta) or the Sheema Classic (mile and a half on turf) in Dubai. If POE did go to Dubai and ran in the Sheema Classic, Graham hoped to use Velazquez on Animal Kingdom in the World Cup.

Animal Kingdom was turning in one terrific workout after another, showing a lot of verve, and tossing in :11-flat furlongs when the notion struck him. Watching him swoop around the stretch curve at Palm Meadows and reel in Badleroibrown never got old and struck rival trainers in the clockers' stand with a sense of awe.

Most trainers will complain their horses are one work away from a good race, but Graham took an opposing view, saying, "I wish the race was in two weeks, not four, because that would give him two extra weeks to recover, in case he does too much in the race. He's ready to run right now!"

As the Gulfstream Park Turf Handicap drew near, English bookies made Animal Kingdom a close second choice for the Dubai World Cup to the mild favorite Royal Delta. The two-time Breeders' Cup-winning mare was trained about an hour north of Gulfstream at Payson Park by Bill Mott, who won the very first Dubai World Cup with the legendary Cigar. Prior to being switched from dirt to Tapeta in 2010, the World Cup had been dominated by American invaders, which accounted for nine of the first fourteen editions, but had been MIA on the Tapeta surface.

Two weeks before he was slated to pilot Animal Kingdom at Gulfstream, Ramon Dominguez was set to ride a full Friday card at Aqueduct before flying down to Florida to receive his third consecutive Eclipse Award as America's leading jockey. He never made it, as his mount in race number seven clipped heels, sending him crashing to the ground. Ramon was hospitalized, where his condition was listed as "critical" for the first 48 hours. He was diagnosed with a "slightly displaced skull fracture."

Five months later he was forced to retire from racing at the peak of his considerable powers. Ramon had been one of our "go to" riders for years, with his best days for us aboard Unbridled Belle when she won the $1-million Delaware Park Handicap and the Grade 1 Beldame Stakes.

Graham and I talked about a replacement for Dominguez. I was getting more and more uncomfortable with a lack of response from Johnny Velazquez's agent Angel Cordero about a Dubai commitment and I pushed to hire a rider who would stick with Animal Kingdom for the prep and the World Cup. I leaned toward Rafael Bejarano, who had ridden AK in the BC Mile, but Graham wanted to use Joel Rosario. Graham was not happy with the way Bejarano was riding in California, so we went with Rosario.

Even though Rosario's agent Ron Anderson was a long-standing friend of mine, dating back to his early days in Southern California when he struggled before brilliantly directing the careers of Jerry Bailey, Gary Stevens and Chris Antley, I asked Ron for something more than a verbal commitment.

Ron's word was good, but he worked for a rider whose word I did not know enough about. In a world where, other than West Coast agent Scotty McClellan, most jockey agents check their consciences at the backstretch gate, Ron dealt on a plane higher than the usual flotsam. But I made him sign a document with a two-race commitment. I wanted to make sure that we were not "spun" before the richest race on the planet.

Twelve days before the Gulfstream race, Graham designed one of his special team drills. Animal Kingdom, scheduled to breeze 6 furlongs and gallop out a mile, worked the first half with Badleroibrown and the second half with our colt English Progress. AK came his third quarter, without being asked, in :23 4/5 and galloped out another quarter in :25. He wound up going a mile in 1:39 2/5, while actually only breezing three-quarters. His strength was prodigious. David Nava told me the work was comparable to AK's final breeze before the BC Mile. He was ready to roll.

Clocker Bruno DeJulio had been the first professional clocker to jump on Animal Kingdom's bandwagon at two. His business partner Molly Rosen was clocking at Palm Meadows. She sent an e-mail to me after the breeze. "As a fan, as a clocker, as a horseplayer, I want to say thank you for how you've managed Animal Kingdom. The work today might be the most perfect drill I've ever seen a horse put in. Credit to Graham for the training, but you and the partners for how you've treated such a special animal."

Animal Kingdom went an easy five-eighths in 1:02 five days before the Gulfstream Park Handicap. I had urged Graham to keep AK fresh, and the horse's workout schedule indicated that Graham had both received and internalized my message.

I reported Animal Kingdom's approach to the Gulfstream race and the World Cup for the partners as follows:

"It's all going to depend on how he's ridden on Saturday. The guy can't give him a hard race, which would be counterproductive for the next one.

"The attitude I have is that whatever he (Animal Kingdom) does, make sure he's not used up. If he wins, great. If he gets beat, I'll be the only guy in the whole stands that is happy, because that will tell me that he didn't get used up. I've drilled this into Motion's head and he's tired of hearing it. Balance on this high wire can be delicate.

"For a recent example, Twice Over flopped twice over in the Dubai World Cup, despite the best efforts of trainer Henry Cecil. Cecil, a six-time Epsom Derby winner, was already one of the top two or three active trainers in the world before the amazing Frankel graced his barn. Twice Over was no Frankel, but he was a perfect fit for the World Cup after winning the prestigious Champion Stakes two years in a row at Newmarket.

"The only question was how to get there. In 2010, Cecil trained Twice Over straight up to the World Cup, and the horse could only finish tenth. The next year, he scored big in a Grade 3 prep in Dubai, but then finished ninth in the World Cup."

Animal Kingdom finished second to Point of Entry in the Gulfstream Park Turf Handicap, but he was beaten by a bonehead move conceived and executed by his own rider. Claire Novak, writing for *The Blood-Horse*, wrote, "An early mid-race move by new rider Joel Rosario may have cost Animal Kingdom the victory in what is planned to be his final start in the United States."

Just before the leader completed a slow :50 2/5 half-mile, Rosario shockingly shot Animal Kingdom through the field to the rail, going from fifth to first in a matter of a few strides, in a move harness racing fans refer to as a "brush." The extravagance of the move was reflected in the :22 1/5 clocking for AK's third quarter of the race, where he shot his bolt.

The head-on replay revealed a trap that wily veterans John Velazquez and Joe Bravo had set for Rosario. Bravo had dictated a slow pace on Salto, with Point of Entry tracking in second under Velazquez. On the backstretch, they both angled well off the rail. Rosario, after sitting back in fifth, could not resist the bait.

Animal Kingdom unleashed his lightning turn of foot to take the lead, but at a place in the race where he would have to sustain it for 5 furlongs to win. Pacesetter Salto came right back at AK, with Velazquez poised outside of them and salivating. AK held off the pair until just inside the stretch, lost the lead, regained it and then could not match Point of Entry's stamina in the end to get beat a length and a half. To make matters worse, Rosario went to his left-handed whip, leading AK to veer to his right, toward the winner, and get off the correct lead, which accounted for most of the beaten margin.

Of the premature gambit characterized by racing pros as a "bug boy" move, John Velazquez remarked, "I know Animal Kingdom well. If Rosario had waited behind me he probably would have beaten me from the quarter pole home. He made a move so big that he changed his style to my horse's style, so it worked out to my advantage. I had my horse running so much by the time we got to the three-sixteenth pole, my horse got his momentum going. It worked out for us."

Shug McGaughey reveled in the win and said, "It was quite a race. We had our tactics. I figured [Salto] would go to the lead and I was hoping we'd break good and be laying second to him without pressing too much and try to make Animal Kingdom commit a little early. It was kind of fun to watch, even though I was leaning a little bit trying to get him in front going around the turn. We're very pleased the way he came back, and to win a Grade I going a mile and an eighth is another feather in his cap."

Upset with himself, Rosario hemmed and hawed almost incoherently when he spoke to Motion after the race. Later, through his agent, he said that he was embarrassed and regretful that he got snookered into the trap. The next day Rosario visited Motion at Palm Meadows and apologized.

In the days immediately following the Gulfstream fiasco, I wanted out of the trap I had created for myself by having Ron Anderson sign the two-race agreement. At the same time, Point of Entry was taken out of consideration for Dubai, which freed Velazquez; Graham indicated he would love to get Johnny back on the horse. I would never unilaterally break an agreement with Ron, but I talked to him about getting out of it. He was embarrassed by the ride himself, but he felt his rider could make amends. So we stuck with our contractual obligation.

I had my office prepare a DVD with all of Animal Kingdom's races, as well as the previous three renewals of the Dubai World Cup. I invited Joel to come to my home to watch and review them with Graham Motion, Brad Weisbord and me. He was very attentive and made some useful comments; he learned a lot about what made Animal Kingdom effective as a racehorse and how the DWC had been run on Tapeta.

The good news about the GPTH was that Animal Kingdom exited the race in tremendous shape and was ready for his final push towards the DWC. Motion gave AK three more breezes at Palm Meadows. Graham reported that AK was unusually sharp for the first one, indicating to him that he had improved again. In the penultimate workout, Badleroibrown broke off 13 lengths in front of Animal Kingdom and the Derby winner ran fast at him, finishing 2 lengths behind, but turning in an excellent final quarter.

Animal Kingdom had his final workout, a five-eighths grass move at Palm Meadows, on March 18 and the next day he was flown on the same plane as Royal Delta to Dubai, where English bookies by then had him as the 6 to 1 third choice for the DWC behind favored Hunter's Light and 4 to 1 Royal Delta.

Graham Motion told me that he could not be happier with the way things had gone since the BC Mile with Animal Kingdom and that everything had gone according to schedule.

Prior to boarding his flight, during the flight itself and upon landing, our horse was treated with an electrolyte protocol developed by Dr. Rob Holland that consisted of special fluids. When Well Armed had flown from California to win the last DWC, run on dirt, in a blowout 14-length victory, I phoned Rob to ask if he had any hand in that invasion because I knew that he worked closely with the colt's owner Bill Casner. Rob told me how he had treated Well Armed and I asked if I could use the protocol in the future.

Our first experience with Dr. Holland's electrolyte formula was with Gitano Hernando, when he shipped from England to Southern California and beat older horses including Casner's homebred Colonel John in the Grade 1 Goodwood at Santa Anita's Oak Tree meeting.

Animal Kingdom went to the track the first time exactly a week before the big race. He was supposed to jog and gallop a bit, just to stretch his legs, but such was his well-being after the flight that he was bouncing off the Tapeta surface. Alice Clapham, whom Animal Kingdom was "giving fits to" according to Graham Motion, had as much of a hold on AK as she could muster, yet AK zipped around the oval. He was not scheduled for a work; however, a clocker caught him going 3 furlongs in :36 2/5. Three days later he officially reeled off another 3 furlongs in :36 1/5.

Over the next week, every time Animal Kingdom came to the track, it was an event. By midweek, it looked like the English bookies would make him their favorite. When Animal Kingdom wound up in post position 12 of 13, the bet-takers backed off, raising his odds and making him the third choice behind Maktoum-owned Hunter's Light and Royal Delta.

Naturally, pundits far and wide dismissed Animal Kingdom's chances for success because of the wide draw. Neither Graham nor I had a concern over the post position, reckoning that AK had a long run to the first turn, he had handled an outside stall in the Kentucky Derby and he did not figure to be on the pace. Ramon Dominguez and Frankie Dettori, whose counsel on selecting a post position was sought by Graham Motion, both told him to stay away from an inside post and take one in the middle if possible. When we wound up with the penultimate stall, the advice became a non-starter.

Graham was very happy with the horse. He was ready for a big race. In an interview with Joe Clancy of thisishorseracing.com, he expressed his pleasure with the position of the horse.

"'It's amazing. Just a year ago, he was sore after his work and we had to scrap plans to go to Dubai,'" Motion said.

"Team Valor's Barry Irwin took that bit of news and went right on thinking big, telling Motion to plan for Dubai 2013."

"'That's a pretty optimistic way to look at things,' Motion said. 'To hear that makes my job a lot easier. A little bit of that is lost. People want to cry about him not running in America, but we lose sight in our sport of what the challenges are. It's 'Who's got the fastest horse?' It's not about 'Let's find the easiest race we can.' It's about taking on new challenges. Obviously, it's a huge purse too, but it's admirable that Barry and the partners have wanted to take on challenges with this horse.'"

The morning after the Wednesday draw, both Kathleen and I became sick. We had elevated temperatures, sore throats, the start of a cough and a general feeling of malaise. We stayed in our rooms Thursday, Friday and Saturday—the day of the race.

On the evening of the race itself, Kathleen started to feel better and was prepared to go racing, but I still felt really sick. Megan Jones checked up on me and urged me to walk over to where the partners had gathered and eat something, as it was just two hours from post time. The short walk from our hotel room to the dining tables was a challenge for me to negotiate, because I was so spaced out. We then encountered trouble getting to our designated seating area because of some mix up with the credentials. By the time we arrived at the tables, it was time to walk downstairs and watch the horse being saddled in the pre-parade ring.

It was very warm outside and I was sweating profusely from my forehead. Animal Kingdom could not have looked better. I had never seen him strip this fit for a race before. Seeing him looking so magnificent picked up my spirits. He was dry as a bone and relaxed. Once the blinkers were put on, Animal Kingdom became a different animal. He knew it was "go time." His ears pricked, he seemed more interested in his surroundings and, for the first time, there was just a hint of white lather between his hind legs.

After the horses left the walking ring and walked onto the racetrack, Kathleen and I stayed in the paddock to watch the race. I planned on winning the World Cup, I was feeling ill and I saw no sense in going up and down stairs in my condition.

On a beautiful, still desert evening, Animal Kingdom went post-ward in good order. When the gates opened he broke nicely. After a furlong he was up right behind the leaders, with three or four ahead of him in the early running, while racing three or four wide in the clear around the first turn and looking very relaxed.

Throughout most of his career, Animal Kingdom had rallied from well back. On DWC night, Graham Motion noticed that the races were being run without much pace. Relying on his observation that AK was sharper than ever during the weeklong lead up to the DWC, Motion came up with a race strategy. He met with Rosario and urged him to get the horse away from the gate as best as he could and to lay closer than usual. Graham said, "He rode a textbook race."

In the run down the backstretch, the favorites—Royal Delta, Animal Kingdom and Hunter's Light—raced 1-2-3. Royal Delta set a measured tempo under Mike Smith, who tried to do a little "race riding" by packing AK wide. Rosario kept his cool, staying about a length behind Royal Delta until the end of the long backstretch. Animal Kingdom crept closer, while still under snug restraint. As the leaders began to curve for home, AK inherited the lead without the rider asking him to do so. When she was passed, Royal Delta retreated tamely, leaving AK with a daylight lead.

Once settled into the stretch, Rosario posed the inevitable question to Animal Kingdom and the powerful chestnut answered with an explosiveness reminiscent of his final furlong in the Kentucky Derby. When AK jetted away from his rivals, the partners who had gathered on the paddock lawn stopped cheering for a moment, turned to each other with expressions of utter amazement at what they were witnessing and could only shake their heads. He immediately pulled away from the field and opened up an advantage of at least 4 lengths.

With his ears pricked, Animal Kingdom raced down the homestretch all by himself. He eased himself in the closing stages, as the race appeared to be in the bag, and he cruised across the finish line a couple of lengths clear of Red Cadeaux. Animal Kingdom was never under any pressure the entire length of the stretch and won with his ears straight up.

English bookies paid off at generous odds of 5 ½ to 1, while horseplayers betting in America drove his odds down to 5-to-2 favoritism.

People always want to know what it feels like to win a big race like the Derby or the Breeders' Cup or the World Cup. My emotional state following wins in the Santa Anita Handicap and the Kentucky Derby was like nothing else I've ever experienced in racing. I was completely overwhelmed with the enormity of the occasion, the historical context and the performances of my horses. In both instances I was completely overcome with emotion.

My feeling after the World Cup was more like "mission accomplished." It was not so much emotional as professionally rewarding. I was happiest of all for the horse himself, because the Dubai win affirmed the quality he first displayed in the Kentucky Derby. Animal Kingdom was a horse of enormous talent and he had seized the opportunity to prove it on the world stage.

I was also very happy for Graham Motion. Like Charlie Whittingham and Neil Drysdale, when he zeroes in on a goal, he does not miss. He had the intellect to recognize what needed to be done and how he needed to do it. He possessed the long-range vision that enabled him to visualize the goal, as well as the presence of mind to make any required adjustments on race day. You cannot ask for more than that in a trainer.

The time I spent standing on the winners' podium next to my partner John Messara and my future partner Sheik Mohammed bin Rashid al Maktoum seemed like an hour, even though it was probably less than ten minutes. I took great pleasure in watching John as he beamed with that world-class smile of his. And it meant a lot to me to see how much Sheik

Mohammed appeared to like Animal Kingdom. He had a look in his eye as he feasted upon the magnificence of Animal Kingdom that told me how much admiration he had for my homebred. That was special and I will never forget it.

An insider told me that Sheik Mohammed has an annual party before the World Cup and attendees make their race selections. When it came time for Sheik Mohammed to give his World Cup pick, he surprised those on hand by bypassing his own horse Hunter's Light, who started as the 5-to-2 favorite with English bookies in the DWC. He said, "I like the American colt." He said that he had a good feeling about him.

The usual sense of exhilaration and euphoria that comes after a huge win did not stop me from feeling faint and ill in the post-race press conference. When a reporter asked me a question, I told those assembled that this victory was especially meaningful to me because it showed my peers back home in America that it was possible to travel a long distance to a foreign land and win the biggest prize on Earth without having to use drugs, especially Lasix.

I also said that as "bonehead a ride as Joel Rosario gave Animal Kingdom in the Gulfstream Park Turf Handicap, he gave him a brilliant ride in the World Cup." The young man definitely rose to the occasion.

After the race, my partners and I made our way back to one of the outside restaurants in the Meydan hotel that was adjacent to the racecourse to celebrate. We had a representative group of partners, including Craig and Holly Bandoroff, who foaled and raised Animal Kingdom at their Denali Stud. Denali Stud client Sue Fletcher was in from Scottsdale. Carl Pascarella, who as the head of VISA had sponsored a $5-million Triple Crown bonus that no horse ever won, was on hand from San Francisco with his wife Yurie, a dressage devotee. Tom Furey, who installed the computer network for the Melbourne Olympic Games as a worldwide traveler for IBM, was in from Marco Island with his wife Julie.

Norton Herrick, who recently had branched out from real estate to produce Hollywood movies and Broadway plays such as the Tony Award-winning revival of *Hair*, had traveled from Boca Raton. Retired Wall Street professional Mark Castellano, one of my personal favorites, was in from New Jersey.

Mark Polivka, who represented me at the Eclipse Awards, was in from Chicago with his wife Gail. Ray Bouchard, who first came to Dubai with Gitano Hernando, returned from Canada. I was happiest of all for my pal, octogenarian Ed Weil. The Chicagoan had come five years earlier with his wife Dia, only to see their filly Irridescence not get a run as the second-favorite for the $5-million Duty Free when she banged herself against a metal railing in the walking ring. Ed also had been a partner in Ipi Tombe when she won the Duty Free, but did not make that trip.

We talked about how Animal Kingdom's first prize of $6,000,000 boosted his lifetime earnings to $8,387,500 and put him behind only Curlin, Cigar and Skip Away among America's all-time highest earners. We talked about the race and how everybody was aghast when he exploded at the top of the lane and sewed up the race in the proverbial "heartbeat." We were Animal Kingdom's biggest fans, his most ardent supporters, yet we were as bowled over as anybody else who watched the race. And we talked about the future. I told them I would meet with John Messara the following morning to chat about what might happen next.

I met with John Messara and Jon Freyer of Arrowfield Stud in the lounge of the Meydan Hotel the morning after the World Cup. I listened to what they had to say about the plans for the future. Fully realizing that I had sold Messara a majority interest in the horse based on a program that included a run at Royal Ascot, I told them that if left up to me, I would never run the horse again, because I thought Animal Kingdom might not top his Dubai performance.

The worth of a stallion and what gives a stallion the staying power to remain popular enough to fill his books for four consecutive seasons is the reputation he has the day he retires from racing. Animal Kingdom had generated an enormous amount of goodwill, worldwide interest, awe and respect with his DWC victory. Knowing full well how daunting the task of filling his book would be following his initial season at stud, I voiced my opinion against further racing.

I had seen what I wanted to see from Animal Kingdom and he had nothing left to prove to me. The risk in running him again was great. I had demonstrated many times over that, when it came to being a sportsman and doing whatever it took to prove my horse with the public, I was fully committed. But now that I had scaled the mountain, I saw no reason to take any further risk. The time had come to think like a businessman.

My recommendation was met without any enthusiasm. John Messara had a new toy and he wanted to play with it. He had a very impressive horse that he wanted to elevate even further. He flirted with the idea of bringing the horse to Australia and running him in a new race that he was inaugurating. But he focused on Royal Ascot.

If I were in John's position, I might feel the very same way; but I had traveled a long and arduous road, I had achieved my goal and I was not interested in incurring any risk that would damage the reputation of Animal Kingdom.

We weighed the prospects of running in the Queen Anne going a mile or the Prince of Wales's going a mile and a quarter. In thinking about Ascot, I had completely forgotten that the Group 1 Queen Anne was run up the straight and not around a turn like the St. James's Palace for 3-year-olds. When my memory was refreshed, I became even more opposed to the notion of racing him at Ascot, especially in the mile. I simply could not visualize Animal Kingdom running a winning race on a straightaway without any previous experience.

At the close of the meeting, it was decided that the horse would be sent to England and prepared to race at Ascot. Graham Motion was tasked with gauging, from firsthand knowledge and reports, whether Animal Kingdom was up for another tip-top race. If Graham approved of a run, then we would choose which race to run in.

When Animal Kingdom showed that he had indeed continued to thrive while training under David Lanigan and being ridden by jockey Ted Durcan on the gallops at Lambourn in England, I warmed up to the idea of racing him at the Royal Meeting. I saw him breeze up the hill and could tell that the seasoned veteran Durcan was suitably impressed. All the signals Graham and I wanted to see were there, as bright as sunshine. We decided to run him in the Queen Anne Stakes on the first day of Royal Ascot.

Animal Kingdom looked as well as I had ever seen him. As a mature horse, he was something incredible to behold in the flesh. He was a true golden boy. I arrived in the pre-parade ring before anybody else and I saw every turn Animal Kingdom made. He was calm and collected.

Because of the time-consuming nature of the Royal Procession, which consisted of horse-drawn landaus transporting The Queen and other Royal Family members along the racecourse, the Queen Anne horses spent an inordinately long period of time in the pre-parade ring.

Being a writer, I naturally needed to get "black on white" to explain what unfolded next, so I wrote the following:

"About 25 minutes after walking calmly around the pre-parade ring at Royal Ascot today prior to the Group 1 Queen Anne Stakes, Animal Kingdom suddenly stopped. He turned his head left as his nostrils flared while he took in a scent, dropped his penis and started acting stubborn.

"Alice Clapham, his traveling 'head lad' from America, managed to lead him forward, turn him right and then immediately left into his saddling stall.

"I walked right over to the stall, told Graham Motion what I had just seen and observed the veins all over Animal Kingdom's body pop out, as he became clearly agitated. It was patently obvious to me that he caught a whiff of the scent from the lone filly in the 13-horse Group 1.

"For the next ten minutes or so, Animal Kingdom advertised his wares to horsemen and women gathered in the paddock prior to the first race.

"I got sick to my stomach, because I knew exactly what was happening: Animal Kingdom was thinking more about the opposite sex than about the task at hand. I could see him transform from a focused competitor to a sex machine.

"It was not a simple matter of Animal Kingdom having unsheathed his sword. The personal member was on display for quite a spell. The horse was gone. I told my assistant Brad Weisbord that I wished I could find a small closet to hide in for the next hour because what was about to happen was not going to be pretty.

"I personally went up to as many members of Team Valor and Arrowfield Stud as I could find, telling them what I had seen and advising them that I was no longer confident that our horse would perform as hoped. So distraught had I became at this circumstance, I didn't even bother to go to the frontside to watch the race in person. I just stayed in the paddock and watched the race unfold on a monitor. All the hard work our teams had put forth was about to go down the tubes.

"In the race itself, Animal Kingdom was rank to place for the first time in his career. He raced closer than usual and never settled. He ran like an agitated horse. When John Velazquez figured it was time to turn the horse loose, the favorite gave him nothing and tamely folded up his tent. He tailed off and was beaten a long ways.

"On the gallop back to the unsaddling area, Animal Kingdom was full of energy and tried to run off, leading the jockey to believe that his mount was not tired at all.

"Other than the Belmont Stakes, in which he was mugged and had exited with an injury that required surgery, Animal Kingdom had never failed to run first or second or fire a big effort.

"Regardless of the circumstances being different in today's race, Animal Kingdom put forth no sort of effort. So what stopped him? Graham Motion suggested that maybe the horse had run one too many races. Others speculated that too much traveling was to blame.

"I am convinced that Animal Kingdom lost his mojo when his stud career began 20 minutes before he ran in the Queen Anne. As one of our racing partners said, "Sex in the workplace is never a good idea."

"Animal Kingdom earlier in the week had shown signs of being studdish while training in Lambourn. Graham Motion saw it, his wife Anita Motion saw it. But nobody thought it would put an end to his Ascot dream."

"I would do it all over again. I think the horse, under normal circumstances, was well up to the challenge. I hope this non-effort does not discourage others from trying. The enthusiasm generated by Ascot and the media was second to none. I feel sorry for Graham Motion, his staff, trainer David Lanigan, his staff and jockey Ted Durcan, because they put their hearts and souls into this venture.

"Okay big guy, we received the message loud and clear. You win! Enough is enough. Best of luck at Arrowfield Stud."

Dave Dillon, an Animal Kingdom partner from Chicago, said, "Barry, you weren't the only one who knew AK was not going to run well after his antics. When my wife Cindy and I saw it, I ran over to the bookies on the apron to see if I could cancel my bet and found they had raised the price on AK from 11 to 8 to as high as 4 to 1. So while the crowd and racing people may not have made the connection to his actions and how he would run, the bookies sure did."

Most people in the game, both domestically and internationally, did not hold the non-effort against him, because the result was simply too bad to be true, especially with the memory fresh in their minds of his dominating the Dubai World Cup.

Flopping at Royal Ascot did not negatively impact his first season books of mares, as he served 100 in Australia and 148 in Kentucky.

CHAPTER 28

Hopes for Clean Sport

American reportage of the Dubai World Cup contained scant reference to Animal Kingdom's winning without the use of Lasix. It was left up to those abroad that were charged with covering the sport to focus on this aspect of the triumph.

Commenting in Ireland's *Independent* below the headline, "Animal Kingdom supreme beyond all borders: Dubai Cup winner provides a glorious example to all would-be rulers of racing across the world stage," Chris McGrath wrote, "True to its billing, as a World Cup, the 18th running of the richest horse race on the planet offered fresh courage and inspiration to those determined that frontiers should no longer be perceived as barriers."

More specifically, McGrath said, "In the United States, brave attempts to fill in a moat of drugs and dirt seem to have been defeated, for now, by vested interests."

Then he lowered the boom, writing, "Animal Kingdom's stunning performance in Dubai showed American conservatives that even a winner of their most cherished prize can adapt to an environment that redressed welfare concerns raised by their stubborn approach to medication and racing surfaces. Having established his caliber on dirt in the 2011 Kentucky Derby, Animal Kingdom has since achieved equivalent status on turf and now on a synthetic surface. In Dubai, moreover, he proved himself in a jurisdiction that prohibits race day medication.

"He has done all this in the silks of a syndicate headed by one of the most vociferous campaigners for new enlightenment on the American Turf."

Animal Kingdom's DWC win was a victory on more than one front for me. Aside from the win of the race itself, the triumph was a singular statement made at a time when Americans were in the midst of a battle over the use of legal and illegal drugs in racing.

The reason few American media outlets focused on the non-use of Lasix is because many of the writers and publications that covered the sport had a conflict of interest and tried to suppress the movement to rid the sport of drugs. Beat writers need access to cooperative trainers. Trainers, to a significant extent, want to be able to race horses on drugs. So, the beat writers take up the trainers' side of the argument. The circumstance is as old as sport itself.

Publications that provide news content are financially tied to racetracks. Most racetracks cater to trainers and are loath to buck their agenda. In an era when "field size" is the focus of every racing secretary in the land, racetracks also have bought into a false premise floated by trainers that medication use helps to increase the number of horses for the tracks' races, thereby generating greater betting turnover on these races and more profit for their business enterprises.

Veterinarians take an oath to put the welfare of the horse first. Two conflicts of interest prevent them from fulfilling this obligation. First, vets want to satisfy their clients, the trainers. Even though horse owners pay the expenses for the horses and trainers do not, vets treat the trainer as though he is the client. Secondly, because of the business model of the vets, their income is, to a great degree, derived from the markup between the wholesale and retail prices on drugs that are dispensed to the animals. The vast majority of vets only make money by giving shots and pills, as they do not charge fees for diagnoses like practitioners for human patients. So vets have a built-in incentive to dispense as many drugs as possible.

I had only been involved in racing for a short time in the early 1970s, when vets and trainers urged racing authorities to usher in the era of so-called "permissive medication," meaning that certain "therapeutic" drugs would be allowed for use on race day. It did not take long for abuse from the proliferation of drugs—both legal and illegal—to get completely out of hand.

I saw how rampant illegal drug use had marginalized my other favorite sport, track and field. I sure as hell didn't want to see horseracing, a game from which I derived my living and indulged my passion for racing, follow in the footsteps of a sport that had lost most of its fan base, when even diehards could no longer support an enterprise rife with cheaters who were typified by the likes of Ben Johnson and Marion Jones.

As my anxiety level rose, I wanted to reach out to participants and overseers of our industry by enlightening them to the dangers, as well as suggesting ways to right the ship, in an attempt to stem the tsunami of drugs from washing away our sport.

I did this by writing Op-Ed pieces in various horseracing publications.

As I had demonstrated during my employment at *Daily Racing Form* and *The Thoroughbred of California*, I was anti-establishment. My controversial piece in *New West* was the first major salvo I fired in 1978. By the 1990s, when I saw the direction the sport was taking, I felt an overwhelming urge to make my voice heard through writing.

Shortly after I moved from Southern California to Central Kentucky in the fall of 1999, I wrote a "Final Turn" piece in *The Blood-Horse* that shook up the commercial breeding community by blaming farm managers for corrupting the breed by authorizing procedures and surgeries that cosmetically altered the front-limb conformation of young horses that were bound for auction. Although the use of screws and wires, as well as periosteal elevation, was well known among commercial breeders, I don't think anybody had revealed the practice to the industry at large or questioned how it might be limiting the number of starts of a racehorse. Perhaps only a child molester would have generated a greater outcry from the hardboots of Central Kentucky.

After illustrating the problem, I finished up the piece as follows:

"The Thoroughbred game is at a crossroads in many areas. Many knowledgeable, sincere participants are rightfully questioning some of the sport's foundations.

"Detroit automakers a decade ago faced a similar challenge and rose to the occasion. It is time those who choose to produce the product upon which our sport is predicated now look beyond the immediacy of the market to a future in the winner's circle."

After that, I started submitting pieces about drugs. In the early 2000s, there was plenty of private debate on whether trainers were cheating by abusing legal drugs or using designer drugs. I remember meeting California horseracing leaders John Harris and Don Valpredo, both members of The Jockey Club, and explaining that, for less than $30,000, the California Horse Racing Board could acquire the testing equipment available to detect whether horses were being milkshaked.

Used to delay the onset of muscle fatigue by buffering the build-up of lactic acid, milkshaking is done by running a tube through the nostril of a horse and delivering a mixture of bicarbonate of soda and powdered sugar. Harris and Valpredo scoffed at the notion that trainers were cheating, Harris citing as evidence the fact that no disgruntled employee had ever filed a complaint with the racing board against a trainer for cheating.

I also explained to Harris, who ran the largest cattle feed lot west of the Mississippi, that clenbuterol was being used for its steroidal impact on horses' physiques and not merely for its prescribed use in treating respiratory issues. Again he pooh-poohed my revelation, even when I pointed out something that he was totally aware of, which is that clenbuterol use had been made illegal by the United States Food and Drug Administration because cattlemen were found to be administering the drug to bulk up their stock.

In the early 2000s, *The Blood-Horse* editor Ray Paulick and I debated a lot about drug use. I would tell him which trainers I felt certain were cheating and he would defend them. A similar scenario played out with my friend Steve Haskin when I told him that I had heard from trainer Eddie Gregson, who was a very close friend of Bobby Frankel, that Frankel had "joined the dark side." Steve refused to consider the likelihood of such a possibility.

I wrote a drug piece with *The Blood-Horse* specifically in mind. Ray Paulick was reluctant to use it. I felt the story needed to be published because it made a very important point. So I did something I hated doing, but I proceeded regardless, because I felt so strongly about the message in my piece: I went directly to the magazine's publisher Stacey Bearse, whom I met when we were both directors of the racing charity The Race for Education. I explained how vitally important I felt my message was. He told me that he loved running my pieces because they always generated more feedback than anybody else's. And he ran my piece. Fortunately, it did not damage my relationship with Ray. Ray and I always got along fine, but I knew he thought my ideas about cheating trainers were fanciful at best.

Ray struggled with his own dependency issues and went through rehab. When he re-emerged, it was with a much more open-mind attitude about the use of drugs in racing. He left *The Blood-Horse*, started the eponymous online racing website the *Paulick Report* and developed it into the most comprehensive site of its kind in the industry. Ray is a fearless and creative investigative reporter who is reminiscent of muckrakers of a bygone era. I could not be any prouder of him. He is one of the most admirable people in racing.

My drug pieces were written to be instructive and provocative. I educated readers about the problems drugs created for the horses, for their competitors and for the image of racing. I am pretty sure I was the first writer to explain that drugs needed to be eliminated from racing because of the optics as perceived by the fan base and general public. When the public perceives that dumb animals with no say in the matter are being shot up and used as tools to break the law, the game is in jeopardy of being lost.

In a 2004 piece in *The Blood-Horse*, I believe I was the first person in racing to suggest in print that the United States Anti-Doping Agency (USADA) should be brought on board to clean up the sport before it was too late. As a track and field fan, I had seen USADA's positive impact on cleaning up a sport that was rife with all manner of drug cheats.

Over the years, I have had numerous Op-Ed pieces published in such outlets as the *Thoroughbred Daily News*, *The Blood-Horse*, the *New York Times* and *Sporting Post* (South Africa). My subjects included instructive pieces on how to break the cycle of drug use in America, the need for an independent agency and on making integrity the number one priority in racing. When I wrote my pieces, I always tried to identify a problem and follow up with a possible solution. I suggested getting state regulators out of racing and getting the Federal Bureau of Investigation involved in racing.

Publishers and editors of my pieces have told me for years that they like running my stuff because it strikes a nerve and creates a stir.

While I considered my Op-Eds to be important, their impact on progress was less than I had hoped for. I always took the position that I would use my energy, passion and skill as a writer to move the ball on hot topics, rather than to join alphabet organizations and work from the inside to foster and promote change.

When the Breeders' Cup and the American Graded Stakes Committee had an opportunity to use their power to take steps that would have eliminated the use of drugs from Breeders' Cup and Graded stakes races and they failed to follow through, I knew that I had made the right decision in not joining these groups.

I did join a new organization that embraced traditional horsemanship and sporting values. The Water Hay Oats Alliance, or WHOA, is a grass roots group set up in Central Kentucky to stop (Whoa!) the use of race-day drugs in America by supporting Federal legislation. Arthur and Staci Hancock of Stone Farm, Roy and Gretchen Jackson of Lael Stable in Pennsylvania and George Strawbridge of Augustin Stable in Pennsylvania started the group, which had strong support from Jeff Gural, operator of The Meadowlands; Bill Casner of Texas; Frank Stronach of Canada; Charlotte Weber of Live Oak Plantation in Florida; Gary Biszantz of Cobra Farm in Kentucky; former HBPA executive director Tony Chamblin; Jon and Sarah Kelly of California; Marylou Whitney and her husband John Hendrickson; former national riding champion Chris McCarron, and trainers Neil Drysdale of California, John Gosden of England and Roger Attfield of Canada.

When I joined, I was asked to submit a statement. My submission was as follows:

"I have been involved in racing since I was hired as a writer for *The Blood-Horse* in 1969. A year later I was a staff writer for *The Thoroughbred of California*. In 1970, when so-called 'permissive medication' was made legal, I was right there on the scene. I have witnessed, written about and observed the transformation of the American-bred racehorse from being the envy of the world back in the 1970s when Secretariat, Seattle Slew and Affirmed raced, to a substandard performer on the world stage during the last 40 odd years. It has not been a pretty sight. I blame a lot of this backward movement by our industry on the negative impact we have experienced because of the widening scope of medication, as well as the huge negative impact of illegal drugs.

"Because of drugs both legal and illegal, it is now virtually impossible in the United States to assess form. How in the heck is any horseman or woman suppose to be able to tell which stallions to breed to when we do not know what has been flushed through their bodies and system? I am in favor of anything that can be done on any level to rid the sport of drugs, including Federal legislation to amend the Interstate Horseracing Act [IHA]. Right now our sport is in crisis. We need help and we need it right now. There is some inherent risk in opening up the IHA because any politician with a wild hair might try to tamper with it and destroy the edge that horse racing has enjoyed since 1978. However, given the current state of affairs, I think the gamble is worth taking, because without teeth in the act that will help us get rid of trainers that cheat, our sport is apt to continue to spiral in a downward direction. We need to clean up our sport both in terms of cleansing the game of bad actors and cleaning the bloodstream of our horses."

So in the second decade of the 21st century, I ratcheted up the intensity of my rhetoric and personal involvement by calling out people and organizations, as part of a concerted effort to motivate change. I gave testimony before a committee of the United States Senate, co-chaired by New Mexico Senator Thomas Udall.

Daily Racing Form's Matt Hegarty wrote about it as follows:

"The U.S. Senate Committee on Commerce, Science, and Transportation has scheduled a hearing on Thursday in Washington, D.C. to discuss "the prevalence and use of medication and performance-enhancing drugs in horse racing," according to a notice the committee posted last week.

"Late on Monday, the committee released a witness list for the hearing. The list includes Barry Irwin, the chief executive of Team Valor; Kent Stirling, the chairman of the National Horsemen's Benevolent and

Protective Association's medication committee; Jeffrey Gural, the owner of several New York harness tracks and casinos; Jim Gagliano, the president of the Jockey Club; Matthew Witman, the national director of the American Quarter Horse Association; Marc Paulhus, a former vice president of the Humane Society; Ed Martin, the president of the Association of Racing Commissioners International; and Dr. Shelia Lyons, the founder of the American College of Veterinary Sports and Rehabilitation.

"Irwin, an outspoken critic of race day medication and the current state of racing regulation, said that he had prepared a 3,600-word commentary for the hearing and would summarize the commentary's content during a five-minute speaking allotment.

"'It's basically what I've been saying all along,' Irwin said. He added that he 'would like to see the federal government get involved in racing, because I don't think the states have been doing a very good job with that.'"

In my remarks at the Senate hearing, I set the table as follows:

"Horse racing is in crisis. The public perceives racing to be out of control. Our image can be resuscitated. But before we can offer a race day program worthy of public trust, steps need to be taken to improve the integrity of the game. The Federal government can help.

"Horse racing is a sport. It began when an owner thought his horse was faster than another fellow's. To settle it, a race was held. It came to pass that if these contests were sufficiently appealing, interest could be generated from the public, which would attend and bet on the outcome. If enough contests were arranged, a racing association could be formed to regularly offer races. Benefits to the public included new jobs, as well as taxes, that could be levied by governments. In order for governments to justify taxing bets on races, states set up commissions to safeguard the integrity of the sport. This is the basis of racing as we know it today.

"But the grand bargain has been broken. State governments have let down their constituents.

"For racing to thrive it must give the public enough confidence to place a bet. State commissions must guarantee a sport that is conducted on a level playing field. Because commissions fail at this, the fabric of the sport has unraveled and the public has lost faith in the product.

"Before the public can be won back, our industry must be able to improve its product. The steps that need to be taken, however, seem beyond the grasp of the racing commissions. This is why we need Federal assistance."

I concluded my remarks as follows:

"Each state has serious conflicts of interest that combine to weaken racing as a whole. If there was a national policy providing uniform drug rules for every racing jurisdiction, all states would be on a level playing field, which is as it should be.

"Putting horses at risk and mistreating them by juicing them with drugs is no way for states to line their coffers, for racetracks to improve their bottom line or for trainers to make a better living. We need to stop drugging thoroughbred racehorses in order to make them the beast of burden that will carry our industry on its back. We should be celebrating this glorious athlete, not trashing it."

The Jockey Club had been an impediment over the years to the implementation of many progressive initiatives and was perceived by most participants in racing to be nothing more than racing's version of a "good ole boys club." While TJC talked a good game each summer at its Round Table in Saratoga about cleaning up the sport by eliminating the use of drugs, its actions told a story of indifference. Still, I became convinced it was the only organization that was capable of moving the chains.

Basically, there are issues with two types of drugs in American racing: known and unknown/illegal drugs. The known drugs are classified and withdrawal times and trace amounts for these drugs have been developed to enable state racing authorities to detect and monitor their use. A model drug protocol was developed of 28 drugs that are considered to be of therapeutic value to a racehorse and its proponents want their usage to be allowed as long as the amounts found in the tests do not exceed limits that indicate they would still be active in the system of a horse on race day.

Unknown drugs are substances that are so-called designer or synthetic drugs, which are man made by chemists that alter the molecular structure of known performance enhancers, exactly as those distributed in the Bay Areas Laboratory Cooperative (BALCO) scandal that involved Marion Jones and Barry Bonds. These can be sourced in China, Mexico, Canada and Europe. Illegal drugs are known PEDs such as uppers, downers, painkillers, mood changers or blood enhancers to increase the delivery of oxygen to the lungs.

Dinny Phipps had long been the most influential individual in racing as the power behind The Jockey Club, which in 2013 promoted a plan for state regulatory bodies to adopt a program that reduced the number of drugs allowed for therapeutic use in racehorses on race day. He concluded his remarks at that year's Round Table by promising to back Federal legislation to rid the sport of drugs if not enough states approved the policy. The statement was used as a threat. Phipps hoped that, by waving a red flag in the noses of conservative elements in racing, it would motivate them to get behind the uniform medication rules he was promoting.

The only trouble with the uniform medication policy was that it still allowed the use of Lasix on race day. Regardless of whether one thought Lasix was effective for its prescribed use of reducing internal bleeding in the respiratory system of a racehorse, the fact remained that it was a race day drug. I was dead set against any use of drugs on race day. If the last race-day drug standing was bute, I would be just as adamant against its use as I was against the use of Lasix. My opposition was not based on Lasix per se, but on the fact that it was a drug. I wanted horses to race clean on race day as they did at virtually every major racing venue in the world.

I thought Phipps' stand was disingenuous because he purported to want a level playing field. In as strong an Op-Ed as I've ever written, I called out Phipps in the *TDN* to be true to his core principles. I was pretty sure that Phipps wanted clean racing. And I thought that a little bullying from me might help give him the confidence and clarity of thought to do the right thing.

Shortly afterward, to my total delight and satisfaction, Phipps announced at the 2014 Round Table that not enough racing jurisdictions had passed uniform medication rules to satisfy him and he decided to throw his weight behind Federal legislation that would name USADA to oversee drug policy and enforcement in horseracing on a national level.

I high-fived Staci Hancock after the meeting and said, "We got game." We had actually succeeded in gaining some traction in racing's version of the "War on Drugs." I was so proud of Phipps for taking this stand that I bought a full-page advertisement in the *TDN* thanking him for his leadership.

My fellow WHOA members and I hope fervently that, sooner rather than later, Congress will install USADA as the overseer of integrity in racing.

One of the major benefits to having uniform drug rules and enforcement would be the elimination of the myriad of different rules in most of the 38 racing jurisdictions in North America. Trainers are constantly getting into trouble because the rules for the administration of therapeutic drugs vary so much from state to state.

Drug use is a complicated issue. There is a legitimate use for drugs in the sport. Therapeutic drugs are used in all forms of athletics to help athletes recover from the rigors of competition and, in some instances, during training and conditioning. If trainers and vets confined the usage of medication to these instances, those who share our philosophy would not have an issue with it.

But there is no place in competition for the use of drugs.

We race horses for one reason and one reason only: to find out which one is best on the day. Anything that tilts the playing field flies in the face of fair competition.

I race horses for the sport of it. I provide entertainment not only for my racing partners but also for the general public. We try to make it financially rewarding, but it is a very difficult enterprise to consistently provide a return on investment in the form of monetary profit. The real return on investment is the amount of pleasure and satisfaction gained from pride of ownership by my clients. Obviously there has been enough return on investment for them to allow me to continue forming racing partnerships for nearly 30 years.

Drug use by trainers falls into two categories. Some trainers honestly feel that using drugs on horses in competition is a legitimate practice because anything that can reduce the stress on a racehorse is advantageous for the well being of a horse. Many veterinarians agree with them.

Other trainers use drugs to make their horses run as fast as possible by artificially altering their bodily systems. They do this because they want an edge over their competitors. They cheat to win.

Cheating by altering the state of a horse in a race can take many forms, but the three most popular methods that constitute the gold standard among chronic manipulators in modern American racing involve reducing pain, enhancing breathing and delaying fatigue.

Pain Management: horses, like many athletes, suffer from skeletal soreness and pain. Medicating joints systemically or by direct injection reduces or eliminates pain from bone inflammation or loss of cartilage.

Improve breathing: stamina in a horse is a result of its ability to process oxygen that is delivered to the lungs through red corpuscles. The greater the number of red corpuscles, the higher the level of oxygen brought to the lungs. Increased volume of red corpuscles can be achieved by administering EPO (erythropoietin), cobalt and EPO-related drugs developed for human medicine to treat kidney patients.

Controlling fatigue. as a race unfolds, horses experience a build up of lactic acid in the muscles, which reduces their efficiency and results in fatigue. Buffering lactic acid delays the onset of lactic acidosis and allows a horse to continue running with less fatigue.

Drugs have been developed that mirror properties already found in humans. EPO, for example, is naturally produced in minor quantities in the body. So using drugs that are already present creates a possible nightmare scenario for drug testing in a laboratory. Unless the use of EPO in a racehorse is tested within four hours of delivery, detection by testing is considered virtually impossible.

A relatively recent technique known as "micro-dosing" reportedly has become a popular way to infuse the human body with illegal drugs that are difficult to detect, but apparently are quite effective in boosting performance. Cyclists and long-distance runners supposedly micro-dose during the evening to both evade detection by USADA investigators and provide enough time for the drugs to sufficiently clear the system.

In trying to wean users off drugs, authorities face a real challenge from both types of trainers because, once trainers see the impact of drugs on a racehorse, they feel that nothing in their normal arsenal of tools as horsemen can match the power of a drug. So even those who try to kick the habit often return to cheat due to feelings of impotence.

Illegal drugs are obtained for use on horses by trainers, veterinarians and owners. In the major leagues of racing, I firmly believe that trainers are the more prevalent seekers of the drugs. Trainers, in many instances, purposely use the most upstanding vets they can hire in an effort to send a message that they run a clean operation. In those cases, legitimate vets suspect their clients are cheating, but they turn a blind eye to these practices because there is such vigorous competition for business among the veterinary community on the backstretch.

Some owners are enablers, who get drugs or arrange contact for the delivery of drugs to trainers, but in most instances, owners of a certain mentality want the benefits of winning races with trainers who cheat but they don't want to know any details. It's simply an unspoken element of the trainer-owner relationship.

Having observed the environment of cheating for so long, I am convinced the only way to stop it is for offending parties—be they trainers, owners or veterinarians—to be banned from racing and never allowed access to the frontside or backside of a racetrack for the remainder of their lives.

I am sure that some offenders could possibly be rehabilitated, but resuscitating a few cheaters by allowing them to return to the sport would diminish the harshness of a message that needs to be sent to would-be cheaters. Cheat and you are gone. This is the only way to stop cheating.

One individual has shown Thoroughbred racetrack operators the way forward. Jeff Gural runs Standardbred tracks in New York and famously in New Jersey at The Meadowlands. Smart as a whip, the billionaire real estate magnate was tired of seeing harness racing trashed by a seemingly endless parade of cheaters. So in order to improve the integrity of racing at his track, Gural hired Brice Cote as his director of security. In addition to running background checks and listening to "the word on the street," Cote conducted searches of the stable area not only at The Meadowlands, but also off site, at training centers where a lot of cheating was believed to take place.

When Cote found incriminating evidence, Gural banned trainers who he considered to be undesirable from stabling and racing at The Meadowlands. Gural was at the forefront in detecting cobalt when it started to have a huge impact on harness racing.

Betting handle at The Meadowlands began to improve in 2013 when Gural started getting tough; proving that ridding the game of cheaters was good business. We in Thoroughbred racing who think along the same lines as Gural are still waiting for his counterpart to emerge in our sport. Jeff gave testimony at the same Senate hearing that I appeared at. He is a very impressive and dedicated sportsman and businessman.

I am not alone in the battle to create a level playing field. And I have not been alone in writing or speaking out about it. Arthur Hancock, Jerry Brown, Gretchen Jackson, Andy Beyer, George Strawbridge, Gary Young, Ray Paulick, Warren Eves and the late Stanley Bergstein have written and spoken out vigorously on the topic.

Any number of newspaper, magazine and TV commentators, on the other hand, have completely avoided the subject or sided with cheaters, including glorifying miscreants because of conflicts of interests or because it was part of their job. Fortunately, over the past half-dozen years I have seen the ranks of these people shrink and the names of those sick of the status quo increase.

Half a dozen or so years ago, most writers and owners were in denial about the rampant use of drugs in racing. The evolution of enlightenment on this issue has been rapid. Acceptance of the notion that cheating definitely takes place in racing is now a given. Today the focus has shifted dramatically to possible solutions.

Stanley Bergstein had always been a hero of mine, along with *The Blood-Horse* editor Kent Hollingsworth. They were, in their time, the most respected figures in Standardbred and Thoroughbred racing, because each stood tall for integrity in racing. And they showed courage.

I first met Stan when he served as master of ceremonies at a harness racing function that I went to as a staff member of *The Blood-Horse*. His love for his chosen sport was immense and his big personality was so infectious that it made others want to embrace buggy racing as well.

In the latter part of his life, Stan banged out a series of Op-Ed pieces for *Daily Racing Form* that took to task cheaters and anybody involved in a position to stop these gangsters from carrying on with their illicit acts. Like me, Stan kept up with cheating in other sports besides our own, and very little escaped his attention. He brought his knowledge to readers through his Op-Ed pieces.

When Bergstein died in November of 2011, I not only felt pangs of loss of a kindred spirit, but an immediate void. I feared that *Daily Racing Form* would not replace him and, instead, allow his brand of Op-Ed pieces to disappear from its pages.

I wanted to encourage turf writers to do more investigative stories. So to keep Stan's flame alive, I inaugurated an annual writing award to honor the best piece of investigative journalism with a racing theme. In order to entice writers to dig deeper and stretch more, as well as to attract as much attention as possible to the Stanley Bergstein Writing Award, I put up a prize of $25,000.

My first thought was to offer the project to the National Turf Writers Association, by providing the funding and having them administer the selection process. The NTWA board thought it was inappropriate for Team Valor to sponsor an award of this nature and *USA Today* turf writer Tom Pedulla suggested that we had an ulterior motive in wanting to offer the award. So they declined our invitation. I never understood the reluctance or the reasoning behind the decision, so with my trusted aide-de-camp Jeff Lowe, a former turf writer who heads Team Valor's media office, we decided to administer and promote the award ourselves.

We instituted a nomination process, recruited highly qualified judges, selected venues, had celebrated sculptor Nina Kaiser create a bronze trophy for the winner and invited guests to attend our inaugural presentation.

In the initial four years, the award ceremonies were held twice at the Thoroughbred Club down the road from Keeneland and once each at the Fasig-Tipton Sales Pavilion in Lexington and in conjunction with the University of Arizona's annual industry confab in Tucson.

Judges for the award have consisted of Frank Deford, Bill Nack, Bill Christine, Richard Eng, Ray Kerrison, Bill Plaschke, Billy Reed, Jeff Siegel, Tom Hammond, Karen Johnson, Tom Keyser, John Pricci, John Sparkman, George Strawbridge, Lynne Snierson, Randy Moss, Steve Haskin and Jon White.

The first four winners have been writers Joe Drape, Walt Bagdanich and Rebecca Ruiz for their piece "Mangled horses, maimed jockeys: death and disarray at America's racetracks" published in the *New York Times*; writer Ray Paulick for his story "Florida Investigation: Vet said Cibelli told him 'Keep me out of it,'" published in the *Paulick Report*; Lucas Marquardt for his piece "Is this the death of synthetic racing? And, if so, why?" published by the *Thoroughbred Daily News*, and Chris Wittstruck for his piece "Watching the Cheaters Cheat" published on the United States Trotting Association website.

Of all the comments that have been made about me in horseracing, it seems that the biggest complaint registered against me over the years has been that I have chosen to "air racing's dirty laundry in public" and thereby "bite the hand that feeds me."

If by challenging the status quo I have rubbed people the wrong way, I do not offer any apology whatsoever because, as a pretty fair country turf writer named William Faulkner was reported to have said, "In literature, one rogue is worth a thousand saints." If my position in racing has been to fill that role, I have gladly accepted it.

As my talented writer wife wrote in the preface to the first Bergstein Award program, "No facet of society can be improved by covering up its problems and hoping no one notices. Only by shining a light upon the problems can they be successfully addressed and overcome."

Using my keyboard to voice my concerns about racing's issues has probably hurt my business in some respects but I feel very comfortable speaking out because, when it comes to promoting the best aspects of the sport, I feel passionate about being on the right side of the issue. I will never stop fighting the good fight. And I have a lot more company now than when I started out.

Racing has been the focal point of my adult and professional life. I find racing to be the most fascinating, exciting and pleasurable activity engaged in by humans outdoors. If our game can find a way to rid itself of drugs and cheaters, we can thrive as a viable major sport. While I would love to see all race day meds stopped, I am not nearly as concerned over the use of therapeutic meds, which I feel are pretty much under control, as I am about the designer or illegal drugs. May the ranks of those insisting on integrity of competition continue to grow.

That is my hope for racing.